The Smart Set

The Smart Set

A Magazine of Cleverness

JAMES MONTGOMERY FLAGG

ONE
CIVILIZED
READER

IS WORTH A
THOUSAND
BONEHEADS

OCTOBER, 1914
25 CENTS

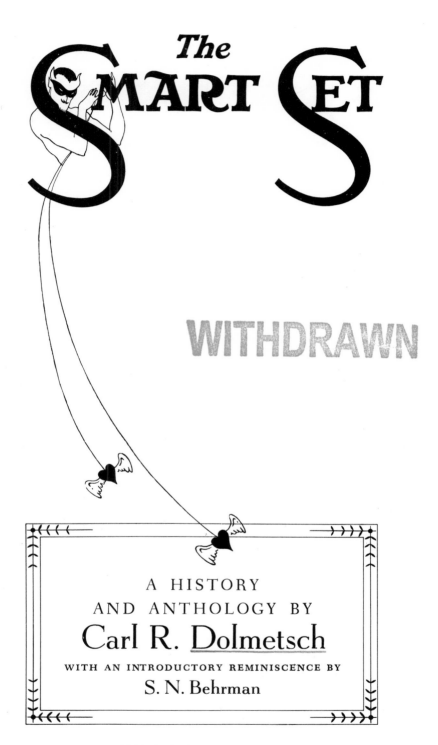

The Smart Set

A HISTORY
AND ANTHOLOGY BY
Carl R. Dolmetsch
WITH AN INTRODUCTORY REMINISCENCE BY
S. N. Behrman

THE DIAL PRESS

NEW YORK 1966

For Joan, Carl and Chris,
who know why.

ACKNOWLEDGMENTS

Acknowledgment is made to the following for permission to reprint material in this volume:

A Cycle of Manhattan BY THYRA SAMTER WINSLOW: Reprinted by permission of Philip Wittenberg for the Estate of Thyra Samter Winslow.

Americanization: A Movie BY WILLIAM GROPPER: Reprinted by permission of the artist.

Three Infernal Jokes BY LORD DUNSANY: Reprinted by permission of Bruce Humphries, Inc. and Curtis Brown Ltd., London.

Union Square BY WITTER BYNNER: Reprinted by permission of the author.

The Education of Paul Gant BY HOWARD MUMFORD JONES: Reprinted by permission of the author.

Cats BY MORRIS GILBERT: Reprinted by permission of the author.

The Librarian BY MARK VAN DOREN: Reprinted by permission of the author.

Roses of a Dream BY ALFRED DAMON RUNYON: Reprinted by permission of the Estate of Alfred Damon Runyon.

A Ghost of a Chance BY O. HENRY: From the book, *Sixes and Sevens* by O. Henry. Reprinted by permission of Doubleday & Company, Inc.

As Played Before His Highness BY JAMES BRANCH CABELL: Reprinted by permission of Margaret Freeman Cabell.

How the Twelve Best Sellers Ended BY CARL VAN VECHTEN: Reprinted by permission of the author.

Mirrors BY ROBINSON JEFFERS: Reprinted by permission of Donnan Jeffers.

That Second Man BY S. N. BEHRMAN: Reprinted by permission of the author.

A Persian Love Song BY JOHN HALL WHEELOCK: Reprinted by permission of the author.

Too Bad BY DOROTHY PARKER: From *The Portable Dorothy Parker*. Copyright 1933, 1961 by Dorothy Parker. Reprinted by permission of The Viking Press, Inc.

Pan Is Dead BY EZRA POUND: From *Personae*, The Collected Poems of Ezra Pound. Copyright 1926, 1954 by Ezra Pound. Reprinted by permission of New Directions Publishing Corporation. Reprinted by permission of the author, Faber and Faber, Ltd., and Arthur V. Moore.

Nina BY MUNA LEE: Reprinted by permission of the author.

Violets BY D. H. LAWRENCE: From *Collected Poems*, Vol. I, by D. H. Lawrence. Copyright 1916 by B. W. Huebsch, Inc.; 1944 by Frieda Lawrence. Reprinted by permission of The Viking Press, Inc., Laurence Pollinger Limited, and the Estate of the late Mrs. Frieda Lawrence.

"SOMETHING PERSONAL"

What becomes nowadays of the back numbers of old magazines? Incinerators, junkyards and scrap drives, I suspect, devour all but a slim fraction. Ponderous bound volumes, the hallmark of a really "cultured" household in Edwardian days, have virtually vanished from private homes in the United States and we no longer build uneconomical houses with great, roomy attics or cavernous understairs closets where stacks of old *Delineators* or *Bookmans* could molder dustily from one generation to the next. To be sure, our major libraries are more vigilant than ever in tracking down and stocking even the meanest and obscurest publications, even as microfilm makes it now unnecessary to preserve the originals. But I fear the present and future generations of youngsters, in permanent bondage to the TV set, are forever barred from one of the small pleasures of my own early childhood—rainy day rummaging through box upon box of seemingly ancient yellowing folios in grandma's deserted "third floor." I was too young to read much then, but what fun it was to leaf lazily through those old illustrations— prim, sweet-faced belles in high necklines and ridiculous "Merry Widow" hats, open-mouthed doughboys charging bravely up some shell-scarred hill at Château-Thierry while Spads and Fokkers barrel-rolled overhead, the Campbell's urchins in chefs' hats riding spoons around a huge, brightly-colored "Pepper Pot."

I never completely satisfied nor outgrew my childish delight in old magazines; hence, the present undertaking. Nevertheless, it is my cherished conviction—and one that has sustained me throughout a decade of sporadic effort to write this volume—that there are others, not born thirty years too late, to share my interest in *The Smart Set,* a once-upon-a-time magazine which, for all practical purposes, faded away in 1924. Yet, more. There are compelling reasons why a detailed account of this little-known (but once-celebrated) journal should at long last see print. For one thing, it is at least a collateral ancestor of several present-day periodicals—*The New Yorker* and *Esquire* chief among them. For another, it is unquestionably one of our best sources of knowledge about what was regarded early in this century as witty, gay, clever, sophisticated, irreverent and iconoclastic reading matter. Finally, to avoid too long a bill of particulars, it is a magazine of neglected, though inestimable, value to literary history as the proving grounds, between 1900 and 1924, of more illustrious literary careers—"O. Henry," James Branch Cabell, H. L. Mencken, George Jean Nathan, Eugene O'Neill, F. Scott Fitzgerald, and hundreds more—than any other journal ever published in America.

Curiously, the story of *The Smart Set* has, despite all this, never before been fully told. Its last issue was not yet off the press (it expired officially in June 1930) before the late Burton Rascoe, with the help of Groff Conklin, set out to write a history of "The Magazine of Cleverness" as an introduction to a projected anthology of the best *Smart Set* pieces. For almost five years Rascoe labored against one frustration after another and when, in 1934, he and Conklin finally

issued *The Smart Set Anthology* (reprinted, minus Rascoe's history, as *The Bedside Companion,* 1940), he had to confess it a botched job. Unfortunately, it was worse than that. It was inaccurate and attenuated, owing to difficulties that were altogether human, however trivial or silly they may seem in retrospect.

Rascoe's stumbling block was his own feud with H. L. Mencken, which made it quite impossible for him to obtain Mencken's cooperation in his project—a *sine qua non* of success inasmuch as this former co-editor of *The Smart Set* controlled perhaps one-third of the extant records of what really happened behind and beyond the magazine's printed pages. Furthermore, Mencken refused to permit any of his own contributions in the magazine to appear in Rascoe's collection (a ruinous exclusion!) and induced his friend and publisher, Alfred A. Knopf, to withhold reprint permissions on all other *Smart Set* pieces then under the Knopf copyright—a goodly share of the best the magazine had had to offer from 1914 to 1923. Out of spite, Rascoe wrote a vindictive thirty-four page introduction, angrily distorting the history of the magazine in order to minimize Mencken's accomplishments in it (which were considerable) while overestimating those of his friend, Willard Huntington Wright, who had edited *The Smart Set* in 1913. Rascoe's narrative grows less reliable and more shrill as it progresses, trailing off into a diatribe against Knopf's supposed conspiracy.

Those old quarrels are now forever stilled and, with the ranks of *Smart Set* stalwarts thinned to a hardy handful, it is feasible for the first time to present a more or less full, documented and balanced account of the magazine. When Mr. Mencken's editorial memoirs, now in manuscript, are finally released a few decades hence (sooner, I hope), more light will undoubtedly be thrown upon the years of his co-editorship with George Jean Nathan, but I am now persuaded that in its crucial points and significant details my presentation will not be substantively contradicted or greatly qualified by further revelations. I have sought, therefore, in my own way to fulfill Burton Rascoe's original aim as historian of *The Smart Set* and I am gratified that, during the last years of his life, Mr. Rascoe followed my progress with enthusiasm and gave me invaluable aid in the form of his copies of the magazine, notes and correspondence from his work and free rein on his extensive library of heavily annotated books about the period.

This is but one of many debts of gratitude I incurred in researching this book—to Messrs. Mencken and Nathan (before their deaths in 1956 and 1958, respectively), to several former *Smart Set* contributors and associates, and to many others—but I have deferred formal acknowledgment of these until an "Afterword," not in a desire to sweep them aside but in order to give the reader a chance to see first what it is that is acknowledged.

To most Americans on the nether side of sixty-five, *The Smart Set* is little more than a vague name, if, indeed, it signifies anything. This is not surprising. Of all the phenomena of literary culture, magazines are certainly the most vulnerable to the whips and scorns of time. Who now recalls, for instance, *McClure's, Munsey's, The Outlook* or *Everybody's?* Yet, these were once enormously popular periodicals, each boasting a circulation ten to twenty times larger than *Smart Set ca.* 1910. Magazines must perforce be sensitive barometers of public taste, at least at certain levels. And if, as Frank Luther Mott claims, the average life-span of American magazines is less than a human generation (*i.e.,* twenty years), it is little wonder that the journals of yesteryear are now so thoroughly forgotten, no matter how many readers once waited eagerly for each issue.

Furthermore, only a few who have some definite recognition of the name "*Smart Set*" have ever actually read the magazine. Extant copies are very rare, mainly because it was considered too disreputable in the innocent days in which it flourished for all but a few shamelessly "advanced" libraries. There are probably not a half-dozen complete sets of *Smart Set* originals in existence today (Princeton, Yale and the New York Public Library have the only ones I know of) and, though it is now available to libraries on microfilm and in photographic reprinting, the costs of sets are beyond ordinary means. For such reason, among others, I have included here a completely new anthology of selections from *Smart Set,* and, since my purpose in doing so is something more than an arbitrary, random sampling, a few remarks about the selection and arrangement seem appropriate.

At the outset, I excluded everything in the Rascoe-Conklin anthology. To be sure, that work is long out of print, but it is still widely enough available in college and public libraries for almost any avidly interested reader to locate as a supplement to this history. Hence, duplications seemed to me quite unjustifiable at this juncture. The same goes for other frequently reprinted pieces. (Exceptions: O'Neill's "Ile," Joyce's "A Little Cloud," and perhaps one or two more—choices dictated by restrictive circumstances involving writers whose exclusion was unthinkable.) Finally, I tried to eliminate works that are intrinsically worthless without thereby giving a better impression of the literary quality of *The Smart Set* than it deserves. This is not to say that some examples were not deliberately chosen on sociological or historical grounds, despite their limited artistic merits, but to have exhumed a whole volume of sub-literary cadavers, no matter how representative they might be, would have been an exercise of futility.

Ultimately, the great problem was not one of exclusion but of an embarrassment of riches. By any defensible criteria there still remains, despite all the picking, choosing, and previous reprintings, enough good material in *The Smart Set* for several more readable anthologies. In fact, my original selection (which I then regarded as absolutely minimal) totaled nearly 500,000 words—enough for several volumes—and this amount had eventually to be pruned by almost four-fifths. My first intention was to include something from each year between 1900 and 1924, something from each "regular" contributor to the magazine regardless of his subsequent stature, and a cross-section of themes, types and genres in about the same proportion as they had originally appeared in the magazine—in other words, to arrange a kind of microcosmic replica of twenty-four years of *Smart Set*. An impossible if not downright fatuous undertaking! Within drastic space limitations (lengthy pieces always had to be vetoed), I soon found that my criteria too often worked at cross-purposes, so that some final decisions inevitably turned upon personal prejudice. Candor forces me to say at this point that another, totally different, selection could present just as valid a picture of *Smart Set* as I have here. But I trust that, after all the agonizing choices, what is included will prove viable and interesting for today's casual reader and that, by juxtaposing the obviously "dated" with what still seems timely and cogent a half-century later, it will provide a few fresh insights for the student of literary history.

I am aware of only one gross omission. During the last decade covered in this history, about twenty percent of each issue of *Smart Set* consisted of a species of short, cynical vignette or sketch of one or two paragraphs each, many of them imitating the "Owen Hatteras" features so famous in the magazine (collaborations of Nathan, Mencken, Wright and others). These had to be eliminated in favor of representing the same themes and attitudes in more substantial pieces. One finished short story or play, it seemed to me, was worth more than its length in several short pieces of such journeyman work. Otherwise, the material here follows the general pattern and format of the maga-

zine itself: the longest piece (a novelette) comes first, plays and special features (such as "Répétition Générale") come somewhere near the middle (amid the plethora of stories and verse), and near the end we have the French story (a standard for twenty years), the *causeries* of Nathan and Mencken, and the "Shopping" column. Such an arrangement, together with the pictorial material, should give the reader who may never have a chance to see a copy of *Smart Set* a reasonably accurate impression of what it looked like.

The first section of this book is a straightforward narrative (with as little backing and filling as possible) of the magazine from its founding until its sale to W. R. Hearst in the summer of 1924. The decision to stop here, with only a bare outline of its subsequent existence (to 1930), arises from the simple fact that the last six years of *Smart Set,* when it was variously a "true story" sheet and a monthly of diet, fashion and cosmetic tips for "the Career Girl" are utterly devoid of interest. (Reading through those issues, for example, I could find not a single piece worthy of being anthologized in company with selections from the earlier years of *Smart Set!*) I have tried here neither to argue a "thesis" about my subject, nor to take sides in the many quarrels that checkered the history of *The Smart Set* and characterized that age of literary ferment, nor yet to be particularly analytical. During my investigation I have obviously formed opinions which I have been at no pains to suppress, but a work about *The Smart Set,* of all magazines, ought to avoid scholarly seriousness without being frivolous. It seems to me that, at its best and most interesting, literary and social history is but a more sophisticated form of grown-up attic-rummaging, and it is in this spirit that I wish this book to be read.

—CARL R. DOLMETSCH

Berlin, September 1965

TABLE OF CONTENTS

——•——

An Introductory Reminiscence

By S. N. Behrman

On a gray afternoon in the winter of 1915, I walked from Weld Hall, my dorm in the Harvard Yard, to cross to Hollis Hall, which was Charles Townsend Copeland's dorm. I was a junior and a member of Copey's English 12. We all had to come weekly to his rooms in Hollis to read what we had written. This seance was, both in anticipation and actuality, an ordeal. If, with the first few sentences, Copey was bored, he would fall elaborately asleep and peculiarly whistling snores would emanate from him. Under this barrage you had to go on reading to the last awful word.

On this occasion I had a short story. I climbed the stairs; Copey's softly-piercing, strangulated voice called "Come in." I entered to encounter the quince-like smile. Copey handed me a red pencil with which to record his comments and motioned me to the usual chair while he sat in his.

For once, he didn't fall asleep, dictated a few corrections while I read—he called for more "verbs of motion," his specialty—and when I was finished asked me to mark myself "B plus." Elated, I went back to my room in Weld and mailed B plus to *The Smart Set*.

In those days, ambitious literati could be

divided, roughly, into two classes: those with a greater grip on reality, who wanted to write for *The Saturday Evening Post* or *Cosmopolitan* and those, more vaporous, who wanted to write for *The Smart Set*. Earl Derr Biggers, for example, just a year ahead of me in English 12, belonged to the realistic group. By the time I ran into him again, twenty years after he had graduated, he had opulently achieved his ambition.

In American colleges when I was an undergraduate (1912-1916), *The Smart Set* magazine, edited by H. L. Mencken and George Jean Nathan, had had an electrifying effect. It was an influence. Along with The New Machiavelli and *The New Republic*, we swallowed *The Smart Set* as part of our regular nourishment. Its editors had already become legendary, Mencken as a Rabelaisian pundit, Nathan as an epicure of forbidden fruits garnered in foreign capitals, whiffs of Continental novelties. We began to look up the Continental playwrights whose exotic names were rattled off so glibly by Nathan. In the literary courses aspirants wanted to write for *The Smart Set*, as, several decades later, they wanted to write for *The New Yorker*. H. L. Mencken himself had tried to make *The Smart Set* and, moreover, with poetry!

By the time I sent my B-plus story from Cambridge, I was already a veteran non-contributor. I had received from Mencken and Nathan letters on earlier submissions that were simultaneously rejections and invitations. (They were true incubators, asking me to send more but not of the same.) Within a week, for the first time, I got a letter from them unaccompanied by my manuscript. But I was somewhat bewildered: Mencken's letter was typed, not on the usual gray-green *Smart Set* stationery but on mauve with pink lettering on the top—*La Vie Parisienne*. Mencken's letter explained that they liked my story very much and that it would appear in their "sister publication." I had never heard of this sister, nor seen her, but I was

happy to be admitted to the family. Moreover, the letter contained a check for fifteen dollars. This was a check! There has never been a sweeter one since.

At my next session with Copey (disastrous, snores) I showed him Mencken's letter. He was pleased, he congratulated me, he asked to borrow it. At the next meeting of English 12, I was startled to hear his opening remarks: "Most of the members of this class send their offerings far and wide without response. But here"—he unfolded the lavender sister—"is a letter from H. L. Mencken. . . ." I squirmed. Dos Passos was a member of that class. I hope he doesn't remember the incident.

Further indication of the hold that *The Smart Set* and its editors had on us may be conveyed by my recollections of the following year (1916), when I was a member of George Pierce Baker's English 47, his course in playwriting. ("Dr. Baker's Ibsenfabrik" was Mencken's way of describing that seminar.) Baker was very businesslike; my experience of him, by the way, does not at all coincide with that recounted by Thomas Wolfe in *Look Homeward, Angel*. There was no aesthetic posing about Baker; he was practical. The first task he set us was to dramatize a short story, any one anywhere that seemed to us dramatizable. Three of the short stories dramatized were from *The Smart Set*. I chose one (natch) from "The Magazine of Cleverness." It was by Major Owen Hatteras. The exotic names of the members of Mencken's and Nathan's stable has always bewitched me: Achmed Abdullah, Lillith Benda, Raoul della Torre, Sherrard Mullikan, George Weems Peregoy. But of all these phosphorescent exotics, Major Owen Hatteras was my favorite. I doted on him. I envied him. What must it be like to be Major Owen Hatteras! He was so prolific, so variegated; no corner of the world was alien to him, no cranny of knowledge. His name itself was an evocation of mystery, of magic, of turbulent powers. How could I know that when I was dramatizing the Major, I was dramatizing a regiment? Much later I found out that Owen Hatteras was an all-purpose pseudonym sometimes camouflaging Mencken and Nathan themselves. He was as multifarious as Homer.

Among its other appeals *The Smart Set* seemed to us electrifyingly avant-garde. With a Nietzschean expansion Beyond Good and Evil, a fellow-member of English 47 picked to dramatize from "The Aristocrat of the Magazines" a story about a dying wife whose husband has an affair with the nurse attending her. Professor Baker was not as advanced as we and *The Smart Set* were. In a pained voice he read this dramatization aloud, and more in sorrow than in anger said that the student had done the job quite well but that he was sorry he had chosen a story in which the hero was such an unmitigated cad. Dear Professor Baker! How canny he was to die before the *nouvelle vague*; how much has been spared him!

It was after I graduated from Harvard that *The Smart Set* began to exert an even more direct influence on me. In a way, it all began with a letter on the gray-green stationery used by "The Aristocrat of Magazines." I still have it. It is signed by George Jean Nathan and it reads:

Dear Mr. Behrman:

Have you a short story? I should like very much to have you in the next number of *The Smart Set*.

There was no way I could have known it, but this letter changed entirely the course of my life. I sent "The Second Man," the story contained in this volume. I was paid fifty dollars for it. But ultimately I got much more.

For years after I left Harvard I had a very thin time. True, as a result of an original play I had written for Professor Baker's English 47 I had had a brief job as assistant to Dave Wallace—William A. Brady's press agent—plugging Brady's current production, a new play by Jules Eckert Goodman. It had been a heady time: Wallace took me to lunch at the Algonquin; I met F. P. A. and Alexander Woollcott, then drama critic for *The New York Times* and an Olympian figure with a manner that made anonymities like me cower. But the job had lasted as long as the play did: two weeks.

I had written three or four plays. But I had quickly found out that it was impossible to sell a play. There were sixty theaters flourishing then in New York, but for an untried playwright to get into one of them, except by buying a seat in the gallery, proved to be chimerical. (Although I should admit that several of Professor Baker's pupils had done it: Edward Sheldon and Eugene O'Neill. Another was Cleves Kinkaid, who had won the Craig Prize while he was in 47.)

So I had had to rely on an occasional short story. I tried all the markets then available and got a few things into most of them: *The Masses, Reedy's Mirror, The Seven Arts, The New Republic, Ainslee's, Town Topics* and *Pearson's,* edited by Frank Harris. I didn't know, when I submitted things to *Town Topics,* that it was the "most degraded paper of any prominence in the United States." It wouldn't have mattered if I did; it was a "market" and paid ten dollars a column.

The Smart Set didn't pay much—fifty dollars was the most I ever got from them for anything—but they did pay and promptly on acceptance. My experience with Frank Harris of *Pearson's* made me look upon *The Smart Set,* from a fiscal point of view, as having the Gibraltar-like solidity of The Prudential Life Insurance Company. I submitted a story to *Pearson's.* Harris wrote me a charming, complimentary letter, accepted the story for twenty-five dollars, which was a windfall, and added, moreover, that he would like me one day, but not too soon as he was then busy lecturing, to drop in to see him.

I was elated by this letter and prematurely felt myself solvent. The story appeared; days, weeks and months went by and I never got the money. I wrote to Harris to call this lapse to his attention. I at once got another charming letter from him inviting me to come to have a cup of coffee with him in his apartment on a Sunday morning. I went. Harris was lying in a four-poster bed in a resplendent dressing gown. His face looked, somehow, as if he had borrowed it but his voice was splendid. He was reading the plays of Middleton and he began talking about Queen Elizabeth, *the first one*. "A lovely bitch," he said admiringly, "a lovely bitch." He talked intimately about her, as if she were a discarded mistress about whom there still lingered, in memory, a certain fragrance. He liked my story so well, he said, that next time he would raise the ante to thirty-five dollars. Somehow, the raise did not stimulate me. I never got the twenty-five.

So my mainstay during the early twenties was *The Smart Set*. You could send them things you couldn't possibly hope to get in anywhere else. For example: I met the English poet Siegfried Sassoon, here on a lecture tour after the first World War. We were in a taxi going someplace. Sassoon was very tall and rather clumsy. He propped his long legs in heavy brogans against the window sill of the taxi. The cab lurched and Sassoon broke the window. There followed an extraordinary dialogue between Sassoon and the irate cabby: metaphysical on Sassoon's part, sternly realistic on the cabby's part. I wrote it up as a one-act play and sent it to Their Majesties. They ran it. I suppose I contributed five or six times that year. It was a busy time. Total income in my top year: $580. But such prosperity couldn't last. My output lessened; rejections multiplied. In 1924, in a doldrum of unemployment and general vacuity—I'll never know what made me do it—I dramatized the story Nathan had bought. It took three weeks. But it took two **years** for my agent to sell it and another year

to get it produced. But when it was finally produced, I was converted overnight into a practicing playwright. So in a way it was *The Smart Set* that launched me. At least I feel that way.

The Smart Set was enhaloed by the personalities of Mencken and Nathan. *The New York Times,* in an editorial, said that Mencken was the most important private individual in America. His reputation was massive, overwhelming and tantalizing. "The sage of Baltimore," as he came to be known, was a pundit but with something new in the pundit line: Socrates in easy wedlock with Rabelais, a one-man Academe swimming sturdily in Pilsener.

Nathan played an irreverent obbligato in the penumbra of this reputation. He was incredibly handsome. Posters of him sprouted all over town as if he were a matinee idol appearing in a Broadway show. But the show in which he had a long-term run was *The Smart Set*.

Nathan took on all comers, including a panjandrum of the era, Alexander Woollcott. One day there burst on the town a bombshell in *The Smart Set,* a piece by Nathan comminating Woollcott. It was called "The Seidlitz Powder of Times Square." It was a sensation. Nowadays it's common enough for critics to bedevil other critics in public; at that time it was unheard of. Nathan stormed the peak citadel of power, *The New York Times* and its proprietor, whom he referred to as Mr. de Ochs. (Even in a blast detonated on 43rd Street Nathan could not forget the Almanach de Gotha!) He took the thesis that Mr. de Ochs was a comic spirit bent on outrivaling as a comedian George M. Cohan whose "The Tavern"—"a lampoon of reason" —was playing across the street from the *Times*. Having already produced a comic masterpiece with *The Times Book Review,* Nathan went on to say, Mr. de Ochs was determined to outdo himself, and he accomplished this by employing Alexander Woollcott to be his drama critic. Nathan slates

Woollcott especially for his dithyrambic style:

"I do not set myself bumptiously to say that the Times's Hazlitt's estimates are always wrong (it is not a question of their rightness or wrongness; they may often be fully right); the style in which they are expressed is the particular bouquet that I invite you to sniff. This style presents an interesting study. It never strikes a mean; it is either a gravy bomb, a bursting gladiolus, a palpitating missa cantata, an attack of psychic hydrophobia, or a Roman denunciation, unequivocal, oracular, flat and final . . . Adulatory frenzy over a certain cabotin sweats itself out in such verbiage as "one swoons at" the splendor of this or that performance. A style, in brief, that is purely emotional, and without a trace of the cool reflectiveness and contagious common sense suited to criticism.

The fact is that Nathan was as stage-struck as Woollcott was. But the backgrounds of the two men couldn't have been more antipodal. Nathan was urban, rich and traveled; Woollcott was a poor country boy, brought up, as Edmund Wilson pointed out in an article written after Woollcott's death, in a phalanstery in New Jersey and was strongly influenced by Fourierism. Alec was indeed somewhat frenzied in style and sentimental in judgment but when his frenzy coincided with a madness that was divine—as when he headed his review after the first appearance of the Marx Brothers: "DANCING IN THE STREETS,"—the collusion was appropriate.

I knew Nathan and took him in my stride. He was amusing enough but after all, when you come right down to it, he was only a drama critic who had been abroad. Every dramatist feels, whether mistakenly or not, that no drama critic can possibly know as much about the subject as he himself does; they were, he feels, writing drama criticism because they couldn't write plays, William

Archer notwithstanding. But Mencken was something else again. I thought him (and still do) a great man.

I was so in awe of Mencken that when Harold Ross, the editor of The New Yorker, telephoned one day in the early thirties and asked me to have dinner with him and Mencken that night at 21, I accepted but with some trepidation. I was young enough to be a hero worshipper.

Clinging hopefully to the Pilsener side of the Mencken legend, I appeared at 21 early. So did Ross. Ross was hailed by a star member of his staff having dinner with his wife. We joined them. Somewhat acidly, Ross congratulated his writer on having succeeded in staying on the wagon for nine days. He had evidently kept count. A jovial acquaintance, carrying a half-filled glass, came up and invited us all to have a drink with him. Ross refused curtly. The hospitable one twitted Ross on his asceticism, and kept urging Ross's star, who virtuously, but rather shiftily, refused. Ross lost his temper. A lion defending his cub, he turned angrily on the bibulous and frustrated visitor.

"When one of my writers," he growled, "no matter how insincerely, refuses a drink, don't you go urging it on him!"

Ross was fuming when he caught sight of Mencken waiting in the hall. We joined him. I was introduced and we went upstairs where Ross had reserved a table.

Ross, still angry, recounted the incident to Mencken. He moaned about the constant battle with alcoholism on his staff.

"When they pass out in the middle of a piece," he explained to Mencken, "you have to imagine what the hell they would have written if they were sober!"

Mencken took Ross's little tempest with, to me, surprising tolerance.

"Writers, I find," Mencken said, "hate to write. It drives them to drink. Artists, on the other hand, love their work. They love to draw, they love to paint. They can't seem to get enough of it. Don't you find that?"

Ross admitted that, by God, he did. It hadn't occurred to him before but, come to think of it, he'd never had any trouble at all with his artists. They always delivered their work on time, whereas with the writers you never knew. Why was it, he wondered.

I interjected that I had visited a painter friend in his studio in Paris not long before. He was touching up a finished canvas with his brush. He had told me that he got sexual pleasure from applying paint to canvas.

Ross said morosely that perhaps that might account for the difference in intensity of application between writers and artists.

I studied Mencken. The most exhilarating writer in America, the wielder of a blunderbuss with the deftness of a fencer, was, in person, quiet, reserved, attentive, courteous. He had written of himself that he was "naturally monkish," but there was certainly nothing monkish in his appearance. He might have been Chancellor of a German University or the Mayor of Hamburg. Also, he had the unassuming air of a great man. Something impelled me to tell him that when I was a Senior at Harvard I had gotten my first acceptance of a short story from him, not for *The Smart Set* but for a publication called *La Vie Parisienne*. "Oh," said Mencken, "we published that *sub rosa*. It made up for *Smart Set* deficits. It came in very handy. We even published good things in it; they slipped in when we weren't looking."

This made me feel cozy. My awe of the sage vanished. I told him how excited we all were about *The Smart Set* when we were undergraduates.

Mencken drank great glass tankards of Pilsener with his dinner. They seemed to warm him up. Deadpan and gravely sober, he launched on a story. He'd had, recently, in Baltimore, to entertain an English visitor, not a writer, one of the landed gentry, somewhat elderly. Mencken asked what he'd like to see, what choice samples of Americana.

"I'd like to see a lynching," said the Englishman.

"Nothing easier," Mencken assured him. "I'll take you to a county fair. They're my favorite diversion. You'll see prize cattle imported from your native land."

"But I want to see a lynching," the Englishman insisted.

"They never have a county fair without a lynching," Mencken assured him. "It tops things off."

They set off for the fair, thirty miles from Baltimore. It was very lively. Mencken showed his guest the prize cattle, bought him frankfurters, offered to take him on the merry-go-round, gave him a chance to display his marksmanship in a shooting gallery. He bought him crackerjacks, popcorn, and ice cream cones. It was all very well, but the Englishman kept asking plaintively for his lynching. Mencken told him he must bide his time. That event was saved for the climactic. Mencken walked his guest's head off; the Englishman was gasping with fatigue, kept alive merely by the promised tidbit ahead of him. At sundown Mencken asked to be excused for a moment while he went to the Administration Building to get the exact time when the main event was to take place. The Englishman waited on a bench in front of a belly dancer's pavillion. Mencken returned with a grave report. The custodian of the chief actor had, regrettably, got drunk and the protagonist had escaped. Drink, he explained, was the great curse of American jailors. Mencken's apologies were profuse but the Englishman's disappointment was abysmal.

Ross enjoyed this account hugely and then told in detail of some of the ingenious and elaborate and diabolical practical jokes contrived by the comedian Joe Cook with whom he spent his weekends.

"Ah," said Mencken, "practical jokes are one thing, but my Englishman was serious. My heart went out to him. He was so disappointed."

My eyes met Mencken's. Without winking, he winked at me. I saw that inside he was bubbling with delight that Ross had swallowed his story whole.

I pumped Mencken about *The Smart Set* and what he thought its place and influence were in the literary history of this country. He talked soberly about the magazine's chief aim: to discover new writing talent and to aerate Puritanic tradition. I told him something of the enormous influence the magazine had had on the college generation of my time. He was well aware of it. "We ran a series, you know," he reminded me, "on the American colleges, the first such investigation I know of." Ross interjected that I had made a play of one of my *Smart Set* stories. "John Colton," I said, "dramatized another *Smart Set* short story, Somerset Maugham's 'Rain.'" Mencken showed no particular interest. I said: "The theater doesn't interest you at all, does it?" "I leave that to Nathan," he said. "I prefer music." I had just read J. F. N. Sullivan's book on Beethoven which I greatly admired.

"Yes," Mencken said, "Sullivan is a Beethoven lover."

He said this as if it were the final accolade he could give a man. He talked a good deal about music to which he devoted his Saturday nights in Baltimore. While Mencken talked about music, Ross took a Sabbatical. He emerged from this to express to Mencken an exasperated wonderment that he seemed to find the time to answer personally every letter, even from callow undergraduates.

"I have the habit of answering letters," Mencken said simply, as if that made it effortless and not in the least time-consuming.

At ten o'clock Mencken got up to go as he said he had work to do. We put him into a cab and Ross and I walked down 52nd.

Ross was full of admiration for Mencken. "He's so God-damn *industrious*," he growled. "Imagine! He writes *The American Language* and still finds the time to answer every God-damn letter!"

I consoled Ross by reminding him that Mencken was German and thorough by inheritance.

The passing of *The Smart Set* in 1924 left me, as well as many others, writers and readers, bereft. To us then, it is as it would be for so many now if *The New Yorker* were suddenly to roll up its shutters. There was nowhere else to turn. No more letters on gray-green stationery from the Aristocrat! Professor Dolmetsch's narrative, which follows, tells what went on behind the scenes while I, and so many others, were aiming at the glittering target. But among the bereft were some—Scott Fitzgerald, Eugene O'Neill, Theodore Dreiser—who survived to form a living aristocracy of their own.

PART ONE:
THE HISTORY

Caviar for Dilettantes

—————————•—•—————————

"Give me New York as it is, with all its glitter and bigness," the handsome young man declaimed, striking a pose. "Give me the millionaires, too, with their vulgar wealth —they know how to spend it; give me the women—heartless, if you like—they know how to make themselves attractive. I am modern to my finger tips, and proud of it."

The deliverer of this ringing paean to modernity was Schuyler Ainslee, standing in the gilded foyer of an opulent Washington Square mansion. This terribly rich, well-bred young Knickerbocker of perhaps twenty-five was the absolute epitome—albeit a fictitious

one—of a turn-of-the-century Manhattan "debonair"—a somewhat more decorous (and certainly far richer) great-granddaddy of to-day's playboy.

Schuyler and the story in which he appears —"The Idle Born," a novelette by Hobert C. Chatfield-Taylor and Reginald DeKoven— have long been blessedly forgotten. But this story had the honor to be the very first item in the premier issue of *Smart Set*, a chic new monthly that arrived almost unheralded on New York's newsstands on the morning of March 10, 1900. Like the new journal's suggestive cover—with its elegant formal couple,

3

its Mephisto, Cupidons and dangling hearts, its swirling vermillion S's—the Schuyler Ainslees and their passion for modernity were harbingers of a new vogue of "smartness" which was about to sweep across the American literary landscape.

To launch this new wave, the lights had burned late into the night for some weeks past in the old St. James Building, at 26th Street and Broadway. There, in the posh offices of the scandalous (but widely read) weekly, *Town Topics,* young Arthur Grissom and two assistants had plotted and patched, sweated and scraped to piece together a presentable magazine that could at least claim to be "by, for and about 'The Four Hundred.'" No blazing comets signalled their achievement. Apparently the heavens are quite impervious to such mundane affairs, however auspicious the occasion for literary history—as the "birth" of this new magazine was eventually to prove.

Nor could ordinary mortals then have foretold the checkered course *Smart Set* would chart during the next quarter-century, or the wake it would leave in the national letters long afterward. To Grissom and his employer, *Town Topics'* preposterous publisher, Colonel William D'Alton Mann—as colorful and incredible an old speculator as ever crossed the American literary scene—the case seemed quite simple. The lucky coincidence of the Mergenthaler Linotype, the highspeed press, rotogravure and the rise of both "muckraking" and modern advertising had brought flush times to magazine publishing. A gaudy scramble for customers had ensued, with nearly every segment of the reading public being thoroughly exploited, and to Colonel Mann's eyes the good pickings were far from over. If 150,000 readers each week devoured his weekly compendium of society news, scandal and social commentary, he reasoned, might not just as many (or more) be eager for vicarious excursions via fiction and verse into the wicked, wicked world reported in *Town Topics?* He guessed

that there were many dilettantes able and willing to pick up a bit of ready cash by fictionalizing what they knew of Park Avenue and Newport peccadillos and that there awaited, untapped, a sizable audience for such a species of literary titillation and snob-appeal, and he was willing to gamble. Thus, in late 1899 he had incorporated his "Ess Ess Publishing Company" in New York and cabled his London and Paris lawyers to stake out publishing charters for him there. It was to prove a very shrewd gamble indeed.

Guessing right had long been a habit with the old dandy who, by 1900, was something of a Fifth Avenue celebrity, to be spotted almost any weekday in flowing white whiskers, flaming red tie and frock coat, consuming a gargantuan lunch and nodding to fashionable acquaintances in Delmonico's. As a Civil War cavalry commandant at twenty-one (whence his military honorific), he had never doubted that he could successfully dodge Rebel bullets at the Wilderness and Gettysburg nor that, having patented an improved infantryman's pack harness, he could milk high profits from War Department contracts. Unscathed at war's end, he narrowly squeaked by an indictment for peddling phony oil stocks and, heading for Alabama as a carpetbagging Internal Revenue official, he soon struck gold again as a cottonseed factor and proprietor of the *Mobile Register,* his first publishing venture. Since most ex-Confederates were disqualified for Federal office, Mann tried his hand at politics, "converting" to the Southern cause and running as a Conservative Democrat for Congress in Mobile in 1869. Elected by a landslide, he was refused certification by Reconstruction officers for reasons that seem to have been only partly political (a horse-whipping for alleged breaches of honor was darkly hinted).

Whatever its cause, the Colonel remained undaunted by this early demise of his political career. The postwar railroad boom was by then in full swing and, casting a shrewd eye at the fortunes being piled up in railroads by the Vanderbilts, Huntingtons, Hills, *et al.*, he built a line of his own from Mobile to New Orleans and patented a highly original (for 1872) "boudoir" sleeping car which became the prototype of today's compartmentalized sleeper. With the American market already dominated by George Pullman, however, Mann sailed for Europe where for nearly a decade he peddled his invention with huge success across the Continent. Selling his Mann Railway Sleeping Car Company (the parent, in fact, of the present-day *Compagnie des Wagons-Lits*) to a Belgian partner, he invaded the U.S. with his luxurious "boudoir car" idea. After a few nearly disastrous seasons, however, he was able to unload his floundering company on Pullman barely a few jumps ahead of his creditors before plunging into the chaotic waters of Manhattan journalism in search of yet another fortune.

Town Topics was to be its source. Founded in 1879 by W. R. Andrews (its original title was *Andrews' American Queen*), this lackluster social gazette had led a hand-to-mouth existence under a succession of editors until, in 1885, it was purchased by a syndicate (headed by Eugene D. Mann, the Colonel's younger brother) in which the Colonel himself had a one-third interest. They not only renamed the paper, they substituted shocking (but well-founded) gossip for dull guest lists and added lively, sophisticated, technically accomplished departments conducted by brilliant young talents. Everything was kept strictly anonymous: within *Town Topics'* flowery and vine-fretted (if innocent-looking) covers, readers began finding scurrilous social notes by "The Saunterer," biting Broadway banter by "The Itinerant," and pungent views on current books by "Der Kritiker," "The Ringmaster," or "The Bookworm." New Yorkers began to take notice and very soon this "Journal of Society" (the paper's subtitle) began showing more than modest returns.

There was just one hitch. In 1876 An-thony J. Comstock had lobbied through Congress a postal law against "obscenity," making it an offense to mail printed matter which said in plain terms that a woman was pregnant or that someone had syphillis or was a fornicator, all matters in which *Town Topics* dealt with (by Victorian standards) inordinate frankness. As a result, the younger Mann brother, as the paper's *de facto* editor, was arraigned in New York for violating the Comstock Act and, slipping South and pleading grave illness to avoid trial, he turned over his interest in *Town Topics* to the Colonel who, in 1891, bought out the remaining partners' shares and assumed full command. He installed as editor Charles Bohm, whose perceptive, almost fanatical devotion to the old pasha's service (he died almost literally of overwork) quickly turned *Town Topics* into a bonanza and established it as a potent social and cultural institution, to be feared or respected, despised or admired but, above all, read by those who wished to keep abreast of the *haut monde*. Under Bohm, indeed, the *ci-devant* weekly of Gotham gatherings and gallivantings became something more than a local gazette, spawning half a dozen imitations across the country (such as Kansas City's *Independent*, which is still going strong). To the critical departments he brought the bright talents of Percival Pollard (a young Anglo-German critic of whom we shall hear more), Vance Thompson and James Gibbons Huneker, co-founders of their own ill-fated journal (*Mlle. New York*) who were then busily transplanting the new European "aestheticism" to America.

Colonel Mann's intention was to make *Smart Set* a literary twin-sister to *Town Topics*. As he conceived it, the weekly would be mostly reportage and commentary; the monthly fictional and "arty." His foremost aim was to attract to the new magazine readable stories and verse from socialite amateurs whose lustrous surnames would sell the magazine quite regardless of its literary merits. It would be "caviar to the general"—and for the *dilettanti* as well. Its columns were to be given principally to "realistic," if nonetheless imaginary, tales of the leisurely life being lived at the top of the American social pyramid. To counteract the monotony of such fare, the tone of the magazine was to be kept light, saucy and irreverent, especially concerning some of the stilted conventions, pretensions and hypocrisies of High Society (for, incredible as it may now seem, there was once a time when the *Social Register* was taken quite seriously and such a class as an enormously [almost immeasurably] rich "High Society" did, in fact, exist in the United States). Subjects other than this were to be admitted to the magazine, of course, but only if treated in a similar vein. All seriousness, practicality, idealism, ideology or advocacy of anything in particular (except *joie de vivre*) was strictly taboo.

Although the specific application to American life may have been the Colonel's invention, the underlying attitudes and assumptions in this approach certainly were not. They had come straight from the English "aesthetic movement" of the 1890's—an Americanized form of the same ideas to be found in Wilde's astringent epigrams and Aubrey Beardsley's *Yellow Book* cartoons. This, one must remember, was the heyday of "The Butterfly" (as James McNeill Whistler, the American painter, was called) when the natural aristocrat of taste could join with the aristocrats of privilege and money to defend the Temple of Art and Culture against the onslaughts of parvenu, Philistine and dangerous democrat. Thompson and Huneker had proclaimed it in 1895 in their short-lived fortnightly, *Mlle. New York*, thus:

> *Mlle. New York* is not concerned with the public. Her only ambition is to disintegrate some small portion of her public into its original component parts—the aristocracies of birth, wit, learning and art and the joyously vulgar mob.

Colonel Mann's first announcement to the press concerning his new venture sounded almost like an echo of this. "The purpose of *The Smart Set,*" he declared, "will simply and solely be to entertain 'smart' people." America then had far and away enough magazines designed to inform, educate, uplift and inspire, he maintained. It even had quite enough fashion magazines, he noted (perhaps sensing that *Smart Set* might be mistaken for one—as, indeed, it repeatedly was). What was needed was a journal devoted exclusively to the evaluation of "Cleverness."

In retrospect it is much easier to say what the Colonel did not mean by this pet term (he subtitled the new journal: "The Magazine of Cleverness") than what he did. He did not mean, for instance, what was *avantgarde* or experimental or even very novel or skillful in ideas and style but, instead, the kind of badinage that echoed in drawing-rooms where the supercilious *bon mot* was as much a status symbol as the diamond stickpin. It was not a literary value but a social one, transferred chiefly to the subject-matter of writing and only tangentially to style. To be "clever" in 1900 was to be *au courant*, One-Up, ahead of the game, a trifle jaded and a wee bit cynical. It was not quite the same thing as being "smart," or fashionable; in fact, it was "clever" to be affectedly careless of fashion. It was fashionable, for instance, to keep an expensive box at the Metropolitan where one could be seen even if he were ignorant of (or hated) opera, to come at eleven when the ball invitations said nine, and for ladies to expose their bosoms in party gowns and keep them tightly wrapped on the beach. It was clever, on the other hand, to know when and how precisely to puncture such hypocrisies and inconsistencies with good-natured raillery.

There was no serious social purpose in this. It was very distinctly not clever to be a reformer ("anarchist" or "socialist" were the standard pejoratives) or to disapprove of great wealth, ostentatious luxury, or the world of High Fashion. On the contrary, the clever person observed society from above. Whether rich or not himself, he identified with and approved the gilded age affluence that had given the United States a flourishing aristocracy of money and an expanding middle-class that imitated them and aspired to their ranks. Now, in the era of Edward VII and "Teddy" Roosevelt (what the French call *"La Belle Epoque"*), wealth and position were to be wedded to intellect, a confined taste and a style of life which the Schuyler Ainslee generation called "modern." To know how to bring this about was caviar to the dilettante and money in the pockets of art dealers, impresarios and the magazine publisher who could exploit the growing climate of "cleverness." Colonel Mann apprehended, however vaguely, that the new aristocracy of money was essentially narcissistic. It wanted to read about itself quite as much as the great middle-classes wanted, with thrills of envy, to peer behind its façade—to see what really happened after the plumed ladies and silk-hatted gentlemen left their carriages (or, with greater frequency, their limousines) in the street and entered the attended doors beyond which so few could pass.

Thus, at the dawn of a new century, his white imperials carefully brushed and the seals of eleven New York clubs spanning his brocaded vest, William D'Alton Mann became a mogul among magazine magnates. His might be a smaller empire by far than those of S. S. McClure, Frank Munsey, Cyrus K. Curtis or William Randolph Hearst but, within its precincts, he was no less absolute. Yet, for all his surface brusqueness and puffing, he exercised power benignly. At his great brownstone on West 72nd Street, he and his glamorous young wife, Sophia Hartog (he had left the first Mrs. Mann in Ohio, the second in the South, years before), liked to entertain with dinners of almost Roman proportions for their fiefdom—the *Town Topics* and *Smart Set* staffs. In expansive moods the Colonel called this gathering

Culver Pictures

Colonel William D'Alton Mann

his "Family" and, at their annual Thanksgiving feasts, small bonuses of Ess Ess Company bonds were sometimes tucked under the plates of the senior staffers. In summers there were frequent weekend outings at the Manns' Lake George cottage for the "Family," sometimes augmented to include regular contributors as well. As a founder and, for a long term, president of the New York Periodical Publishers Association, the Colonel promoted annual bacchanales at a New Jersey country club for the better part of the male New York literary world (lady authors, however "emancipated," were never invited). At such dinners, well-heeled and established authors (like Booth Tarkington) were not above candidly and gratuitously giving the Colonel their low opinions of his enterprises, but, with one eye on his spiraling circulation figures, he would wave them off good-naturedly with a bit of salty chaff.

In the *Smart Set* offices—first established in the St. James Building, then moved (in June 1902) uptown to the Knox Building on

Fifth Avenue—the atmosphere created by the old gilded age grandee was no less convivial. The suite itself was sumptuously appointed, even by the lush standards of 1902. Each editor and sub-editor had his own partitioned office opening onto a long, deeply carpeted corridor, at one end of which was a burgundy and gilt reception room furnished with horse-hide sofas, massive mahogany tables and potted palms. (One contributor remembered that it "looked more like a club than a magazine office.") At the corridor's other end the Colonel had his "Editorial Chambers," as he grandiloquently styled a spacious room done in polished mahogany and red plush with gilded fringe and tassles. The crowning touch of this room (almost literally) was a cigar-lighter in the shape of a gold Cupid suspended from the ceiling just above the Colonel's oversized desk by a chain of gilt hearts.

Preoccupied with *Town Topics,* Colonel Mann rarely graced these glorious "chambers" with his corpulent presence for more than a few hours a month. According to Charles Hanson Towne, who served the magazine throughout most of its first eight years, the Colonel's perpetual absence was a key factor in the unusually harmonious atmosphere which prevailed in the *Smart Set* office. The Colonel's deputy was his twice-divorced daughter by his first marriage who called herself *Miss* Emma Mann-Vynne and who read manuscripts *ex officio* at *The Smart Set* for a decade. But, adds Towne, she was an unobtrusive, bovine, somewhat dull woman and it was an easy matter for the staff to manipulate her into thinking she had some part in decisions which, in fact, they were themselves making.

For all practical purposes, then, the editor and staff of "The Magazine of Cleverness" enjoyed an autonomy that was as rare in their profession in those days of strong, one-man editorships as it is today in the area of corporate, hierarchical decision-making. The Colonel established basic policies, to be sure,

and held a tight rein on the purse-strings but, as long as the circulation climbed satisfactorily, his editors were left free to improvise according to their own lights. This was to prove a saving grace. In his plans for the magazine, Colonel Mann had made an important miscalculation—in supply, not demand. To produce a magazine of society fiction and verse palatable both to the so-called "Four Hundred" and the *hoi polloi* was quite feasible, even easy, but to sustain it solely by contributions from those in or near the social register was a patent impossibility. There was not enough literary talent among the American leisure classes to keep such a journal afloat for long. Fortunately, Editor Grissom foresaw this. His stratagems in the face of it not only rescued *The Smart Set* from an early grave but gave it a special character which, in effect, was to determine its destiny.

Grissom's ingenuity was evident from the first. In his pre-publication publicity, he had induced the Colonel to advertise a series of enticing prizes for manuscripts, ranging from $10 to $50 for "witticisms" (sketches, jokes and epigram-fillers), $50 to $250 for poetry, $100 to $500 for short stories, up to $1,000 and $2,000 for novelettes. These were continued for several months after the magazine was actually underway, effectively bringing in a flood of contributions and, thus, giving the magazine a reservoir of material to draw upon until it could make its own reputation. One of the items in the first competition was the novelette mentioned above, "The Idle Born," which received a $1,000 prize for prose satire (although the satire today seems to extend no further than giving socialite characters names like Mr. and Mrs. Ferry Dobbs). Its authors, Chatfield-Taylor and DeKoven, were actually professional writers who, if they were not precisely blue-bloods, had suitably aristocratic-sounding names. So, Grissom gave this "society romance" the place of honor in the first issue and thereby established a pattern (of opening with the novelette) which was to be almost rigorously followed in *The Smart Set* during the next twenty-four years.

But these were not the only high-sounding names in early tables of contents. There was often a title or two: The Countess of Warwick, Prince Vladimir Vaniatsky, Countess Loveau de Chevanne, The Infanta Eulalie, Prince Albert of Monaco, *et al.* There were also a few *bona fide* Knickerbocker signatures: Minna Irving, Edgar Saltus and Mrs. Van Rennselaer Cruger among them. An aristocratic Southern lady, Mrs. Burton Harrison, contributed reminiscences of a summer's travels in a quaint and far-off land—Russia—and Richmond author, John Regnault Ellyson, often represented (and wrote about) the First Families of Virginia. Other contributors to early issues who dwelt at least on the outer edges of the socially elite were A. V. Winterroth, Frederic Fairchild Sherman, Eliot Gregory, Caroline K. Duer (who, with her sisters, Elizabeth, and Alice Duer Miller—both highly talented writers—was to reappear regularly), S. E. Benét (father of two poets) and Charles F. Nirdlinger, whose nephew (George Jean Nathan, then a Cornell freshman) would one day play a most decisive role in the future of *The Smart Set.*

Literary *éclat* was signalized in the first few issues by contributions from Nathaniel Hawthorne's only son, Julian, then a popular author on his own. (In one early article, incidentally, Julian Hawthorne observed: "It seems highly improbable that American ladies, as a body, will ever seriously take up smoking.") There were others, too, just as popular: Ella Wheeler Wilcox, Bliss Carman, Gertrude Atherton, Emerson Hough, Temple Bailey, Gelett Burgess, Gouverneur Morris, Theodosia Garrison, Justus Miles Forman (who died on the *Lusitania*) and Anna Katherine Green—to mention but a few who once led best-seller lists but may now be (at best) but dimly remembered. A complete roster of *Smart Set* contributors over the period from 1900 to 1924 would contain perhaps 2,000 names—without doubt a more representative cross-section of American writers during two generations than any other periodical then or since. There would also be an amazing continuity in such a list; six contributors to the first number of the magazine, for example, were still appearing there two decades later!

From the very beginning there were also a few signatures in each issue that had a definite Social Register ring to them but were not readily identifiable. Who, one wondered were Cecil Carlisle Pangman, Charles Huxton Going, Dancan Campbell Scott, or Van Tassel Sutphen? (In early *Smart Set* usage almost everyone had three names as *prima facie* evidence of social standing.) In plain fact, many of these high-sounding names were among Grissom's deliberate ruses—fanciful pseudonyms concocted by him or his colleagues for their own works as well as the second (and sometimes third and fourth) pieces in an issue by stalwarts like Burgess, Forman, Garrison, *et al.,* who could be counted on for a steady supply of material having all the earmarks of coming straight from "inside" the *haut monde.* Hither and yon in early issues one also came across such blatant *noms de guerre* as "Florida Pier," "John J. a'Becket," "Pomona Penrin," "Onoto Watonna," or "Bert Timoney." Merely an expedient at first, the use of pseudonyms (whether aristocratic or fanciful) soon ripened into a tradition which, in due course, would save the magazine more than once from imminent oblivion.

The kind of things *The Smart Set* would print for the next decade and beyond—both as to genre and line of attack—were also delineated by Grissom and his assistants. Each issue (160 pages) would contain, in addition to the novelette (perhaps a fourth of the space), a short play, a dozen or so stories of varying lengths, a dozen poems (again, depending upon length), and as many "witticisms" as needed to fill up the bottoms of pages without overcrowding—vignettes of incident or character, a joke in dialogue form, or epigrams (singly and in groups). Sometimes "cleverness" was far from apparent in such heavy-footed fillers as:

HE PROVED IT!

Mother—I told you to tell that young man he couldn't kiss you.

Daughter—But, Mama, he could.

Or, in others, the archness of what the 1900's called "chaff" was more than obvious: "The song of life is often a duet in A flat, with incidental minor accompaniments." Fortunately, time brought some improvements to *Smart Set* fillers.

Only occasionally in the first few years were non-fiction articles introduced into the magazine and then they were of a deliberately non-controversial nature: Mrs. Harrison's trip to Russia or "A Bit of the Yale Blue" (personal reminiscences), Arthur Symons' "Aspects of Verlaine" (literary), or an occasional article on the New York theater scene by some popular playwright like David Belasco, Clyde Fitch, or Thomas A. Daly. Even after the introduction of regular critical departments (theater and literature), the percentage of space in the magazine devoted to non-fiction was minute. It was and remained, above all, a magazine of fiction and verse. Even the verse, after the first few numbers, was limited largely to short lyrics, although the first volume saw the publication of a 19-page poetic satire (another prizewinner) on Newport ("The Charge of the Four Hundred," by "Momus, Jr."), and in November 1900 appeared a 10-page, unfinished (posthumous) satire by Richard Hovey, a supposed "Canto XVII" to Byron's "Don Juan" which included such stanzas as:

His father's name was Smith, and later Smythe;
He was Van Smythe, completely Knickerbockered.
His father had begun with spade and scythe;

He, from his cradle had been coaxed and cockered.
His father had the wit to take his tithe
(And wed a widow who was richly tochered),
But never quite got into good society;
He belonged to its most select variety.

The Parvenu—Hovey's target in this extract—was a favorite theme in *The Smart Set* for many years, and, more often than not, he defeated the social lions who obstructed his climb, repulsive and gauche as he was. Another favorite theme in the magazine's stories and plays, early and late, was "The New Woman"—the independent, strong-willed female who flouted convention by divorcing and remarrying successfully or by engaging in a public career (such as journalism or the law) or merely by violating some sewing circle taboo. She was sometimes an object of ridicule, especially if she gave herself to uplifting "causes," but more often she was an unsentimentalized heroine. Then there was the "horse sense" approach to the inanities of society, usually from the point of view of a foreigner (especially a Far- or Middle-Easterner) or a yokel ("country cousin") or even an animal. In the first issue of the magazine, for example, a stage horse poked fun at some of the more obviously ridiculous conventions of opera by supposedly giving his reminiscences of playing the part of *Grane,* Brünnhilde's trusty steed. But if one of the vulgar mob—especially a "hayseed,"—were used as a satirizing device, he was never more than merely a vehicle and never, by contrast, approved. One vacationed —but never *lived,* really—in the country, and one of the most popular features for several years were the vignette-fillers by Tom P. Morgan of the hilarious crudity of his "Arkansaw" characters, the precursors of present-day Dogpatch.

Perhaps Grissom's greatest editorial coup was the negotiation of a long-term contract (it eventually ran twenty years) with a Parisian authors' league, the *Société des Gens de Lettres,* for an annual supply, *en bloc,* of short French manuscripts for the incredibly low yearly stipend of twenty-five dollars. Within a few months *The Smart Set* began flaunting in each issue a short story, play, or poem (sometimes more than one type) in the original French. Before the contract expired in 1921, a long roster of Gallic authors —among them such distinguished names as Gautier, Mendès, Edmond Jaloux, Paul and Victor Margueritte and Anatole France (as well as numerous lesser lights)—had graced the magazine's pages. It would be fatuous to conjecture at this point the proportion of *The Smart Set*'s patrons who actually enjoyed such things. But in an age when boarding-school French and an eventual trip to Paris was practically a *sine qua non* of genteel education, the inclusion of such exotic fare was not as precocious as it might now seem. Whether or not one was really fluent in French mattered little if he could display a copy of the current "Magazine of Cleverness"—casually opened to the French item, perhaps—on his kidney-shaped library table. It was like the finely-bound sets of George Borrow, Browning or Ruskin which, with uncut pages, adorned one's shelves. In the new affluence, "Culture" for Americans was a matter of having, not being.

Despite the lush prizes, Grissom had to manage not only these French contributions, but everything else on a monthly budget that would send today's editors into screaming fits. One cent per word for prose and twenty-five (sometimes stretched to thirty-five) cents a line for poetry was the going rate—not only for *The Smart Set* but for the generality of American magazines which then accepted unsolicited manuscripts. Occasionally a well-established author—like the perfumed, elegant Richard LaGallienne—could blackjack the Colonel out of as much as two cents-a-word, but even most "Big Name" writers, like the English exotic, Edgar Fawcett, were content with $250 for a *Smart Set* novelette without

grumbling until *Collier's Weekly* upset the American market in 1904 by announcing a five cent rate for prose.

Once, however, an irate poet returned a check for five dollars for a 20-line contribution with this note:

> Dear Editors of *The Smart Set:*
> Now I know why you call yourselves the smart set.

To this Grissom quipped (mimicking Col. Mann's arrogance): "Poets are born, not paid!"

But the joke was not bitter. If the pay-scale was low so, too, was the cost of good living in those halcyon days. A struggling author could stretch his $25 check for a *Smart Set* story a long way. He could buy a good suit of clothes, pay a month's rent on a sizable city apartment or house, or spend five days in a palatial suite in a first-class New York hotel for such a sum. If he came to Manhattan from the hinterlands for a big splurge, he could enjoy for one dollar en route, according to an early *Smart Set* ad, a seven-course meal in a New York Central dining car that would include, among other choice viands, Blue Points, filet mignon Bordelaise, roast squab with watercress, and a delectable compendium of vegetables, salads, fruits, cheeses and sweets.

Editorial salaries, office assistance and even the rent and maintenance on the Colonel's sumptuous offices were correspondingly low. Although exact figures are unavailable, it seems likely that, in the early years at least, the inclusive cost of an issue of *The Smart Set* did not exceed $6,000. It was probably less. Yet, with the magazine priced at twenty-five cents (a luxury in the era of the ten-cent monthly) and with two dozen pages of advertising (at $150 per page) in each issue, it is not difficult to calculate the old Colonel's rate of profit at the end of the first year when the circulation hit 100,000 on its way up. Furthermore, the Colonel, as we have seen, had prudently organized a London affiliate of his Ess Ess Company which published an

English edition, reprinting the contents of the New York magazine for a handsome tribute which he did not have to share with the contributors, who sold their wares outright (though the American reprint rights were immediately returned to the author). Whatever talents Editor Grissom may have had as a sharp bargainer in the literary marketplace, he was clearly no match for the dollar-squeezing Colonel Mann.

It would, in fact, be quite unfair to suggest that Grissom was in any sense either ruthless or arrogant. He unquestionably belonged to that rising generation of tough-minded, raffish, hard-drinking newspapermen who were just then revamping American journalism. He was cut from the same cloth as George Ade, Finley Peter Dunne and, in due course, H. L. Mencken, Ring Lardner, Damon Runyon and "F. P. A." Like them, his alma mater was the city room of a metropolitan daily—in his case, the *Kansas City Star*—and he had come East to Printing House Square in the late '90's to seek his fortune in the mushrooming magazine market. He had a flair for the kind of *vers de société* then in vogue in *Town Topics*, as well as *Puck, Judge* and the old *Life* magazine (all satirical weeklies to which *The Smart Set* bore more than a little kinship). Almost effortlessly, he could turn out rhymes like:

> If I were King Cophetua
>   And you a beggar maid,
> Oh, what a wealth of love, parfay,
>   Would at your feet be laid!
>
> But since you are of love the queen,
>   And I a troubadour,
> You go upon your way serene,
>   And I am very poor!

Who could imagine a cynical newsman unabashedly tossing out such gallant pleasantries today? Such was the paradox of Arthur Grissom's personality (a not unusual paradox in his time) and it was precisely this com-

bination of the practical journalist and the articulate *bon vivant* that allowed him to succeed with his "Magazine of Cleverness." According to an associate, he was hardly a man of wide learning or culture, although he had sincere respect for literature and the arts. Somewhat slow-moving and methodical, he was nevertheless a hard and aggressive worker whose devotion to the magazine brought him to the office on many a Sunday morning when the staff enjoyed their only respite from the standard six-day work week. His work was indeed his life and to correspond with—even better, to be called upon—by well-known authors titillated this midwestern boy almost inordinately.

Barely thirty-one when Colonel Mann tapped him from among his *Town Topics* associates to edit *The Smart Set*, Arthur Grissom was dead of typhoid fever in October 1901, before his infant magazine was halfway through its second year. In a very real sense the "Magazine of Cleverness" was his legacy, owing as much to his resourcefulness and devotion as to the Colonel's gambling instincts. It bore his stamp long years afterward. In the April 1902 number an anonymous colleague or contributor penned a saccharine, if nonetheless sincere, elegy ("In Memoriam—A. G.") which concluded with the comforting thought

> That God is gentle to his guest
>   And therefore may I gladly say,
> "Surely the things he loved the best
>   Are his to-day."

Earlier that same year Queen Victoria also died, ending an epoch. But, though *Smart Set* ingenues might sip Alexanders on Newport terraces or nonchalantly puff a Murad on a motor outing while, in their clubrooms, their beaus traded tips on how to avoid the snares of matrimony, not far beneath this veneer of presumed sophistication, the old Victorian sentiments endured.

The Colonel versus Mrs. Grundy

———•—•———

Two days after Arthur Grissom's funeral Colonel Mann called his *Smart Set* minions together in his *sanctum-sanctorum*. The associate editor, Marvin Dana, three assistant editors—Charles Hanson Towne, Henry Collins Walsh and Charles G. Sheldon—and the Colonel's laconic daughter, Mrs. Mann-Vynne, comprised the solemn gathering. "Our magazine faces a grave crisis," the publisher officiously began, adding that he knew he could depend upon his "family" to carry on the work bravely. Then he got down to business. There would, he announced, be a general upward shift for everyone present:

Dana would be editor, Towne and Walsh associates, and Sheldon the new assistant editor-at-large. New subordinate readers would be hired to replace the former assistants. These, as it happened, were a succession of comely, if wholly untrained and untalented young ladies (mainly genteel daughters of the Colonel's impecunious Southern cronies) whose obtuseness, says Towne, cost *The Smart Set* more than one first-rate manuscript. The old dandy, it seemed, was a flinty bargainer with businessmen and authors but a pushover for a sweet face with an Alabama drawl and what is today known on American campuses as "the *Mademoiselle* Complex."

Marvin Dana, an Upstate New Yorker with a superb Vandyke, a refined taste in Saville Row suits and French wines, and a penchant for intellectual ladies of easy virtue, was a popular (if perhaps inevitable) choice as the new editor, despite his office nickname ("the Professor"). Indeed, for a magazine office of that era, Dana possessed an inordinate set of academic credentials: degrees in English from Middlebury, law from Union, and three years' graduate study at Columbia and N.Y.U. After a stint on the old *New York Herald* he had worked for two years in the Boston Public Library as a researcher for Dr. John Clark Ridpath, editor of the enormously successful "Library of Universal Literature" series. A facile writer, Dana soon found the rewards of journalism and *belles-lettres* greater than those of scholarship or the law, so in 1896 he took an editorial job in London with a short-lived competitor of *Punch*. In November 1899, he was back in New York, working briefly for *Town Topics* and thence to the first *Smart Set* staff where he became Grissom's closest friend and confidant. By 1902 he had two novels to his credit (*The Woman of Orchids* and *A Puritan Witch*) and an impressive string of stories and poems in a variety of American and foreign periodicals.

But, for all his learning and literary skill, Dana was neither an imaginative nor energetic editor and he was able to add little, if anything, to the foundations already laid by Grissom. Instead, he was rather inclined to accept the *status quo* in the magazine, observing dourly that "in our day at least, there are no mute, inglorious Miltons—though there are many, alas! neither Miltons, nor mute, only inglorious."

And why not? There was little need to experiment with new approaches at this point. In its first two years *The Smart Set* had established itself firmly with its audience (still continuing to grow in 1902) and with

a dependable coterie of contributors (workhorses like Katherine Metcalf Roof, G. Vere Tyler, Miriam Michelson and Frank Dempster Sherman could keep several magazines afloat for years!) and Dana saw no compelling reasons to want to change things.

Then, quite without warning, came a challenge from a very unexpected quarter. For two and one-half years, *The Smart Set* held a virtual monopoly on its special brand of literary cleverness. Suddenly it had a competitor: *Ainslee's Magazine*. Had it been *Youth's Companion* or *The Ladies Home Journal*, Dana and his staff could not have been more astounded.

Since 1897 *Ainslee's,* a Street & Smith family magazine ("An American Magazine for the American People" was its subtitle) had struggled along as one of many profusely illustrated monthlies of innocuous fiction and verse, timely articles and household hints. Its single noteworthy achievement in those years was early publication (a few months before *The Smart Set* also "discovered" him) of a very clever fellow who signed himself "O. Henry" (which *Ainslee's* sub-editors insisted on emending to "Oliver Henry"). Hardpressed in competition with successful giants like *Everybody's* and *Cosmopolitan*, Street & Smith decided to seek greener pastures for *Ainslee's*. The field in which *The Smart Set* grazed contentedly alone looked most enticing.

Thus, the October 1902 issue of *Ainslee's* arrived on the newsstands looking for all the world like *The Smart Set*'s twin. It had the same size, shape, format, type-face and pattern of contents and a new subtitle: "The Magazine of Clever Fiction." Its table of contents was composed almost exclusively of *Smart Set* "regulars"—such as Edward S. Van Zile, Bliss Carman, Arthur Ketchum, Arthur Stringer, Emery Pottle, Rovert Loveman, Theodosia Garrison, *et al.* There was even an untranslated French story and, perhaps the unkindest cut in this brazen imitation, a poem by Charles Hanson Towne. Finally,

Richard Duffy and Gilman Hall, *Ainslee's* co-editors (themselves contributors to *The Smart Set*), announced a new editorial stance that could well have been written by Colonel Mann:

> . . . It is a truism to say that men and women read a magazine to be amused, rather than to learn the sorrows of life. That is why the zest of humor, sprightliness and sparkle will be the dominating characteristic of the contents of *Ainslee's*.

To *Smart Set* eyes, such a bald proclamation amounted to running up the black flag.

At first there was consternation and anxiety in the *Smart Set* office, but the Colonel and Dana remained outwardly unflurried. After a steady rise, the circulation had levelled off at around 135,000 and the Colonel saw no reason why this comfortable figure could not be sustained without new "gimmicks" or without increasing payments to attract "bigger" names to the contributors' roster. Whatever lures *Ainslee's* might offer at first, he knew that, as a fifteen-center (underselling *The Smart Set* by ten cents), it could not afford for very long to pay authors more than the standard rates. Moreover, *The Smart Set* was firmly established with its advertisers and the Colonel reasoned that his clientele would remain loyal rather than desert to a magazine that had, until then, a very different market and reputation and an uncertain future.

Once again the Colonel was right. In its new imitative guise *Ainslee's* indeed thrived (it eventually gained a circulation of 250,-000) but not at the expense of *The Smart Set*. On the contrary, the latter's sales actually rose perceptibly year by year until, in 1905, "The Magazine of Cleverness" hit its peak of 165,000—in the proportions of today's magazine audience equivalent to perhaps five times that number. Vying for material, the rivals editors also found that they could "share" contributors and even cross the battle lines themselves—Towne, Walsh and even Dana himself appeared now and again in *Ainslee's* and returned the favor to Duffy,

—*New York Public Library*
Marvin Dana

Hall and their associates. In fact, one of the most remarkable phenomena of the New York magazine scene in that era was the coterie atmosphere in which such editorial exchanges were commonplace. Among the *Smart Set's* "regulars" during this period, for instance, were the editors of *Life* (Tom Masson), *Judge* (R. K. Munkittrick), *Munsey's* (Robert H. Davis), *St. Nicholas* (Albert Bigelow Paine), *The Woman's Home Companion* (Arthur Guiterman), the associate editor of the newly-invigorated *Saturday Evening Post* (Reginald Wright Kauffman) and several more. In those days, it was the editors, not the critics, whose chairs formed a charmed circle!

Nevertheless, with such an expanded market for their contributors' wares, Dana and his staff had to be more sharply alert than ever for signs of promising new talent. In this respect they did remarkably well. One day, for instance, a shy young lady with a euphonious name—Zona Gale—fresh from the fields of Portage, Wisconsin, and with a brand-new job on the *New York World*, called at the *Smart Set* office with a bundle of ballads and a letter of introduction to Towne. When these were accepted she sent in more poems, then stories, then plays and soon joined the growing roster of "regulars." But recognition came slowly to Zona Gale. It was not until 1920—eighteen years of constant good writing after her *Smart Set* debut —that her novel and play, *Miss Lulu Bett*, finally brought her the Pulitzer Prize and a richly deserved fame.

Another *Smart Set* "find" who, in 1901, was only on the threshold of a spectacular success was William Sydney Porter ("O. Henry"). Despite three or four earlier appearances in *McClure's* and *Ainslee's*, Porter was still earning less than enough from his writing to keep the proverbial pot boiling. In Pittsburgh, he studied the magazines—especially "The Magazine of Cleverness"—assiduously and, one day, sent in a piece exactly tailored to its customary vein. The story actually totalled over 2,000 words but, in an accompanying note, the author offered a 50% "discount" for cash on the line as he desperately needed money to buy a train ticket to New York. The story, "The Lotos and the Bottle," was accepted forthwith (published January 1902), Porter caught the next train to Gotham and immediately began his meteoric ascent, with its feverish round of publishing, that ended in his untimely death in 1910. Few appreciate the extent to which his style and technique were actually influenced by *The Smart Set*. The "surprise ending," with its semi-ironic, semi-sentimental twists, was a specialty of the magazine from the very outset, though, admittedly "O. Henry" did it better than most of his competitors or the myriad imitators he was to inspire in the next two decades.

Another mail brought in a beautifully handwritten novelette (entitled "Araby"), bearing a Swiss postmark. It happened to be well-written and interesting, but the author's signature alone—Baroness Bettina von Hutten—would have sufficed to insure it huzzahs from the staff had it been frankly inferior. Soon, pieces by the Baroness were turning up in almost every issue of *The Smart Set*. It was months before the truth leaked out that the exotic Baroness was plain Betsy Riddle, from Erie, Pa., who had gone abroad to study and (in 1897) had met and married an impoverished German nobleman who mistook her for an heiress. Until she divorced the Baron in 1909, she made a living for both of them by her literary talents. In 1905 her novel, *Pam* (then considered a "shocker") became a best-seller and over the years she published some twenty-three popular books, many of them developed from her *Smart Set* pieces. But when she died in a London convent in 1958 at an advanced age, the Baroness von Hutten had been almost entirely forgotten.

As the magazine glided through its first four years numerous interesting newcomers rallied 'round the swirling S's. From New England, for instance, the editors received good manuscripts from fledglings like Dorothy Canfield Fisher, Martha Dickinson Bianchi (Emily Dickinson's niece and executrix) and the erudite Henry Seidel Canby, father of The Book-of-the-Month Club. The urban East Coast provided, among many another, Agnes Repplier, Stewart Edward White, Ludwig Lewisohn, Mary Heaton Vorse and—a recent arrival from St. Louis and Chicago—the charming, Vienna-born Helen Woljeska ("Mme. Leandre" as she became known in *The Smart Set*), who was not only mistress of the cynical epigram, but an artist and stage designer of great ability as well. From the Far West came still more lustrous names: Frank Norris, at last acquiring fame on the eve of his premature death; Jack London, on his way to becoming the decade's *beau ideal* of the American storyteller; and the now almost forgotten "Joaquin Miller" (Cincinnatus Heine Miller).

From the somnolent sub-Potomac came a fastidiously typed manuscript (still a rarity in 1902) signed, in the most pristine copperplate imaginable, by a young scion of two of the Old Dominion's oldest families—James Branch Cabell. The story ("As Played Before His Highness") was Cabell's first fiction to be accepted by a national magazine. Like the fourteen other pieces that would follow it from Cabell's seemingly immaculate typewriter to the pages of *The Smart Set* during the next twenty years, this would eventually find a place in the immense tapestry of mythic satire woven between 1902 and 1929 by this eccentric Virginian whom Joe Lee Davis has called "the Boccaccio of the second American Renaissance." (Retitled, it is one of the *"Dizaine des Fêtes Galantes"* in Vol. 9 of "The Biography of the Life of Manuel.") Eventually, too, it would be a *Smart Set* story ("Some Ladies and Jurgen") which, expanded into a novel at the suggestion of H. L. Mencken, would bring Cabell fame, fortune and, briefly, a reputation as one of the three or four most important American novelists of the 1920's.

The story of Cabell's *Jurgen* and its relationship to the magazine belongs, of course, to a later chapter of this history, but it would be very hard to find another author who better typifies the cluster of attitudes and postures cherished by those who rallied to *The Smart Set* in its earliest years. Cabell was *Smart Set* "cleverness" incarnate. His imagination dwelt in such exotic and aristocratic realms as the courts of Louis XIV and Charles II, the romantic medieval world of Aucassin and Nicolette and, ultimately, in his own fantastic Never-Never Land of the indefinite past—"The Land of Poictesme"—which he peopled with "moderns" who, like himself, hated hypocrisy, vulgarity and cant and exulted in a rarified urbanity that mocked all pretensions. Indeed, *The Smart Set* was Cabell's ideal vehicle and, though he was accepted ere long in a half-dozen other periodicals, he never forgot it. His mannered prose, his use of the unhistoric past as a club to beat the present, and his emphasis upon a kind of modernized Byronism (in part, no doubt, deriving from Edgar Saltus) typify

—*New York Public Library*

Charles Hanson Towne

much of what, in the first years of the twentieth century, was beginning to look like a "Smart Set School" in American writing.

Although the influences of any given magazine in literary styles and attitudes of its time are always too nebulous for precise delineation, there can be little doubt in the mind of anyone who takes the trouble to read the American magazines of that period that such a "school" was developing. Month upon month the list of new contributors grew as the young writers of the land heeded the patient advice of Dana, Towne and Walsh —to the rejected as well as the accepted— and learned from them that even "cleverness" had its formulas.

Near the end of 1904, however, Dana received an irresistible call from a New York newspaper and Charles Hanson Towne inherited his editorial chair. Although he was but twenty-seven at the time, Towne had worked on three periodicals since leaving college at the end of his freshman term, eight years before, and had been with *The Smart*

Set almost since its inception. The editorship was the "big break" he needed toward what was to be a long and varied editorial career —on *The Designer, The Delineator, McClure's* and, finally, *Harper's Bazaar.* In the 1930's he would write a syndicated daily column for the New York *American* and, in the last decade of his life, embark on a wholly new career in the theatre, acting with success the part of the Anglican clergyman in the record-breaking Broadway hit, *Life with Father*—a role admirably suited to his genial, yet gentle, nature. Affable "Charlie" Towne was an efficient editor and a prolific writer of stories. As the late Burton Rascoe once observed, "Charlie was the model commercial magazine poet's poet." Nevertheless, his published memoirs provide one of the very few reliable glimpses into the inner workings of *The Smart Set* during his period. Unluckily, his three-year editorial tenure fell during the magazine's most dismal hour.

Flushed with success, Colonel Mann had assaulted new fields. For some years past he had successfully operated, via *Town Topics,* a "Financial Advisory Service," giving patrons (for a fancy price) Wall Street tips by telephone, telegram and daily letter. Now he proposed a similar service for *Smart Set* readers: "personalized advice" by subscription on fashions, interior decor, resorts, restaurants, etc. After three months, however, the service had not attracted enough business to pay for itself, so it was quickly and quietly abandoned. Next, the Colonel turned his attention to the seeming interest of *Smart Set* readers in the magazine's foreign contributions. Why not, he wondered, a magazine devoted exclusively to such matter? So, he launched a new monthly called *Transatlantic Tales* or, more properly, he refurbished a by-product periodical in which, for many years, he had reprinted monthly the fiction offerings of *Town Topics* for sale in the hinterlands. The editors of *Transatlantic Tales,* which was designed to reprint English and expertly translated stories from the European

magazines, were James G. Huneker and Edward Clark Marsh. Through their efforts a surprisingly large number of leading Continental and British writers of the most advanced schools received their first (and, as it happened, premature) publication in the United States. The American audience that followed *The Smart Set* in that decade was not yet ready for a greater degree of literary sophistication and the Colonel found the bothersome copyright convention blocking his filching of material without adequate payments. Hence, *Transatlantic Tales* was allowed to expire early in 1908.

The losses sustained in the "Smart Living Service" and *Transatlantic Tales* were to prove a pittance compared with the Colonel's third new venture—an annual entitled *Fads and Fancies of Representative Americans at the Beginning of the Twentieth Century.* It was superbly bound in gilded morocco, printed in ornamented type faces on hand-made, gilt-edged paper and expensively illustrated. The price: $1,500 per copy! Naturally, the Americans the Colonel found "representative" were all very rich: industrialists, financiers with Knickerbocker patronymics, gentleman-politicians and the like. The idea appeared quite harmless, if expensive. It recounted the successful and glamorous lives led by these people and gave titillating anecdotes about their careers, hobbies, travels, social engagements and other leisure activities. To innocent eyes it all seemed innocent enough.

Not so to the practiced eye of Mr. Norman Hapgood, the intrepid editor of the rival *Collier's Weekly.* Pressed for a *Cause célèbre* wherewith to compete in the "Muckraking" craze with Lincoln Steffens' "Shame of the Cities" series in *McClure's* (exposing urban political corruption), Tarbell and Baker's shocking revelations of Standard Oil chicaneries in *The Outlook* and Thomas W. Lawson's Wall Street confessions ("Frenzied Finance") in *Everybody's,* Editor Hapgood thought he spied a rat—or perhaps two rats

—in *Town Topics'* murky undergrowth. In mid-summer of 1906, several weeks before *Fads and Fancies* made its long-delayed appearance (it was "in the works" for over four years) another such enterprise, unfortunately called *America's Smart Set*, had been exposed by a prominent New York broker, Edwin Post (husband of Emily Post, of later *Etiquette* fame), as a shake-down operation. Post had, in fact, acted as live bait to catch a solicitor for this blackmailing operation and in the subsequent investigations three high ranking members of *Town Topics,* including the editor, had been directly implicated.

Colonel Mann had been spending the summer in France when the scandal about *America's Smart Set* broke and, though he had immediately issued a strong denial of its connection with *Town Topics* and had fired his weekly journal's editor, Charles Stokes Wayne, the suspicion yet lingered that Colonel Mann and Justice Joseph M. Deuel were at the very least working only a different side of the same street. Hapgood intended to make the most of it for his magazine and he enlisted in his cause the headline-seeking William Travers Jerome, New York's enormously popular "reformist" District Attorney. Their plan was simple: to goad Mann into an action for criminal libel and let him incriminate himself.

In this they had the connivance and enthusiastic support of Robert Collier, the 29-year-old editor of the weekly magazine his Irish immigrant father had founded in 1888, who had frequently been a target for "The Saunterer's" biting aspersions in *Town Topics.* Cautiously at first, Hapgood (a lawyer by training himself) began to jab at Colonel Mann, Justice Deuel and their real or alleged enterprises. Each week the blows became a bit thicker and heavier.

Meanwhile, *Town Topics* put its (or the Colonel's) head obligingly into the paper noose. In reporting the appearances of Alice Roosevelt (President Theodore Roosevelt's twenty-year-old daughter) at several Newport summer parties, "The Saunterer" had indulged in some blatant innuendos about her too-costly "Alice-blue" silk undies, her "fancy dances for the edification of men," and her alleged imbibing, *sans chaperon,* of "stimulants," concluding:

> There may be no reason for [Mrs. Grundy] making such a fuss about it, but if the young woman knew some of the tales that are told at the clubs in Newport she would be more careful in the future about what she does and how she does it.

At this Rob Collier—an enthusiastic "T. R." supporter and personal friend of the Roosevelts—saw red. To Hapgood's latest crusading editorial (in the August 16, 1905 *Collier's*) he appended a personal barrage, asserting that the Colonel was well-known as "something worse than . . . an ordinary forger, horse-thief, or second-story man" and heaping calumny upon Justice Deuel into the bargain. Even with such provocation, it took several weeks of reprinted accusations and billingsgate sniping between the two weeklies before the Colonel and his associate were constrained (on *Collier's* dare!) to prefer the desired charges of criminal libel. District Attorney Jerome lost no time obtaining the necessary indictments.

By some mysterious means the separate actions of the Colonel and Justice Deuel, as plaintiffs, charging Hapgood, both Colliers (father as well as son) and *Collier's Weekly* with willful and malicious defamation with intent to damage their good repute and destroy the Colonel's magazine were simplified into one of Deuel vs. Hapgood, with the Colonel as the star witness for the prosecution. The trial, which dragged through a fortnight (in January 1906), swept everything else off the front pages of New York's daily newspapers. Nevertheless, Hapgood and the Colliers remained unperturbed. They brought up a battery of the best legal minds in the country, enlisted a cadre of *Social Register* witnesses, and dug in with gusto. Newspapers throughout the land had, of course, caught up the story and with every headline and news lead the name of *Collier's Weekly* was mentioned. It was the kind of advertising you could not buy, as the mushrooming circulation figures soon showed.

Meanwhile, the *Smart Set* office was in a state close to panic. Advertisers cancelled contracts with each new revelation and contributors began shying away. At the outset of the scandal, the circulation seemed to rise, then drop noticeably as it became apparent to sensation-seeking readers that the magazine would remain unflinchingly aloof from the whole tawdry mess. After all, Hapgood had levelled no charges at "The Magazine of Cleverness"; he had, on the contrary, gone out of his way in one of his anti-Mann tirades to praise *The Smart Set's* high level of writing and taste. But every trial dispatch that mentioned "the notorious" Colonel Mann identified him as "publisher of *Town Topics* and *The Smart Set*" and Mrs. Grundy (society's name for outraged self-righteousness) and the American penchant for guilt by association did the rest.

In an era known for its "Society" trials (that of Harry K. Thaw for the triangle slaying of the fashionable architect, Stanford White, occurred in the same year) the two-week process of Deuel vs. Hapgood was a veritable social carnival. To be sure, *Collier's* eventually produced only a few *bona fide* socialites to testify in person for the defense but, throughout several days' grueling cross-examination, their lawyers wangled, wheedled and pressured enormously damaging confessions from the Colonel. A dozen or so Wall Street financiers, many of them socially prominent, had made him long-term, low-interest and (in most cases) unsecured loans totalling nearly $200,000 during the previous decade, he was compelled to admit, and the defense was able to show that in numerous instances there was a marked difference between the treatment accorded these gentlemen by "The Saunterer" before and after such baksheesh. The Colonel was also shown to have kept paid informers in some of the "best" houses—servants and disgruntled social climbers, and the like—and to have boasted that his office safe "contained the reputations of 'The Four Hundred'." (When, as social historian Lloyd Morris reported, it actually was opened after his death in 1920, the year Prohibition began, it was found to contain but a few rare bottles of Cognac Extra!) Nevertheless, as Jerome declared in his equivocal summation for the plaintiff, there was really "not a scintilla of evidence Colonel Mann blackmailed anyone."

The jury took just seven minutes to reach a verdict of "Not Guilty." But long before this event the metropolitan newspapers had acquitted Hapgood. The journalistic fraternity closed ranks, as it were, against a renegade scoundrel in their midst lest his methods cast suspicion upon them all, and the interpretation they put upon the outcome was not that Justice Deuel had failed to satisfy the legal requirements of his complaints—to demonstrate unquestionably that Hapgood's editorials indeed constituted a palpable libel (a difficult proposition in any court)—but that the two "extortionists" had engaged in all the nefarious practices alleged against them by the *Collier's* editor. The prompt arrest of Colonel Mann for perjury following this trial lent credence to his blackest public image and, though he was quickly cleared of the charge, his brief trial and exoneration were noticed only perfunctorily in the back pages of the metropolitan press.

Both the Colonel and *Town Topics* quickly recovered their equanimity and, though slightly chastened for a time, went doggedly on their way. Paradoxically, *The Smart Set* did not. Although it had only been on the periphery of the scandal, it was left in deep distress—permanently and irreparably maimed.

To those of its readers (a goodly company, apparently) who really belonged on the upper slopes of High Society, the pale blue cover with the dangling red hearts had suddenly lost its appeal. It was no longer "smart" (quite the contrary!) to be seen reading it in the best clubrooms or in the salon cars of expresses headed beyond New Haven. Since *Town Topics* continued to function as New York's only social gazette, one regrettably found it indispensable even if one had to read it surreptitiously or subscribe in a servant's name. But . . . the deliberate, cynical creations of an unmasked, arrant bounder . . . why, what had one *ever* really seen in it (one asked with a bored yawn) that was all that *clever*? To the *hoi polloi* the name *Smart Set* thereafter gave off a faint odor of blackmail, scandal and perfumed pornography which, though it might lure the smuthounds, was an effective deterrent to finding a stable new audience to replace the defectors. The circulation plummeted in 1906: some 25,000 readers departed in that year, and perhaps 10,000 more slipped away during each of the next four years. In the magazine's advertising pages, its "carriage trade" clients—luxury hotels, fashionable boutiques, expensive jewellers, etc.—gave way to ads for Milwaukee breweries and convention hotels in Atlantic City.

Fortunately, more sensible attitudes prevailed among most of the magazine's steady contributors or, at least, there were still authors around who were brave, brazen or desperate enough to remain doggedly loyal. One such daring young man was Harry Sinclair Lewis, making a tentative start on the long career that, three decades later, would make him America's first Nobel laureate. Fresh from the Yale campus, Lewis was then living at Upton Sinclair's utopian socialist colony in New Jersey, "Helicon Hall," where (dropping his first name in admiration for Sinclair) he began turning out reams of lyrics by lamplight for *The Smart Set*. One of these

brief "crimes of my youth" (as Lewis later described his juvenilia) which now lies buried in surviving copies of the July 1907 *Smart Set* was this filler:

THE ULTRA-MODERN
I know one strangely skilled in tone and
    scent,
  A subtle master of exotic hours;
Yet broods he joyless in his Orient,
  Forgetting how to love the roadside
    flowers.

As poetry it may not be much (though hardly the "crime" that Lewis called it), but it is an excellent example of the undertone of frustrated romanticism that echoes through the surface of what passed in that era for hard-nosed anti-romanticism. Furthermore, "Red" Lewis conveniently forgot in later years how proud he had once been of such effusions. When, for example, in the winter of 1907 he went fortune-seeking in Panama, he could think of nothing more prestigious to take along by way of credentials than a letter from the editor of *The Smart Set* acknowledging his published "works" there.

Another budding *Smart Set* poet of those years who would soon find the Muse too harsh a mistress for life-long courtship was Alfred Damon Runyon, then "laureate of the *Rocky Mountain News*." Young "Al" Runyon (a news editor would soon thereafter make him plain Damon) was already finding sports-writing more lucrative than poetry but perhaps it was the *poète-manqué* in him that eventually gave him such a splendid ear for the speech rhythms of ballplayers and gangsters and their inchoate yearnings for romance, chivalry and poetry. Whatever the cause, there is no doubt that as chronicler of America's underworld, Runyon remains without peer—a strange literary career to have come out of *The Smart Set!*

More typical than either Lewis or Runyon—in his early success in the magazine and the effect it would ultimately have on his writing and his later popular success—was another young Southerner, Henry Sydnor Harrison. Late in January 1907, Harrison sent to the magazine his very first short story ("Rhoda Gaines, M.A.") about a bluestocking's successful ruse in getting a man to propose to her by letting him think she is someone else. Towne accepted the story immediately, sending the astonished author a check for $75.00. Thrilled by his first success, Harrison deluged the magazine, according to Towne, with a spate of "gay, satirical yarns (that) captivated our whole staff." One of the letters that Towne wrote to Harrison has survived and is worth quoting here as a typical example of the way *Smart Set* editors (and Towne in particular) wooed potential winners:

April 27, 1907

Dear Mr. Harrison:—

Your story, "Rhoda Gaines, M.A.," seems to have made a definite impression on numerous readers, for we have heard many delightful things about it, and it may interest you to know that O'Henry [*sic*] remarked that it was the best short story he had read in a magazine for many months. Dr. Maurice Francis Egan wrote us that he would like to know who Mr. Harrison was. In view of all this we hope we can see another manuscript of yours very soon. Stories like "Rhoda Gaines" are not found every day, and we are glad that it has been appreciated as it should be.

Very sincerely yours,

The Editor

Typically, too, other magazine editors caught the sweet smell of Harrison's impending success. A *McClure's* editor wrote to verify "O. Henry's" enthusiastic reaction, adding that he wanted some of the same for his maga-

zine. From a Maine vacation a few weeks later, Witter Bynner (a *Smart Set* poet himself), chief editor at Holt's, wrote that he was "much taken" with "Rhoda Gaines" and wished Mr. Harrison would consider doing a book for his publishing house.

The book for Holt—*Queed*—was soon forthcoming. It was an enormous popular success and so, a few years later, was *V. V.'s Eyes*. He continued for several years thereafter to give *The Smart Set* "first refusal" of his short stories in gratitude for his first successful appearance in a national magazine.

Few writers had Harrison's loyalty. In its pay-scale, the magazine did not keep pace with the mass-circulation market and, when it ceased to compete, most of its luminaries quickly departed for more lucrative shores. The staff was understandably demoralized to see authors they had "discovered" or, at least, nurtured achieve a success in the magazine and use it as a springboard to more remunerative writing elsewhere. Nevertheless, fighting a declining circulation and a malodorous reputation, the Colonel could not see his way clear to increasing authors' rates "simply to hold on to a few favorites." The magazine, Towne complained bitterly, had become a literary Grand Central Station where the best contributors were constantly catching trains to better stations. Faced with what he regarded as a highly unstable (if not intolerable) situation, Towne was easily lured away in the spring of 1908 to the editorship of *The Delineator,* under Theodore Dreiser (then editor-in-chief of all Butterick Publications).

When Towne left *The Smart Set,* it was at last crystal clear to the Colonel that his beleaguered journal "by, for and about The Four Hundred" must soon change course or go under.

"For Minds That Are Not Primitive"

———•———

By the spring of 1908, the horsehide on the reception room sofas in the *Smart Set* office showed distinct cracks. On the great oval mahogany table, between late numbers of *The Smart Set, Town Topics* and *Transatlantic Tales,* scratches were plainly visible. The potted palms looked dusty, the red plush trappings frankly shabby. What the Great Scandal of 1906 had not done to the magazine's profits, the business panic of the following year had. Gone were the misplaced Southern belles—the Colonel's "charity" readers. Gone, too, were Towne, Walsh, Sheldon and the old air of ease and conviviality. To economize, the Colonel had assumed the editorship himself (at least nominally), but to do the work he had hired an earnest, ambitious 22-year-old, Fred C. Splint (with the title, "Managing Editor"), and an old Baltimore newspaper hand, Norman Boyer, as Assistant Editor, as he cast about desperately for new tactics.

In the end it was *Ainslee's* that pointed the way. While the fortunes of *The Smart Set* declined, those of the erstwhile "Magazine of Clever Fiction" (changed now to "The Magazine That Entertains") were on the ascendant; it was now the imitator's turn to be imitated. As early as October 1903, Duffy and Hall (*Ainslee's* co-editors) had begun sporadically to print anonymous book reviews in their magazine. (Their first was a laudatory notice of Jack London's first best-seller, *Call of the Wild*.) A year or so later this had become a regular feature in *Ainslee's* under the pen of Archibald Lowery Sessions and was followed in March 1904 by a monthly theatre column conducted, in turn, by Alan Dale and Channing Pollock. With the addition (in March 1905) of frontispiece portraits of leading contributors, *Ainslee's* now looked much less like *The Smart Set* than it had a few years earlier.

In due course each of these innovations found its way into *The Smart Set*, sometimes with odd twists. Instead of photographs of authors, for instance, *The Smart Set* introduced in December 1905 a series of frontispiece portraits of *grandes dames*: the Duchess of Marlborough (Consuelo Vanderbilt), Mrs. Potter Palmer, the Countesses of Warwick and Winchilsea (both American heiresses), Elizabeth Mills Reid, *et al*. Instead of theater reviews, *The Smart Set* deviated in its imitation at first by soliciting general theater articles of timeliness from Broadway personalities. This interesting series was discontinued in 1907, however, when the Colonel shamelessly raided *Ainslee's* staff and engaged Channing Pollock to do a regular monthly theater column for *The Smart Set*.

Finally, in the summer of 1908, Colonel Mann decided to follow *Ainslee's* lead in the third innovation—a monthly book column—and he authorized Splint to engage a "literary editor" for the magazine. After a few inquiries, Splint sent off a letter to a Baltimore newspaperman who, ironically, had failed some years earlier to sell his verses to *The Smart Set*, Henry Louis Mencken. Would Mr. Mencken, the editor inquired, be at all interested in writing book reviews regularly for the magazine? If so, would he please come to New York at an early opportunity to discuss the matter? Henry Mencken replied in

the affirmative, took the next train to New York and was instantly engaged with what he later called "a strange and suspicious absence of parley." Then he was handed an armful of books and taken to lunch by Norman Boyer. Writing his memoirs thirty years later, Mencken inquired of Splint (then a physician) about the matter and discovered to his amazement that it was actually Boyer who had suggested him for the job in the first place. At the time he had jumped to the conclusion that it was his friend, Channing Pollock, then *The Smart Set*'s drama critic.

Mencken at twenty-eight had previously written only a handful of newspaper reviews although by then he had published three books of his own (*Ventures into Verse*, 1903; *George Bernard Shaw: His Plays*, 1905; and *The Philosophy of Friedrich Nietzsche*, 1908) and knew first-hand what it was like to be on the reviewer's skewer. By the standards of our day he was abysmally untrained and ill-equipped to run the critical department of a national magazine. He knew no more of literature than one could then acquire with a city high school education and a passion (unsystematic and idiosyncratic) for leisure reading. But he compensated, at least in part, for the huge gaps in his knowledge by having the practiced eye of a master reporter (with nine years' service on three Baltimore papers) and a freewheeling style admirably suited to the magazine's still-unwavering claims to "cleverness." His penchant for paradox and vivid, sometimes caustic, phrases had already brought him a modicum of fame in circles outside Baltimore and his mandate from Splint was simple: "Write what you damn well please as long as it's lively and gets attention!"

Thus, the concluding item in the November 1908 *Smart Set*—as in 181 succeeding issues—was a book review column signed by "Henry L. Mencken" (the shortening to "H. L." came several months later). Mencken singled out Upton Sinclair's *The Moneychangers* for denunciation. Of Henry James' essays, *Views and Reviews,* he remarked guardedly that "some are in the English language," but he found good things to say about Mary Roberts Rinehart's first thriller, *The Circular Staircase,* and he praised at least faintly a novel, *Holy Orders,* by Marie Corelli—in future years a favorite target for his derision. Such a beginning was certainly a far cry from the unbridled, unbuttoned Mencken of the next decade.

By spring (1909), he began to chip away with less restraint and more assurance at a whole bundle of his "prejudices"—against democracy, the Common Man, sentimentality, joiners, socialism, politicians, Christianity, romantic love and women—mindful of the advice that the public attends more to gaudy negations than to judicious criticism in letters, as in life. He also began beating the drums for his darling Nietzsche ("Only *The Ladies Home Journal* and the *War Cry* [a Salvation Army paper] have yet to find him out," he proclaimed) and for the primacy of *Huckleberry Finn* among American novels (an opinion he repeated in the magazine, according to William Manchester, no less than twenty times from 1908 to 1914 alone and at least as often thereafter). Fortunately for Mencken's development and for American criticism (then at low ebb), Fred Splint meant what he said about giving the critic *carte blanche* and, although it had lately been too much given to Graustarkian romance, the traditions and general tone of *The Smart Set* offered excellent nurture for the aesthetic and social viewpoints then taking shape in Mencken's mind. In more than one way, then, Mencken the critic, like Mencken the editor, would be a product of the magazine whose destiny would be directly linked with his career during the next fifteen years.

On one of his infrequent trips to New York (then, as later, Mencken did his writing in Baltimore) in late May, 1909, he was awakened at his hotel one morning by a telephone call from Norman Boyer, asking him to come to the *Smart Set* office (still at Fifth Avenue and Fortieth Street) later that day. "I want you to meet someone who's going to work on our staff," Boyer explained. The new man turned out to be a twenty-seven year-old Indianan from Fort Wayne by way of Cornell, two years' study in Italy, and a two-year stint in theatrical reviewing for Manhattan newspapers and weeklies. His name was George Jean Nathan. Channing Pollock had resigned the drama column effective with the June issue and young Mr. Nathan was to be his replacement. Slender, handsome, sartorially elegant and more than a little snobbish, Nathan posed a strange contrast to the unfastidious, round-shouldered, genial Baltimorean as they stood in Boyer's office. But fifteen minutes later they were seated at a table two blocks away (at the Beaux Arts) downing Tavern cocktails against a background of schmaltzy music (Mencken later remembered first hearing there the Viennese waltz, *"Ach, Frühling, wie bis Du so schön!"*) and swapping ideas "about everything under the sun," as Nathan recalled nearly fifty years after. It took less than another fifteen minutes for the two fledgling critics to discover that, despite great discrepancies in their backgrounds, education and basic interests, they shared more than mere attitudes and, as Nathan said, "a common liking for the same kinds of alcoholic refreshment." Above all, they were agreed that the people who then ran *The Smart Set* were "a pack of asses," but that they could have some "fun" with the magazine. Thus began, quite undramatically and without fanfare, a fifteen-year friendship and collaboration that would eventually transform not only *The Smart Set* itself but certain aspects of American literary culture as well.

George Jean Nathan's first appearance in *The Smart Set* was not a review but a facetious essay, "Why We Fall in Love With Actresses," in October 1909. The following month he commenced his regular theatre column, the cover of that issue advertising "A Sparkling Comment on the Plays and

New Books," and his article ("The Drama Comes Into Season") immediately preceding Mencken's book *causeries* in the book—an order that endured uninterrupted until December 1923. The opening paragraph was scarcely "sparkling":

> The drama, like the oyster [*Nathan commenced haltingly*] comes into season with the first autumn month having an "R"—September; but several recent cases of dramatic ptomaine suffered by early theatergoers from partaking of unripe products seem to argue that equal caution should be exercised at the outset in approaching both the theatre and the bivalve.

After discussing the various reasons for so many early-season flops on Broadway (a phenomenon that yet endures), Nathan gave a Cook's tour of the current productions, seeming to follow the old saw, "if you can't praise, don't dispraise!" His harshest thrust in the column was no stronger than "the play, in general, must be criticized for its unnecessary loquacity." So, too, in hindsight, must the early Nathan—a far cry from the economical, biting wit with which he was to decimate many a pretentious production in the years just ahead. Here also "The Magazine of Cleverness" would provide a hospitable training ground for the development of an influential critic—nay, the most influential in the history of the American theatre, one may safely claim.

Unfortunately, there is no evidence to indicate that the addition of critical departments made *The Smart Set* more attractive to the general public, nor did the addition in 1910 of a third department—"Shopping for the Smart Set," in which new fashions, gift ideas and new phonograph recordings (hardly a review, but one of the first columns to pay heed to such newfangled things) were noticed. As the circulation continued to sag (gently but firmly), the Colonel came to the office less and less frequently and devised fewer and fewer stratagems for luring readers. Now past seventy, he was plainly old and tired of the magazine wars. As far as he was concerned, *The Smart Set* was now an uninteresting "loser" and he longed to be rid of it—but at a price no one yet seemed willing to pay.

As the magazine celebrated its first decade, Splint and Boyer were forced to break its long-standing rule against dealing with agencies. An occasional "name" piece by E. Phillips Oppenheim, George Barr McCutcheon, Jacques Futrelle, Irvin S. Cobb, John Kendrick Banks or Roi Cooper Megrue—purchased through agents, often at double or triple the magazine's accustomed prices—seemed the only desperate alternatives remaining. These were sandwiched between pieces of old stand-bys and respectably dull verses. Ella Wheeler Wilcox, the queen of magazine "poetesses," had long since been permanently alienated from the magazine by some waggish compositor's change of "My soul is a lighthouse keeper," to "My soul is a light housekeeper."

Sometimes there were interesting newcomers like the vagabond socialist, Harry Kemp, or Joyce Kilmer, or even younger aspirants—such as Deems Taylor, John Erskine, Carl Van Vechten (fresh to New York music criticism from Chicago and Cedar Rapids), and Carolyn Wells—all of whom fame would one day tap in sundry ways. After Mencken and Nathan joined the staff, the epigram-fillers began to show occasional slight improvements, or, at least, affected a slightly greater degree of cynicism. It was not long before Splint knew he could count on the two critics for yards of fillers like "There is nothing like the clutch of conventionality for squeezing the breath out of individuality"; or, "Why do we labor in this world? The attainable nobody wants; the unattainable nobody can have"; or, "Love is a witching chimera—life's most beautiful optical illusion."

For the most part, however, *The Smart Set*

had settled into an uneasy mediocrity by the end of 1910, its name besmirched, its sad decline a clubroom joke. Then, quite without warning, the Colonel got a nibble on his line and a prospective buyer broke water! So eager was the prospect—a gentleman with the sterling New England name of John Adams Thayer—that on February 20, 1911, the Colonel was able to close out the sale and relinquish *The Smart Set* at last for the handsome sum of $100,000 (worth perhaps thrice that amount in today's dollars). At a press conference he made this carefully dissembling announcement:

> *The Smart Set,* which, since I founded it in 1900 has made profits of over one-half million dollars, has been sold. . . . I did not wish to sell *The Smart Set* [but] I wanted a publisher for it, and after reading Mr. Thayer's business autobiography . . . I picked him as the ideal co-worker. Frankly, I offered him, free of payment, almost a half interest, as the potential value of the property with the right publisher would have been very great.

What actually happened was that Thayer had swallowed this "come-on" whole and insisted on nothing less than full, outright ownership, each demurrer whetting his eagerness to pay through the nose. There was also a small unpublicized matter of some $100,-000 in twenty-year debenture bonds on the magazine for which Thayer assumed liability (whether knowingly or not is unclear). Colonel Mann retained the copyright on the name *"Smart Set"* and the English reprint rights for the Smart Set Publishing Company, Ltd., of London, in which he owned a controlling interest.

The "business autobiography" to which Mann referred in his press statement *Astir: A Publisher's Life Story* (1910, rev. 1912), belonged to a species of blatant self-advertising which has blessedly fallen into disuse in the American business community. In terms that might have made Horatio Alger blush for

modesty, Thayer told how he rose from the status of a poverty-stricken printer's devil at the age of fourteen to become co-owner of *Everybody's Magazine* and a millionaire gentleman of leisure at forty-five. Nevertheless, beneath its braggadocio, its tumid style, studded with platitudes about "business ethics" and the rewards of "clean living" and "hard work," *Astir* is an impressive document of the kind of "self-made" success on a grand scale that was still common in the American experience at the turn of the century.

Born in Boston to a hard-working family whose straitened circumstances forced him to leave school and earn his livelihood at an early age, Thayer went to work as a printer, first for the Riverside Press in Cambridge, later for various presses in Boston, Chicago and Philadelphia, rising to become an expert printer and typefounder. In 1892 he successfully answered a "Want Ad" in the *Boston Herald* for a "first-class man to take charge of the advertising pages . . . of *The Ladies Home Journal.*" Magazine advertising was still in its cradle and though Cyrus K. Curtis, the *Journal's* publisher, and Edward Bok, its editor, desired only a competent printer to compose and design lay-outs, Thayer went much further, hustling new accounts himself and advancing, within five years, to the newly-created post of advertising manager. During the next eight years he held similar positions with *Munsey's,* the *Boston Globe* and, finally, *The Delineator,* under George Warren Wilder, who built the Butterick Publications empire.

While he was working on the latter magazine, Thayer met the energetic editor, Erman J. Ridgway and, in 1903, he, Ridgway and Wilder bought the nearly defunct *Everybody's* on notes for $75,000. They engaged a Boston capitalist turned reformer, Thomas W. Lawson, to do a series of sensational "muckraking" exposés of Wall Street peculations ("Frenzied Finance") which boosted the circulation of the magazine to over 1,000,000 within a year. As a result of

Thayer's "clean and honest" policies plus the magazine's skyrocketing sales, ad rates rose from $150 to $4,500 a page in an equally short time. In 1906 the partners disagreed over the future development of *Everybody's* and disbanded, Thayer and Ridgway selling their shares to Wilder for $3,000,000. Thus, Thayer had parlayed a borrowed $25,000 into a million and a half in the short space of three years!

In those days a prudent American of wealth could live in Europe in very high style on about half of what it cost to live luxuriously in an American city. So Thayer took his millions into "retirement" in Paris, where he bought a fine house. But, lacking family, school or club connections or high office, he possessed none of the touchstones of acceptance into the realms of international society. Thayer was distinctly a parvenu and, in retirement even before the onset of middle-age, time hung heavily upon him. After four years of idleness, he returned to New York, brought out the memoirs he had composed while abroad, and began shopping for a publishing venture to absorb his energies. Colonel Mann had let it be "leaked" in various Manhattan clubs that *The Smart Set* "might be" for sale and at this point Thayer's inclinations and the Colonel's converged. The sale was consummated on Thayer's fiftieth birthday.

Just why a man like John Adams Thayer wanted to own a magazine like *The Smart Set* is anyone's guess. Certainly he had no special talents or penchants for a literary journal, *per se,* and his experience had all been with mass-circulation periodicals. Perhaps he thought he could achieve another spectacular success with it, as he had with *Everybody's.* Perhaps he thought it a stable, well-established magazine that would provide him a modest, but comfortable return without great expenditures of time or money in the ensuing years. Or perhaps, as Burton Rascoe suggested, he naïvely believed that this would give him entrée into New York

society—an incredibly fatuous notion for anyone aware, as Thayer must surely have been, of the reputation of the magazine and the nuances of social eligibility along Park Avenue. Whatever the case, he was soon to learn that he had paid exorbitantly for what was, at best, a risky investment.

The new publisher's first task was to hire a new editor, Splint having taken the opportunity to resign in order to enter upon his long-delayed medical studies. At the time of the sale the March issue was already on the stands (or in the mails) and there was barely time to pull a page of material from the April number to insert a statement reassuring old subscribers that the magazine would continue without radical changes—"business as usual." The May number was fairly well "blocked out," so Thayer had a few weeks' reprieve before a new editor actually became an imperative. He offered the chair first to Mencken, then to Nathan, both of whom rejected, giving "personal" reasons to cover their apprehensions that Thayer would take far too strong a hand in the magazine for any editor with a mind of his own. Next, he tried unsuccessfully to woo back Charles Hanson Towne. Ultimately, he was stuck with Norman Boyer, the hardy perennial, to whom he gave the title "Managing Editor" (signifying, as Mencken and Nathan feared, the publisher's desire to be, in reality, his own editor-in-chief); Louise Closser Hale, who had served as an editorial reader with the magazine for upwards of a year, was raised to "Associate Editor." Thayer's own additions to the staff were Mark Lee Luther, an affluent New York attorney and author, whom he brought in as a second "Associate Editor" (and "Business Manager") and Howard P. Ruggles, who was appointed *The Smart Set*'s first "Advertising Director."

Mark Lee Luther was an interesting personality who, in background and inclinations, closely resembled Colonel Mann's dilettantes of the previous decade, but he was as ill-qualified as a Brooklyn stevedore for an editorial position. Amiable, learned and rather preciously literary, he and his wife (Grace Richmond, also a writer) were intimates of the Booth Tarkingtons with whom they enjoyed membership in a vagabond set of American authors who toured Europe incessantly on royalties from potboilers. Thayer had met Luther under such circumstances in Paris ateliers and on the Riviera and, when he acquired *The Smart Set,* Luther happened to be in New York and was easily prevailed upon to invest in a few shares of the newly-formed John Adams Thayer Corporation and come onto the staff at a handsome salary. Since Luther's acquaintances in the literary marketplace were legion, Thayer naturally thought him a good man to scout manuscripts and generate ideas which Boyer, as titular editor, could execute. There was only one trouble—Luther was not a man of ideas.

Nor was Thayer himself, for that matter. He had a mind that worked in slogans, a satisfactory attribute for a typesetter or ad-man, no doubt, but hardly adequate for the formation of sound editorial policies and practices. Nevertheless, he decided that he must come up with a new "Smart Set Idea," without seriously alarming the old-guard patrons. The result was a masthead motto (June 1911 and thereafter): "Its Prime Purpose is to Provide Lively Entertainment for Minds That are not Primitive." To be sure, it was alliterative and eye-catching, but what it meant no one (least of all Thayer) could say. What was a "primitive" mind or, by indirection, the "nonprimitive"? If Thayer intended this as a gimmick to recapture the all-but-vanished interest of the socialite audience of the magazine's palmier days under Colonel Mann, he was quite unsuccessful. It seemed merely decorative.

Also decorating the June issue was a brand-new cover design by another of Thayer's Paris acquaintances—James Montgomery Flagg, a well-known American artist-illustrator. "Brand-new" is perhaps not quite the right designation since Flagg's drawing was

a more or less "updated" version of the old Womrath cover picture. The curtseying belle now wore a more *décolleté,* less frilly gown with a huge corsage of red carnations pinned to a wide black sash. Her hair was dressed in the more stylish "Empire" coiffure of 1911, and her fan was less feathery. Her tail-coated escort now looked somewhat older (a bit of gray showing at the temples)—definitely a more suave lothario, gallantly holding his top hat before him while bowing ever so slightly from the waist. Flagg's gentleman betrayed a slightly wolfish ogle, his lady a more coquettish look; beside his, Womrath's original couple appeared a pair of innocents. However, amid the swirling red S's of the title and around the borders, the masked Mephisto continued to dangle winged hearts at which a single impish cherub now aimed a single arrow. Apparently Flagg's orders were to retain as many as possible of the hallmarks of the old cover while simultaneously "modernizing" the scene so that it would still be recognizable to newsstand readers (the bulk of the magazine's patrons, then as always) yet would convey a definite sense of "improvement."

Inside was a luxuriant frontispiece—not one of the Colonel's *grandes dames* of five years earlier, but a two-color reproduction of a painting by Rose Cecil O'Neill (another prominent American artist-illustrator, then the wife of a popular humorist, Harry Leon Wilson), which purportedly "interpreted" Keats' poem. "La Belle Dame Sans Merci," apropos of nothing at all in the issue. For the next eighteen months succeeding frontispieces would include (again, with no particular relevance to the contents of the magazine) Vernon Howe Bailey's pencil sketches of French scenes, André Castaigne's impressions of such classic lovers as Dante and Beatrice, Hero and Leander, Anthony and Cleopatra, *et al.* It proved a costly way of trying to infuse the magazine with a "higher tone" or "air of luxury and sophistication."

To stimulate readers' reactions to these innovations, the new publisher also opened in his first issues a chatty editorial department ("Something Personal"), inviting patrons' comments. The responses were mixed. Some newspaper commentators and readers' letters praised the new look and new slogan; others—mainly disgruntled old subscribers—felt that what had been good enough to endure for a decade should not be discarded so lightly. Thayer remained adamant: "A Magazine of Cleverness," he rejoined, "should be clever from cover to cover." To one reader who suggested that he go even further and change the name "to something less odious," he gave an emphatic "No!" explaining that the old title was an apt designation for what he proposed to do with the journal (in truth, the terms of his purchase prohibited change!). After six months, however, the new Flagg cover was quietly put aside (it would reappear at intervals later on) in favor of different designs on each issue—colored pictorials of courtship, domestic life or office ogling with such captions as "A female of the species [is] more alluring than the mail," or "The Man Who Never Goes Out Deserves a Wife Who Never Stays In!" All this, complained one reader, was nothing more than "just fresh icing on a stale cake."

As might be expected, Thayer shone in one area—advertising. In his first issue, Ruggles (the new advertising man) announced a six-point program (formulated by Thayer) in a "house ad." The magazine would, he said, provide frank statements of circulation, insist upon conformity to its style and typography in all copy, disdain "medical and other questionable" ads, and refuse trade or exchange contracts and agents' discounts. Ruggles concluded his manifesto by solemnly promising that the magazine would "limit its advertising section to a reasonable number of pages to prevent burdening the reader with a bulky paper and assure our clients a good return." In short, the old expedient of "snob appeal" and "exclusiveness" once again. Soon the magazine bulged with new advertisements and, in May 1912,

surveying his first year with *The Smart Set,* Thayer boasted that the volume of accounts had risen some 166% over the previous year. With such an increase in revenue he was able to defray even the costs of his extravagant gilding on the lily despite the nagging failure to find many new subscribers.

Throughout 1911 and 1912 the circulation fluctuated between 80,000 and 90,000, mostly at the lower figure. The figures are deceptive because there is some evidence that there had been, during the previous five years, almost a complete turn-over in the readership of *The Smart Set.* By 1912 a new generation was arising (born mostly in the late 1880's) to whom the magazine was a long-accustomed institution, its name synonymous with "cleverness," "sophistication," "daring" or the "risqué." This impression was reinforced when parents refused, as they often did, to allow the magazine in their homes or when the local librarian (in the few libraries that bothered even to take it) pursed her lips and raised her eyebrows when asked for a copy. In one sense, the magazine's undeserved reputation for naughtiness had begun to boomerang—to attract, rather than repel. Down in King George, Virginia, for instance, young Nancy Byrd Turner, daughter of an Anglican clergyman and up to her elbows in flour and lard making "light bread" in the rectory kitchen, received one day an unexpected *Smart Set* acceptance (with check) for her first poem. Her "liberal" father, she recalls

> was so proud of having a genius at his hearth that he took to carrying the magazine around (on horseback, some of the time) when making his parochial calls. . . . However, the devil-and-Cupid outside cover began to strike me as inappropriate for a parson to show around, even though I could see no other objection, whatever there may have been—so we made him stop.

But "inappropriate" or not, Miss Turner did not stop contributing her verses.

Out at the University of Missouri a journalism coed from Fort Smith, Arkansas—Thyra Samter—sent in a very maudlin poem (the result of a college romance, she later remembered) and felt herself "a great success" when it was accepted. Thus encouraged, she went on to a Chicago and New York newspaper career and eventually as Thyra Samter Winslow, and variously as Bruce Reid, Laura Kent Mason, Betting Calvert and under a host of other pseudonyms (from 1914 to 1923) became the magazine's most regular regular, the editors only excepted. Although other young literati — Djuna Barnes, Ezra Pound, John Hall Wheelock, Paul Hervey Fox and the incomparable lyricist, Sara Teasdale, among them—sometimes found the magazine hospitable, Boyer was, for the most part, wary of newcomers. He preferred to rely on "gimmicks," such as story-naming contests (with $100 prizes) and sexy cover ads for novelettes that turned out to be as sexless as a Shaker meeting, as cliché-ridden as a sales convention, by innocuous old standbys like G. Vere Tyler, Rebecca Harding Davis and Arthur Wallace Peach. For a brief period in 1912 he even tried a resort, restaurant and cabaret department ("Where Shall We Go?" by Philip Ames) but with no greater success than Colonel Mann had had with his "Smart Living Service" eight years earlier.

While the American *Smart Set* floundered, its English counterpart flourished. When he sold his Ess Ess Publishing Company to Thayer, it will be recalled, the Colonel kept control of its London subsidiary, the Smart Set Publishing Co., Ltd., in the Strand. In 1905 the London *Smart Set*, under the editorship of William James Thorold, began to be something more than merely a reprint sheet, adding photographs of leading British socialites and theatre personalities, cartoons, fashion columns, social notes and, occasionally, English fiction and verse that did not find its way into the New York edition. In the reorganization that followed on the heels of the sale of the American edi-

tion in 1911, Thorold quit the magazine and the editorship fell to H. J. Gillespie, who remained for another four years. He, in turn, was succeeded by James W. Milne, who purchased the English rights after Colonel Mann's death, becoming the sole proprietor until 1925, when it was merged into *Standard Stories,* another English periodical. Kitty Shannon was the last London editor, from 1924 to December 1925. Always more heavily illustrated than its American parent and lacking the topical items in the New York edition and those with peculiarly American reference (all of the editorial departments and reviews, for instance, were omitted), the English *Smart Set* was really a distinctive periodical whose story is really tangential to this account. Most of the magazine's American readers (and, indeed, the contributors themselves) remained blissfully unaware that there ever was such a thing as a London *Smart Set* and, to tell the truth, so did the vast majority of the British reading public. Even so, it prospered—in part because it had no need to wrestle with the problems that beset the parent journal (these were all solved before the material crossed the ocean), in part because, as a minor periodical with a very low "overhead," it was content with a small stake in the Fleet Street market.

The New York *Smart Set* might have done likewise and stressed a kind of quiet quality had Thayer not had delusions of grandeur. By the end of his first year with the magazine, however, he saw his dreams dissolving, his initial hopes for achieving success in appealing to "Minds That Are Not Primitive" coming to grief in the desert of ideas in his editorial office. Under Boyer and Luther, as Mencken observed to a friend, the magazine had settled down to a "pallid imitation of Smith's [*Ainslee's*] magazine."

But there were those in the editorial basement, so to speak, (Mencken and Nathan among them) who were not content that it should remain so. A desperate John Adams Thayer was at last ready to heed them.

Owen Hatteras in Eruption

Thayer's slogan was not totally useless. However vague or ambiguous it might seem, it at least afforded a sense of direction by re-affirming *The Smart Set*'s old commitments to "entertainment" (as opposed to topicality) and, on the negative side, it committed the magazine to avoiding what was "primitive." This term was certainly imprecise, but it suggested a whole cluster of associations: "old-fashioned," "traditional," "prudish," etc. Inversely, it denoted modernity, novelty, un-conventionality, daring. "Primitive" minds were presumably the steady customers of, say, *Scribner's, The Century, The Atlantic*

Monthly, et al. (staid "quality" monthlies) or, on the other hand, the audiences of the popular, mass-circulation ("family") maga-zines. Unwittingly, Thayer had thus elim-inated popular appeal as an aim of his mag-azine and had prepared the ground for it to become truly *avant-garde*.

What was needed at this juncture was an editor of vigor, imagination and resource who could infuse meaning into Thayer's hollow slogan, translating it into viable policies and a definite editorial program.

Just such an editor was Willard Hunting-ton Wright. He took command of "The

Magazine of Cleverness" on New Year's Day 1913 and held it for precisely one year—by any measure the most tumultuous and decisive year in the labyrinthine history of *The Smart Set*. If Wright virtually bankrupted The John Adams Thayer Corporation in the process, he also succeeded in transforming the magazine and assuring it a permanent place in American literary history.

Willard Wright came to his editorial chair by a somewhat devious route. Born in Virginia in 1888, he was a precocious child who studied an astonishing range of subjects at three colleges between his fifteenth and eighteenth years, leaving Harvard in 1906 without a degree "because they had nothing more to teach me." He then went to Paris to study art briefly with his older brother, Macdonald Wright, a well-known "Futurist" painter (probably the first important American post-impressionist) and returned to California (where his family had settled) to become literary editor of the *Los Angeles Times* at the age of nineteen. In 1908 he gave an extended, highly laudatory review to Mencken's *Philosophy of Friedrich Nietzsche* and, when Mencken wrote him a "thank you" note, a correspondence developed which eventually catapulted him to *The Smart Set*.

Meanwhile, in April 1911, Percival Pollard, literary editor of *Town Topics,* published a critical volume entitled *Masks and Minstrels of New Germany* which caught the imagination of literary-minded intellectuals across the land, especially those in Willard Wright's generation. The book had no very great sale, but those who read it with fascination were members of a rising generation of journalists, authors, critics, editors and publishers upon whom its influence was decisive. Pollard's subject was the *"Uberbrett'l* Movement" in Central Europe which had arisen more or less spontaneously and without program in the late 1890's in the beer cellars and small *avant-garde* cabarets of Berlin, Munich and Vienna. Rendered literally, *Uberbrett'l* means "over the staves" or, in other words,

a movement conducted upon the makeshift stages made of planks thrown across empty beer and wine kegs in cellars and brewery gardens—the Teutonic version of France's *L'Art Pour L'Art* or England's "Aesthetic" Movement of a decade earlier.

Pollard discussed with obvious delight in his book a host of Central Europeans who had previously been only exotic names to the American literati: Mann, Rilke, Wedekind, Ludwig Thoma, Hauptmann, Schnitzler, Roda-Roda, Hugo von Hofmannsthal, and a half-dozen more. Diverse as these writers were in other respects, they shared irreconcilable opposition to the kinds of bourgeois sentimentality and *biergemütlichkeit* provincialism that was stifling creativity in the Hapsburg and Hohenzollern empires. Their weapon was satire and they founded (or rallied round) two new magazines: *Jugend* and *Simplicissimus*. The truth is that by 1911 the movement Pollard's book chronicled was no longer virulent, having been emasculated by the success of its individual members, but this neither lessened its attractiveness for Pollard's readers nor detracted a whit from his invidious comparisons with the tameness, timorousness and shallowness of current American letters. Pollard exhorted his youthful readers in ringing tones to follow the example of their Germanic counterparts. He offered no specific proposal; he merely reiterated that ". . . if you are minded to tilt at windmills—to start an *Uberbrett'l* in New York or London—the way is easy and not far."

This was just the sort of siren song that many a creative young American, chafing under village taboos and the literary restraints of a "Puritan" Establishment, yearned to hear. Out in the prairies, Burton Rascoe, Ben Hecht, Carl Sandburg, Sherwood Anderson, Harriet Monroe, *et al.* shared dog-eared copies of Pollard's book and laid plans for *Poetry* Magazine (1912) and, in due course, *The Little Review* (1914)—focal points of the Chicago "Renaissance." In New York, his words echoed in gatherings of excited youngsters who flocked from hinterland crossroads to the congeries of flats south and west of Washington Square coming to be known in literary and artistic circles simply as "The Village." Here, as if in answer to Pollard's reveille, a rash of "little" magazines broke out and, if most of them died of inanition after a few issues, they at least gave a few budding poets and novelists their first spilled ink.

This is not to imply that *Masks and Minstrels* . . . was in any demonstrable sense a direct cause of the tremendous upsurge in literary creativity ("the tuning of the fiddles," in John B. Yeats' familiar phrase) that became so remarkable all over the land *ca.* 1912. It was merely another straw in the fresh winds that blew in from Europe in a happy hour. Its timing was undeniably fortuitous, coming at precisely the right psychological moment to reach an eager (if limited) audience. Few books in American literary history have had such a reception.

What, one wonders, might have happened in American letters had Percival Pollard lived to take command of this growing army of admirers and disciples—among whom, certainly, were Mencken, Nathan and Willard Huntington Wright. (Mencken once acknowledged Pollard as one of the two greatest influences in his literary criticism.) But the ink was scarcely dry on *Masks and Minstrels* . . . before Pollard fell ill of what proved to be a brain tumor and, after an unsuccessful operation at Johns Hopkins Hospital, died in December 1911. Mencken, who was with him at the end, and Ambrose Bierce (whom Pollard had championed in the way Mencken would later champion Dreiser) were two of the six who attended his simple funeral.

Pollard's untimely death (he was barely 42) created a sudden vacancy in the literary editorship of *Town Topics*—a post he had held for more than a decade. At Mencken's prompting—and with his recommendation—Willard Wright successfully sought the appointment as Pollard's successor. However,

he had already signed a contract in Los Angeles to continue for a year his literary editorship of the *Los Angeles Times,* so it was not until October 1912 that he was at last able to come East to take up his new duties with *Town Topics* (which in the interim he carried on by correspondence). His arrival in New York coincided with the resignation from the *Smart Set* staff of subeditor Louise Closser Hale, and Wright lost no time (again, with Mencken's machinations) moving into this job, retaining his *Town Topics* chair on the side. Moreover—as Mencken correctly foresaw—once "on deck" at *The Smart Set,* Wright's brilliance so overawed the desperate John Adams Thayer that, within two months, he was able to talk his way into the editorship. How all this came about is not quite clear ("Hypnosis!" was one former colleague's joking explanation) but, whatever the means, Wright prevailed upon Thayer to demote Norman Boyer and make him editor-in-chief with *carte blanche* to do with the magazine as he wished. In New York, at least, the way to an *Uberbrettʼl* was indeed "not far" now.

No other editor of *The Smart Set* ever enjoyed such power and none exercised his editorial prerogatives with quite such ruthless abandon as the 25-year-old Willard Huntington Wright in the twelve issues of the magazine that were to comprise his regime. Compared with the changes he wrought, those of his predecessors seem glacial, those of his successors imitative, or at best derivative. In his very first issue (February 1913) he commandeered the publisher's column, "Something Personal," to announce himself (under Thayer's signature, of course) as one who "for years has waged war against effeminacy and formalism in American letters." The following month (and thereafter through 1913) the department appeared over Wright's own name as he gave forth his manifesto, thus:

I believe that this is a day of enlightenment on the part of magazine readers. Men and women have grown tired of effeminacy and the falsities of current fiction, essays and poetry. A widespread critical awakening has come, and with it a demand for better literary material. The demand for pious uplift, for stultification, and for the fictional avoidance of the facts of life has diminished. The reader of today demands truth.

And "truth" Wright proposed to give them. He would, he promised, sweep away "the wool-tidy fiction of yesterday, with its reticence, its superficial moralities and its unreal characters" and replace it with "stories which deal with life truthfully and frankly," stories in which "virtue need not necessarily triumph over vice." He concluded:

> It is not altogether true that America is incapable of producing literature such as is being brought from overseas every season. I believe that only an outlet is needed to prove that American writers are capable of meeting European writers on an equal footing.

The Smart Set, he declared, would be that "outlet"—the American *Simplicissimus.*

The general attitude Willard Wright thus made explicit as his editorial credo was not, however, an altogether new departure in the magazine. A year or so earlier Mencken and Nathan had proposed to Thayer the founding of an outspoken new weekly (they even suggested a name—"The Blue Review"—after an idea in H. G. Wells' *New Macchiavelli)* which would attack, mainly by satire, traditional American mores and shibboleths. ("Anti-puritan" was Mencken's coinage for this approach.) Much to their surprise, Thayer had responded enthusiastically, but he had also demurred "for the moment," explaining that he wanted to put the circulation "on firmer ground" before venturing into "new waters." As an alternative ("a temporary expedient," he called it), he then suggested sending up trial balloons among *The Smart Set* clientele by "experimenting" with

the "anti-puritan" approach in a new department. Before the publisher had had time to realize that this would, in fact, undermine his tacit commitment against topicality, Mencken and Nathan had plunged into the breach with a new column, "Pertinent & Impertinent," in the April 1912 number, thus preceding Wright's arrival and foreshadowing his bold policies by several months.

At the outset, it had been decided to make "Pertinent & Impertinent" pseudonymous so that the collaborators could lay about them freely without risking too much unpopularity among their own following. The *nom de guerre* concocted for this purpose was "Owen Hatteras"—a choice, according to Nathan, of no more than ten minutes' cogitation. The choice of surname—that of the blustery North Carolina cape—was quite deliberate, Nathan recalled, to connote an irascible, swaggering, mercurial character. (Forty-three years later Nathan sentimentally chose the Cape Hatteras waters for his marriage to actress Julie Haydon aboard the S.S. *Santa Rosa.*) "Owen" was a last-minute inspiration, Nathan added, replacing "John" on the galleys because "it sounded somehow more capricious."

Thus was born an estimable literary *persona* and personage. At his debut an editorial note in the magazine flatly predicted: "This is a name that will some day be as well-known as 'Mr. Dooley' or 'George Ade.'" That "Owen Hatteras" did not, in truth, become such a household name during the course of the next twelve years (his life-span) is an accident of literary history, partly owing to the fact that he was too urbane a fellow ever to join company in popular fancy with such folksy characters as "Mr. Dooley" *et al.* All the same, "Owen Hatteras" very early acquired—like "Artemus Ward," "Sut Lovingood" and other such creatures of the pen —a distinct personality and existence quite apart from his creators', however much it may have resembled theirs. As a collaborated creation (not the mask or spokesman of a single author only), he is perhaps unique as an American literary "mouthpiece." Moreover, after his arrival in the East, he, Wright, was also invited to join the Hatteras collaboration, meeting Mencken and Nathan on mid-month weekends in Philadelphia to compose the new department (and other pieces by Hatteras) over countless bottles of *Pschorrbräu*. After 1914, "Owen Hatteras" also became a "house pseudonym," occasionally being signed to the second or third pieces in an issue by some regular contributor, often to the writer's amazement. Once, for example, when the poet John McClure appeared under the Hatteras disguise, he was overheard to remark: "So that's how that guy can be so versatile!"

Most *Smart Set* readers, as well as most contributors, remained quite unaware that "Owen Hatteras" was a pseudonym. He received fan mail which the collaborators dutifully answered and invitations—to lecture, to dine, and even to contribute to other journals—all of which were politely "regretted" for him, usually because of "acute dyspepsia." In 1917 "Owen Hatteras" published a slender mock-biography of Mencken and Nathan *(Pistols for Two)* which immortalized him in the Library of Congress catalogue. But the good Congressional librarians were at a loss for vital dates for him until someone remembered seeing his "Conclusions of a Man of Sixty" series in *The Smart Set* and arbitrarily assigned him a birth year of 1862—good reasoning, perhaps, if poor arithmetic. In April 1919 his creators compounded the hoax by supposedly bringing him back from World War I a decorated hero: "Major Owen Arthur James Hatteras, D.S.O." Presumably he died in December 1923 when his collaborators founded the more sober *American Mercury*; whereupon (according to Betty Adler's bibliography) his obituary was noticed in several newspapers. In November 1913 an "Amelia Hatteras" (another Mencken-Nathan-Wright concoction) appeared as the author of a *Smart Set* sketch, but whether she was intended as a pseudonymous helpmeet to the ubiquitous Owen is unclear because the "lady" vanished thereafter.

"Owen Hatteras" was an interesting compendium of the variegated traits of character, personality quirks, postulates and prejudices of his creators. To characterize him adequately one would need to compile an extensive editorial psychograph of the magazine during the dozen years of his existence therein. Still, a few simple characteristics are quite clear. He seems to have been born, for instance, prematurely old and utterly without illusions. He jeered at marriage, romantic love, sentimentalism in all forms. He scoffed at reformism, conventional piety and all types of supernaturalism. He whooped at optimism and enjoyed nothing better than an invidious implied paradox in the "idiot" idealistic utterances of some self-seeking politician, preacher or professor. He revelled masochistically in the kind of self-scourging that seeks expression in long lists of pet peeves: bores and boors, flatulent chauvinists, maudlin moralists, tendentious cliché-coiners and platitudinous publicists among them. His *Codex* of nightmares and aversions was strung through dozens of misanthropic "litanies," "meditations," "panoramas," "Conclusions" and "rosemarys." Yet, beneath a façade of unalloyed hatred for pretension, cant, hypocrisy and downright fraud there was always a detectable sense of *joie de vivre,* a relish of life's fun and games.

Although there can be little doubt that Wright took his editorial cues from the apparent success of the early "Owen Hatteras" experiments (which, as we have noted, preceded him by a few months), his policies were in no sense imitative. Much as this young Nietzschean editor might pose in discipleship to Mencken and Nathan for selfish ends, he was too much the individualist to play the sedulous ape for long.

"Handsome, arrogant, erudite and corrupt" —this is the impression Wright left with many of his contemporaries, as Odell Shepard (then a struggling young poet, later an eminent literary scholar) clearly recalls. To Ernest Boyd, the Anglo-Irish critic, he was "the most interesting and attractive *unlikable* man I have ever known, a brilliant talker and a good listener." Wright delighted in larding his brilliant marathon conversation with shocking obscenities. To "emancipated" women in bohemian gatherings he hinted broadly at incredible acts of orgiastic diabolism. When friends remarked that he resembled the German Kaiser, he dyed his hair, cultivated an upturned Junker mustache and spread a rumor that he was "related in a morganatic way" to the Hohenzollerns!

All such foolishness to the contrary notwithstanding, the intellectual proclivities of this erratic *poseur* are beyond dispute. He could compose sonatas in the "new" manner of Debussy, toss off a fair Baudelairean sonnet, or paint a post-impressionist gouache with equal ease. In 1915 he published the only book on the contemporary art of that period by an American that is worth reading, and he was a brilliant student of post-Romantic philosophy from Schopenhauer to Bergson. As a critic, he was certainly more learned than either Mencken or Nathan, if less adroit at phrase-making than they, but as an editor he displayed disastrous rashness.

Evidently Wright ingratiated himself with Thayer by praising the publisher's "For Minds That Are Not Primitive" slogan, saying it was a great idea that could only be realized with bold, unconventional strokes. Thayer was delighted. (Curiously, this stodgy printer-publisher liked to think of himself as "unconventional.") Thus hoodwinked, it was several months before Thayer realized that he and Wright did not share quite the same ideas as to what constituted the non-primitive. What Wright intended (covertly) was to pattern *The Smart Set* along the lines of Ford Madox Ford's *Eng-*

Williard Huntington Wright

lish Review, a London journal of *belles-lettres* and criticism that printed the works of young Britons and Continentals who were fearless in the expression of unpopular ideas or new techniques.

Hence, one of Wright's first editorial gambits was to engage the expatriate poet Ezra Pound, then in London and already acting as foreign editor for *Poetry* Magazine, to help him scout manuscripts from Europeans and young Americans living abroad. Likewise, from Frank Harris, erstwhile editor of London's *Saturday Review,* he solicited a long satire on academic piety ("An English Saint") that captured the fancy of the American college crowd as few *Smart Set* pieces had ever done. He also solicited (and, to his surprise, got) an article from "The Incomparable" Max Beerbohm and, on a summer tour subsidized by Thayer, called at the Paris apartment of playwright André Brieux (then fashionable, now forgotten) for some plays and stories he translated for the magazine himself. Finally, he garnered some of the idolized *Uberbrett'l* authors—Wedekind and Schnitzler, above all

—along with Italy's leading poet (D'Annunzio) and such worthies from England and elsewhere as W. L. George, George Moore, D. H. Lawrence, May Sinclair, William Butler Yeats, Robert Bridges, Joseph Conrad (whose only play, *One Day More,* he published) and August Strindberg—surely an imposing list for a single year in any periodical!

To the native literati he spread the word that he was interested only in the kinds of material shunned by the popular magazines. When New York author Barry Benefield brought in a short story about prostitutes ("Daughters of Joy") which, he said, had been rejected by virtually every other magazine in business, Wright told him, "that is the very best recommendation you can give it!" and printed the story. From George Bronson-Howard he purchased a series of satirical stories exposing the seamy side of Broadway theatre life and another series of "tough-guy" stories about a character named, simply, "Raegan" by Albert Payson Terhune (later famous, ironically, only for his sentimental dog stories). Theodore Dreiser sent him some of his mystical plays and there were sketches in the magazine by such Greenwich Village exotics as André Tridon (the first American champion of Sigmund Freud and Havelock Ellis) and Achmed Abdullah, an enigmatic Moslem who contributed yards of epigram-fillers and atmospheric short stories during the next decade.

Now it was the "old-timers'" turn to find their pieces sandwiched in between these choice morsels. Even Owen Hatteras was sidetracked while his material appeared undisguised in the departments of Wright and the two critics and in several new signed series. One such dealt satirically with the great American metropolis—deflating civic pride mercilessly in articles like "Los Angeles —the Chemically Pure," or "Washington— Home of the Climber," or "Philadelphia— City of Seven Sundays." For horrible contrast, Wright and Nathan took a trip to Europe

(subsidized by Thayer) to gather material for a series on "The Night Life of Europe," describing the various European capitals in language so lush as to make a tourist agent blush. (Mencken, who had been to Europe earlier, also contributed to the series and the whole was gathered into book form as *Europe After 8:15,* published in the summer of 1914—one of the worst bits of timing in American publishing history!). To this Mencken added a series of fiercely clinical dissections of "The American" (the essay on language later became the basis for HLM's magnum opus, *The American Language*), while Nathan did some first-rate parodies ("Scenes from The Great American Drama") and began a catalogue of palpably false and silly notions cherished by Americans—"The American Credo"—which he and Mencken later expanded to book length.

All this was not without its high costs, financial and otherwise. Wright believed in paying for what he wanted and, with a free rein on the magazine's exchequer, he startled newcomers and regular contributors alike with his largesse. For example, Ludwig Lewisohn, who had counted himself lucky to get five dollars from *The Smart Set* for a poem suddenly found himself receiving $100 checks from Wright by special delivery. For the short stories and novelettes he liked Wright paid ten times the magazine's customary rates. *The Smart Set's* new munificence became the talk of American literary circles.

The talk in the clubs that John Adams Thayer frequented, however, was of a different nature. Many of the advertisers he had so carefully cultivated were angered by the new "bohemian" and "radical" tone of the magazine. When a few hard-won advertising contracts were cancelled, Thayer became alarmed. His alarm changed to outrage when ten pages of precious advertising were dropped between October and December and nasty letters began arriving from old readers who wanted to cancel their subscriptions. Finally, when he went down to the

MARCH
1900

VOL. 1 NO. 1

PRICE 25 CTS

THE
SMART SET

A
MAGA
ZINE
OF
CLEVERNESS

ESS ESS PUBLISHING COMPANY
NEW YORK

LONDON

PARIS

office in mid-November for a look at Luther's books, his rage turned to panic. The circulation had fallen well below 60,000 and Wright's expenditures, if continued, would produce at least a $20,000 deficit in 1913.

During the fearful uproar that followed, Wright refused to concede anything, reminding Thayer that their contract gave him an absolutely free hand and demanding that the terms be strictly met at least until the end of the agreed-upon period (still six months off). In due course new readers and, if necessary, new advertisers could be found, he baldly told his publisher. With his legalistic turn of mind, Thayer could not but concede that Wright had won the first round, but he was not yet ready to surrender his magazine to what he regarded (perhaps rightly) as certain doom.

In the ensuing moves and counter-moves, Mencken and Nathan played somewhat anomalous and equivocal roles. It is easy to say in hindsight that these two friends, who had helped Wright into the editorship and were in general agreement with his aims and views, should have supported him on principle. Would Thayer have retreated from his demand that Wright change policies or resign had his literary and theatre editors threatened resignation? Probably not. His maneuvers during late November and early December were clearly those of a desperate man who was ready to risk all to salvage his *Smart Set*.

Whatever the case, Thayer shrewdly and carefully sounded out Nathan before making his next moves. It was a "messy business" in which he had no wish to be involved, Nathan told the publisher. He did not approve of the idea of trying to terminate Wright's contract before expiration, he admitted candidly, but neither did he approve wholly of Wright's "mussing the magazine up with pornographic stuff" (a harsh judgment in retrospect). Privately he conceded to Wright that Thayer was indeed "an ass" but his

counsel was one of moderation: "Tone it down. . . . Don't be foolhardy!" he advised the editor.

Buoyed up by Nathan's mild stand, Thayer descended on Baltimore, roused Mencken from bed in the wee hours of a cold December day and harangued for four hours on Wright's failures with, as Mencken later reported, a few pointed adversions "on my own lack of piety" for good measure. At the outset Mencken tried cautious and diplomatic counter-argument but, seeing that Thayer was irreconcilable, he fell silent. Would the literary editor, Thayer petulantly asked, "bolt" the magazine if Wright were somehow forced to resign? Mencken replied sarcastically that he "was not a breaker of contracts" but, in his relief at this, the heavy irony was evidently lost on Thayer. Immediately after the interview Mencken sent a play-by-play description of it by special delivery to Wright, advising him quite frankly that

> . . . the situation is hopeless — *i.e.*, that the only thing for you to do in decency is to clear out. [Thayer] seems to have convinced himself that the only sort of magazine that has a chance is one appealing to all the right-thinkers, and it's apparently useless to try to convince him to the contrary. . . . If he is determined to get out a conventional sheet, and equally determined to see disaster in every fluctuation of circulation under the present plan, I think the one and only thing to do is to let him have his way.

Mencken was apologetic for leading Wright into "this past vain and disheartening year," concluding: "Get a lawyer and look into this, and *don't make any propositions of abrogation yourself.*"

Meanwhile, upon his return to New York, Thayer had found an even better pretext for Wright's dismissal. Without the publisher's knowledge or consent, Wright had ordered a "dummy" issue of *The Blue Review* (the "anti-Puritan" weekly he, Mencken and

Nathan still dreamed of) made up and printed at *Smart Set* expense. The bill was only fifty dollars but, to the infuriated Thayer, it was nothing less than a gross embezzlement. He gave Wright twenty-four hours' notice to clear out.

A suit for breach of contract now seemed Wright's only alternative. Whereupon Thayer threatened a counter-suit to recover losses from Wright's "mismanagement"—a move that the horrified staff foresaw as ruinous to *The Smart Set*. For days emissaries scuttled back and forth between the antagonists and the office routine dissolved in a series of huddles. In the end, Wright was prevailed upon to accept a cash settlement in lieu of his six months' notice and Thayer was persuaded to let the matter rest there. Luckily, Mencken had heard that Frank Adams was about to leave a $100-a-week job (a high salary for those days) as literary editor of the New York *Evening Mail* and, on his tip, Wright quickly snagged the post and, with it, a contributing editorship on *The Forum* in the bargain.

Back to his former "Something Personal" column came Thayer in the March 1914 *Smart Set,* informing readers of the return to innocuous mediocrity. He quoted laudatory remarks from the *Boston Transcript* that "during the past year *The Smart Set* has been gathering laurels unto itself as a unique magazine for those who desire to keep abreast and ahead of modern literary currents." But, Thayer noted in his breast-beating,

> together with this academic approval we have received stout protests. Many of our most valued readers have written us that they did not like the innovation.

The Smart Set, he confessed, had been "too serious as regards the relations of literature to life." In future, he promised, the magazine would be "more like the old days" with "a good round measure of romantic and humorous relief . . . not ultra in any respect."

If the purpose of a commercial magazine is to make money for its publisher (and who can gainsay it?), then Thayer was quite justified in sacking Wright and trying to give his customers what he thought they wanted to read. But the hour had grown late for the "Zenda stuff" and the innocent joshing of yesteryear. If the readers of *The Smart Set,* by and large, were not yet ready for the kind of literary sophistication that Wright tried to give them (a "sophistication" which seems terribly tame today), they had at least outgrown the Colonel Mann conception of "Oh, you kid!" cleverness. Figuratively speaking, a new earnestness had come upon the land in concert with the new creative energy we have already noted. In the White House, President Wilson expounded with seriousness a progressive idealism ("The New Freedom") and those who wished to find fault with the social order could find better targets than the foibles and furbelows of the *haut monde.* In Europe, "The Guns of August" were already primed; their first volleys would forever obliterate the wide ocean barriers behind which America could safely slumber in rural content.

Far from bringing the magazine into tune with these changing times, Wright's exit had left *The Smart Set* bereft of even a semblance of a program. A young assistant editor, Harry Torsey Baker (in later years a venerable English professor at Goucher College) tried vainly to carry on for a few weeks, then he too departed, leaving *The Smart Set* in the listless hands of Mark Lee Luther. All through the spring and summer of 1914 the magazine drifted like a rudderless ship, saved only by a backlog cargo of good manuscripts purchased during Wright's regime. Its circulation continued to erode as the readers who had been attracted by Wright were repelled by Thayer and turned instead to such journals as the radical *Masses* or the numerous new "little" magazines.

The subsequent career of Willard Huntington Wright, while not properly a part of *The Smart Set's* history, is an astounding and little-known story of personal tragedy, degradation and ultimate triumph.

For some three or four years after his dismissal from *The Smart Set*, Wright prospered, his star clearly in the ascendant. By 1915 he had added another contributing editorship (*International Studio*) and, in 1916 and 1917, he published a successful book on Nietzsche as well as his *Modern Painting* and his widely denounced but brilliant attack on the *Encyclopaedia Britannica* ("Misinforming a Nation," an essay-length work). Then, in October 1917, Wright's flair for the dramatic overcame his common sense and cost him his job, his friends and his reputation. A few months earlier the United States had entered the fighting in France and war hysteria was at fever pitch. Since Wright was notoriously pro-German and the *Evening Mail*, where he worked, was suspected of harboring treasonable leanings, the Creel Press Bureau—the government's watchdog in journalism (similar to the O.W.I. in World War II)—asked Wright's secretary to keep alert for signs of her employer's covert disloyalty and, if necessary, inform on him. The frightented girl began keeping carbon copies of Wright's correspondence and, when he discovered this, he played a perverse joke by deliberately dictating a letter to a newspaper friend in Washington full of obviously phony double-talk hinting at plans for cloak-and-dagger espionage and sabotage for "our glorious Kaiser."

Halfway through the typing of this letter, Wright burst in upon the stenographer, demanding to know why she was making extra carbons. At this the frantic girl jumped up, grabbed her note pad, snatched the letter from the typewriter and ran down the stairs and into the street toward the nearest telephone booth with her boss in hot pursuit. She was on the verge of phoning the police when Wright arrived to grab the telephone and the ensuing fracas was described in a *New York Times* sub-headline with wonderful understatement as "Exciting Time in Telephone Booth at Corner Drug Store." The stenog-

rapher refused to lodge charges, so Wright was not arrested, although he was questioned at length by the police concerning his "unpatriotic" sympathies. The unfavorable publicity that attended all this gave the jittery editor of the *Evening Mail* an excuse to fire both Wright and his correspondent, the Washington reporter.

Mencken and Nathan were shocked and incensed by what they considered Wright's "idiotic" behavior. In their view he had senselessly victimized an innocent mutual friend and thereafter they neither spoke to nor of him again. He found himself virtually blacklisted by many American publications and, going West, he was forced to seek a living by pseudonymous free-lancing and menial copydesk work for long hours and short wages. Under the strain of this his health broke and, as a result of long periods of sedation, he became a narcotics addict.

In 1922 Wright went to Paris for "the cure" in a small private clinic operated by a French psychotherapist. This learned doctor put him in virtual solitary confinement for six months, allowing him to read nothing heavier than detective novels, which he devoured by the hundreds. They reminded him of the somewhat anemic mystery stories he sometimes concocted pseudonymously for *The Smart Set*. This brought upon him the urge to write again and the purposeful excitement this entailed enabled him to live without relying on narcotics. Slowly at first, then with quickening pace, he began to carve a new career for himself, not as Willard Wright, but as "S. S. Van Dine"—the popular author of *The Benson Murder Case* (1926), *The Canary Murder Case* (1927) and ten other best-selling detective novels during the next decade. (Curiously, each title had six letters in the principal word—the same number as "Wright.") "S. S. Van Dine's" popular detective hero—Philo Vance—now widely regarded as one of the classic figures in that genre—is an idealized Willard Huntington Wright.

On April 11, 1939, Wright succumbed

suddenly to a coronary thrombosis in his Park Avenue penthouse where he had lived in great style during his last eight years. By this time, "S. S. Van Dine" was a literary institution—such as Ian Fleming or Georges Simenon have become in more recent years—and *The New York Times* saw fit to eulogize him not only with an obituary but an editorial as well, summing up his life thus: "He was a master of his favorite form. There was a kind of subtler splendor in his way of life. He who had killed so many harmlessly knew how to live with enjoyment."

No doubt "Owen Hatteras" would have appreciated that!

"Good Lord, Deliver Us!"

"Good Lord, Deliver Us!"

———•—•———

The spring and summer of 1914 were joyous seasons for the arts in America. In the Midwest a full-blown literary "renaissance" was in progress, with *Reedy's Mirror,* in St. Louis, and *Poetry* and *The Little Review,* both in Chicago, discovering new geniuses in every issue. In New York the Armory Show of the previous year and Mabel Dodge's continual "salon" had brought barriers down and people were meeting each other at parties to listen to Emma Goldman and "Big Bill" Haywood outline Armageddon, to Alfred Stieglitz expound photography as "an art," to Isadora Duncan articulate the blessings of corsetless, free-form dancing. New voices were heard in literary criticism in *The Masses, The New Republic* and elsewhere as Max Eastman, Joel Spingarn, Randolph Bourne and Van Wyck Brooks, following the leads of Huneker, Pollard, Mencken and Nathan, added their muscle to the long task of sweeping out the cobwebs left by Brander Mathews, Hamilton Wright Mabie and Henry Van Dye. Freud had been discovered by Americans and was already being widely misunderstood. So was Havelock Ellis—the hero of the emancipated. Everywhere in the land, for the self-conscious "intelligentsia," the air was vibrant

43

with new ideas, new passions, new movements.

Amid this aesthetic and philosophical revelry, *The Smart Set* was down in bed with what looked alarmingly like a mortal illness. The deficits run by Wright had to be met and, with advertisers deserting in droves and the circulation slippage continuing, John Adams Thayer was in no mood to give ear to dulcet harmonies wafting in from the West and up from MacDougall Alley. After a year with "whores and horrors," as Mencken put it, the magazine was once more "as pure as the *Christian Herald*," but those who had been attracted by Wright's editorial hijinks (and they were considerable, despite Thayer's refusal to acknowledge it) were repelled by the namby-pamby policies of Luther and Boyer and by Thayer's evident kneebending before the dour gods of the "right-thinkers." Only the reserves of foreign manuscripts purchased by Wright saved *The Smart Set* during these months from utter fatuity. To Mencken and Nathan the situation looked hopeless; both resolved to quit the magazine altogether come October, when their contracts were due to expire.

Then: Sarajevo—six weeks of uneasy negotiation—and the outbreak of war in Europe. The American stock market convulsed violently. As prices plummeted with war news, Thayer saw his Liliputian kingdom dissolve. Panic seized him and, early in August, he begged his chief creditor, Colonel Eugene R. Crowe, head of Perkins-Goodwin Company (*The Smart Set's* paper suppliers), to assume receivership of his ailing magazine in return for a release on the $6,000 owed by the John Adams Thayer Corporation to Perkins-Goodwin and for Crowe's assumption of the magazine's remaining obligations. Thus Thayer made his exit, as Mencken said, "to a low comedy tune"—a $100,000 investment, plus over three years' toil, scuttled for debts amounting to $24,000!

Crowe had not the least interest nor desire to own any part of *The Smart Set* but he foresaw no alternative if he wished to salvage anything at all from an otherwise bad debt. This was not the first time he (and Perkins-Goodwin) had fallen heir to periodicals in their death agonies. He had, in fact, formed a partnership for just such purposes with an up-and-coming young midwesterner, Eltinge F. Warner, who had shown amazing proclivities at the business of rehabilitating nearly-defunct magazines or, at the very least, of milking the assets of those beyond all hope. With such talents he was then on his way to building a publishing empire that would eventually include over forty magazines before his retirement in the late 1940's. A native of Minneapolis, Eltinge Warner came to publishing straight from Princeton, rescued *Field & Stream* Magazine from imminent oblivion, and turned it into a huge success as undoubtedly the greatest magazine devoted solely to hunting and fishing in the United States. Almost the *beau ideal* of the American sportsman himself, the energetic Warner was superbly equipped to publish *Field & Stream* but he had, quite rightly, some misgivings about running a journal like *The Smart Set*.

Fortunately, for Warner, for Crowe and, above all, for *The Smart Set,* there had occurred a few weeks earlier on board the S. S. *Imperator,* steaming toward New York on the return trip of its maiden voyage, one of those chance encounters which, in retrospect, seem almost providential. Among the passengers were Mr. and Mrs. Warner and a certain Mr. George Jean Nathan, whose reputation as a reviewer was rapidly growing but whose face was not yet familiar (as it would one day be) to millions as the awesome "dean" of New York drama critics. On the next-to-last day out, the Warners and Nathan happened to decide simultaneously upon a late morning stroll on the promenade deck but, as the brisk breezes were blowing off the North Atlantic, both donned, for the first time, gray homespun surtouts that had been "exclusively" tailored for them in London. The coats were identical—and, when the two gentlemen saluted each other and remarked the "coincidence," they discovered to their amused chagrin that they had patronized the same Bond Street tailor who had made the same protestations of "exclusiveness" to each. There seemed little for it except to make a joke of it and adjourn to the bar to toast their duplicitous tailor—which they promptly did.

Thus, when Colonel Crowe came to Warner with his *Smart Set* proposition, Warner recalled his shipboard *tête-à-tête* and dimly remembered that Nathan was on the staff of that magazine. Up to that moment, Warner later recalled, he had never seen a copy of *The Smart Set,* but Nathan had been impressive in his elegant bearing. "I may know just the man to edit it for us," Warner responded and immediately set out, with some difficulty, to locate the drama critic—at the apartment on the top floor of the Hotel Royalton where he lived from 1908 until his death fifty years later. If Nathan was surprised with the offer of editorship coming from such an unexpected quarter, it was certainly no novelty. Three years earlier, as we have already noted, he had declined a similar offer from Thayer. But something in Warner's detached and "straightforward" business approach struck a responsive chord. The man obviously had no "Smart Set Idea" or program of his own to promote, only an interest in turning a profit by any means at hand. This, in turn, persuaded Nathan that Warner was quite sincere in his avowals not to "meddle or muss in the editorial conduct of a literary magazine."

"All right," Nathan consented, after some thought. "I'll give it a try if Mencken will come in with me." The publisher was nonplussed: "Who the hell is Mencken?" was his reaction. He was no longer finding out than it takes for a long-distance phone call to reach Baltimore. Mencken's acceptance was neither immediate nor unconditional: he must, he asserted, be permitted to remain in Baltimore. But how could a magazine be edited in two different cities? Over

Eltinge Warner

this point Nathan, Warner and Crowe forthwith began to negotiate. Meanwhile, Mencken wrote (on August 11, 1914) a "confidential" note to his friend, Theodore Dreiser, begging a two-week option on three one-act plays that Dreiser had just finished and that Mencken desperately wanted to "blaze out" with in *The Smart Set.* (The three—"The Blue Sphere," "Laughing Gas," and "In the Dark"—were published there in, respectively, December 1914, and January and February 1915). "If the thing goes through," he told the novelist-turned-playwright, "there will be a future in it for both of us [him and Nathan]," adding that

> The S.S. [*sic*] is losing very little money, and the cutting off of certain excessive overhead expenses—high rent, extravagant salary to Thayer, etc.—will quickly make it self-sustaining. And we are associated with a truly excellent man of business—one who is no mere talker, but has actually made a success elsewhere.

Three days later Mencken went to Manhattan to take part in the final settlement. The "scheme" he and Nathan proposed was admirable in its simplicity: Nathan would take on the office routine in New York; Mencken would act as chief "reader," winnowing manuscripts in Baltimore; twice monthly the two would get together for editorial conferences. As they would be "co-editors," each with an absolute veto, little need for protracted discussions or close daily contact was envisioned. Nevertheless, they would not be complete co-equals: Nathan, as "editor in residence," so to speak, would be the "senior" partner. His name would appear first on the cover and masthead and he would be empowered to make the "on-the-spot" decisions in emergencies.

For his part, Warner would assume all the tasks of getting and spending—circulation, advertising, bookkeeping and the like. The editorial and business sides would thus be kept quite separate, neither permitted to infringe upon the other except by general consent. After a weekend of bibulous sessions at a New Jersey country club Colonel Crowe had bought for himself (he liked golf but hated the "boors" who inhabited most golf clubs), all these arrangements were ratified by Warner and Crowe and the compact sealed by which *The Smart Set* would operate for the next decade.

Ultimately, this divorce of the magazine's editorial and financial responsibilities would prove a mixed blessing at best. On the one hand, it freed the editors for purely literary endeavors; on the other, it tied them to conservative fiscal policies not of their own choosing, cramping their budget and preventing changes in format, typography and illustration that might have improved the magazine. It was an advantage to Warner to be relieved of dreary editorial conferences (over matters he cared little for) but, though he might dislike what the editors selected (especially in later years) he felt powerless to object. Under this schism it was several years before either Nathan or Mencken saw a subscription list. From readers' letters and friends' comments they formed some idea of

the nature and tastes of their audience, but it was their standing office joke, Mencken told Percy Marks that *The Smart Set* was "read mostly by women of superior intelligence but perhaps inferior virtue—among them, by the higher ranges of kept ladies," and he professed horror in 1922 when, at his first glimpse of the lists, he found them headed by an Elks Club and spotted "a great many solemn dodoes, including even some clergy" among their faithful readers.

The morning after these arrangements were concluded (August 16, 1914), the September issue hit the newsstands with a hideous, hastily-concocted "war" cover—picturing soldiers going "over the top" and advertising a "war" novelette (also hastily-written)—"Through 'Hell' to Peace"—by Donn Byrne. This was the only time in four years that the magazine, or any of its contents, would make anything more than very oblique reference to the existence of World War I! On the same morning, *The New York Times* carried this quiet disclosure in its back pages:

> *The Smart Set* Magazine has changed ownership, John Adams Thayer having disposed of his interest in the corporation bearing his name. The purchase price has not been disclosed. The magazine will be continued on similar lines, but will be published in connection with another magazine, thereby decreasing overhead charges and increasing profits.

On the heels of this discreet announcement Crowe's attorney, James P. Brady, began contacting holders of the $100,000 in five percent debenture bonds that Thayer had inherited as a liability from Colonel Mann, offering them cash at ten cents on the dollar or a one-for-ten exchange on ten-year bonds in the newly-created "Smart Set Company." By this shrewd maneuver, the new organization was able eventually to acquire most of Colonel Mann's bonds at very little outlay and thus reduce the liabilities of the magazine to manageable proportions. The Smart Set Company had a triumvirate ownership: Crowe and

Warner each owned one third, with the remaining one-third interest divided between the co-editors. (At Crowe's death in 1921, Warner purchased his share and held a two-thirds interest until the sale to Hearst in 1924.) In addition to sharing (one-sixth each) in whatever profits would be forthcoming, Nathan and Mencken were to receive salaries of $100 a month, plus the regular contributors' scale (one cent per word) for their monthly columns and whatever else of their own they printed. Although supposedly a temporary expedient, this arrangement remained in force throughout the hand-to-mouth decade of their editorship.

At the outset, Warner and his colleagues faced a situation that would have turned the hair of many a more experienced head. Despite Mencken's bravura claims to Dreiser ("The S.S. is losing very little money . . .") the magazine was in desperate straits. Thayer's $24,000 deficit increased during August and September by nearly $2,000 each month. Circulation had dropped to the 40,000 mark, mostly in unreliable newsstand sales. With the war jitters affecting business, advertisers were reluctant to give long-term contracts to a magazine with a record of instability. Under such circumstances it is a tribute to Warner's acumen that he was able to keep *The Smart Set* afloat at all much less make it pay its way.

In the end, the trick was turned by stringent economy. Warner moved the magazine from its spacious, expensive "editorial chambers" in Fifth Avenue (engaged twelve years earlier by Colonel Mann) into an austere $35-a-month cubicle adjoining his *Field & Stream* office at 456 Fourth Avenue. The staff was reduced to one all-purpose secretary—Miss Sara Golde—a Brooklynite pillar of *The Smart Set* for a decade thereafter. "Goldie," as the co-editors nicknamed her (Nathan claimed never to have known her real name!), virtually ran the magazine herself at times—during Nathan's trips abroad and the two or three days each week that he

—*Brown Brothers*
H. L. Mencken and George Jean Nathan

did not come to the office. She guarded the editors' inner sanctum against the incursions of obnoxious literary agents and the "phony" poets whose names did not appear on the "approved" list given her by Nathan and Mencken—or so it was rumored among the young literati, in whom Miss Golde struck awe. Even the editors themselves were a little awed by her frightening efficiency and proprietary manner.

In addition to these drastic reductions in overhead, Warner turned loss into profit by binding together back issues and current returns and shipping them into hinterland villages as a ten-center, *Clever Stories*. All bills and payments to contributors were settled immediately out of current proceeds and one-third of all income for the first eight months was ploughed into debt reduction even though this meant that, for six months, the editors went salary-less and Crowe and Warner without profits. But, by the end of the seventh month, Warner's bush-beaters were scaring up new advertising contracts for six to twelve months, the returns were steadily declining as the new regime at last began to find an audience, and Mencken was able to confide cautiously to Dreiser: "I begin to believe we'll put it over. But what a sweat!"

The "sweat" he referred to was really on the editorial, not just the business side of the house. When the new regime commenced the September 1914 issue, as we have seen, was already on the stands and the October issue was ready to go into galleys. The November issue, thus, was the first to be wholly edited by Nathan and Mencken and even that had some "left-over" material in it. That number of *The Smart Set* is certainly one of the greatest curiosities in the history of American journalism, more than half of it being written by the editors themselves under a gaudy variety of fanciful pseudonyms. Under his own name, Mencken himself wrote the novelette of the month ("The Barbarous Bradley") and, as Janet Jefferson, Marie de Verdi, Harriet Morgan, Herbert Winslow Archer and Pierre D'Aubigny he contributed poems, the last of these being signed to a farcical "Ode to Munich," which was nothing more than a *vers libre* arrangement of Munich brewery names—*Pschorrbräu, Löwenbräu, Spatenbräu, et al.*—the kind of spoof the co-editors delighted in throughout their regime. For his part, Nathan premiered what was planned as a new series of literary burlesques—"The Return of Baron Münchausen"—under the name Ronald V. Cross, but he lost interest in the series after a few numbers. Back from a three-month "vacation" came the needling Owen Hatteras, to be joined by a host of fictitious colleagues—Raoul della Torre, George Weems Peregoy, Sherrard Mullikin, Francis Clegg Thompson, William Fink, R. B. McLoughlin—Mencken's brainchildren all!

Much as they enjoyed these *tours de force,* the editors could not continue indefinitely to be their own chief contributors. New voices had to be found quickly to swell the chorus of "old standbys" like the Baroness von Hutten, Helen Woljeska, Achmed Abdullah, Lee Wilson Dodd and Hayden Carruth in the Nathan-Mencken version of "cleverness." To a dozen editorial colleagues —William Marion Reedy, Ellery Sedgwick (of *The Atlantic Monthly*), and T. R. Smith (of *The Century*) among them—they sent requests to "pass the word" in the marketplace that *The Smart Set* was once more searching for good, young talent, and, especially, for unconventional material that might be unacceptable elsewhere. Still, they were determined to avoid the pitfalls of "whorishness" that Wright had fallen into by playing up the lighter side, making the magazine "a sort of frivolous sister to *The Atlantic*."

By sheer accident, the first Nathan-Mencken issue turned up a major new talent in a 22-year-old Vassar graduate, Edna St. Vincent Millay, but it was as fictioneer, not as poet, that Miss Millay made her debut in *The Smart Set*. Nevertheless, the word soon began to spread among the literary "bucks and wenches" of the land that the magazine was once more open for their business, and other eager youngsters were not long to follow.

Nathan, meanwhile, looked eastward, soliciting manuscripts from the British and French writers he admired, often with little hope of positive response. One of these was the Anglo-Irish playwright, Lord Dunsany, who astonished the editors not only by replying enthusiastically but by sending along a huge packet of manuscripts as well. "The Bureau d'Echange de Maux," a haunting story *à la* Huysmans in which sinister men come and go in a Parisian cafe, trading in their sins and vices for new ones, was Lord Dunsany's first appearance in an American publication (in the January 1915 issue). Over the next three years there was at least one Dunsany piece in every second or third issue (sometimes oftener) and it can safely be said that the "Dunsany vogue"—which, though it has faded past recovery, was very strong in America in the 1920's and '30's— actually began in *The Smart Set*.

From London, Ezra Pound responded to their pleas for fresh material by sending over the "Dubliners" stories of his latest "discovery"—James Joyce. Two of the stories ("A Little Cloud" and "The Boarding-House") appeared in the May 1915 number and the editors would have taken all of them had B. W. Huebsch not scheduled the collection for book publication during that very season.

As it is, these constitute Joyce's first publication in the United States. Pound also sent the page proofs of the English edition of Joyce's *A Portrait of the Artist as a Young Man,* which the editors sorrowfully had to reject because of length. They did not publish serials and, Mencken told the author, they knew it would "do unpardonable violence" to his story to whittle it down to the size of a *Smart Set* novelette (*i.e.,* under 30,000 words). As late as 1917 the editors were still corresponding with Joyce, then living in Zürich, in the hope of arranging another appearance for him in their magazine, but Joyce had ceased to write short stories or poems and everything else he then had in progress was too long for consideration. So it was left to *The Little Review* to begin serial publication (in 1918) of *Ulysses,* resulting in one of the most flagrant cases of censorship and suppression in the history of American letters.

But the "name" writers that Nathan and Mencken ardently desired for their magazine—like Dreiser, Dunsany, Conrad, Anatole France, Beerbohm and George Moore—were difficult to attract, especially at the "starvation" rates (unchanged from Colonel Mann's day) which were all they could afford. Nor could they compete with *The Saturday Evening Post* for a popular figure like Harry Leon Wilson (author of *Ruggles of Red Gap, Bunker Bean,* etc.) even though Wilson was an admirer and close friend for many years. In the main, they had to content themselves with whatever they could get of value from promising novices and ultimately, as we shall see, they made a virtue of this necessity.

One of their early "discoveries" was Harris Merton Lyon, a Dreiser protégé from Texas by way of Kansas City and *Reedy's Mirror,* whose story ("The Pact," December 1914) about a banker who lures his mistress into a false suicide pact and is panicked into poisoning himself as well when a confused drunk

(who he mistakes for the police) tries to enter his hotel room, is the quintessence of *Smart Set* "cleverness." Another was Scammon Lockwood's "The Twelfth Juror" (April 1915) in which a man takes bizarre revenge on his wife's lover when he is impanelled as a member of a jury trying the lover for a murder that he did not commit.

There were also stories in the early issues of the Nathan-Mencken regime that had more real substance than cleverness. Waldo Frank's "The Fruit of Misadventure" (July 1915), for instance, anticipated Nabokov's *Lolita* by nearly forty years—and with impunity. One of the best stories ever published in *The Smart Set* was Lee Pape's "Little Girl" (April 1915) in which a college boy picks up a shopgirl and, in an evening of innocent love-making in a series of cheap dance halls and bars, falls genuinely in love with her, only to realize (as she does also) that the social distinctions that separate them make such an affair hopeless. Jean White's stories of New York's Chinatown ("The Singing Girl," July 1915, and others) were also told with a realism and a poignancy that compared favorably with Joyce's *Dubliners,* for instance, and gave further proof that *The Smart Set* would soon outgrow the "O. Henry formula" stories which it had helped to create in the first place.

Not everyone shared the satisfaction of Nathan and Mencken with their efforts to "lift the thing" at the end of their first half-year. Dreiser, for one, protested that their magazine was too light—"like a diet of soufflé." Mencken countered:

I am sorry that *The Smart Set* doesn't please you. As it stands, of course, it represents a compromise between what we'd like to do and what the difficulties that we face allow us to do. We had to buck a falling circulation and a bad reputation. The former has swung back; the latter we are trying to live down. We haven't money enough to take long chances. We have to give them, to some extent at least, what they seem to like, and more particularly, what we are able to get. . . . Read the novelettes in the other magazines; you will find that they are even worse than ours. I know it because I have read most of them in manuscripts and declined them.

But the light touch you protest against is what we want. *The Smart Set*—consider the title!—is no place [for] revolutionary fustian. . . .

But let it go! We are not trying to shock 'em, but to entertain 'em!

Nathan and Mencken both agreed with Dreiser, however, that much of what crossed their desks—and some of what they had, in desperation, to publish—was indeed execrable. Early in 1915 they tried to improve the situation by publishing a "Note to Authors," listing some of their aims and interests, and a four-page pamphlet listing twelve items of "Don't Send Us," and eight strictures of "What We Want." This they enclosed with clever pithy notes in lieu of a "rejection slip."

Sometime early in 1915 it also occurred to them that they might turn a neat profit from some of the second-rate material they received by publishing an admittedly inferior "by-product" magazine. With Warner's backing, they capitalized on the then current war interest in France with a magazine entitled *Parisienne*, beginning in July 1915. All stories judged inferior for *The Smart Set* were shunted over to this "louse" magazine, as the editors nicknamed these ventures, where they were "doctored" and their locale changed to France before being published. *Parisienne* was an immediate success, selling 150,000 copies and bringing in profits of $4,000 an issue to the co-editors. In 1916 they sold their interest in the magazine to Warner and Crowe and repeated the process with another 15-cent "thriller" pulp monthly — *Saucy Stories* — deliberately designed to compete with *Snappy Stories* which Colonel Mann had started, using the

swirling S's of his old *Smart Set*. Within a year, *Saucy* was circulating in excess of 120,000 copies per month and, soon thereafter, Nathan and Mencken were able to sell out their interests to their partners for $10,000 apiece. This, they promised themselves, would be the last of their "louse" ventures and, despite the prospects dangled by J. W. Glenister (Warner's business manager)—an all-Negro pulp was one of his lucrative ideas — they kept their vow for nearly three years.

Then, in April 1920, they succumbed again. This time the "louse" by-product of *The Smart Set* was to be a mystery magazine par excellence—*Black Mask*—which has been credited by some historians of popular culture with playing a major role in the development of modern detective fiction. *Black Mask* was a popular triumph, soon selling a quarter-million copies and bringing another sales "deal" with Colonel Crowe which, Mencken facetiously reported, "sufficed to relieve Nathan and me from want permanently." He was not far wrong. Crowe was then dying of old age and knew it. He had grown fond of the two editors and gave them extremely liberal terms for *Black Mask* which, though never publicly disclosed, were rumored to be "in excess of $50,000" for each. Thus they were able to wrest from these pulps the profits *The Smart Set* failed to provide, fishing shekels from the dustbin, so to speak. Although writers were sometimes startled to have pieces they had submitted to *The Smart Set* accepted by Wyndham Martyn or Florence Osborne (editorial hirelings) on behalf of *Parisienne, Saucy Stories* or *Black Mask,* there is no record of anyone objecting to the higher rates of pay these "louse" pulps were able to afford.

As we have already seen, the availability of really first-rate manuscripts was a continual problem for Nathan and Mencken, as it had been for some of their predecessors, and the problem became increasingly acute as *The Smart Set* fell behind in the marketplace for lack of money. Even so, it made a strong showing among the top ten or twelve magazines surveyed in O'Brien's annual *Best Short Stories*. The typical magazine story of that era had a "formula" plot peopled with stereotyped characters. Some idea of what these were like may be had from an early "Owen Hatteras" litany ("Litany for Magazine Editors," February 1915) which Nathan also published in a symposium in *The Bookman* in 1916 in which leading magazine editors discussed their reasons for rejecting manuscripts and what their journals wanted most to receive from contributors. Here is an excerpt:

> From stories in which a rising young district attorney gets the dead wood upon a burly political boss named Terence O'Flaherty, and then falls in love with Mignon, his daughter, and has to let him go; and from stories in which a married lady, just about to sail for Capri with her husband's old *corpsbruder,* is dissuaded from her purposes by the news that her husband has lost $700,000 in Wall Street and is on his way home to weep on her shoulder; and from one-act plays in which Cornelius Van Suydam comes home from The Club at 11:55 P.M. on Christmas Eve, dismisses Dodson, his man, with the compliments of the season, and draws up his chair before the open fire to dream of his girl, thus preparing the way for the entrance of Maxwell, the starving burglar, and for the scene in which Maxwell's little daughter, Fifi, following him up the fire-escape, pleads with him to give up his evil courses; and from poems about the war in which it is argued that thousands of young men will be killed before it is over, and that their mothers will regret to hear of it . . . and from epigrams based on puns, good or bad; and from stories beginning, "It was the autumn of the year 1960"; . . . and from stories in which the gay nocturnal life of the Latin Quarter is described by an author living in Dubuque, Iowa; . . . and from newspaper stories in which a cub reporter solves the mystery of the Snodgrass murder and is promoted to drama critic on the field; . . . and from stories in which the dissolute son of a department store owner tries to seduce a working girl in his father's employ and then goes on the water wagon and marries her as a tribute to her virtue. . . . GOOD LORD DELIVER US!

Could it be that popular fiction in America has improved in the last fifty years?

Pistols for Two

———•———

"It is the policy of this magazine (copiously supported by the gratitude of its readers) to avoid any discussion of the war, even in fiction and poetry," the editors of *The Smart Set* flatly enunciated in August 1916. Despite some wishful hyperbole about readers' "gratitude," this was no mere caprice but a firm policy clearly apparent in the magazine from the outset of the Nathan-Mencken regime and unswervingly pursued until after the Versailles Peace Conference of 1919. Incredible as such a stance would seem today, *The Smart Set* officially ignored the most catastrophic world war then known to man!

The reasons for this—as for virtually all else in the Nathan-Mencken strategies—were purely personal. Mencken was overtly pro-German before American entry into the war, covertly thereafter. (Perhaps it would be fairer to say he was less "pro" German than anti-British, seeing the conflict simply as one between entrenched British imperialism and the ambitions of a renascent Germany, the issues and stakes of which were unrelated to American self-interest.) For his part, Nathan regarded all war *per se,* irrespective of the belligerents, as essentially idiotic, a negation of those peculiar human sensibilities which over the ages had bridged the great gulf between the Neanderthal and the Metropolitan. It was, in fact, his open boast that he spent the day of the war's bloodiest battle calmly composing an essay on aesthetics and, unruffled amid the simian hysteria of the mob, finished it by consuming his "normal quota" of cocktails in studied disdain.

Thus, to have discussed—or to have allowed partisan discussion—of the war in their magazine would have been to risk the veriest hypocrisy on the one hand, suicidal unpopularity on the other. In the face of such prevalent attitudes, silence seemed the only sensible solution for *The Smart Set*. Yet, this course too was fraught with perils, as Mencken hinted to Ernest Boyd (then in Ireland) in early 1917:

> The war has naturally affected all publishing ventures, but I don't think there will be any very formidable paralysis. The people will stop reading magazines for a while, but sooner or later they will tire of the newspapers and go back to the magazines. Nathan and I are so firmly convinced of this that we are sticking to our resolution to print nothing about the war. When the reaction against alarms and headlines comes we'll pick up the circulation we now lose.

Nor was loss of circulation the only wartime difficulty, as Mencken told Boyd, later that same year:

> The war taxes here threaten to become impossible. If the proposed increase in postage rates goes through the S.S. [*sic*] will probably take the hemlock. Meanwhile, paper continues to soar. The paper manufacturers are making enormous fortunes, and all efforts to combat them have so far failed. . . . The war has cut magazine sales to pieces and raised all the costs of production. The result is that I tremble on the verge of bankruptcy, and may have to get a job before the end of the year.

As the editors feared, postal rates did increase (some 600%!) and, added to these woes, the New York post office lost one complete issue of the magazine in the mails. Paper costs, even with the influence of Crowe behind them, rose from $3.60 per pound for good paper in 1914 to $5.50 "for the most horrible toilet paper," as Mencken said, in less than two years, and the brittleness of their pulp pages led Nathan to joke grimly: "Never fear, Henry, if our subscribers desert we can always chop up the magazine and sell it for toothpicks." The flow of foreign manuscripts slowed from fifteen a week in 1914 to merely a trickle of two or three a month in 1917, and the editors had to comb the agencies for even mediocre English and Continental material.

Faced with these difficulties, the editors went without salary for months on end and began to foresee "blood upon the moon" for their magazine. In June 1916 *The Smart Set* moved to comfortable, if modest, quarters in the newly-opened Printing Crafts Building (Eighth Avenue at Thirty-Fourth St.) but in September 1918 Mencken lamented to Boyd:

> Our building has been seized by the War Department and we must move. Our printer also—a formidable business. . . . Warner rented a nice place at an advance in the rent of $1,500, plus $500 for moving and $750 for erecting partitions, but before we could get into it, it was seized by the Creel Press Bureau. We now have another building in sight. But the thing is very vexing and costly.

Worst of all (but blessedly never known to Nathan and Mencken), they were actually being "spied" upon from April 1917 to November 1918—by no less a person than their employer, Eltinge Warner. Since his patriotism was beyond question, he was appointed by George Creel to a vigilance committee of leading publishers who could be relied upon to report strange machinations or signs of incipient disloyalty in newspaper, magazine and printing offices. At the committee's inaugural meeting a list was circulated of "suspicious" persons to be put under unofficial surveillance. Among them were the co-editors of *The Smart Set* and Warner was assigned to keep a cautious eye on them—an assignment which he took somewhat lightly since he never seriously doubted the fundamental loyalty of these amiable colleagues, however much he disapproved their political opinions and their policies *vis-à-vis* the war.

Through all these rigors of publishing, *The Smart Set* picked its precarious way and somehow endured. By 1916 its co-editors had become potentates of the literary arts in America. Each issue of the magazine contained their *causeries* in its back pages and these had become by far the most stimulating and attractive portions of the magazine. Many a reader opened his monthly issue of "The Magazine of Cleverness" to the back, as if it were written in Hebrew or Chinese, beginning his perusal with the critical essays of Mencken (the last item) or Nathan (next-to-last), according to his penchant.

Nathan perhaps had the fewer followers if only because the Broadway theatre (and, in summers before and after the war, the European stage) was of somewhat less general interest to those outside metropolitan New York than the new books. Nevertheless, his impact upon the American theatre in the mid-Teens of this century was beginning to be discernible and this would grow until, by the early 1920's, he would be indisputably the *arbiter elegantiarum* of our native drama.

That George Jean Nathan was a frustrated actor or a *dramatiste-manqué*, as some have suggested, is far too simple an explanation for the brilliant and complex intellect that lay behind a sybarite's mask that was itself a work of great art—the elegant fashion-plate (with his blue cornflower *boutonnières*, his fabled collection of overcoats to match his thirty-eight suits), the bachelor-connoisseur pursued by

actresses and feared by producers, the arch-snob whose *hauteur* and sardonic quips repelled strangers and conferred upon friends a special aura of belonging. His spiritual homeland was that of the *boulevardier* in the Paris of Toulouse-Lautrec, Huysmans, Antoine's *"Théâtre Libre."* He was a Gallic wit —a Rochefaucauld a de Musset, or a Sainte-Beuve—"exiled" to New York and, like Miniver Cheevy, "born too late." Reviewing a book of Nathan's criticism in *The Smart Set* (December 1917), Mencken publicly acknowledged his continual bewilderment at Nathan's "peculiar taste." Mencken scoffed at the theatre and rarely attended plays himself (although he had earlier served as a drama critic in Baltimore), but of Nathan he said:

> . . . at the brink of forty years, he remains faithful to the theatre; of his books, only one does not deal with it, and that one is a very small one. In four or five years he has scarcely written of aught else. . . . I sometimes wonder what keeps such a man in the theatre, breathing bad air nightly, gaping at prancing imbecilities, sitting cheek by jowl with cads. Perhaps there is, at bottom, a secret romanticism —a lingering residuum of boyish delight in pasteboard and spangle, gaudy colours and soothing sounds, preposterous heroes and appetizing wenches. . . .

"Not so!" declared Nathan in a series of mock-rebuttals in *The Smart Set,* stoutly maintaining that he was not enthusiastic about the "fripperies" of the theater as such, adding: "I am constitutionally given to enthusiasm about nothing." What fascinated him, he extenuated, was "the surface of life: life's music and color, its charm and ease, its humor and its loveliness." In this much, he and Mencken were in accord, but they differed over "the great problems of the world— social, political, economic and theological," which absorbed Mencken's interest but left Nathan utterly indifferent. "I care not who writes the laws of a country," he echoed, "so long as I may listen to its songs." As for religion, one church seemed no better than another then (although late in life he became a Catholic) because he never entered one except "to delight in some particularly beautiful stained-glass window, or some fine specimen of architecture, or in some great, throbbing organ."

But his "great toy," the theatre, held him, he admitted, because

> . . . it is one of the best subjects in the world with which to fashion a variegated assortment of predicates. It is almost impossible for a writer on politics to use politics as the hook whereon to hang his opinions, say, of music or cow diseases. . . . The theatre, on the contrary, by the very nature of its diverse constituent elements and its peculiar ramifications offers to the man who writes about it a hundred convenient opportunities to air his views *con sordini* on nearly everything under the sun, and what a writer craves are such opportunities. . . . Life, to me, is artificial; all my criticism of drama is based on the theory that drama is artificial life. There isn't so very much difference, in my way of looking at things, between life as it actually is and life as it is shown in the theatre.

If such views seem inconsistent or paradoxical, the stamp of the *fin de siècle* is unmistakably upon them, and they contain the fervent negations of a latter-day Swinburne, Pater or Wilde—*"le dernier cri"* which, as Oscar Wilde himself lamented, has no echo. Perhaps his seeming narrowness of concern may serve to explain why, even in his brightest years on *The Smart Set,* Nathan was persistently regarded as the lesser of the two critic-editors—a shadow of the "colossus of Baltimore." Who could be bothered to cut through his mazes of witty comment on current productions to contemplate Nathan's "variegated assortment of predicates" upon life in general? Undoubtedly, he knew the

risks inherent in such an oblique approach to ideas, but he remained baffled by the apparent failure of his public to follow him beyond the pasteboard, the spangles and the magical names of Broadway stars.

From beginning to end, Nathan's *Smart Set* criticism was one long gasp of exasperation at the inadequacies of the American drama, especially as compared with that of Europe. By the early 1900's, the Continental and British theater, revived from the Victorian nadir *ca.* 1875 by Ibsen, already boasted a distinguished roster of playwrights. But by 1909, when Nathan first took up the cudgels in *The Smart Set,* the United States had produced nothing remotely comparable to these dramatists. David Belasco, Augustus Thomas, Clyde Fitch, William Vaughan Moody, Edward Sheldon and Charles Klein were the "geniuses" of the American theater then. These writers, and a horde of less noteworthy imitators had achieved a facile compromise between the sentimental melodrama of earlier years and the newer techniques of naturalistic stagecraft imported from abroad, consisting mainly of smoking "real" cigarettes on stage, fetching "real" dinners from Sherry's to be eaten before drooling audiences, shelving "real" books in drawingroom sets, and laying "real" Karastans on stage floors. It was this superficial "realism," as well as the prevailing tendency among American critics to review the performance rather than the play itself, that Nathan attacked full tilt —and vanquished almost single-handedly— in the pages of *The Smart Set.*

His predicament in having to write "reviews" for a monthly magazine was not an easy one. His articles had to be composed at least a month in advance of publication and, although he had leisure to polish phrases and clarify impressions without the pressures of midnight deadlines that beset his newspaper colleagues, he was in the unenviable position of being a "second-guesser" who must find something fresh to say about plays that had already been discussed in the dailies and weeklies. Even so, there always remained the chance that, by mid-month (when *The Smart Set* appeared), he would be caught feeding oats to a dead horse, so to speak—lavishing extended discussion upon some play that had already closed! Finally, in addressing a national audience, most of whom lived outside the metropolitan New York area, his commentaries had to appeal to those yearning readers in the corn rows for whom Broadway might be as fantastically inaccessible as, say, Katamandu.

To solve these puzzlers, Nathan developed a pattern of reviewing calculated to be as invulnerable as possible to the vicissitudes of time and distance. His yearly cycle of *Smart Set* articles looked something like this:

> November-May: reviews of current New
> York productions;
> June: a retrospect of the previous season
> July-August: reviews of European productions;
> September-October: essays on dramaturgy and critical theory (some of his best).

But whatever the topic at hand—from the "art" of vaudeville slapstick to grandiose outdoor stagings of Euripides by Granville-Barker—his object was always to shock the native public into questioning the values, the taboos, the "archaic" practices and the crass commercialism of the American stage.

Firmly convinced that most American drama critics were either fuzzy-minded academicians who perverted their craft in irrelevant displays of erudition or (sometimes unwittingly) the hirelings of vested commercial interests, Nathan was determined to be fiercely independent. If this sometimes meant reckless irresponsibility, sacrificing some corner of truth to achieve a clever phrase or piquant pose, well, then, Nathan asked, "and why not?" Being earnest (Wilde's pun notwithstanding) was, he claimed, quite unimportant: "Your true artist

is seldom, if ever, sincere; for he realizes that to write only what he believes is to confess his pettiness, narrowness and his inflexible limitations." For Nathan, then, as for Mencken, the Unpardonable Sin was to be caught with one's ideals showing.

Admittedly, Nathan was a destructive critic in his *Smart Set* period. "Art and the artist," he claimed, "cannot be developed by mere back-slapping . . . I am a destructive critic . . . because I deal chiefly with elements that are themselves most often artistically destructive." Before the United States could develop a "good drama" of her own, he argued, the whole stultifying claptrap of Belasco "realism" had to be swept away. "Good drama" he defined with characteristic looseness as "anything that interests an intelligently emotional group of persons assembled in an illuminated hall." The key word here is "illuminated"—not the darkened halls of the cinema! If Nathan's interest could encompass even vaudeville and the Ziegfeld Follies, he jealously guarded the portals of the legitimate stage against the incursions of "the hooligan at the gates"—his pet phrase for the movies, which he vilified as "the outhouse of the arts."

A thorough-going Romantic in an age when romanticism was said to be moribund, Nathan's favorite term connected with the drama was "emotion." "Drama in its entirety," he reiterated, "consists in the surrender of accurate and judicious thinking to emotionalism." Not mere sentiment—so often mistaken for genuine emotion, Nathan insisted, but "intelligent emotion" informed by a broad and amoral experience, a subtle intellect, and a refined taste. Whatever burden of ideas a piece of dramatic writing might contain, he contended, must first be "felt" before it could be intellectualized. In appealing to the emotions, there were no rules of dramaturgy that genius could not disregard—whether the genius of George M. Cohan for popular comedy, or of "Flo" Ziegfeld for lush spectacle, or of Bernard Shaw for "saying the obvious in terms of the scandalous," it was all one to Nathan.

Despite his pertinacity, there always lurked at the back of Nathan's mind, even in his surest moments, gnawing doubts about the importance of the drama. In one of his most brilliant essays in *The Smart Set* (August 1922), he gave voice to his questionings, observing:

> Of all the higher arts, drama is perhaps the simplest and easiest. Its anatomy is composed of all the other arts, high and low, stripped to their essentials. It is a synthesis of those portions of these other arts that, being essential, are most easily assimilable on the part of the multitude. It is a snatch of music, a bit of painting, a moment of dancing, a slice of sculpture, draped upon the skeleton of literature. At its highest, it ranks with literature, but never above it. . . . Drama, indeed, is dancing literature. . . . Whatever emotions drama may succeed brilliantly in evoking, another art succeeds in evoking more brilliantly.

What fired Nathan's critical steel was not black doubts that the drama might, indeed, be a second-rate means of evoking "beautiful emotions" but that too often the emotions evoked were themselves second-rate. In his view, it was a rare audience in America that did not joyously surrender itself to specious sentiments and his contempt for shoddy dramaturgy was surpassed only by his disgust with audiences who permitted themselves to be duped by appeals to "crowd psychology," by snuffling idealism and by the "pious piffle of the Uplift." He was willing to concede that the drama was "a democratic art," but he steadfastly held that this art rose to greatness only when it appealed to aristocratic tastes over the heads of the groundlings. What passed for "great" drama among the *hoi polloi,* he constantly argued, was merely a bagful of obvious technical tricks or specious miming. Hence, he con-

centrated his fire upon the intrinsic merits of a play, not upon the qualities of its performance, often ignoring altogether the technical aspects of a production and even the most celebrated acting.

However, Nathan did not decry acting and stagecraft *per se.* On the contrary, drama could not live, he maintained, except in the living theatre which stood in the same relation to the written text as the art gallery does to painting: "The printed drama is like a bubbling and sunlit spring, encountered only by wanderers into the hills and awaiting the bottling process of the theatre to carry its tonic waters far and wide among an expectant and emotionally ill people." The imagination of the average reader is defective, he argued, and even that of a cultured man may be inferior to "the combined theatrical imaginations of Gordon Craig, Max Reinhardt and Eleanora Duse operating jointly upon the same play—three or four 'readings' instead of one." Thus, Nathan concluded, only the actual theatrical production of a play could most closely approximate the *intention* of the playwright if the parties involved were sufficiently sensitive and intelligent.

If some inconsistency appears in this, Nathan's defense was simple: "Show me a consistent critic, a critic who sets himself a critical creed and abides by that creed with never a sidestep, never a whispered doubt, and I will show you a critic who is generally wrong." The fact is nonetheless that George Jean Nathan, for all his caprices, his wish to put wit above creed, his penchant for making Ego the whole measure of art, was more consistent than perhaps even he realized. Whatever contradictions appear in the decisions he rendered under his own "Aesthetic Jurisprudence," a single overriding theme pervades his *Smart Set* criticism—that the ordinary fare of the American theatre constituted "stupidity" raised to the level of "a fine art." Although he improvised scores of variations upon this theme, he stated it forthrightly and forcefully in the November 1916 issue, thus:

> "The stupidity of the native professional stage has attained a splendour so grand and unmistakable that one opens one's mouth in dazzled awe before the very majesty of the thing. It is stupidity not of a mean and lowly order, but stupidity brought to its highest point of perfection, stupidity so full-bloom and fascinating as to betoken something akin almost to genius. . . .

Never one to lose a chance at paradox, Nathan maintained that this alleged "stupidity" was indeed salutary. It would, he predicted, "awaken the latent interest in the playhouse," by attracting to it "erstwhile rebels" who, "exasperated by merely mediocre plays and merely mediocre mummering" would seek to reform the native drama and raise it above the level of "current complete idiocies." In restrospect we can easily see that he was right, of course, and that he deserves credit for having led the rebellion he preached. It may well be that such playwrights as O'Neill, Maxwell Anderson, Rice, Howard, Behrman, Sherwood, and Kaufman might have arisen anyway, without Nathan thundering in "the Methodist Desert," but this does not detract from his having been among the very first to recognize them and plead their cause.

For Nathan's *Smart Set* readers, however, his attractions were not only in these Jeremiads against mediocrity but in the piquant mannerisms of his reviews as well. Few critics have been so obsessed with matters of style, with finding precisely the right word to pinion a dull playwright, an obtuse producer, or an errant actress. A prodigious reader of dramatic literature, Nathan was fond of larding his critiques with oblique references to the ancients, to Shakespeare, to the French neo-classicists and to a host of modern Europeans—Yeats, Dunsany, Synge, Molnar, Hauptmann, Schnitzler, and Thoma

were among his special favorites. Soundly grounded in music, painting and sculpture, he delighted in startling analogies between plays and the works of Old Masters. With an encyclopediac sweep of his own field of criticism, he lost no opportunity to make passing allusions to Lessing, or Lewes, Hazlitt or Lemaitre. All this was done with a touch that dispelled suspicions of pedantry, cleverly intimating that the reader was a member of "the intelligent minority." Never patronizing or condescending to the reader, Nathan subtly invited him to share in his own sense of superiority to the canards of the vulgar.

This is not to say that Nathan's style was precocious or lofty. Keenly aware of the shock value of American slang and the humorous possibilities of homely metaphors, he shunned the exalted tones of the academic critics as he shunned their commonplace opinions. His favorite device for dismissing a totally bad play was a pithy one sentence or even one word review: "flapdoodle," "whangdoodle," "boloney," "pish-posh," or "flapper food." One bad English play was "imported from London to enchant the native hoddy-doddies," another was "a clumsy steal" from a play that "Plautus cabbaged from Menander three centuries before the birth of Christ," and a French playwright with an inflated reputation was "a Krupp gun firing spitballs." To engage in criticism, Nathan well knew, was to engage in argument—to invite the reader's resistance, then to overpower him with rhetoric. If he often stacked the deck mercilessly, Nathan played the critical game of "losers weepers, finders keepers" with awesome fury and spectacular success and no one who reads his *Smart Set* reviews of plays and seasons long ago lost to memory can fail to be infected by his insouciance and bravado even now. To do so is to understand why, by 1925, "George Jean Nathan says . . ." was the ultimate judgment in the Broadway theatre and was to remain so for at least another generation and why he is the *Stammvater* of all American dramatic critics of the present.

Nathan's bugaboos, then, were puerility, pretension and provincialism. These Mencken shared and to them he added a fourth —"Puritanism"—a venerable word to which he gave, almost single-handedly, an entirely new signification. He did not refer in any real sense to the historical Calvinism of New England but to the pervasive middle-class morality of the United States which, surviving from the late Victorian Age (an age more "Victorian" in America than in Britain!), blindly and mindlessly resisted from entrenched positions the social and cultural changes which impended in the first three decades of this century. Mencken's criticism and editing in *The Smart Set* is, in fact, shot through with his picturesque efforts to pinpoint the "Puritan" both syllogistically and symbolically in such a way as to enlist the sympathies and support of the natural "anti-Puritans" of the younger generation. He succeeded beyond his wildest expectations and much of what is characteristic of American literature in our time stems from that success.

No greater contrast could be imagined to Nathan's debonair aestheticism than the catholicity of interest of the boisterous Henry Mencken. Literature, politics, music, social philosophy, theology, medicine, philology, gadgetry—and more—came under the rapacious curiosity of the editor-critic of *The Smart Set* who was even then being called "The Sage of Baltimore." That Mencken was never truly a "sage" in any profound sense is unimportant. He held a public opinion on almost every conceivable subject and his readiness to pass sentence upon everyone and everything within his ken made him a pundit, a sage and, finally, a patriarch in the eyes of an adoring public. Thousands of words have been lavished in portraits of Mencken, most of them laudatory (but some, like Charles Angoff's scurrilously vindictive) in biographies, memoirs, critical studies and social histories,

yet the essential man remains an elusive bundle of contradictions, humanly defying all categories. Like Nathan, he was never thoroughly at home in the America of his day. Whether in his beloved Baltimore or in New York (which he loathed), his *lares et penates* remained those of the smug world of his ancestral Bavaria—a world (or so he thought) of Strauss waltzes, Wagner operas, *biertisches* and *gemütlichkeit*.

He has been called a latter-day Swift or Voltaire and, in criticism, the heir of Goethe, Carlyle, Arnold and Benedetto Croce. Among his countrymen he freely acknowledged debts to Poe, Whitman, Twain, Bierce and, of course, Pollard and Huneker, but the essential Mencken was both more and less than an amalgam of these myriad influences. His voracious, if unsystematic, reading was impressionistic rather than analytical; of the English classics he knew scarcely more than the superior high school graduate of his day; there were large gaps in his reading of American literature, and of the ancient classics and modern French and Russian authors he remained almost wholly ignorant. Had he been college-bred among the professors he affected to despise, Mencken might well have become a great scholar, as his monumental studies of the American language give evidence. As it was, he was often forced into absurd postures and specious positions by his defensiveness as a self-taught "amateur" against the encroachments of academic specialization in the humane arts. Yet, such was the glitter of his astringent rhetoric, with its vocabulary of invective, sprinkling choice Latin, Italian and German with American slang, that he was able to simulate a learning of far greater depth than was actually his and to parlay this into power and influence unequalled by any other critics in the history of American letters.

Again like Nathan, the stance of the angry social critic and pungent phrasemaker was a public image beneath which Mencken himself was generous and sociable almost to a fault, salty and prosaic of speech. Never fastidious of attire, his hearty tastes ran to Pilsener Urquell and the heavy dishes of Lüchow's. With women he was, until comparatively late in life, the bachelor-cavalier, and among men he could be coarse or courtly, jovial or sedate, according to the company. He was always somewhat ill-at-ease in the drawingroom, but he was equally at home in sleeve-garters and eyeshade, cigar clenched between his front teeth, amid the raffish uproar of a political convention or a newsroom, or in "galluses" swapping yarns with the yokels of Dayton, Tennessee or the oystermen of the Eastern Shore. The stories of his witty remarks are mostly apocryphal; he saved his best for the printed page and, in his prime on *The Smart Set,* he worked diligently at his trade, reading and writing long hours of the day and night.

Altogether Mencken must have reviewed or briefly noticed at least one hundred books a year in the fifteen years he was associated with *The Smart Set*—a prodigious quantity of criticism, perhaps unequalled in American reviewing history. Many of these articles he pruned, expanded, revised or combined to form the chapters of five books: *A Book of Prefaces* (1917) and the first four *Prejudices* volumes (1919-1924). In this guise his literary criticism reached a wider audience than merely the readers of *The Smart Set* but, because these essays were purposely recast to eliminate their immediacy, the latter-day reader who knows Mencken as a critic chiefly through them will surely fail to grasp the interest, excitement and enthusiasm his pronouncements evoked in the magazine. Moreover, in adapting his reviews, Mencken often performed a kind of literary lobotomy upon them, extracting the generalities and leaving the specifics on the cutting room floor. In the process, much of the life went out of what then appeared not as book reviews at all but as breezy discussions of *allerlei wissenschaften.*

To be sure, *belles-lettres* interested him almost solely as a mirror of social thought and, though he was abysmally untutored in techniques and prosody, he could spot an inimical idea and blow it into oblivion with his verbal howitzers before the ink in which it was written was scarcely dry. If Mencken did not invent the "slashing attack" in American reviewing, he certainly deserves credit for perfecting it to the level of a fine art in the pages of *The Smart Set*. For this reason, among many others, it is a pity that no full-fledged study of H. L. Mencken as a literary critic has yet been published.

Like Nathan, he was an eclectic who professed no aesthetic credo but, unlike his colleague, he rarely troubled himself or his readers with extensive excursions into aesthetics and critical theory, regarding all such disquisitions—like "all metaphysical speculations"—as "a huge bore." The closest he came to stating his premises explicitly was in a review of Joel E. Spingarn's *Creative Criticism* (August 1917) in which he observed that

> the really competent critic must be an empiricist. He must conduct his explorations with whatever means lie within the bounds of his personal limitations. He must produce his effects with whatever tools will work. If pills fail, he gets out his saw. If the saw won't cut, he seizes a club. . . .

In place of "creative," Mencken suggested "catalytic" as a better word for what the critic does, explaining that

> it is his [the critic's] business to provoke the reaction between the work of art and the spectator. The spectator, untutored, stands unmoved; he sees the work of art, but it fails to make any intelligible impression on him; if he were spontaneously sensitive to it, there would be no need for criticism. But now comes the critic with his catalysis. He makes the work of art live for the spectator; he makes the spectator live for the work of art. Out of the process comes under-

standing, appreciation, intelligent enjoyment—and that is precisely what the artist tried to produce.

There is more than a hint here of the professorial compulsions which go a long way to explain the jealous disparagement that Mencken heaped upon his rivals in academia.

The key word in Mencken's statement here is "effect." The critic, he contends, must "produce his effects" at any cost. This was precisely his weakness as a critic just as it was, paradoxically, his strength as a pundit. Preoccupied with producing his own incandescent "effects" he was often all too willing to overlook those really intended by the author whose work was under his scalpel. Small wonder, then, that he distrusted poetry, where the manner is everything, and praised or condemned inordinately out of hand. Customarily, he devoted one article a year, usually in the April or May issue, to a collective review of the new volumes of poetry (sometimes fifteen or twenty in a clump) under such revealingly facetious titles as "The Burbling of the Bards," "The Rough House on Parnassus," "The Poets That Bloom in the Spring, Tra-la!" or even "Tra-la! Tra-la-la! Tra-la-la-la!" and, quite candidly, "Notes of a Poetry Hater." Once, in an unguarded moment (the May 1910 Smart Set) he tried to ameliorate his harshness toward poets and "to spread some balm upon the wounds of these bards" by confessing "that I myself used to be a poet, and that I failed at the trade. I thus qualify as an orthodox critic, for I am a failure barking at the heels of unrecognized genius." His reviews of poetry were never analytical. Poets, he said, "were creatures apart" whose works could not be analyzed, only appreciated. Analysis of poetry was something akin "to performing an autopsy on a butterfly with a crowbar." His technique was to quote a few lines or mention a few subjects in passing, usually with a sneer, but on those he liked

—notably such Smart Set poets as Louis Untermeyer, Sara Teasdale, John V. A. Weaver, Lizette Woodworth Reese, Erza Pound, John McClure and even occasionally (though seldom) the cigar-puffing Amy Lowell—he conferred festoons of superlatives, even while he could dismiss Frost as "Whittier without the whiskers" and Conrad Aiken as "Sigmund Freud reduced to doggerel."

In his reviews of fiction Mencken's batting average is perhaps a bit higher, though even here favoritism often played a distressingly large role in his judgments. Works that showed the hallmarks of regionalism and naturalism were, prima facie, praiseworthy. So was any book banned in Boston or elsewhere and so, too, anything published by Theodore Dreiser, Joseph Hergesheimer, James Branch Cabell, Carl Van Vechten, Sinclair Lewis, F. Scott Fitzgerald, Willa Cather, John Dos Passos, Anatole France, Frank Harris, James Joyce, Aldous Huxley, and Lord Dunsany. Mencken was perhaps one of the first to enunciate what has become a basic tenet of American literary criticism; namely, that it is de rigueur for a popular bestseller to be a bad book. Hence, all the writers of such novels in his day came sooner or later upon his cruel hook.

"My critical labours, in the main," he once observed, "have ever been on the side of the younger generation. I have protested sforzando against the schoolmastering of our letters—against setting the artist in bondage to his inferiors" (December 1922). He constantly reiterated invidious comparisons between the tameness of American belles-lettres and the seriousness of that of most European countries; thus:

> When one turns to any other national literature—to Russian literature, say, or French or German or Scandinavian—one is conscious immediately of a definite attitude toward the primary mysteries of existence, the unsolved and ever-fascinating problems at the bottom of human life, and of a definite preoccupation with

some of them, and a definite way of translating their challenge into drama. . . . But it is precisely here that the literature of America . . . is most colorless and inconsequential. . . .

Yet, he maintained he had not "the least lust to improve American literature," adding that

> if it ever came to what I regard as perfection my job would be gone. . . . My motive [is] simply and solely to sort out and give coherence to the ideas of Mr. Mencken, and to put them into suave and ingratiating terms, and to discharge them with a flourish, and maybe with a phrase of pretty song, into the dense fog that blankets the Republic.

There was, however, one tenet to which H. L. Mencken, in literary criticism and out, held unswervingly: absolute freedom of expression for those he reviled and denounced as well as for himself and his own kind. As a champion of American literary expression in a crucial hour against the strangle-hold of Anthony J. Comstock, Charles Sumner and the New York Society for the Suppression of Vice, The Legion of Decency, the Ku Klux Klan—indeed, against all of our insidious forms of censorship, private and official, his achievements are beyond dispute. In this one respect he was passionately libertarian.

Mencken's second great service to American letters in *The Smart Set* was as a popularizer of a kind of culture that had hitherto been beyond the reach of all but a handful of urban sophisticates. He made Mark Twain, for instance, the archangel of our novelists. Of *Huckleberry Finn,* "nothing has ever been written in America to surpass" it, he reiterated in *The Smart Set* in September 1921, adding that "it is rather more than a book; it is almost a whole literature"— a judgment that is all but sacrosanct to this day. He set Americans to reading Conrad and, from thence, to rediscovering (in the early 1920's) Herman Melville. He was the first American critic with a popular follow-

ing to champion Walt Whitman. He introduced Americans to Henrik Ibsen and Flaubert and, by his clever allusions, piqued their curiosity about Stendhal and Goethe. Indirectly but surely, he helped to foster a whole new era of cheap reprints (such as the Modern Library) of standard American and foreign authors, the end of which, with the techniques of paperback publishing added, is not yet in sight.

These are no mean achievements in themselves. But the truth is that what gave Mencken his following in *The Smart Set* and makes him continually readable is not what he said but how he said it. In his case, the style was truly the man and, for tens of thousands, the man the style. Indeed, his whole tactic as a reviewer was based, as he frankly admitted, on his awareness that "readers and connoisseurs of criticism delight in brutality and esteem a critic in proportion as he is lethal" (March 1916) and being "lethal," he knew, required a pungent style. For all its bombast, his manner of critical writing was crisp, direct and idiomatic in a way that no other American had then achieved. The man who could make "pish-posh," "flapdoodle," "buncophagous" and "piffle" into technical terms of literary analysis, who could describe the music of Puccini, for example, as "silver macaroni, exquisitely tangled," and who could coin one aphorism after another ("I have never met a thoroughly moral man who was honorable," or "Man, at his best, remains a sort of one-lunged animal, never completely rounded and perfect, as a cockroach, say, is perfect") —surely holds as much fascination for us today as he did forty years ago, and he probably always will.

The lines of attack which *The Smart Set* would follow in its onslaughts on American civilization in the decade of the Nathan-Mencken regime were clearly implicit in the literary and theatre departments but they were by no means confined there, as they had virtually been before the editorship of

Willard Wright. After November 1914 the ideas and attitudes of the editor-critics were reflected by and large in the growing monthly non-fiction budget. At first, these were merely epigram-fillers—used by the thousands—in which everything under the sun was defined (a whole new *Devil's Dictionary* could be gleaned from those pages) or lampooned, including even an epigram itself—"A strut is something everybody wants to forget in such a way that no one can help remembering it." (February 1918.) Then there were skillful compilations of implied criticisms: a mock "Who's Who in America" in which six or eight prominent citizens would be listed, all of whom were immigrants (*Cf.* January 1915, *et al.*), or a half-page entitled "Purling of the Platitudinarians" in which a group of prominent public figures were quoted in some ridiculously unprofound or asinine cliché (December 1914, *et al.*)

During the war years (April 1917-November 1918) when even such mild, implied criticism as these would have been considered subversive, the magazine resorted to such innocuous items as a series on "The Sins of the Four Hundred" (throughout 1917) supposedly "by one of themselves," written from Paris. Then there was an "Enchanters of Men" series (1918-1919) by "Thornton Hall" (probably a pseudonym for Albert Payson Terhune who published such a series in book form in 1918) which gave capsule biographies, cleverly done, of such voluptuaries as Ninon de Lenclos, Adrienne Lecouvreur, Catherine the Great, Grace Dalrymple and eight other courtesans of the eighteenth and early nineteenth centuries. Then there were Mencken's endless lists ("Thesaurus") of American synonyms for "whiskers," euphemisms for "drunk," etc. done as "James P. Ratcliffe, Ph.D., LL.D." and equally endless lists by various hands of characteristics of "The Ideal Woman," "The Ideal Husband," etc.

After the war the attack on the gaucheries of American life was hotly joined in a new department, *"Répétition Générale,"* begun in April 1919 and continued until the end of the Nathan-Mencken regime. Significantly, the department was signed "H. L. Mencken and George Jean Nathan," reversing the masthead order of the editors' "seniority." Most of the monthly column of about seven pages of comment and passing observations on nearly everything imaginable was written by Mencken, but Nathan contributed a goodly share. The department began mildly enough with observations on love, flattery, etc. but, in June 1919, Nathan opened a salvo on "The American Credo" with a list of eleven patently false ideas cherished by most loyal citizens of the Republic. The number was later expanded to several hundred (in subsequent columns) and a compilation under that title published in book form. In later months *"Répétition . . ."* often contained several of the following sub-divisions:

1. *The Jazz Webster*—clever epigrams
2. *American Eminence*—lists of nonentities who make up such organizations as the National Realty Board, American Association of Funeral Directors, National Institute of Arts and Letters, etc.
3. *100%*—lampoons of super-patriotism (example: May 1921 listing of roster of newly-established National Symphony Orchestra of New York, William Mengelberg, conductor, with most of the players being Germans and Italians)
4. *Vox Populi, Vox Dei*—asinine pronouncements by small town mayors, leading Fundamentalist preachers, etc.
5. *Monthly Award of 3½" by 4¾" Custard Pie*—to the most pretentious, hollow, utterly meaningless platitude uttered by some Episcopalian bishop, Midwestern governor, soap company executive, *et al.*

No institution, no public official (including—perhaps especially—Presidents Harding and Coolidge and "Prof. Dr. Wilson"), no religion and, above all, no tradition or convention was immune from the raucous ridicule of *"Répétition Générale."* Its overriding theme was simply that America was one great human comedy and that humor was the intelligent man's only defense against a political and social system deliberately calculated to keep him in bondage to the likes of George F. Babbitt. Living in the postwar United States was, according to *The Smart Set* like being in continual attendance at a vaudeville show—"incomparably the greatest show on earth"—or "The Nietzschean Follies," as another series of essays (contributed to discerningly by Thomas Beer, Arthur Symons, Benjamin DeCasseres, Frank Pease, and Walter E. Sagmaster) was aptly named. One of the repeated fillers in the *"Répétition . . ."* department was a supposed query from a lady who wrote in: "If you find so little that is worthy of reverence in the United States, why do you not go elsewhere?" to which Mencken and Nathan responded with the question: "Why do men go to zoos?"

Soon the contributors began imitating the *"Répétition . . ."* series with echoing essays of their own. John Macy, in "Rum, Reading, and Rebellion" (November 1921), for instance, spoke for a generation of young Americans who found reading "impossible" under Prohibition, concluding: "Someday I shall go to Paris or Florence or Munich and sit in a cafe next door to a bookstall and read and read and read and drink and drink and drink." Louis Sherwin noted that Sycorax ("The Goddess of Ugliness") is our national idol and Joseph Wood Krutch in "Threnody upon a Decadent Art" lamented that suicide was no longer a fine art, but sloppily done. But probably the most outrageous and "far-out" imitation of the editors' stances was an article entitled "The Yellow Hope" by Edward E. Paramor, Jr. (a Princeton classmate and friend of Edmund Wilson and F. Scott Fitzgerald) who envisioned the great benefits that would occur to American intellectual and artistic life when, after World War II, the United

States would be subjugated to Japan—this nearly twenty years before Pearl Harbor!

In retrospect, one of the most ingratiating series in the latter days of *The Smart Set* (late 1921 to mid-1923) was one on "The Higher Learning in America" in which recent graduates described their colleges. Nathan and Mencken thought they would get some truly acid exposés when they gave the young alumni a chance to even old scores in a national magazine but, to their surprise, what came in were mainly quite balanced, judicious and, often charming, reminiscences and appraisals of the kind of education available in a dozen or more of America's leading universities. Henrik Willem Van Loon wrote a fine historical piece about Cornell, W. Carl Whitlock did the same for "Mr. Jefferson's University" (Virginia) and G. D. Eaton repined that *Mme. Bovary*, Schnitzler's *Reigen* and "anything else risqué" was reserved "for Faculty only" in the university library at Michigan. John Peale Bishop led off the series with a retrospect of Princeton, concluding that if he had a not-too-bright son, he would certainly send him to Princeton but that, if he had a genius, he would lock him in a library until the boy was old enough to go to Paris! John Gunther asked: "And what does one learn at the University of Chicago? Unless one is an egregious numbskull, one learns a lot." And Sarah Addington came to similar conclusions about Columbia, President Nicholas Murray Butler (one of Mencken's favorite targets) notwithstanding.

The last—and in some respects, most interesting—of the departments to be started in *The Smart Set* was the "Americana" section, by "Maj. Owen Hatteras, D.S.O." which began in May 1923. This was a column made up solely of representative newspaper stories from around the country, re-printed without comment, which illustrated and corroborated the *Smart Set* editorial line *vis-à-vis* American inanity and insipidity. Here was an appalling monthly compilation of florid boosterism from some small-town Rotarian in West Virginia, high-flown prophecies of doom or great miracles from a Kansas evangelist, a South Dakota super-patriot calling for the blessing of God upon the local Ku Klux Klan, and the like. Granted that the *Smart Set* editors were lucky in their targets—Prohibition, Fundamentalism, anti-Darwinism, racism, censorship, and a dozen more wildly bizarre elements in post-World War I America—in columns such as "Americana" they made the most of their opportunities, it may safely be said.

Even with the mask of Owen Hatteras to protect them, there was always more than a little self-consciousness in this attack on the part of Nathan and Mencken. As if their ideas were not sufficiently explicit in their reviewing and their other departments, the editors were always at some pains to address their readers obliquely and explain their positions. They did this in a mock double biography by Hatteras, *Pistols for Two* (1917), in a promotional pamphlet, *A Personal Word* (designed, in 1922, to boost circulation but netting only twenty new subscribers) and, most entertainingly, in a series of "Conversations" as "set down by Major Owen Hatteras" from August 1920 to March 1923. There were nine of these altogether: on literature, politics, dress, women, marriage, anatomy and physiology, "the darker races," theater-going and editing. These imaginary Socratic dialogues often took place in odd locations: the Lackawanna ferry slip at Jersey City at 4 o'clock on a winter afternoon; a dormitory at "Muldoon's Health Farm" at 5 A.M. Here are some typical excerpts from the conversation "On Editing a Magazine" (June 1921):

> *Scene:* Campbell's Funeral Church
>
> *Time:* Between two funerals

Mencken: . . . The magazine editor is simply a scoundrel. In his dealings with authors he is utterly without conscience. . . . His one aim is to sell his puerile and scabrous magazine. If he can do it by debauching and degrading an author, he never hesitates an instant. The beaches of beautiful letters are covered with the carcasses of his victims. . . . No man can pass through the magazines without gross damage to his spiritual kidneys. For this the editor is to blame.

Nathan: As an author, I agree with you. But as a magazine editor, I file a caveat. . . . Show me an author that I have thus brought down. . . . I never give a hoot about the public taste; for all I care, the public may rot away in its wallow . . . all [authors] have to do is send in something that happens to tickle me—and then you—and the cheque goes out on Thursday.

Mencken: A simple and honest system, but it has its drawbacks nevertheless. Suppose you happen to be bilious? What then?

Nathan: The bitter goes with the sweet. True enough, there are days when I am full of acids, and nothing seems good to me. But on the other hand there are days when I feel like a girl at her first party, and then I am surely an easy mark.

Mencken: It is on such days that I earn my honorarium. If the stuff that you vote for actually got into the magazine, then the barber shops would begin to take it in as a comic paper.

Nathan: Maybe so. . . . Many a time, within a day or two after some elderly wench has smiled at you, you have passed to me manuscripts so bad that their publication would have ruined both of us. Fortunately, every such occasion has found me suffering with a ringing in the ears or spots before the eyes, and so I have saved the magazine. . . .

Nathan: They are bringing in the next coffin. Let us depart.

Mencken: Where's my hat?

Nathan: Which hat was it?

Mencken: The one I bought six years ago and always wear.

Nathan: Doubtless in the coffin.

Finally, in June 1923 ("*Répétition Générale*"), the editors of *The Smart Set* jokingly announced their "candidacy" for the office

65

of President and Vice-President of the United States and, in the following two issues, put forth their platform of some 110 "planks." Among other items in their program was an agreement to make no speeches, Nathan's promise "never to accept an invitation to visit the place of his birth, Fort Wayne, Indiana and to meet and speak to the residents," and their pledge to remove "In God We Trust" from the coinage and to change the name of the Virgin Islands "to something more in accord with the genius of the inhabitants." They also agreed to make the ex-Kaiser Governor-General of West Virginia, to "order the Honorable Charles E. Hughes seized by the military, to have his whiskers cut off, and to have photographs of him made and distributed, that the world may see what he actually looks like." Their final "plank" was "to suspend by executive order all statutes against the Mormons, and to let the Saints exhume their plural wives from their storm-cellars and live with them openly, as God hath commanded them."

Strange to say, in the Presidential election of 1924, they actually received a scattering of "throw-away" write-in votes. It would be interesting to speculate what might have been the subsequent history of the United States if, in some wildly fantastic turn of fate, they might actually have drawn enough attention to get themselves elected!

"The Aristocrat Among Magazines"

Each Monday and Friday for nine years a carefully tied brown paper packet arrived at the row house in Hollins Street, Baltimore, addressed to "H. L. Mencken, Esq." in the pristine secretarial hand of Miss Sara A. Golde. These packets contained semi-weekly accumulations of *Smart Set* manuscripts. At their arrival Mencken dropped whatever he had in hand and, within hours, completely disposed of the lot. He could spot (so he claimed) a usable story from its opening paragraph, so those that immediately failed to capture his fancy were laid aside for rejection. When he had finished the prelimi-nary sorting, he read again through the "interesting" stack. If on second perusal a manuscript seemed genuinely worthy, he gave it his *"Nihil Obstat"* and sent it off in his weekly packet to Nathan, who then made his choices from what Mencken had already approved. Those that also "amused" Mr. Nathan ("amusement" was their sole announced criterion) went into the magazine as soon as possible. Surely few periodicals have handled the business of selection with greater dispatch or less discussion.

Since one "Nay!" sufficed to keep a piece out, wrangles and long, soul-searching editorial sessions were avoided and favoritism minimized. There was little editorial tampering. Either a piece amused or it did not. It might be returned to the author for the elimination of minor gaffes or the author might be asked to permit such slight editorial emendations, but there was never a *Smart Set* steamroller (as on many another magazine, then as now) to standardize rough diamonds and give each contribution a special stylistic surface. If there was ever a "Smart Set School" it was one of attitude and outlook rather than style, the numerous imitators of Nathan and Mencken notwithstanding. Occasionally a questionable piece by some famous author or a "regular" might merit more than a horseback judgment from the co-editors but even then the atmosphere in which they conducted such discussions was scarcely serious.

A case in point is a "disagreement" between the co-editors in November 1921 over a novelette by a Philadelphia chemist, L. M. Hussey (director of a biological research laboratory) who contributed more than sixty times (perhaps still more under unidentifiable pseudonyms) between 1916 and 1923. Hussey, in fact, was typical of a number of non-professional writers whose publishing careers are virtually contained within the pages of *The Smart Set* because they were so "attuned" to the magazine that they could turn out acceptable pieces by the ream. He had evidently spent some time in Latin America, judging from some of his best *Smart Set* stories, and in one piece he had used a tippling Venezuelan priest as a main character. Fearing repercussions from the pious if they printed the story, Mencken pinned this editorial memo to the manuscript:

> I am against the last Hussey story. It is a capital piece of work, but it would offend the Catholics and set every priest in the land to whooping against us. . . . Give Hussey a bottle of vermouth, and he will be glad to change the priest into a Presbyterian.

To which Nathan responded, in character:

> I'll be good and damned if I give Hussey a bottle of vermouth to change the padre into a Presbyterian. I'll offer him a pint of Acker, Merrell and Condit's California No. 2, but that's as far as I'll go to promote literature in America. . . .

Even without a potable bribe, however, Hussey was quite amenable. "Let me know, when you are ready, what changes you think would make [the novelette] more suitable," he obligingly wrote Nathan, and dutifully made the suggested revision.

As a result of their peculiar "veto" system, Mencken had to write most of the rejections, Nathan or Miss Golde most of the acceptances. Checks were sent immediately, regardless of delays in printing a contribution, and authors were returned their copyrights upon publication. The prospect of a quick response, of prompt payment (when one needed ready cash) and of free rein on republication rights went a long way to make up for the cent-a-word scale, unchanged since the days of Colonel Mann. There are no records to indicate how many manuscripts the editors considered each month, but it is a safe guess that the number often exceeded a hundred. During the war years (1917-1918), of course, the total was very much lower and there were then many months when perhaps half the fiction in an issue was written by Thyra Samter Winslow and Ben Hecht under fanciful pseudonyms. Good manuscripts in certain categories (notably novelettes and short plays) were always in distressingly short supply, though short stories, sketches and lyric poems were usually plentiful, especially in the post-war years.

To handle the prodigious correspondence this influx of manuscripts demanded, the editors developed pithy, short-answer techniques, like these random examples:

> (HLM to Vincent Starrett)—"Unluckily, nay. It is a bit too pianissimo for us."
> (HLM to Carl Van Vechten):—"If it

were not for a depressing overstock of stories, poems, essays, dithyrambs, etc. about death, I'd take this at once. Something less mortuary, in God's name! Our safes, bins, vats, etc. are like morgues, etc."

("The Editors" to Will F. Jenkins)— ". . . You seem to know precisely the sort of epigrams *The Smart Set* needs, and we shall be very glad to have you submit this sort of material to us regularly."

Sometimes to writers with whom they were on intimate or easy terms, they would send spoofing letters, like this one from Mencken to Untermeyer early in 1919:

Gents:

I have went through your samples, and have decided to lay in two models. Our check will reach you by return mail, so to speak. These goods are stylish, and we expect a good spring trade with them, as it were. On one model we notice some bum trimming. The tag is "Betrayal." You have used one "stabbed" in the front and then hung on another. Please have your designer fix this. Otherwise the model greatly pleased our Mr. Blumblatt.

We would be glad to inspect more models Mar. 1, May 2, July 3, Sept. 4, Nov. 5, u.s.w.

In later years many a former contributor remembered that, even with such "pat" phrases, Nathan and Mencken could often communicate tersely more about what was really wrong with a rejected piece than could most editors in paragraphs of polite explanation. From the editors' standpoint, the important thing was to keep the writer from feeling discouraged. Through rejections and acceptances alike, therefore, ran such refrains as "What else have you?"; "Haven't you something more within the tastes of our customers?"; "Please send more of the same soon." (Though such "come-ons" could be stimulating, the poet Leslie Nelson Jennings recalls his exasperation [mixed with amuse-

ment] at such a solicitation in his first *Smart Set* acceptance after more than a dozen rejections there!) In brief, Nathan and Mencken gave hospitality and tutelage verging upon paternalism to the novices, even if they acknowledged little altruism in their desire "to give the boys and girls a chance." They insisted that they were merely making a virtue of necessity (the cent-a-word scale virtually excluded well-established writers) and they steadfastly denied they had ever "discovered" anyone. There was no false modesty in this. As Mencken told Jim Tully, he and Nathan were merely "looking for good copy, not for orphans to rescue."

Despite accumulated testimonials in the memoirs of aging authors who, in the 1950's and '60's, fondly remember *The Smart Set* as "my alma mater" or its co-editors as patron saints, the actual results seem to bear out Nathan's and Mencken's realistic appraisal. Only a handful of those who published their early work in *The Smart Set* gained unqualified success in *belles-lettres*. For every one who did, scores sought and dozens found distinction in other fields—chiefly in journalism and academia. A goodly number of leading university pedagogues (in later years) were *Smart Set* "alumni." Some of the dozens of *Smart Set* novices who later distinguished themselves as journalists include John Gunther, John McClure, Burton Rascoe, *et al.* —an impressive roster, surely.

On the other hand, a goodly company (perhaps fifty percent) of the young *literati* who were drawn to *The Smart Set* eventually developed into what might be termed "interesting journeymen" in letters, pursuing a lifetime of popular authorship with but modest rewards and limited recognition outside the marketplace itself. Such a writer, for instance, was Thyra Samter Winslow (1888?-1961), who holds the record for the total number (between 80 and 100) of noneditorial contributions to the magazine. Indeed, scarcely an issue passed between 1914 and 1923 without at least one Winslow item, either under her own name or with such fanciful signatures as "Laura Kent Mason," "Bruce Reid," "Betting Calvert," "Seumas LeChat," *et al.* In numerous ways Mrs. Winslow's career is thoroughly typical of what might be called "the *Smart Set* generation" of American writers—eager youngsters who moved into New York *en masse* from hinterland villages in the teens and twenties of this century and kept the literary agents in business long years after—so a brief review of her thoroughly uneventful life and nearly-forgotten works may not be inappropriate here.

She liked to acknowledge that she was "born and raised in a hick-town in the sticks" (Fort Smith, Arkansas) which formed the background of some of her best short stories. Just when she was born there is anybody's guess, for she had the knack of successfully shaving a few years from her vital statistics every decade or so. Sometime around 1930 she settled on 1893 as a good year to have been born in and she stuck to it, but earlier references give her birth date as 1888 and still earlier ones as 1883! It matters not. The fact is that "Siren Thyra," as some of her admiring male contemporaries called her, was ageless. She wore her years so well and contrived to look so much younger than she could possibly have been that she was able to earn her living during her last decade by writing diet and health books—*Look Younger, Live Longer* and *The Winslow Weight Watcher.*

Her first published work was in *The Smart Set:* a maudlin poem in 1911 when she was a student at the University of Missouri's School of Journalism, whence she had gone after two years' disappointing study at the Cincinnati Art Academy. That same year she left Missouri to become a chorus girl, then a dancer and finally an actress on the Chicago stage. There she met and married Mr. Winslow (they were divorced in 1927) and was "discovered" by Burns Mantle, feature editor of the *Chicago Tribune,* who gave her

a newspaper job that brought her to the outer edges of the Chicago Renaissance, then in full sway. Dreiser was the man of the hour and all the young Chicago newspaper people were trying to write like him. So Thyra Winslow tried her hand at a short story about the rise to stardom of a chorus girl through a succession of hedonistic love affairs and blackmail—an amalgam, she admitted, of *Sister Carrie* and a few of her own theatre experiences. The story ("In the Case of Lou Terry") was accepted by Nathan and Mencken for their first issue (November 1914) because it had this superbly "shocking" first sentence: "The sexes seem to have changed places since the days of the first man."

A few more *Smart Set* appearances and young Mrs. Winslow was emboldened to try her luck in the New York literary world. So, leaving Mr. Winslow behind in Chicago, she took a job as a "sub" in the drama department of the *New York World* under Percy Hammond, who occasionally assigned her to review the plays he suspected of being "turkeys." This renewed contact with the theatre and theatrical people, as well as the newspaper world, gave her material for story after story in *The Smart Set* dealing vividly with the distinctly unglamorous side of backstage life with bright, vivacious Midwestern girls blighted and imprisoned by small-town life, with the aching dullness of penny-pinching urban "cliff-dwelling." Her success soon brought her to the periphery of the Algonquin *Stammtisch*—the crowd of literary people (mostly from *Vanity Fair,* but a few from *The Smart Set* also) who lunched together frequently at the Algonquin Hotel and, according to some contemporary accusations (partly true), dominated American letters *ca.* 1920. She liked to give splashy parties for these *illuminati* which, despite her picturesque name for them ("pig rassles") were only slightly less decorous or more bibulous than the usual Manhattan literary gathering during Prohibition. Invitations to these "pig

"THE UNEXPECTED" by Charles Caldwell Dobie--A COMPLETE
SHORT NOVEL

The SMART SET

A Magazine of Cleverness

"The Pernicious Influence"
by Lilith Benda
A really remarkable short story

"Should a Pretty Woman Eat?"
by Frank Pease
An impudent little essay

JULY, 1916
25 Cents

"THE SIREN", by C. Vere Tyler—A

The SMART SET

A Magazine of Cleverness

N.B.A

AUGUST 1916

25 Cents

rassles" always came on the sedate stationery of "The Seven Arts Club" of which Mrs. Winslow was founder, president and, in fact, sole member—a hoax that few of her guests ever discovered.

Much of what we think of as characteristic of American fiction in the 1920's is actually foreshadowed in Thyra Samter Winslow's *Smart Set* stories nearly a decade earlier. One of these, for example, ("A Bad End," February 1917) begins with a description of the ladies of Leffingwell, Kansas "sitting on their porches in the summer, rocking in cadence with embroidery needles"—a detail of "local color" more than a little reminiscent of the porch rockers of Sinclair Lewis's *Main Street* a full three years later. She was also one of the first to write with compassionate insight about the growing assimilation of the urban Jew into American life (see "The Cycle of Manhattan" in the anthology of this book)— a persistent theme in some of our best writing in recent years.

By the spring of 1923, Mrs. Winslow had a long list of first-rate *Smart Set* stories to her credit. (She had, indeed, almost completely confined herself to publishing in that magazine.) She was not therefore greatly surprised by an invitation to lunch one day with the co-editors of *The Smart Set* (old acquaintances, by now) at the Algonquin. The usual light banter between "The Professor" (Nathan) and "Heinie" (Mencken) flowed easily until, over coffee, the conversation suddenly turned serious and Nathan leaned across the table to hand Mrs. Winslow a slip of paper containing the titles of a dozen of her *Smart Set* stories. "What would you say to this as a good book?" Nathan asked, adding that he and Mencken had prevailed upon their publisher, Knopf, to bring out a collection of her magazine stories during the coming month. Astounded, she could only think to blurt: "But what on earth shall I call it?" Nathan had already chosen a catchy if innocuous title: *Picture Frames.* (Out of gratitude, Mrs. Winslow kept the practice of letting Nathan supply titles for

the four other collections of stories she eventually published.) When the book appeared, Mencken naturally gave it a lavish play, concluding his review (July 1923) with: "I know of no realist in practice among us today . . . with greater skill than Mrs. Winslow." At least a half-dozen books published by Knopf in the early years of the Borzoi imprint had the same genesis.

When Nathan and Mencken left *The Smart Set* to found *The American Mercury* Mrs. Winslow accompanied them as one of the exclusive list from whom contributions were solicited and accepted, but she never really "outgrew" the magazine where she had served her apprenticeship. When the kind of story that pleased *The Smart Set* went out of vogue, she had little recourse—an occasional piece in *McCall's, Good Housekeeping* or *Cosmopolitan,* perhaps, and, very occasionally—*The New Yorker.* More and more often she was thrown back onto non-fiction articles for which her agent had a good market. Toward the end of her life she lived at The Royalton (a few floors below Nathan and across from the Algonquin) where she raised Pekingese (one of them, "Lord Calvert," sometimes "answered" her thinning fan mail from old admirers), and lived off the proceeds of her diet books and the labors of "Laura Kent Mason," "Bruce Reid," *et al.* in the "true story" pulps—an interesting eccentric to the last. Even before the end of her life a few anthologists and schoolbook text editors had discovered some of her early *Smart Set* pieces. Finally, she moved to a dingy housekeeping flat on West Fifty-Seventh Street and, on the Fourth of July, 1961, she suffered a fall in which she broke several vertebrae and was left partially paralyzed. When death came six months later, Thyra Samter Winslow was a name that only a few old *Smart Set* readers and a handful of others remembered with respect and affection.

Another Nathan-Mencken "discovery" whose literary career was almost solely confined to *The Smart Set* was "Lilith Benda," the pen-name of Lucia Bronder. Miss Bronder was by no means as prolific as Mrs. Winslow (she only contributed some twenty times), nor did she achieve even Mrs. Winslow's modest stature and reputation, but she wrote some excellent novelettes for the magazine and her career illustrates the lengths to which the editors would sometimes go to cultivate good writing and talent where they found such.

Late in the summer of 1915 a packet done up in blue ribbons arrived at *The Smart Set* office containing a manuscript of several sketches and an interesting, if somewhat crude, novelette handwritten on scented blue stationery. It was the sort of thing, according to Nathan, that was ordinarily rejected on sight but it happened to arrive in a "dry" season and, when read, it proved to contain some impressive writing. Nathan and Mencken immediately accepted some of the sketches but they returned the novelette to its author —"Lilith Benda"—with some detailed suggestions for improvement. Miss Benda's reply to this was indeed bizarre. She was grateful for the suggestions but, she added, she was not really a writer, only a poor immigrant girl from Flatbush longing to meet a man who would give her some "intellectual companionship." If the editors of *The Smart Set* cared to try personal coaching, she hinted, she might be able to revise her novelette. The idea was not without its fascinations for the two bachelor co-editors. So, at the toss of a coin Mencken won the chance to meet "Lilith Benda" and assist her literary endeavors in person.

The address was in Sheepshead Bay where Miss Benda's father, a Polish immigrant, kept a seafood restaurant and gambling casino. It was in the back room of this establishment that, under the watchful eye of Papa Bronder, H. L. Mencken gave a practical lesson in creative writing to the daughter (who turned out to be a shy, wistful girl with delicate features and an alarming case history of tuberculosis) —with bumpers of Pilsner Urquell and heaps of steamers on the side. The incident pro-

voked this typically Menckenian editorial memo:

> We will simply have to make a change in the editorial conduct of the magazine. My assignment to make love to lady novelette writers in order to get decent novelettes for the magazine is proving too strenuous. Last week, as you know, I took out three different literary wenches, bought and drank at least fifty dollars' worth of alcoholic liquor, and made enough love to inflame a dozen Marie Corellis, and didn't get home until dawn, and what will we get? Not a damned thing worth printing! And my health is gone! It's your turn, my boy!

But Mencken's prediction proved baseless; the magazine ultimately reaped much that was worth printing from "Lilith Benda," including (in August 1916) a novelette, "The End of Ilsa Mentieth," about the effects on a group of Brooklyn tenement-dwellers of the suicide of a lonely girl who lives in a neighboring apartment. Each of her neighbors constructs his own version of what happened, reading into the event his own neurotic distresses. In the end we learn that Ilsa (the suicide) was suffering from an incurable physical illness. This story, in fact, was quite prophetic: some years later, "Lilith Benda," suffering the progressive ravages of tuberculosis, took her own life.

Two other interesting *Smart Set* "regulars" were Lilian Foster Barrett and her brother, Richmond Brooks Barrett, of Newport, Rhode Island—*bona fide* socialites who should have belonged to the magazine's palmy days under Colonel Mann and Arthur Grissom instead of the plebeian regime of Nathan and Mencken. Miss Barrett also formed another link with the literary past that might have amused the co-editors had they known about it. She was vacationing with her parents in Jacksonville when the glamorous Stephen Crane came ashore there to a hero's welcome after the dramatic sea rescue he immortalized in "The Open Boat." Miss Barrett went down to the port for his arrival and pushed through the throngs to get his autograph—an experience that inspired her first published effort, in a Jacksonville newspaper.

Several years later she concocted a "deliberately lurid" tale—"Gold Dust," a study of a narcotics addict (modelled, so Miss Barrett said, upon the mother of a friend)—and sent it off to *The Smart Set* because, she explained:

> I had heard that Mr. Mencken and Mr. Nathan themselves read every single manuscript that came into the office [and] I was intrigued with Mr. Nathan's theatre criticisms. There was an affected, smart-aleck style about them but the spark was there.

The prompt acceptance of "Gold Dust" was followed by sixteen more—mainly novelettes of Newport society that would have sent earlier editors of *The Smart Set* into ecstasies. Several of these she combined at Nathan's suggestion into a novel, *The Sinister Road,* which Knopf (again, with Nathan's influence) published. Nevertheless, Miss Barrett's literary career was short-lived and almost confined to her *Smart Set* appearances. She had become interested in the theatre, and tiring of *belles-lettres,* gave up writing to become manager of the Newport Casino Theater—one of the few successful American repertory theaters outside New York.

During his sophomore year at Yale, Richmond Brooks Barrett decided to emulate his sister and send a story (his very first effort in fiction) to *The Smart Set*. Since this was during the war years when good manuscripts were in painfully short supply, the co-editors were delighted to see it and, to young Barrett's astonishment it was not only accepted but flamboyantly advertised on the cover of the issue (September 1917) where it appeared—as if "Richmond Brooks Barrett" were a "name" author. This was soon followed by some two dozen novelettes and stories which Barrett contributed, under his own signature and as "Paul Brooks." One of these stories, "The Daughter of the Bernsteins," an excel-

lent dissection of the roots of anti-Semitism in American life, Barrett expanded into his first novel, *The Enemy's Gates* (again, a Knopf imprint), which was well received in both its New York and London editions and, translated into German in the *Roman der Welt* series edited by Thomas Mann, it had a considerable vogue in pre-Nazi Germany.

Richmond Barrett was one of those whose talents Nathan and Mencken quite deliberately cultivated and promoted ("advised, encouraged, scolded, spanked and praised . . ." he recalls) and he remembers the astringent effect on his writing of a one-word rejection note from Nathan: "SHAME!" He had a talent for subtle comedy and witty understatement that the editors prized and they came to depend on him to put flesh on the bare bones of plot ideas and themes they had no time to work up themselves. Nathan remembered a case in point: a story ("The Sins of the Fathers" was its title) in which the son of a toilet seat magnate falls in love with the daughter of a toilet paper manufacturer and each tries vainly to conceal the "sins" of the father from the other. According to Nathan, such a story was the very epitome of "cleverness" ca. 1920, although it would be difficult to imagine a magazine accepting it today.

As one might expect, such "cleverness" attracted some strange birds of the literary skies. Scarcely a week passed without bringing its share of daffy fan letters (some of them probably pranks) signed with outlandish names and reading like wild parodies of the magazine itself. Nathan preserved one particularly juicy specimen which opened:

> How do you do George?
> I have just finished focussing my binoculars on your August number of the "Aristocrat Among Magazines."
> After lamping all of the other magazines on the news stands including the "squirrel" issues it certainly does elevate a "bird" to scan your publication. You use no abracadabras when you say "The

Aristocrat Among Magazines" is a swell sheet. . . .

and so on in this vein, running to several pages. Yet, none of the magazine's lunatic fringe readers could have been more bizarre than certain of its regular contributors. There was, for example, Harry Kemp, "The Tramp Poet," who had stolen Upton Sinclair's wife and afterwards wrote a salacious autobiography (*à la* Frank Harris) describing his numerous amours in almost clinical detail; there was Jacques L. Morgan, a Kansas City dilettante who, in rare moments of sobriety, sent *The Smart Set* a series of hilarious stories (only slightly fictionalized) about the escapades of a bibulous Kansas City judge and his club cronies; there was the "super-Nihilist" philosopher, Benjamin DeCasseres, who boasted lineal descent from Spinoza; there was Aleister Crowley, the English ocultist who conducted Black Masses for New York's literati. Most exotic of them all, however, was Achmed Abdullah.

Whether Abdullah was, as he claimed, a Middle Easterner with an adventurous past, extending from Afghanistan to Shanghai and beyond, or (as his detractors maintained) a phony Brooklynite with a fantastic imagination, a photographic memory and a flair for the ultra-dramatic, would be difficult to determine beyond dispute. Verifiable records about him are scarce, vague and sketchy and no two accounts agree in particulars. In some he is a Turk, in others an Egyptian and still others a Persian. Like André Tridon (self-styled "Physician of the Soul"), he was one of those drawn to the magazine by Willard Huntington Wright and there he remained for a decade—under his own name as well as "Sulamith Ish-Kishar," "Yar Nadir Khan," "A. A. Nadir," and perhaps other pseudonyms. He could be counted upon whenever the magazine needed some exotic leavening ("The Color of Cairo," "The Soul of Pekin" are among his stories) or whenever the sup-

ply of French stories ran low. As a De-Maupassant imitator, Abdullah was probably without peer.

He gave his full name as "Captain Syyed Shaykh Achmed Abdullah Nadir Khan el-Iddris-syieh el-Durani" and claimed to have studied at Oxford, Paris and Cairo, where he supposedly took a doctorate in Koranic law. Thereafter, according to one account, he was a soldier of fortune for the Turks in the Balkan War and for the British in India, winning countless decorations for bravery. He was also an exceptionally adroit linguist (so he claimed), fluently speaking Turkish, Hindi, Kurdish, Arabic, Tibetan, Manchu, as well as English, French, Russian, Italian and German with a Berliner accent.

During his *Smart Set* years, Abdullah maintained an apartment in Waverly Place where he gave hasheesh parties for the literati, often greeting his guests at the door clad only in a turban. The apartment itself looked like something out of *The Arabian Nights*—or an Oriental bazaar—with prayer rugs, embroidered Persian cushions, scimitars, fourteenth century Indian bronze deities, enormous Chinese porcelain incense burners, samurai swords and scores of other objects of exotic decor instead of conventional furniture. Although Abdullah's invitations were sought after by some of his titillated *Smart Set* colleagues, the co-editors themselves tried (not always successfully) to avoid such gatherings, repeatedly disparaging them as "bohemian shenanigans" or "the naughtiness of second-rate high school boys"—an attitude which prompted Sinclair Lewis's coinage of the pejorative "Hobohemia" for Greenwich Village.

All the same, the trappings of the *Smart Set* office itself (located, after 1918, at 25 West 45th Street) were not far removed from what one might expect to find in the writers' bohemia below 14th Street or in the workrooms of a college humor magazine. (Indeed, several collegiate magazines of that era conscientiously imitated the *Smart Set* office decor.) In the outer room, where Miss Golde was sovereign, the walls displayed framed originals of covers by Flagg (the up-dated *Ur*-cover); John Held, Jr.; Alexander King (who signed his covers "A. Rose"); Gene Kessler; and Archie Gunn, creator of the "Cupid's Bow" mouth. Opposite Miss Golde was a visitor's bench—a golden oak church pew—and on a nearby table were late issues of the Warner publications and trade journals (those of undertakers' and plumbers' suppliers were favorites) together with a stack of two-page brochures entitled "SUGGESTIONS TO OUR VISITORS"—a list of some twenty-six "house rules," which included the following:

> Visitors are kindly requested to refrain from expectorating out of the windows. . . .
>
> Solicitors for illicit wine merchants are received only on Thursdays, from 12 o'clock noon until 4:30 P.M. . . .
>
> Interpreters speaking all modern European languages are in daily attendance, and at the disposal of visitors, without fee. . . .
>
> A woman Secretary is in attendance at all interviews between the Editors, or either of them, and lady authors. Hence, it will be unnecessary for such visitors to provide themselves with either duennas or police whistles. . . .
>
> Visiting English authors are always welcome, but in view of the severe demands upon the time of the Editors, they are compelled to limit the number received to 50 head a week. . . .
>
> The Editors regret that they will be unable to receive visitors who present themselves in visibly inebriated conditions. . . . [and]
>
> The objects of art on display in the editorial galleries are not for sale. . . .

This last item doubtless referred to the decor of their inner-sanctum where Nathan and Mencken sat at opposite desks surrounded by beer posters, a French temperance placard (about the frightful effects of absinthe), an Atlantic City pennant, pictures of Follies "cuties" and such long-deceased notables as Nietzsche, Beethoven and Otto von Bismarck "personally autographed" to the editors, and a large streamer imploring: "GOD BLESS OUR PRESIDENT!"

In studied disarray were such items as a huge yellow tea cosy woven from hundreds of cigar bands, reposing on a disordered bookcase a tasselated tapestry of a Newfoundland dog rescuing a baby, thrown over a hideously claw-foot gilt chair. When the chair was in use by a visitor, the tapestry served as cover for a makeshift table of saw horses and an alabaster slab that Mencken had filched from an abandoned Maryland graveyard. During the long work sessions when Mencken was in town, this slab served as a *Biertisch* for the prodigious lunches they had sent in from "The Klosterglocke"—a nearby German cafe. Above the slab they tacked a sign—"POETS' FREE LUNCH" —but they hastily draped the lugubrious tapestry over the victuals when a notorious freeloader such as Harry Kemp was announced. Near his desk Mencken (a lifelong cigar-chewer) kept two oversized brass cuspidors which Warner thought were "undignified" (in contrast to Nathan's ubiquitous vase of blue cornflowers, which he liked), so the editors had black crepe covers made to shroud them decorously whenever the publisher came to confer. Such surroundings were intentionally symbolic of the tastelessness and vulgarity of American bourgeois culture, but they also created a kind of carnival atmosphere in which the editorial business of *The Smart Set* became a harlequinade.

Once each month Mencken went to New York by train for a five-day stay to help make up the issue. Customarily, he arrived late of a Sunday afternoon, checked in at The Algonquin and phoned Nathan (across the street, at The Royalton) to begin a convivial evening—often with Carl Van Vechten, Joseph Hergesheimer and other friends at a favorite bar (later to be a speakeasy) in Hoboken where Czech beer remained illicitly available throughout Prohibition or at parties given for the literary Establishment by Zoë Akins, the Burton Rascoes, or Zelda and Scott Fitzgerald at Great Neck. Despite these diversions, the editors would be at their desks by ten the next morning, though they steadfastly held to a vow never to speak to each other (or to anyone else, if possible) before 11 A.M. Some of the hijinks with which they conducted even their routine business may be glimpsed from the editorial memoranda which passed between them and which they preserved with a view to publishing a comic history of their collaborations (a project which, regrettably, did not materialize). In one note Nathan observed: "We surely get very little out of the magazine save the fun that is in our jobs, so why bother ourselves with questions of 'advisability' and the like? . . . Let us assume that there are thousands of other Americans who have just as little virtue in them as I have, and just as little taste as you . . ." To this Mencken rejoined: "What you say about the lofty principles of magazine editing diverts and instructs me. You have reached such a stage of cunning that you can put my own ideas into such ingratiating phrases that they convince even me." In another, Nathan scolds: "Your last literary review is very sour, doctor! Almost as bad as my play review. We are getting stale. We have been writing too much lately. I am tired of work and think I shall marry a rich widow. I shall name the child Henry. . . ." Mencken pleaded guilty to this, explaining: "I go stale about once a year, and write such stuff that I am almost ashamed to print it. But they get their money's worth during the other eleven months. To get eleven such

arituclcs [*sic*] for $4. is really a great bargain. We don't charge 'em enough."

At another point they made a game of concocting slogans and subtitles for the magazine, having decided at the outset of their regime that "The Magazine of Cleverness" seemed to smack too much of the unsavory past. They conjured up hundreds of these and actually used some thirty, including:

> "No Smart Set author has ever lectured at a chautauqua"
> "The magazine that other magazine editors read"
> "The magazine that's read in the Pullman"
> "The only American magazine read by royalty"
> "The magazine of the civilized minority" and even
> ". . . Angels could do no more" or *"Qui vit sans folie n'est pas si sage qu'il le croit"*

In the end none of these *bon mots* seemed to be quite as satisfactory as the first one they had devised, in December 1914—"The Aristocrat Among Magazines"—so they revived this in mid-1918 and left it on the masthead for the remainder of their regime.

From the standpoint of format, contents or clientele the term "Aristocrat" was certainly a misnomer. During its Nathan-Mencken era the magazine was printed on cheap pulp paper, its format was undistinguished (if conservative), its literary qualities were uneven and its customers were anything but aristocrats. Nevertheless, the slogan did not seem pretentious then, nor does it in retrospect. It quite appropriately signified the "aristocratic" bias of Nathan and Mencken. Men of noble tastes and superior intelligence, they addressed (so they claimed) a select group that had at least the makings of an American intellectual aristocracy: "Our purpose in running the magazine is primarily to please ourselves, and secondarily to entertain those Americans who happen, in general, to be of our minds." Their list of negations included "the sentimental, the obvious, the trite and the maudlin" and

> . . . all such ideas as come from the mob, and are polluted by its stupidity: Puritanism, Prohibition, Comstockery, evangelical Christianity, tin-pot patriotism, and the whole sham of democracy.

To make certain they were not identifying themselves with the Marxist intellectuals who attacked some of the same targets, they denounced socialism and came out for capitalism, but carefully adding that "Capitalism [as practiced] in the United States is ignorant, disreputable and degraded and . . . its heroes are bounders."

Such ideas, they freely acknowledged, were bound to be unpopular with all *but* a "civilized minority." Hence, *The Smart Set* could never hope to be a mass-circulation magazine and while this fact certainly made for some tight budgets, it also freed the magazine "from taking a hand in the Uplift and pretending to be made sad by the sorrows of this world." Thus emancipated, *The Smart Set* could continue to uphold "the dignity of the fine arts, and regard Beethoven and Brahms as far greater than Wilson and Harding." To this end, in October 1921, the editors gave forth one of their rare explicit statements of *Smart Set* policy. Their program, they explained, had five interrelated points: (1) "To discover new American authors as they emerge, and to give them their first chance to reach an intelligent and sophisticated audience"; (2) "To present the point of view of the civilized minority"; (3) "To introduce the best foreign authors to America"; (4) "To leaven the national literature with wit and humor"; (5) "To encourage sound poetry."

To what extent and with what merit, we may well ask today, did Nathan and Mencken realize the aims they set for "The Aristocrat Among Magazines"? The "proof of the pudding," of course, is not alone—not even

primarily—in the later careers of those to whom they gave their "first chance"—a number well in excess of a thousand. Nor is their achievement in introducing (with the help of Ezra Pound and others) scores of foreign authors—including, in the latter days, such figures as Walter Hasenclever, Leonid Andreyev, Luigi Lucatelli, Stacy Aumonier, James Stephens and Aldous Huxley—under dispute. But what of the "point of view of the civilized minority," and what of "sound poetry?" We must look to what these and other writers actually wrote for *Smart Set* publication.

Judging from the fiction contributions (and fiction always bulked largest in the contents of *The Smart Set*) the "civilized minority" of American readers in the post-World War I era was tiring of "clever" coincidence, concealments and "surprise" plot twists—the O. Henry-Guy deMaupassant formulas that had captivated the magazine's customers in the previous two decades. There is a perceptible increase in those years of the magazine in stories of character rather than incident and in psychological analysis. Escapist fiction—such as detective, mystery, horror and adventure stories (like those by a young novice named Dashiell Hammett)—continued to account for perhaps one out of every five *Smart Set* tales and novelettes, but the tendency after 1918 was definitely to satire, with the principal targets of ridicule being matrimony, small town life, academic life and what for want of a better term might be called simply "success."

An excellent example of the attacks on "success" (a kind of reverse Horatio Alger formula) is one by Donald Ogden Stewart entitled, appropriately enough, "The Secret of Success" (November 1921) in which an ambitious young man endeavors to practice all of his officious employer's business platitudes about hard work and efficiency until he discovers and emulates his boss's real "secret"—marrying the boss's daughter, which entitles him thereafter to spout the same pompous sentiments. This was but one of hundreds of *Smart Set* variations upon the "anti-success" theme. Business eminence, if we can trust *Smart Set* fiction in the early 1920's, was then achieved at the sacrifice of artistic yearnings, love and romance, was founded only in utter hypocrisy and dishonesty, was the handmaiden of political corruption, could only be tolerated by the stupid and the timorous—and a list of numerous other predicates, all satirically demonstrated.

Matrimony also took quite a beating in *Smart Set* fiction. The conventional romance, with wedding bells or a passionate embrace to end all complications on the last page, became less and less frequent after 1915 and faded away almost entirely in the post-war years. In place of the older formulas came a new "anti-formula" story in which courtship is depicted as a contest of wills between the sexes, the plot turning upon the ruses by which the poor, outwitted male is entrapped and marched unwillingly to the altar. In the sequels, old-fashioned "domestic bliss" was shown to be so excruciatingly dull that infidelity becomes a virtue in itself. Again, as in the "anti-success" story, satire was the weapon for this massive attack on the old conventional marital patterns. "Such a pretty little picture!" the neighbors remark in a Dorothy Parker story (in September 1922), for example, when they stroll by a house where a handsome young husband is clipping the hedge while his lovely wife babbles pleasant inanities from the porch swing, the neighbors symbolizing a society that is unaware (as the reader is by the incidents in the story) that the sweet wife is a domineering Gorgon whom the husband hates and yearns to abandon or murder.

Another favorite target in these years was the horror of small town existence. Hell was a locatable entity for followers of *Smart Set* fiction: a crossroads in Iowa where the creative spirit was stifled in lace-curtain propriety. What Carl Van Doren first called "the revolt from the village" in American writing *ca.*

1920 is too well-known a phenomenon to warrant much discussion here but almost any issue of *The Smart Set* in that era will supply copious working examples of that pervasive theme. One of the best of these was by the archdeacon of the "anti-village" movement himself—Sinclair Lewis—who published in *The Smart Set* (in August 1916) a story ("I'm a Stranger Here Myself") that had been rejected by no less than four other magazines although it was, as Mark Schorer has pointed out, "the first sustained work recognizably written by the author of *Main Street.*" In this story a comfortably middle-class couple from a small midwestern town set out on an eight months' "see America" tour of Florida, the urban East and New England, only to be dissatisfied and ill-at-ease with everything they encounter that is not exactly like "back home." In the end they return to tell their fellow-villagers proudly: "Why, we haven't seen a single place that begins to come up to Northernapolis [the home-town]."

During World War I, Nathan and Mencken had rejected some of Sherwood Anderson's *Winesburg, Ohio* stories (another famous "anti-village" work) as "too frank," but after the war the magazine was crowded with stories that unquestionably bore the stamp of Anderson's influence. Some were, indeed, even "franker" than Winesburg. The best of these came from John T. Frederick, who sent in poignant tales of blasted hopes and thwarted lives in the drab, stultifying towns of Minnesota and the Dakotas, and from Ruth Suckow (1892-1959), whom some have called "an Iowa Willa Cather." When Miss Suckow published her first story in the November 1921 issue of *The Smart Set*, Mencken sent a copy of the issue proudly to Sinclair Lewis (then in England, at work on *Babbitt*), announcing:

> I lately unearthed a girl in Iowa, by name Ruth Suckow, who seems to me to be superb. . . . She follows after you, Dreiser, and to some extent, [Sherwood] Ander-

The SMART SET

A Magazine of Cleverness

718329

Vol 53.
Sep–Dec.
1917

NBA

"THE CRUCIFIXION OF ANNE GILBERT," by Richmond B. Barrett

An Unusual Complete Short Novel

FOURTEEN EXCELLENT SHORT STORIES

HALF A HUNDRED AMUSING BURLESQUES, SATI

son, but she is also a genuine original. She is now at work on a novel.

The novel was *Country People* (1924), which Mencken persuaded Knopf to publish (the first of several such) and which enjoyed a *succès d'estime* and a good sale. But this frail beekeeper from Earlville, who was probably Iowa's best local colorist, never achieved great popularity with her excellent realistic stories of the grain elevator towns and the "American Gothic" farmers she knew so well, probably because she was less satirical and sensational and more compassionate in her treatment of the subject than those who (unlike her) fled the provinces to give the American myth of rural virtue such a drubbing from the safety of Manhattan or the Left Bank.

A unique feature of *The Smart Set* for over fifteen years was the inclusion in each issue of a short play or playlet (sometimes more than one) and these works dealt with some of the same themes and attitudes that were endemic in the magazine's fiction. In the Nathan-Mencken era of the magazine the emphasis in the one-act plays was upon novelty. "Anything to avoid a monologue into a telephone!" was Nathan's admonition to would-be playwrights. So there were exotic pieces like Cabell's "The Jewel Merchants" (still performed), set in sixteenth century Florence; a play by George Sterling in which all the characters are rabbits who think the owner of their hutch is God (with obvious implications); a lugubrious farce by George M. Cohan in which all the characters are detectives, each of whom is trailing the other as a criminal; a "Futurist" play by Maxwell Bodenheim and Ben Hecht in which the "characters" are five animated love-letter clichés; parodies of Socratic dialogues by John McClure, and dozens of others equally "clever" in the inimitable *Smart Set* ways. Nathan occasionally appeared in the magazine as a playwright himself, parodying some popular dramatist or some hit play he disliked and, at the beginning of their regime, even Mencken got into the act (three to be exact) by writ-

ing "plays without words" for the magazine.

As a purveyor of "sound poetry" the achievements of *The Smart Set*—and, especially, the claims made for it by the editors—are somewhat doubtful. The period of the Nathan-Mencken editorship coincided with one of the most intense periods of poetic experimentation and creativity in the history of American letters, yet *The Smart Set* scorned the "free verse" movement and all experiments more radical than the milder forms of Imagism. For a time, in fact, the magazine counterattacked the new movements in poetry with fillers by Owen Hatteras like this in January 1915:

VERS LIBRE
Kiss me on the other eye
This one's wearing out.

Then there were parodies, like this one by Lucretia H. Burgan (May 1917):

THE FUTURISTIC RIVER
(after Leo Ornstein)
Gurgla bubbla trickla rolla
Burpla murmla tala dola
Smoothel slowthal soothal dothal
Shadla sunla ripla gothal.

Nevertheless, there was experimentalism in *Smart Set* poetry—cautious at first and, later in the period, a bit bolder. It was experiment in subject-matter, however, not in form, as the minnesingers of the magazine clung tenaciously to the sonnet, the ballade and the iambic quatrain for poem after poem. To be sure the "sweet lies" (as Mencken viewed poetry) of Abigail Cresson, Grace Hazard Conkling, Amanda Benjamin Hall, Lizette Woodworth Reese, and others of that school, abounded, but there were also the unsentimental lyrics in increasing proportions by Leonora Speyer, George Sterling, David Morton, Witter Bynner and a nineteen-year-old St. Louisian named George O'Neil. To be sure, the editors rejected as "too highbrow" some of the early poems of T. S. Eliot (which Pound sent them) but Pound himself was there and so, too, were Louis Untermeyer, William Rose Benét and (his wife) Elinor Wylie, Sara Teasdale and a host of others who certainly knew what "sound" poetry was and how to write it.

But by far the most frequent contributors of verse to *The Smart Set* in its post-war years were two Oklahomans—a school teacher and a journalist, Muna Lee and John McClure. Miss Lee eventually gave up pedagogy (after winning a $100 prize from *Poetry* Magazine and a trip to Chicago) to try her luck in the New York literary world. There she met and married a young Puerto Rican journalism student at Columbia—Luis Muñoz Marin, later to become Governor of the Commonwealth of Puerto Rico, who also published his early stories and poems in *The Smart Set*. As Señora Muñoz Marin, she gave up writing to return with her husband to San Juan and many years later (after their divorce), she went to work for the State Department, in Washington, where she became a world-renowned advisor on Latin American affairs—a long way from a rural school in Oklahoma or even *Smart Set* sonnets.

A classmate of Miss Lee's at the University of Oklahoma, John McClure, was for many years before his death in 1955 literary editor of *The New Orleans Times-Picayune*. McClure was immensely talented and versatile—as his sixty-odd poems and a score of stories, plays, sketches and epigram essays in *The Smart Set* indicate—and he had a deep love of classical learning which gave his work an exotic quality. In his poems, plays and stories he used backgrounds and forms drawn from Greece, Babylonia, Hellenistic Egypt (Alexandria), and Old English. In this and other respects some have likened him to a less intellectualized Ezra Pound without Pound's bitter intensity. In January 1921, McClure and two friends—Basil Thompson (himself a *Smart Set* contributor) and Julius Weis Friend—founded a literary magazine in New Orleans, *The Double Dealer,* which was quite self-consciously modeled upon *The*

Smart Set (they even wrote to Warner's business manager, J. W. Glenister, for advice on running their journal) and they made it one of the focal points of the Southern literary renaissance, then beginning. They followed the *Smart Set* practice of using gaudy pseudonyms (*e.g.,* Fritz Oolong, Banbury Cross, Sumet Gawn) and boasted a roster of contributors a majority of whom were *Smart Set* regulars, including their Chicago, New York and London "editors" (Vincent Starrett, John V. A. Weaver and Arthur Symons, respectively). But their major achievement was the first publication of Ernest Hemingway, Thornton Wilder and William Faulkner. Nevertheless, the ultimate truth is that, despite his influence as an editor, John McClure did not really fulfill his great promise as a poet and, ere long, he too lapsed into silence and obscurity.

Luckily, there is a small group of really distinguished contributions in the latter-day *Smart Set* which, if all else in the magazine had been worthless nonsense, would have sufficed to insure the journal a permanent place in literary history and legitimize its claim to being "The Aristocrat Among Magazines" in its time.

One of these is W. Somerset Maugham's "Miss Thompson" (April 1921), a long story (featured as a "novelette") which became the basis for the enormously successful play, *Rain*. Indeed, the story itself (retitled later to conform to the play) is widely regarded as a classic of modern short fiction and, as such has been anthologized in dozens of outstanding collections. Certainly its wicked heroine, Sadie Thompson, the "fallen woman"—portrayed on Broadway by Jeanne Eagels and in movie versions by at least three reigning Hollywood queens—is one of the most famous prototypes in twentieth century fiction and drama of the modern Circe. Maugham had sent this story to his New York agent (James B. Pond) who, in turn, had sold it at a handsome figure to Ray Long, then managing editor of the Hearst magazines, for publication in *Cosmopolitan*. In doubt about its propriety, Long took the story home to his wife, who read it and told him frankly that he could print it only if he wished to raise a furor among the ladies who formed the magazine's clientele. The *Cosmopolitan* staff concurred in this opinion and, after some delay, he regretfully returned the story to the agent. It then went the rounds of virtually every magazine office in New York before ending in Nathan's lap over cocktails one evening at The Royalton. Nathan and Mencken snapped it up since, by this time, the price tag had been marked down drastically and Maugham had given orders to his agent to "unload" the story wherever he could for whatever he could. But, to protect Maugham's market, the *Smart Set* editors agreed to permit a rumor that they had "mortgaged their souls" to the extent of $200 (which would be known as an enormous sum for the magazine in those days) instead of divulging the actual sale price—$20.00! When the issue with "Miss Thompson" emblazoned across the cover hit the newsstands, it sold out within hours.

Another literary "coup" for *The Smart Set* (though hardly a financial bonanza into the bargain) was the publication of James Branch Cabell's short story, "Some Ladies and Jurgen" in July 1918. As we noted earlier Cabell had published in *The Smart Set* off and on for sixteen years and, by then, he had enjoyed a modest success with several novels and collections of stories. He was earning a respectable living from his magazine contributions and book royalties but was not widely known. This story recounted the experiences of Jurgen, a naif-rogue pawnbroker, who tires of conventional matrimony and, Faustus-like, dallies with some of the great beauties of history, only to conclude that marital life may be dull but may compensate with its comforts. It was very much in the vogue of the magazine's general onslaught in fiction upon "domestic bliss" and might have ended as simply one

of many such were it not that it captured Mencken's fancy. He could foresee the possibilities of expansion to novel-length in the story and he said so to Cabell, who got to work on the idea immediately, and, a year later, produced the full-fledged *Jurgen* (1919), a minor classic of exotic modern fiction and probably Cabell's best novel. *Jurgen,* however, would probably have gone the way of Cabell's earlier novels—to a modest sale and early "remainders"—despite laudatory reviews from Mencken and his growing circle had it not had the good fortune to be banned in Boston, suppressed in New York and proscribed by the postoffice. The censorship of *Jurgen* boomeranged, as such things usually do, and Mencken turned it into a *cause célèbre*. For a time (until the ban was reversed) black market copies of *Jurgen* brought fantastic prices and every college boy and girl in the land simply *had* to read it. Cabell found himself a celebrity and, more important, began to be taken seriously as one of the great literary artists of the day, and he capitalized on his sudden success with a series of sequels to *Jurgen* (*Domnei, The High Place,* etc.) and revised and rearranged his earlier volumes to conform to what had become a celebrated "Cabellian" theme and mannered style, the whole forming a series which Cabell called "The Biography of the Life of Manuel" with what seems like wonderful redundancy. And it all started with a *Smart Set* story!

During the same period as "Some Ladies and Jurgen," the magazine also gave first national publication to a new American playwright who signed himself "Eugene G. O'Neill" (later dropping the G.). Here it was Nathan's turn to be mentor, sponsor and champion. O'Neill, an alumnus of Professor George Pierce Baker's drama workshop at Harvard, had already received limited recognition from fellow-artists in experimental theatre groups (such as the Provincetown Players) but he had yet to find a wider audience when he sent the first of his "foc'sle" plays, "The Long Voyage Home," to Nathan. Its immediate acceptance and publication in *The Smart Set* (in October 1917) brought two more O'Neill one-acters to the magazine and a meeting between O'Neill and Nathan which began a lifelong friendship. It was, in fact, through Nathan's persistence and influence that O'Neill's first Broadway productions were mounted soon thereafter and, with these, O'Neill was set upon the road that led to the Nobel Prize and to the most distinguished career yet recorded in the history of the American theatre.

Ironically, it was O'Neill who, some years later, was indirectly responsible for the end of the Nathan-Mencken editorial partnership. O'Neill had given them "first refusal" of serial rights on his short plays out of gratitude for his first publication in *The Smart Set* and Mencken in 1920 exercised his right of veto against *The Smart Set* publication of "The Emperor Jones" because it would take up more than one-third of the magazine and might thereby set a bad precedent. Nathan was rankled by this but held his peace. However, when Mencken also voted against including "All God's Chillun Got Wings" in an early issue of *The American Mercury* on the same grounds, Nathan decided to terminate their long association.

Finally, there can be no doubt that *The Smart Set*'s discovery (and in this case that word is no exaggeration) of F. Scott Fitzgerald, the highest literary deity of "The Jazz Age," must rank among the magazine's finest accomplishments. "Isabelle and Stephen were distinctly not innocent, nor were they otherwise" was the paradoxical opening of the second section of a frankly erotic story which Fitzgerald entitled "Babes in the Woods" and sent off to *The Smart Set* with little hope of acceptance. Back from the wars and repining for the love of the beauteous Zelda Sayre, Fitzgerald was surviving by writing streetcar ads in a stuffy Manhattan office while, at night, writing unsalable stories

in the stuffy Claremont Avenue room that he had festooned with rejection slips when, in June 1919 (a week after he had sent his "hopeless" story off), he received a check for $30 from *The Smart Set*. "Babes in the Woods" was published in the September 1919 issue of the magazine and, with it, Fitzgerald's career was launched.

It mattered little that the story had actually been written while he was a Princeton undergraduate. He had at last found an outlet, and by October (1919) he was earning some $215 a month from *Smart Set* stories and could afford to quit his job and put the finishing touches to a long-projected novel about modern college life. As a regular contributor to *The Smart Set* (appearing in five out of six issues), he found it considerably less difficult to convince the publishing house of Charles Scribner's Sons to take his work seriously. By July 1920, when his excellent short story, "May Day" appeared in *The Smart Set*, the editors could advertise it proudly as "by the author of *This Side of Paradise*" which was then breaking all previous sales records for a first novel. Soon all the mass circulation magazines that had once rejected Fitzgerald were clamoring for his work and accepting stories they had earlier turned down.

Nevertheless, what Fitzgerald was to bring to *The Saturday Evening Post* (where he soon became a regular), *Cosmopolitan* and, eventually, *Esquire* was something of *The Smart Set*. Long years afterwards he echoed the biases of its editors (in an article in the April 1924 *Smart Set* under Morris Gilbert he asserted that Mencken and Dreiser were "the two greatest living Americans"), and his subjects, his light serio-comic style, and his penchant for dramatic irony (as in *The Great Gatsby*) were the very elements that had characterized the best in "The Aristocrat Among Magazines" from its earliest times. Fitzgerald's novelette, "The Diamond As Big As The Ritz," for instance, would have been accepted with as much alacrity by Grissom, Dana, Towne or Willard Wright as it was in the summer of 1922 by Nathan and Mencken. Here—in the work of this tragic, bright young man who had been in diapers when Colonel Mann had first conceived his venture, "The Magazine of Cleverness" had at last come to its finest flower.

The Costs of Cleverness

Sneering at *The Smart Set* became fashionable in the literary parlor games of the winter of 1922-1923. In certain circles—notably among *The Little Review* crowd and other "far-outs" for whom publication in *The Smart Set* put one dangerously close to commercial success—the magazine had been derided for a long time. But such scorn was the obvious tactic of rivalry, real or fancied; it could be endured, even encouraged for its net publicity value. Now, however, a wider spectrum of the "civilized minority" began sneering and such stalwarts as Ernest Boyd, Theodore Dreiser and Burton Rascoe felt compelled to come out publicly in defense of the ailing journal. Its editors were still (perhaps more than ever) the Grand Chams of American criticism, but the shafts now being levelled at their magazine were more subtle, insidious and incontrovertible than those that had come in former times from the Stuart Shermans and Irving Babbitts, on the literary Right, or the Max Eastmans on the political Left. Blood was unmistakably upon the moon.

Few realized then that, by the actuarial standards of American publishing, *The Smart Set* was already a venerable old party, having survived longer than a human generation and throughout at least two literary life-cycles. What really ailed the old journal was a chronic circulatory condition with a case history running clear back to the Great Scandal of 1906. Sales of *The Smart Set* had, of course, never recovered to anything approaching prescandal levels. By the outset of the Nathan-Mencken regime, the circulation had hit "rock bottom" (around 40,000) and, despite wartime fluctuations, had risen to 50,-000 again by 1920. Now, the old unnerving slippage began again and nothing—not promotional mailings, combination subscription offers, new departments, occasional cartoons, bright new names—seemed to avail against relentless defections. A "quality" journal, such as Scofield Thayer's refurbished *Dial,* could survive with 7,500 readers, highbrow prestige and subsidies from an independently wealthy publisher (for Thayer *The Dial* was simply an expensive hobby); "little" magazines, such as *The Little Review* or *The Double-Dealer,* might piece out a month-by-month existence for a few years with perhaps 1,500 customers (most *tendenz* journals had far less). But, measured against its real competitors—*Life, Judge* and *Vanity Fair,* all of whom could show yearly gains in five figures—*The Smart Set* could not hold its own in the marketplace. Indeed, it had ceased to compete for advertisers unaided and, by 1922, was combined with a dozen Warner pulps into "Newsstand Group" contracts for tasteless ads selling cheap diamonds, body-building schools and correspondence courses in ballroom dancing.

Paradoxically, what brought the "Aristocrat Among Magazines" to this sorry pass was the success of those very tendencies in American writing it had championed for so long. Realism and naturalism, for example, had long since carried the day and, with Cather, Lewis, Dreiser and Dos Passos in high favor, the public of 1923 wanted less of the "josh" and "kid" that had titillated their elders. Much of the fire had been stolen from the magazine. For years *The Smart Set* had ridiculed pushers and boosters but after *Babbitt* (1922), for instance, what could one say freshly about Rotarians? After the conviction of Sacco and Vanzetti, what new remained to be said of bigotry and social injustice under a supposed democracy?

The Smart Set had pioneered very well in the publication of foreign authors; by 1923 there were five or six popular American magazines that welcomed a Thomas Mann, an Aldous Huxley or a Leonid Andreyev to their pages. The Young Intellectuals were taking over. By the mid-'20's some of the leading publishers—Knopf, Covici, Farrar, Liveright, Huebsch, *et al.*—were men in their twenties and thirties. A rank novice like Stephen Vincent Benét could step from the college campus into an editorial chair on the newly-founded *Time* Magazine, for instance, and a dozen of his contemporaries held similar posts. With O'Neill, the Theatre Guild, designers like Lee Simonson and a whole covy of bright young dramatists and producers who followed Nathan's tutelage, the American theatre was at last coming of age, the new-fangled movies having fallen heir to its earlier childish claptrap. Readers were no longer content merely to read about such developments in Nathan's commentaries; they left his magazine unread and, heeding his advice, headed to the theatre itself.

Nor was this all. Urged on by Nathan and Mencken who themselves "stood on the dock, wrapped in the flag," droves of the young *literati* had set sail for Paris, Rome, Vienna—anywhere, as Mencken counselled, "to escape the shambles" of American life—to study art and literature, to write the Great American Novel and, most of all, to drink openly and as freely as the proceeds of Papa's post-war prosperity would permit. Unlike *The Little Review* (which moved to Paris), however, *The Smart Set* could not follow its constituency abroad. The problems it faced were not to be solved so dramatically or decisively.

Early in March 1923, Nathan, Mencken and Warner huddled in the *Smart Set* office to discuss ideas for reversing the magazine's inexorable decline. It was a fruitless session that foreshadowed even deeper troubles, the editors vetoing every suggestion the publisher put forth (they had long agreed privately that most of his ideas were "idiotic") and offering very little of their own that did not alarm Warner, who had grown increasingly irritated at their incessant "boob-bumping." Mencken had frankly tired of *belles-lettres* and, still dreaming of his *Blue Review* of the long-dead days of Thayer and Wright, suggested they establish a new non-fiction adjunct to *The Smart Set*. This was quite out of his line, Warner replied; he wanted to stick to what he knew—sports (*Field & Stream* remained his first love) and pulp fiction. For his part, Nathan saw no reason why they could not experiment with *The Smart Set*, trying out different ideas for a time until they hit a winning combination. Warner feared this cure might prove more fatal than the disease and drive away the present clientele before the right combination was hit upon by such dangerous gambling. So it went—with nothing being decided.

A week later Mencken and Nathan, lunching with Knopf, brought up the *Blue Review* idea. Knopf was impressed. As a result, either he or his father (the reports are conflicting) tentatively approached Warner through a mutual friend to find out if perhaps Warner was interested in selling *The Smart Set*. Warner, however, was incensed. He accused Nathan and Mencken of plotting the proposed sale and thought the price suggested (reportedly $30,000) a deliberate insult. "And besides," he roared as he stalked out of their office, "I'm not going to sell *The Smart Set* to that damned Jew no matter what he wants to pay!" For once, the highly articulate editors were left speechless.

As spring turned to summer and Nathan made preparations for his annual European trip, things at *The Smart Set* were on dead center. The magazine was now listing heavily to port and drastic action was long overdue if it was to be saved. Mencken and Knopf talked with infectious enthusiasm about the possibility of founding an entirely new magazine and Nathan finally agreed to come along, with the added proviso that he and Mencken would continue to operate *The Smart Set* as a companion monthly devoted exclusively to *belles-lettres*. Mencken could be the "senior editor" on the new review; Nathan would keep his place at the top of the *Smart Set* masthead. It seemed like a good compromise to all parties, so there the matter rested until mid-August.

Meanwhile, President Harding set out on his fateful trip to Alaska, fell ill and, after lingering for tense days, died on August 2, 1923. A funeral train was organized to bring Harding's remains from California back to Ohio for burial and the contrast between the saccharine, hypocritical efforts of the press to drum up national mourning for this amiable nonentity and the legendary Lincoln cortège from Washington to Springfield, struck many an American intellectual as ludicrous if not downright vulgar. Nathan and Mencken had repeatedly lampooned Harding in life and they saw no reason to "speak well of the dead" to an audience who (they were confident) shared their views. Such feelings prompted a brief, mildly satirical bit about the Harding funeral train for "Répétition Générale" in the September issue, then in press. But when the copy reached The Charles Francis Press (their printers) a compositor who had agreed to "keep an eye" on the contents of the magazine for Warner called the publisher: "Have you seen what those guys are printing about President Harding?" he inquired in shocked tones. Of course Warner had not and when the printer read the copy to him over the phone, he was furious.

A terrible row ensued. To Nathan and Mencken, Warner's behavior was clearly a betrayal of their long-standing compact against such interference with the magazine's contents. To Warner, the unflattering references to a deceased President were irreverent and unpatriotic to the point of treason. "I don't give a damn what you thought of him," he stormed, "Harding was our President, after all." "In a nation of mules, any jackass can be president," Mencken undiplomatically snorted. Besides, Nathan tried quickly to explain, the issue was already made up and locked in press. Finding new material to fit that space at such a late date would be difficult, if not well-nigh impossible. "Write something else, run it blank— I don't give a damn! But I won't have that kind of disrespect in *my* magazine. And I can tell you this much: you won't do it again. *The Smart Set's* for sale!"

And so it was. In the end, Nathan used his prerogative as "senior editor" (for the first and only time) to kill the Harding piece and insert an innocuous filler. But the editorial arrangements under which they had worked for nearly a decade had obviously been jeopardized to such an extent that, had Warner relented, the old amity could never have been restored. So Mencken and Nathan turned their attention immediately to plans for their new magazine. All of the shares in The Smart Set Company were signed over to an escrow account which was to be divided proportionately among the shareholders if and when a sale took place. (The co-editors eventually realized $15,000 apiece from this.) On October 10, 1923, thousands of copies of the following broadside went through the mails to *Smart Set* subscribers, contributors and other interested persons:

> The undersigned announce that they are relinquishing the editorship of THE SMART SET with the issue for December, 1923, and that they have disposed of all their holdings in The Smart Set Company, Inc.
>
> They have had this step in mind for several years; lately, on their completion of nine years' service as editors of the magazine, they decided upon it definitely.

> For six years before they assumed the editorship they were regular members of the staff. Thy [*sic*] have thus put in fifteen years of continuous service.
>
> They are withdrawing from the work so long carried on together because they believe that, in so far as it is accomplishable at all, the purpose with which they began in 1908 has been accomplished. That purpose was to break down some of the difficulties which beset the American imaginative author, and particularly the beginning author, of that time—to provide an arena and drum up an audience for him, and to set him free from the pull of the cheap, popular magazines on the one side and of the conventional "quality" magazine, with its distressing dread of ideas, on the other—above all, to do battle for him critically, attacking vigorously all the influences which sought to intimidate and regiment him. This work is obviously no longer necessary. The young American novelist, dramatist or poet is quite free today, and the extent of his freedom is shown by the alarm and dudgeon of the pedants who still protest so vainly against it. That protest, in 1908, was yet potent and damaging; today it is only ridiculous.
>
> The undersigned have enjoyed the combat and do not tire of it. They are not eager for a rest; they are eager for another round. But their desires and interests now lead them beyond belles-lettres and so outside the proper field of THE SMART SET. They could not carry the magazine with them without changing its name, completely revolutionizing its contents, and otherwise breaking with its traditions—a business plainly full of practical difficulties. They have thought it wiser and more comfortable to withdraw from the editorship, dispose of their stock in the publishing company, and devote themselves to setting up an entirely new magazine. This they are now engaged upon in association with Mr. Alfred A. Knopf, the publisher. The new magazine will be THE

AMERICAN MERCURY; its purpose will be to discuss realistically, not only American letters, but the whole field of American life. The first issue will be as of January, 1924.

> [s] George Jean Nathan
>
> [s] H. L. Mencken

A day or two after this announcement went out, Morris Gilbert, a 23-year-old New York newspaperman, received a letter from Nathan asking him to "drop around" to the *Smart Set* office at an early opportunity. Young Mr. Gilbert, a lowly re-write man on the staff of the *New York Tribune,* had been a regular contributor to *The Smart Set* since the tender age of fifteen when he had sent the magazine a brief sketch based on Al Jolson's blackface at the Winter Garden and, by October 1923, he was contributing stories and poems to a number of magazines and newspapers. He was not, therefore, surprised by Nathan's request for a meeting. Although most of his business with *The Smart Set* had been handled by mail, he had been to the office twice before and, on one occasion, had chatted with the editors about ideas for stories. When he arrived at *The Smart Set* a day later, however, both Nathan and Mencken were present and the air with which they received him hinted that this was not to be a casual chat. They came straight to the point: Would he like to edit *The Smart Set*? To Morris Gilbert the question seemed almost rhetorical. Who could possibly consider rejecting such a fantastically wonderful opportunity?

Nathan and Mencken had promised Warner they would find him a suitable editor before they abandoned ship. After all, *The Smart Set* might not find a buyer for months —even years—Warner reminded them, and in the meantime the circulation would have to be built up to make the property attractive. But just how or why they had settled on young Gilbert as a likely candidate, he never knew

and, some thirty years later, they could not precisely recall. They both agreed that he had probably been recommended by some mutual friend and, of course, they were well-acquainted with his previous work in their magazine. If he was ambitious, industrious and skilled in the craft of writing in the *Smart Set* vein, he was not a young man of very great originality or aggressiveness. Nevertheless, it might be interesting to speculate on what he might have done with the magazine had he been given a free hand to edit it according to his own lights and resources.

As it was, his "orders" were quite clear. Mencken and Nathan would have their hands full with the new *American Mercury,* but they would set up a list of prescribed policies for him to follow, they told him. He was to leave the office routine in the capable hands of Miss Golde and not to spend more than $50 for a contribution without consulting Mr. Warner. As parting advice, they recommended that he follow their rule not to speak to anyone in the office before 11 A.M.

Gilbert was given no hint then that *The Smart Set* would be put up for sale, nor was he told that Nathan and Mencken had actually "signed off" the magazine and would have nothing more to do with it. He took the job with the understanding that for the time being he would be in a subordinate position —editor in name more than in fact—but nothing was said of the future. In due course he was to learn the rueful facts but neither then nor later did Gilbert feel ill-used or put upon as, with justice, he might have. "It was an awfully glamorous job for a youngster in those days. . . . I probably would have taken it under any conditions," he reflects ungrudgingly today.

If Morris Gilbert's *Smart Set* (January-September 1924) was undistinguished, it was at least gay, lightsome and in keeping with the best established traditions of the old "Magazine of Cleverness." Shorn of its Nathan-Mencken *causeries* and departments, the issues looked more like 1904 than 1924, as this "ad" on the January cover hinted:

> With this issue, the SMART SET becomes an All-Fiction Magazine—*As It Was When America's Most Popular Monthly!*

There was a backlog of usable material in the office files and, as long as the magazine continued, several old hands could be counted on to keep the stock replenished. There remained, for instance, Charles G. Shaw, an artist-illustrator of means with the world's largest collection of cigar-store Indians, who (as "John Torcross," "Jay Jarrod," "André Saville," "Stuyvesant Hilliard," "Banbury Cross" and other such squirish gentlemen) supplied the magazine with reams of humorous sketches, epigrams and articles (his series on "American Institutions" was excellent) for over eight years. There was also Helen Woljeska (the "Mme. Leandre" of twenty years' standing!), A. Newberry Choyce (an enormously prolific English poet), G. Vere Tyler (another veteran of Colonel Mann's *Smart Set*), the budding playwright, F. Hugh Herbert, and dozens more of considerable merit or promise. There was even a fairly good D. H. Lawrence novelette ("The Borderline") waiting for rescue from the office mortuary— a relic, probably, of Willard Wright's purchasing spree eleven years earlier.

Warner's strategems, faithfully carried out by the efficient young editor, worked wonders. With the price slashed to twenty cents per copy and pretty flappers adorning the covers, the circulation began a rapid ascent. By April a buyer was nibbling—the grand mogul of American magazine tycoons himself, William Randolph Hearst. The negotiations between Warner and Hearst, conducted through a sales broker, were complex and protracted and it was not until early July that Arthur W. Sutton, Warner Publications business manager, could report agreement on all sides concerning terms and conditions. The sale price was $60,000, of which Nathan

Morris Gilbert

and Mencken each netted one-fourth, Warner one-half. Hearst agreed to pay half the brokerage fee and transfer expenses, Warner the remainder. The morning after the sale contract was signed, a gentleman by the name of George D'Utassey presented himself at the *Smart Set* office and announced to Morris Gilbert: "I'm your new boss."

Mr. D'Utassey was, in fact, general manager of the Magus Magazine Corporation, a Hearst-owned subsidiary, which henceforth would operate *The Smart Set* and his arrival was the first confirmation Gilbert had had (although he had heard rumors of sale negotiations) that the magazine had indeed been sold out from under him. But, D'Utassey explained soothingly, no changes would be made for the present; Gilbert should proceed with his normal routine, unmindful of the presence of anyone new in the office. While the "lame duck" editor sweated over his September issue (the August 1924 number was already out), D'Utassey quietly set about his own tasks of making over the magazine for October. He invited Gilbert to stay on as an assistant but, one glimpse at the Hearst manager's plans sufficed to convince Gilbert that his future lay elsewhere. He called Dwight Perrin, managing editor of the *Tribune* (just then being merged with the *Herald*), asked for his old job back, got it, and left *The Smart Set* at the end of August 1924. Precisely ten months after his exhilarating engagement interview with Nathan and Mencken, Morris Gilbert was "ex-editor" of *The Smart Set*.

Despite Burton Rascoe's estimate that Gilbert "had the makings of a great editor," he was never again to edit a magazine. He has spent the remainder of his life with New York and Paris newspapers, and for the most of the past two decades has been a feature writer and member of the Sunday staff of *The New York Times*.

It was small wonder Gilbert was revolted by his preview of the October 1924 *Smart Set*. The format was drastically altered and sepia-toned photographs were introduced to suit the new sub-title: "True Stories from Real Life." In an editorial (headlined: "We're Here to Fight—In Which We Describe the Spirit of a New Idea") the Hearst management baldly declared:

> Always, whatever we do, we will strive toward one ideal—to make *Smart Set* an influence for good. We want our magazine to leave the world just a little better every month. We want it to leave happiness in the homes of the readers, and we want it to reach out to those less fortunate than we and make them happy.
>
> We believe in the American people. We believe in Main Street. We believe in the farmer, the laborer, and the mechanic. To *Smart Set* we comprise one people, indivisible, with our eyes set on a goal.

Less than a year earlier such incredible balderdash—a travesty on twenty-four years of *Smart Set* policy—would easily have won the monthly "Répétition Générale" award of the

3½"x4¾" custard pie for flatulent nonsense.

Inside the magazine worse horrors awaited: inspirational, folksy verses by Edgar A. Guest and Harry Lee, an inspirational editorial by Dr. Frank Crane (a Baptist preacher who, as author of *Sane Sex*, was one of Mencken's favorite targets), and even a sermon on "Clean Living" by the Rev. Billy Sunday. The stories interspersed with these features were anonymous. Who could unblushingly sign his name to such pieces as

"Is One Wife Enough?"

"Gypsy Love"

"Black Regrets"

"Buying Beauty at $22 a Week"

"Quong Kee's White Wife"

"The Freedom I Craved"?

It was almost as if D'Utassey and his staff had deliberately set out to parody the old magazine by including at least one item of each kind of cheapness and vulgarity attacked by all the previous editors from Nathan and Mencken back to Arthur Grissom. Many an old subscriber must have blinked incredulously and turned back to the cover to see if it really did have those familiar swirling S's. But if some fell soon by the wayside, their places were quickly taken by hordes of new readers. Exploiting to the full the magazine's long, undeserved reputation for perfumed pornography, Hearst's *Smart Set* could soon write its sales in six figures—a sorry datum of H. L. Mencken's cynical epigram: "Nobody ever went broke underestimating the taste of the American people."

With such razzle-dazzling success *The Smart Set* naturally could not be allowed an honorable death. The Hearst management had still further plans for it. In 1926 *McClure's*—another turn-of-the-century giant now down at heels—came on the block and into the Hearst dominions and, in 1929, it was merged with *The Smart Set* under the general management of James R. Quirk (publisher of *Photoplay* and new president of a reorganized Magus Publishing Co.). The combined journals were retitled *"The New Smart Set,"* and sub-headed: "The Young Woman's Magazine." The editor of this "new" periodical was Margaret E. Sangster, ironically a contributor in the old Nathan-Mencken days herself, and the contents (as one might expect) were given over almost entirely to advice on clothes, diet, cosmetics, "career tips" and romantic serials with an occasional innocuous poem as filler material.

The winter of 1929-30 was a hard one for all American magazines. Following the Wall Street debacle of October 1929, most Americans tightened their pursestrings, and as always, one of the first "luxuries" to be sacrificed was publications of all sorts. Magazine subscriptions were not renewed except on journals that had a very stable following and long-established policies and even these suffered losses. Newsstand sales, always a Depression bellwether, were cut to ribbons. *The New Smart Set* was one of the first to be in deep trouble. Nevertheless, the undaunted and resourceful Hearst minions had some bright ideas for its rescue. They would "tone up" the magazine and run it in

competition with *Vanity Fair*—in effect, a reversion to "cleverness" and the policies of Nathan and Mencken! As the right editor to put through such a program they lured Arthur Samuels away from the staff of *The New Yorker* (in 1925 the astute Leonard Ross had picked up the market abandoned by the old *Smart Set*). Gradually, in the early months of 1930, something akin to *belles-lettres* began to return to *The New Smart Set* under some familiar names of bygone years: Frank Adams, Faith Baldwin, Mary Carolyn Davies, Donald Ogden Stewart and Charles B. Driscoll, among them.

The hour was late for such changes. The Depression had settled over the country in earnest and in the face of increasingly stringent measures for economy, Samuels' project had to be abandoned before it could be put into full effect. Indeed, the Hearst empire itself had to be retrenched, its "losers" discarded. So, with neither a bang nor a whimper—not even an audible death rattle—*The New Smart Set,* which contained at least the bones of its former self, was allowed to expire quietly on June 15, 1930.

Ringing the Changes

———•—•———

There were no elegiac editorials over the passing of *The Smart Set* nor need of public tears for its inglorious demise. In the new American literary world of the sobering Thirties, it would have seemed incredible that one had ever joined *The Smart Set* in making sport of The Uplift or crusading zeal; in retrospect, the innocent merriment of previous decades seemed at best quaint, at worst indecently irresponsible amid the grim headlines of a collapsed economic order, of militant Fascism, of rampant racism and mounting criminality on every hand. Had the old *Smart Set* somehow managed to survive unchanged into the 1930's, it would have looked as misplaced and anachronistic in the Proletarian Decade as a cocked hat and farthingales on a West Side subway. Having no job to go to *ca.* 1930, one had plenty of time to plan all sorts of ideal societies, but none of them looked anything like the Edwardian world to which *The Smart Set* so completely belonged. Indeed there never was a time in our history when nostalgia was less fashionable.

Of *The Smart Set's* movers and shakers, those who were still around at the end were otherwise too preoccupied to take much notice. Colonel Mann had gone to his grave full of years a decade before (in May 1920). John Adams Thayer, his interest in publishing long ago lost, divided his time between an advertising office and his Westport home, where he died in 1936, and Eltinge Warner, like Hearst, was busy shoring up his own magazine empire against the Depression's ravages. Of the living ex-editors (only Grissom and Boyer had died), Dana and Splint had foregone journalism for the law and medicine, respectively; Towne was editing *Harper's Bazaar;* Wright was now the best-selling "S. S. Van Dine"; Gilbert was in Europe for *The New York Times.*

H. L. Mencken, of course, was then still editing *The American Mercury* (where he continued until 1933), but George Jean Nathan spent his time writing widely syndicated Broadway reviews and a monthly critical column for *Esquire.* Their *Mercury* had been a great success from the beginning, though it never actually reached more than about 70,000 readers. Its staid green cover peeping out of a jacket pocket was the college boys' badge of intellectual respectability and "the Merc" was quoted far and wide by schoolteachers and heterodox Rotarians who fancied themselves "advanced" thinkers. Some eighty-odd *Smart Set* regulars had followed Nathan and Mencken into the pages of the *Mercury* (*i.e.,* on the "approved" list from which contributions were solicited) and many of the ideas and insights one encountered there were familiar ones from "The Magazine of Cleverness," refurbished and institutionalized. In short, no one could actually call the *Mercury* "witty," "gay," "charming," "sophisticated," "spontaneous," or "clever"—all adjectives applied to *The Smart Set*; from first to last, everything in it was quite thoroughly predictable. Within a year of its founding, Mencken and Nathan had quarrelled and their great partnership was at an end. Even that might have been predicted.

What remains to be said of the old *Smart*

—*The Stork Club*

Nathan and Mencken at a reunion at The Stork Club in 1948

Set? The returns are all in now, as indeed they have been for a good many years. There seems no longer any valid reason to postpone further the ringing of the changes.

"There never *was* anything really quite like it," was Nathan's judgment a quarter-century later (in 1955) as the shadows lengthened one afternoon along 44th Street. Then he added:

> But there ought to be. Where can the beginning writers of today get that kind of audience? And look at our puerile criticism—merely intellectual back-slapping in life and in the arts! I would give a lot of money, if I had it and could find some bright young editor, to start the *Smart Set* up again. I think it just might "go" today. Well, . . . maybe not, after all. You couldn't be as outspoken as we were then. When you denounce the conformities today you must do it *sotto voce.* If Menck and I wrote today as we did then, we'd probably be jailed.

A highly biased opinion, no doubt, but one that would certainly be hard to gainsay. Surely, *The Smart Set* was *sui generis*—its "descendants" a far, far cry from what it was itself. Not the least of its uniqueness is the fact that, through most of its history, the magazine itself was but an extension of its editors' personalities. In the last era of individualism, it could be intensely individualistic—a luxury that no magazine can afford in this day of corporate decision-making and computer analysis. Its successes and its failures followed from this fact.

We should not continue to judge these successes and failures of *The Smart Set* from the somewhat somber viewpoint of the 1930's, still less from the current romanticizing of "La Belle Epoque." To have published the work of perhaps two thousand writers, most of them young and a vast majority of them unknown was no mean feat. (How much does it matter that only a relative handful became literary lions?) To have provided the opportunity for the publication of perhaps 8,000 works of the creative spirit, many of them defying prevailing literary taboos and a goodly number of them scornful of the political and social conformities of the moment was no small accomplishment. It matters little that only a few of these pieces have the bite and sting today that gave them immediacy and force in their own time, nor does it matter greatly that not many are even minor masterpieces. It would have been enough to insure *The Smart Set* a place in our literary firmament that it produced only an O. Henry and a Cabell, an O'Neill and a Fitzgerald, "Miss Thompson" and a handful of exquisitely wrought lyrics by Sara Teasdale. Few magazines can claim more. If, in other words, we read that old magazine today in the proper historical context, we can readily see that its only great failure was its inability to change with the changing times and keep alive the fragile spirit of "cleverness" that animated it.

There can be no doubt of Nathan's *"ought."* Every age that wishes a vital literature should have a magazine "of last resort" where the fledgling can get a hearing before a national audience without pandering to public taste. Such a magazine stimulates writing by just being there. Moreover, it would indeed be interesting to put to the test Nathan's assumption that, despite our lifting of all the old "obscenity" taboos, a stricter censorship of unpopular opinions now prevails. Meanwhile, in the vaults and stacks of the New York Public Library and a few other places, the volumes of what we may certainly call "the aristocrat among magazines of cleverness" are crumbling to dust. Buried in those moldering pages, in the first "Répétition Générale" column (May 1919) is an "Epitaph" of the *Smart Set* spirit:

When I die, as die someday I must, I pray to God that it shall be on a warm, lazy late afternoon in the early Springtime of the year, and that my best friend among men shall sit himself down quietly and alone in Sherry's and order two of our old cocktails, and that my best friend among women shall be waiting, as always, near her telephone and that when, the minutes passing, it fails to ring, she may at last for one small fleeting moment doubt that I am up to some deviltry with another girl.

FINIS

94

JUNE, 1922   35 Cen

The SMART SET

Edited by
George Jean Nathan
and
H.L. Mencken.

"The Diamond as Big as the Ritz"
By F. Scott Fitzgerald

LEMBER, 1922   35 Cen

The SMART SET

Edited by
George Jean Nathan
and
H. L. Mencken.

"The Yellow Hope"—A Forecast of the Japanese
Conquest of the United States.

PART TWO:

THE ANTHOLOGY

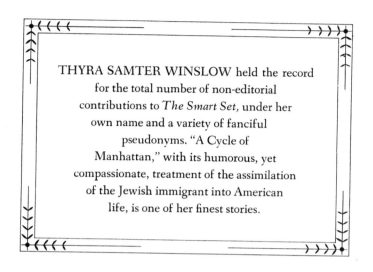

THYRA SAMTER WINSLOW held the record
for the total number of non-editorial
contributions to *The Smart Set,* under her
own name and a variety of fanciful
pseudonyms. "A Cycle of
Manhattan," with its humorous, yet
compassionate, treatment of the assimilation
of the Jewish immigrant into American
life, is one of her finest stories.

A Cycle of Manhattan
ABRIDGED

BY THYRA SAMTER WINSLOW

THE Rosenheimers arrived in New York on a day in April. New York, flushed with the first touch of Spring, moved on inscrutably, almost suavely unawares. It was the greatest thing that had ever happened to the Rosenheimers, and even in the light of the profound experiences that were to follow it kept its vast grandeur and separateness, its mysterious and benumbing superiority. Viewed later, in half-fearful retrospect, it took on the character of something unearthly, unmatchable and never quite clear—a violent gallimaufry of strange tongues, humiliating ques-

tionings, freezing uncertainties, sudden and paralyzing activities.

The Rosenheimers came by way of the Atlantic Ocean, and if anything remained unclouded in their minds it was a sense of that dour and implacable highway's unfriendliness. They thought of it ever after as an intolerable motion, a penetrating and suffocating smell. They saw it through drenched skylights—now and then as a glimpse of blinding blue on brisk, heaving mornings. They remembered the harsh, unintelligible exactions of officials in curious little blue

FROM VOL. 58, MARCH 1919

coats. They dreamed for years of endless nights in damp, smothering bunks. They carried off the taste of strange foods, barbarously served. The Rosenheimers came in the steerage.

There were, at that time, seven of them, if you count Mrs. Feinberg. As Mrs. Feinberg had, for a period of eight years—the age of the oldest Rosenheimer child—been called nothing but Grandma by the family and occasionally Grandma Rosenheimer by outsiders, she was practically a Rosenheimer, too. Grandma was Mrs. Rosenheimer's mother, a decent, simple, round-shouldered "sheideled," little old woman, to whom life was a ceaseless washing of dishes, making of beds, caring for children and cooking of meals. She ruled them all, unknowing.

The head of the house of Rosenheimer was, fittingly, named Abraham. This had abbreviated itself, even in Lithuania, to a more intimate Abe. Abe Rosenheimer was thirty-three, sallow, thin-cheeked and bearded, with a slightly aquiline nose. He was already growing bald. He was not tall and he stooped. He was a clothing cutter by trade. Since his marriage, nine years before, he had been saving to bring his family over. Only the rapid increase of its numbers had prevented him coming sooner.

Abraham Rosenheimer was rather a silent man and he looked stern. Although he recognized his inferiority in a superior world, he was not without his ambitions. These looked toward a comfortable home, his own chair with a lamp by it, no scrimping about meat at meals and a little money to put by. He had heard stories about fortunes that could be made in America and in his youth they had stirred him. Now he was not much swayed by them. He was fond of his family and he wanted them "well taken care of," but in the world that he knew the rich and the poor were separated by an unscalable barrier. Unless incited temporarily to revolution by fiery acquaintances he was content to hope for a

simple living, work not too hard or too long, a little leisure, tranquillity.

He had a comfortable faith which included the belief that, if a man does his best, he'll usually be able to make a living for his family. "Health is the big thing," he would say, and "The Lord will provide." Outside of his prayer-book, he did little reading. It never occurred to him that he might be interested in the outside world. He knew of the existence of none of the arts. His home and his work were all he had ever thought about.

Mrs. Rosenheimer, whose first name was Minnie, was thirty-one. She was a younger and prettier reproduction of her mother, plump and placid, with a mouth inclined to petulancy.

There were four Rosenheimer children. Yetta was eight, Isaac six, Carrie three and little Emanuel had just had his first birthday. Yetta and Carrie were called by their own first names, but Isaac, in America, almost immediately gave way to Ike and little Emanuel became Mannie. They were much alike, dark-haired, dark-eyed, restless, shy, wondering.

The Rosenheimers had several acquaintances in New York, people from the little village near Grodno who had preceded them to America. Most of these now lived in the Ghetto that was arising on the East Side of New York, and Rosenheimer had thought that his family would go there, too, so as to be near familiar faces. He had written, several months before, to one Abramson, a sort of distant cousin, who had been in America for twelve years. As Abramson had promised to meet them, he decided to rely on Abramson's judgment in finding a home in the city.

Abramson was at Ellis Island and greeted the family with vehement embraces. He seemed amazingly well dressed and at home. He wore a large watchchain and no less than four rings. He introduced his wife, whom he had married since coming to America, though she, too, had come from the old country. She wore silk and carried a parasol.

"I've got a house all picked out for you," he explained in familiar Yiddish. "It isn't in the Ghetto, where some of our friends live, buts it's cheap, with lots of comforts and near where you can get work, too."

Any house would have suited the Rosenheimers. They were pitifully anxious to get settled, to rid themselves of the foundationless feeling which had taken possession of them. With eager docility, Yetta carrying Mannie and each of the others carrying a portion of the bundles of wearing apparel and feather comforts which formed their luggage, they followed Abramson to a surface car and to their new home. In their foreign clothes and with their bundles they felt almost as uncomfortable as they had been on shipboard.

The Rosenheimers' new home was in Mac-Dougal Street. They looked with awe on the exterior and pronounced it wonderful. Such a fine building! Of red brick it was! There were three stories. The first story was a stable, the big door open. Little Isaac had to be pulled past the restless horses in front of it. The whole family stood for a moment, drinking in the wonders, then followed Abramson up the stairs. On the second floor several families lived in what the Rosenheimers thought was palatial grandeur. Even their own home was elegant. It consisted of two rooms—the third floor front. They could hardly be convinced that they were to have all that space. There was a stove in the second room and gas fixtures in both of them —and there was a bathroom, with running water, in the general hall! The Rosenheimers didn't see that the paper was falling from the walls and that, where it had been gone for some years, the plaster was falling, too. Nor that the floor was roughly uneven.

"Won't it be too expensive?" asked Rosenheimer. Abramson chuckled. Though he himself was but a trimmer by trade, he was pleased with the role of fairy godfather. He liked twirling wonders in the faces of these simple folk. In comparison, he felt himself quite a success, a cosmopolite. Just about Rosenheimer's age, he had small deposits in two savings banks, a three-room apartment, a wife and two American sons, Sam and Morrie. Both were in public school, and both could speak "good English." He patted Rosenheimer on the back jovially.

"You don't need to worry," he said. "A good cutter here in New York don't have to worry. Even a 'greenhorn' makes a living. There's half a dozen places *you* can choose from. I'll tell you all about it, and where to go tomorrow. Now, we'll go over to my house and have something to eat. Then you'll see how you'll be living in a few years. You can borrow some things from us until you get your own. My wife will be glad to go with Mrs. Rosenheimer and show her where to buy."

The Rosenheimers gave signs of satisfaction as they dropped their bundles and sat down on the empty boxes that stood around, or on the floor. This was something like it! Here they had a fine home in a big brick house, a sure chance of Rosenheimer getting a good job, friends to tell them about things —they had already found their place in New York! Grandma, trembling with excitement, took Mannie in her arms and held him up dramatically.

"See, Mannie, see Mannischen—this is fine —this is the way to live!"

Things turned out even more miraculously than the Rosenheimers had dared to hope. After only three days Rosenheimer found a job as a pants cutter at the fabulous wages he had heard of. He could not only pay the high rent, twelve dollars a month, he would also have enough left over for food and clothes, and to furnish the home, if they were careful. Maybe, after the house was in order, there would even be a little to put by. Of course it was no use being too happy about it, he told Mrs. Rosenheimer.

"It looks fine now, but you know you can't always tell. It takes a whole lot to feed a big family."

Although secretly delighted, he was solemn and rather silent over his good fortune. Abraham Rosenheimer was a cautious man.

Mrs. Abramson initiated Grandma and Mrs. Rosenheimer into New York buying. It was fascinating, even more so than buying had been at home. There were neighborhood shops where Yiddish was spoken, and already the family was beginning to learn a little English. Mrs. Rosenheimer listened closely to what people said and the children picked up words, playing in the street.

The next weeks were orgies of buying. Not that much was bought, for there wasn't much money and it had to be spent very carefully, but each article meant exploring, looking and haggling. Grandma took the lead in buying—didn't Grandma always do such things? Grandma was only fifty-seven and spry for her age. Didn't she take care of the children and do more than her share of the housework?

Grandma was supremely happy. She liked to buy and she felt that merchants couldn't fool her, even in this strange country. A table was the first thing purchased. It was almost new and quite large. It was pine and bare of finish, but, after Grandma had scrubbed it and scoured it it looked clean and wholesome. It was quite a nice table and only wobbled a little when you leaned on it heavily, for the legs weren't quite even. One was a little loose and Grandma didn't seem able to fasten it. Assisted by Mrs. Rosenheimer and Yetta, she scrubbed the whole flat, so that it equaled the new table in immaculateness. There were families who liked dirt—Grandma had seen them, even in America—but she was glad she didn't belong to one of them.

Then came chairs, each one picked out with

infinite care and much sibilant whispering between Grandma, Mrs. Rosenheimer and Mrs. Abramson. There was a rocker, slat-backed, from which most of the slats were missing, though it still rocked "as good as new." The next chair was leather-covered, though the leather was cut through in places, allowing the horse-hair stuffing to protrude. But, as Mrs. Abramson pointed out, this was an advantage, it showed that the filling wasn't an inferior cotton. There were two straight chairs, one with a leatherette seat, nailed on with bright-colored nails, the other with a wicker seat, quite neatly mended. There was a cot for Grandma and a bed for Mr. and Mrs. Rosenheimer and Emanuel. The other children were well and strong and could sleep on the floor, of course. Hadn't they brought fine soft feathers with them?

All of the furniture was second—or third—hand and the previous owners had not treated it with much care. So Grandma got some boxes to help out, and she and the Rosenheimers worked over them, pulling and driving nails. Finally they had a cupboard which held all of the new dishes—almost new, if you don't mind a few hardly noticeable nicked edges—and decorated with fine pink roses. Some of the boxes were still used as chairs, "to help out." One fine, high one did very nicely as an extra table, with a grand piece of brand-new oilcloth, in a marbled pattern, tacked over it. They had a home now.

Grandma and Mrs. Rosenheimer marketed every day at the stores and markets in the neighborhood. Rosenheimer sometimes complained that they used too much money, but, then, he "liked to eat well." The little Rosenheimers grew round and merry.

Grandma and Mr. and Mrs. Rosenheimer, looking at the children and at their two big rooms—all their own and so nicely furnished—could hardly imagine anything finer. Grandma and Rosenheimer were absolutely at peace. But Mrs. Rosenheimer knew that, with more money, there were a lot of things you could buy. She had walked through Washington Square and up Fifth Avenue. She had seen people in fine clothes, people of her own race, too. She didn't have much, after all. Still, most of the time she was content.

Gradually, too, Rosenheimer saw shadows of wealth. He heard rumors of how fortunes were made overnight—his boss now, a few years before, had been a poor boy. . . . Nevertheless, smoking his cigarettes and reading his Yiddish paper after his evening meal, or talking with Abramson or one of the men he had met, he was well satisfied with New York as he had found it.

As the months passed, the Rosenheimers drank in, unbelievably fast, the details of the city. Already the children were beginning to speak English, not just odd words, here and there, but whole sentences. Already, too, they were beginning to be ashamed of being "greenhorns" and were planning the time when they could say they had been over for years or had been born here. Little Mannie was beginning to talk and everyone said he spoke English without an accent.

Yetta and Ike started to school. Each day they brought home some startling bit of information that the family received and assimilated without an eyewink. Although most of the men at the shop spoke Yiddish, Rosenheimer was learning English, too. He even spoke, vaguely, about learning to read it and write it, and he began to look over English papers, now and then, interestedly. Mrs. Rosenheimer also showed faint literary learnings and sometimes asked questions about things.

Ike was always eager to tell everything he had learned. In a sharp little voice he would instruct, didactically, anyone within hearing distance. He rather annoyed Rosenheimer, who was not blinded by the virtues of his eldest son. But he was Mrs. Rosenheimer's favorite. She would sit, hands folded across her ample lap, smiling proudly as he unrolled his fathomless knowledge.

"Listen at that boy! Ain't he wonderful, the way he knows so much?" she would exclaim.

Yetta's learning took the form, principally, of wanting things. Each day, it seemed, she could find out something else she didn't have, that belonged to all American children. And, no matter how penniless Rosenheimer had just declared himself to be, unsmilingly and a bit shamefacedly, he would draw pennies out of the depths of the pocket of his shiny trousers.

Only Grandma showed no desire to learn the ways of the new country. She didn't mind picking up a little English, of course, though she'd got along very nicely all of her life without it. Still, in a new country, it didn't hurt to know something about the language. But as for reading—well, Yiddish was good enough for her, though she didn't mind admitting she didn't read Yiddish very easily. Grandma had little use for the printed word.

Each week the Rosenheimers' clothes changed nearer to the prevailing styles of MacDougal Street. Only a few weeks after they arrived, Mrs. Rosenheimer, overcome by her new surroundings, bought, daringly, a lace sailor collar, which she fastened around the neck of her old-world costume. As the months passed, even this failed to satisfy. The dress itself finally disappeared, reappearing as a school frock for Yetta, and Mrs. Rosenheimer wore a modest creation of Red plaid worsted which Grandma and she had made, huge sleeves, bell skirt and all, after one they had seen in Washington Square on a "society lady."

Just a year after they arrived in America, Mrs. Rosenheimer discarded her *sheidel.* She even tried to persuade Grandma to leave hers off, but Grandma demurred. There were things you couldn't do decently, even in a new country. Mrs. Rosenheimer made the innovation in a spirit of fear, but when no doom overtook her and she found, in a few weeks, how "stylish" she looked, she never regretted the change. She was wearing curled bangs, good as the next one, before long.

Little Ike had a new suit, bought ready-made, his first bought suit, not long afterwards. The trousers were a bit too long, but surely that was an advantage, for he was growing fast, going on eight. They couldn't call him a "greenhorn" now. He came home, too, with reports of how smart his teacher said he was and of the older boys, unbelievers, whom he had "got ahead of" in school. His shrill voice would grow louder and higher as he would explain to the admiring Mrs. Rosenheimer and Grandma what a fine lad he was getting to be.

Other signs of change now appeared. Scarcely a year had gone by before lace curtains appeared at the two front windows. They were of different patterns, but what of that? They had been cheaper that way, as "samples." By tautly drawn strings, white and stiff they clung, adding a touch of elegance to the abode. Only three months later a couch was added, the former grandeur of its tufted surface not at all dimmed by a few years of wear. Yetta and Carrie slept on it, luxuriously, one at each end. It was a long couch and they were so little.

Then a cupboard for dishes appeared. Grandma bought it from a family that was "selling out." It had glass doors. At least there had been glass doors. One was broken now, but who noticed that? In the corner of the front room, opposite the couch, it looked very "stylish." And not long afterward there was carpet in the front room, three strips of it, with a red and green pattern. Then, indeed, the Rosenheimers felt that they could, very proudly, "be at home to their frends." They had company now, families of old friends and new, from the Ghetto and from their own neighborhood. And they visited, *en masse,* in return.

There wasn't much money, of course. Rosenheimer was getting good wages, but children eat a lot and beg for pennies between meals. And shoes! But like many men of his race and disposition, Rosenheimer never contributed quite all of his funds to his household. Nor did he take his women into his confidence. He felt that they could not counsel him wisely, which was probably right, for neither Grandma nor Mrs. Rosenheimer was interested in anything outside of their home and their friends. Besides this, he had a natural secrecy, a dislike of talking things over with his family. So, each week, he made an infinitesimal addition to the savings account he had started. He even considered various investments—he knew of men who were buying the tenements in which they lived on wages no bigger than his, living in the basement and taking care of the house outside of working hours. But he felt that he was still too much the "greenhorn" for such enterprises, so he kept on with his small and secret savings.

In 1897 another member was added to the family. This meant a big expense, a midwife and later a doctor, but Rosenheimer had had a raise by this time—he was, in fact, now a foreman--so the expense was met without difficulty. There was real joy at the arrival of this baby—more than at the coming of any of the previous children. For this was an American baby, and seemed, in some way, to make the whole family more American. The baby was a girl and even the sex seemed satisfactory, though, of course, at every previous addition the Rosenheimers had hoped for a boy.

There was a great discussion, then, about names. Before this, a baby had always been named after some dead ancestor or relative without much ado. It was best to name a child after a relative, but, according to custom, if the name didn't quite suit, you took the initial instead. By some process of reasoning, this was supposed to be naming the child "after" the honored relative. Now the Rosenheimers wanted something grandly American for the new baby. Grandma wanted Dora, after her mother. But Dora didn't sound American enough. Ike suggested Della, but that didn't suit, either. Finally Yetta brought home Dorothy. It was a very stylish name, it seemed, and was finally accepted.

Little Emanuel, aged four, was told that "his nose was out of joint." He cried and felt of it. It seemed quite straight to him. It was. He was a handsome little fellow, and, when Mrs. Rosenheimer took him out with her, folks would stop and ask about him. She was glad when she could answer them in English. And as for Mannie—at four he talked as if no other country than America had ever existed.

Very gradually, Mrs. Rosenheimer grew tired of MacDougal Street. She tried to introduce this dissatisfaction into the rest of the family. Grandma was very happy here. With little shrugs and gestures she decried any further change. Weren't they all getting along finely? Wasn't Rosenheimer near his work? Weren't the children fat and healthy? What could they have better than this—two rooms, running water, gas and everything? Didn't they know people all around them? Rosenheimer was indifferent. Some of his friends, including the Abramsons, had already moved "farther out." Still, he didn't see the use of spending so much money; they were all right where they were. Times were hard; you couldn't tell what might happen. Still, if Minnie had her heart set on it— The children were ready for any change.

Mrs. Rosenheimer, revolving the matter endlessly in her mind, found many reasons for moving. All of her friends, it seemed, had fled from the noise and dirt of MacDougal Street. On first coming to New York she had been disappointed at not living in the Ghetto over on the East side. Now, when she visited there, she wondered how she had ever liked it. When she moved she wanted something

really fine—and where her friends were, too. She had a good many friends outside of the Ghetto now. On arriving in America she hadn't known MacDougal Street was dirty. She knew it now. And the little Italian children in the neighborhood—oh, they were all right, of course, but—not just whom you'd want your children to play with, exactly. Why, every day Ike would come home with terrible things they had said to him. And their home, which had looked so grand, was old and ugly, too, when compared with those of other people. Of course, Grandma liked it, but, after all, Grandma was old-fashioned. Mrs. Rosenheimer discovered, almost in one breath, that her mother belonged to a passing generation, and didn't keep up with the times—that she, herself, really had charge of the household.

Out in East Seventy-seventh Street there were some tenements, not at all like those of MacDougal Street nor the Ghetto, but brand-new, just the same as rich people had. Each flat had a regular kitchen with a sink and running water and a fine new gas stove. The front room had a mirror in it that belonged to the house—and—unbelievably but actually true—there was a bathroom for each family. It had a tub in it, painted white, and a washstand—both with running water—and already there was oilcloth, in blue and white, on the bathroom floor. The outer halls had gas in them that burned all night—some sort of a law. Those tenements were elegant— that was the way to live.

Rosenheimer got another raise. There was some sort of an organization of cutters, a threatened strike, and then sudden success. Mrs. Rosenheimer never understood much about it, but it meant more money. Now Rosenheimer had no legitimate reason for keeping his family in MacDougal Street.

So he and Mrs. Rosenheimer and Grandma went out to the new tenements and looked around. Mrs. Rosenheimer acted as spokesman, talking with the woman at the renting office, asking questions, pointing things out. At the end of the afternoon Rosenheimer rented one of the four-room flats in a new tenement building.

On the way home, Mrs. Rosenheimer leaned close to her husband:

"Ain't it grand, the way we are going to live now?" she asked.

"If we can pay for it."

"With you doing so well, how you talk!"

"Good enough, but money, these days—"

"Abe, do you want to do something for me?"

"Go on, something more to spend money on."

"Not a cent, Abe. Only, won't you—shave your beard? Moving to a new neighborhood and all. Not for me, but the neighbors should see what an American father the children have got."

Rosenheimer frowned a bit uneasily. Mrs. Rosenheimer didn't refer to it again, but three days later he came home strangely thin and white-looking—his beard gone. Only a little mustache, soft and mixed with red, remained.

Before the Rosenheimers moved they sold the worst of their furniture to the very men from whom they bought it, five years before, taking only the big bed, the table and the couch. It was Mrs. Rosenheimer who had insisted on this.

"Trash we've got, when you compare it to the way others live. We need new things in a fine new flat."

On the day they were moving, Yetta said something. The family were amazed into silence. Yetta was thirteen now, a tall girl, rather plump, with black hair and flashing eyes.

"When we move, let's get rid of some of our name," she said. "I hate it. It's awfully long—Rosenheimer. Nobody ever says it all, anyhow. Let's call ourselves Rosenheim."

"Why, why," muttered her father, finally, "how you talk! Change my name, as if I was a criminal or something?"

"Aw," Yetta pouted, she was her father's favorite and she knew it, "this family of greenhorns make me tired. Rosenheimer—if it was longer you'd like it better. Ike Rosenheimer and Carrie Rosenheimer and Yetta Rosenheimer! It's awful. Leaving off two letters would only help a little—and that's too much for you. Since the Abramsons moved they are Abrams, and you know it. And Sam—do you know what? At school they called him MacDougal because he lived here on this street and he liked it better than Sam, so he's calling himself MacDougal Abrams now. And here, you old-timers—"

"She's right, Mamma," said Ike, "our names are awful!"

Mannie didn't say anything. He sucked a great red lollypop. At six one doesn't care much about names. Nor did Carrie, who was eight.

There was a letter-box for each family in the entrance hall of the new tenement building and a space for the name of the family just above it. Maybe Rosenheimer had taken the advice of his children. Perhaps he wrote in large letters and couldn't get all of his name in the space made for it. Anyhow, Rosenheim was announced to the world as the occupant of Flat 52.

[Mrs. Rosenheim was delighted with her new four-room flat on East Seventy-seventh Street. She persuaded Grandma to take off her *sheidel*. Ikey decided to call himself Harold, but the family insisted on Irving.

Rosenheim and Abrams became partners in The Acme Pants Company and prospered, and Mrs. Rosenheimer decided to move from the tenement on East Seventy-seventh Street. Yetta convinced them to move to the Bronx.]

One of the startling changes of the new régime was the name above the letter-box. A simple and chaste A. G. Rosen was announced in Irving's most careful writing. Rosenheim explained that, at the factory, everyone called him Rosen for short and it might make it confusing to keep the old name. The family hailed Rosen joyfully. Surely they were real Americans, now.

[Yetta begged Rosen to buy a piano for the new apartment. The children grew.]

. . . .

Carrie was quieter than either Yetta or Irving, but she observed a great deal. She liked to spend money, begging it from her parents. "We're rich, why can't I have more things?" she would say, buying unnecessarily expensive ribbons and purses. She liked to correct the family, too, and, when her mother grew vocal and her voice took on the sing-song of her native tongue, Carrie would say, "Don't talk so loud, Mother. We aren't deaf, you know," or "This is America. We try to speak English here." Mrs. Rosen would check herself rather shamefacedly, instead of "calling the child down," as she felt she should have done. Carrie liked expensive clothes and she liked putting them on and taking long walks with just one girl friend, talking quietly. She thought Yetta's crowd awfully loud. Mannie and Dorothy were good-looking little children, still coaxers of pennies and both quite spoiled.

. . . .

A year later, when she was eighteen, Yetta became, suddenly, Yvette. The crowd she was going with thought Yetta an awful name, old-fashioned and foreign. And certainly there was nothing foreign about her. She had seen Yvette in a book—and, with the right initial and all—Yvette Rosen sounded fine. After that she frowned at anyone, even old Grandma, if the old name crept in.

. . . .

It was Irving who first spoke dissatisfaction with the Bronx apartment. Irving was to enter Columbia University in the fall and he wanted to be a little nearer his school.

"You don't know how it is," he said, one night at dinner. "Everyone laughs at the Bronx. I went to a vaudeville show with Yvette last week, though Heaven knows why she goes to it, and at a mention of the Bronx everyone laughed. It isn't only that. Here we are in a walk-up apartment, when we could have something better. I'm starting—to—to make friends. I've got to make a place for

myself. I'm eighteen. When we were younger it didn't make much difference, now we ought to get out of here."

[The new apartment was on West 116th Street.]

. . . .

That winter Mrs. Rosen went to a beauty parlor for the first time. The women of her set were going, it seemed. It made your hair thicker to have it shampooed and waved, especially when it was starting to get grey. Though it did hurt a little, she grew used to manicures, too, after a while. Mrs. Rosen even considered dieting. But, after a few attempts she gave it up. Just the things she shouldn't eat were the ones she liked best. After all, she was forty-four, though she knew no one would ever guess it, and, if, at that age you are a little plump, who is there to say anything against it? She bought a fur coat that winter, seal, of course, with a great sweep to it and a hat to match, with a curved feather. Now, let one of her neighbors say something! She knew she looked mighty fine —as good as any one in her crowd. Why shouldn't she? Wasn't her husband a well-known manufacturer?

Rosen wasn't quite as busy as he had been, though the Acme Pants Company was getting along splendidly. But with things in good condition there was time to spare. He could have spent more time with his family had he cared to, but it seemed tiresome when he did. Irving annoyed him more than ever with his debates and arguments. In the evening he fell asleep over his paper—he didn't care for other literature except an occasional trade magazine. He still played cards with a few old friends he had made when he first came to America, and who, like himself, had prospered. He kept his coat on in the evenings now or wore the smoking jacket Carrie had given him. What if their friends came in—he had to look nice for their sakes, didn't he? There was a little room, off the living room, which the family spoke of as "Papa's den." There was a couch here, brought over from the Bronx, and a desk. Under pretense of being busy, Rosen would read in there, until he fell asleep.

The next year there was a great change in the Acme Pants Company. An opportunity came almost overnight and he and Abrams, after long discussions—at the factory this time—joined the Rex Pants Company, McKensey and Hamberg, partners, and the four formed the Rex Suit Company, Gentlemen's Ready-Tailored Suits. Ready-tailored suits, it seemed, were more in demand every day. The four had capital enough to swing something good and to introduce a new name. Until then, most ready-made suits were mere trade goods. But a few firms had learned the value of a trade name and advertising, and Rosen and Abrams agreed with McKensey and Hamberg that there was room for one more and great possibilities in the idea. They rented an immense loft building and were soon making and selling a line of ready-made suits under the name of the King Brand. They hired an advertising man, giving him an absurdly high salary, an office of his own, with a stenographer and all of that, and agreed to pay exorbitant rates to magazines just for the privilege of a half or a quarter of a page of blank space on which to advertise their wares. A few months later, tall, exquisite young men, in graceful poses, accompanied by impossibly thin young women or sporty dogs looked at you from the magazines under such captivating captions as "King's Suits for the Kings of America" or "Every Inch a King in a King Brand Suit."

Rosen was interested again. Here, expenses were mounting, though profits might mount, too. Now he could figure again, and plan and talk things over with Abrams. Abrams, however, was Abrams no longer. He was Adams, now. He had signed himself Adams when the new firm was organized. Even Rosen's name had changed — he dropped one more letter. The indefinite

Abraham G. had been altered and he blossomed forth as Abraham Lincoln Rose, to the delight of his children.

Irving was going to Columbia. He had joined a debating club and even his mother had to admit that, at this time, he was pretty much of a bore. He even called his father "Governor" on occasions and twirled a cane on holidays. He was "getting in with fine people" and dined at the homes of new friends, bringing back stories of families who didn't interrupt when you were talking and who had servants who knew how to serve meals. He felt he was going to be quite important and he wanted his family to live up to him.

Carrie was going to a private school—the only kind of school suitable for rich girls. It was in Riverside Drive, and she met some mighty fine girls there. Like Irving, she brought home stories showing the heights of other and the degradation of her own family.

"—We are such rich people and still we never have anything."

Carrie objected to her name, too, it seemed. "Carrie" was such a cheap name. Nobody would know you were rich with a name like that. She was going to be Carolyn after this. Carolyn Rose was a pretty name, wasn't it?

Carolyn loved to spend money. She had decided that the family was really wealthy, that it was all bluff about hard times and saving. She wanted a gold mesh bag and got it before Yvette even knew there were gold bags in the world. Carolyn had a fur coat as expensive as her mother's, but with a smarter, more girlish cut. She disregarded the stupid idea, made up by some one who didn't have the money, probably, that diamonds were for older people, and persuaded her parents to give her a big diamond ring, set in platinum, for her seventeenth birthday.

Yvette's clothes were always a bit loud, too extreme, even cheap looking. Although she paid big prices for them they were still tawdry. Carolyn's tastes were not quiet, but she managed to look "expensive." Her hair was black and sleek and she knew she had "style." She liked collars a bit higher than anyone else wore, when they were high, a bit lower, when low collars came in. She was no slavish follower of fashion, like Yvette. She added a bit of "elegance" to whatever fashion had dared ask for. She liked smooth broadcloth suits, much tailored, for day wear, and elaborate, chiffon evening frocks. She talked with an "accent," but not the kind her mother had. She said "cahnt" when she could remember it, and thought that one ought to have "tone." She had languid airs.

Mannie was growing into a nice child. He was quiet and he started to read when he was just a little fellow. Now you could find him, any time, curled up with a book he'd brought home from school. He didn't care much for out-of-door games. He was the first of the family to have literary leanings, though Dorothy read, too, when she couldn't find anything that pleased her better.

Dorothy was petted and spoiled by the whole family. She got things even before she could think to ask for them. Because there was never anything for her to be cross about the family said she "had a wonderful disposition," though she had a pouting mouth and did not smile very much.

Dorothy was "a little beauty." Although the family kept always with their own race and declared, on all possible occasions, their great pride in it and their aversion to associating with those of other faiths, the thing that delighted them most about Dorothy was, for some unexplainable reason, that everyone said "she looked like a Gentile." Mrs. Rose would repeat to her friends that people had said, "you'd never guess it—just like a Gentile that child looks." Her friends agreed and there was nothing in their minds but cordial congratulation over the fact. Dorothy had lighter hair than the others and grey eyes. She was a slender little thing, quiet, determined, impatient.

"We ought to have an automobile," she said, one day. That was in 1909, before cars had become as much of a necessity as they are now, and Dorothy was only twelve. Two weeks later, after many hugs, her father bought a car, a red one that would hold any five of them. Irving soon learned to drive it and later Carolyn and Dorothy learned, too. Grandma could never be persuaded to enter the car—it didn't look safe to her. Mrs. Rose rode, but it was always sitting stiffly erect with unrelaxed muscles. Rose asked Irving to drive him places, occasionally, when he was in a hurry. He never liked the automobile except as a convenience.

That year Grandma died. She was sick only a few days and didn't complain even then. The doctor came and fussed over her and finally a nurse came, but Grandma persuaded her daughter to send the nurse away. Grandma seemed quite content to die, and though the family was fond of her, her going did not cause any undue emotion. Mrs. Rose wept loudly at the funeral and Rose looked unusually solemn in the weeks that followed. He had been very fond of Grandma and had appreciated the little things she always loved doing for him. But, after all, as Mrs. Rose would say to her husband, "it ain't as if she was a baby at 72. It ain't as though Mamma ain't had everything money could buy, these last years. A grand life she's had, nothing to do and her own room and all. Many times she spoke of it. It's good we was able to give it to her. She was a good woman, but now she's gone and I can say I ain't got nothing to reproach myself for."

In 1910, when Yvette was twenty-four, she became engaged to marry MacDougal Adams. Already MacDougal was sales manager for the Rex Suit Company, and he was doing finely. He had grown into a handsome fellow who would be quite fat, one day, if he didn't diet carefully. He was crisply black-haired, ruddy-faced. He made friends easily and was jovial most of the time. He had no subtleties, but Yvette was not the one to notice. She considered him very modern and liked the way he "caught on to things." Her friends—and the announcement Yvette mailed to the newspapers—spoke of the affair as "a childhood romance," as indeed it was. It pleased the Roses and the Adams, too. They gave a reception at a hall on 125th Street to celebrate the occasion, each of the family inviting their special friends, with Dorothy and little Helen Nacker to pass flowers to the guests. There was a band behind artificial palms, and waiters in white aprons passed refreshments. Yvette wore a dress of pink and Carrie wore yellow. Carolyn didn't think the party fine enough, and Mannie and Dorothy didn't like it much, either. The rest of the family thought it a successful affair.

Mrs. Rose, Yvette and Carolyn spent the following weeks shopping. Yvette had to have a complete trousseau, starting with table linens and ending with silk stockings. Three months later Yvette and MacDougal were married at the Waldorf, with Carolyn and Maurice Adams as attendants. Only the most intimate friends were invited to the elaborate banquet which followed, though later there was an "informal reception" with much wine. MacDougal had just bought an automobile—black, though Yvette would have preferred a gayer color—and, after a short Atlantic City honeymoon the young couple took a new and elaborate apartment in Central Park West and settled down, with two maids, to domesticity.

"Ain't it grand, Papa?" Mrs. Rose had said to her husband after their first call on the young couple. And even Rose had to agree that even Yvette was getting all that could be expected.

Carolyn was "the young lady of the family," now. She was not as easily satisfied as Yvette had been. She called Yvette's crowd "loudly vulgar," though she was a trifle loud, herself, at times. She raised eyebrows and

drew away when fate included her in her sister's parties. She was glad when her sister married—now she could entertain her loud friends in her own home. Maybe Yvette would even tone down a little; she laughed too loud and had terrible taste in clothes. Her mother talked loudly, too, except when she tried very hard to remember—and it was terrible the way she shrieked and sing-songed when she grew excited—but, at least you could remonstrate with her.

The Harlem apartment didn't suit Carolyn at all. Here she was, out of school, nearly twenty—and living in—Harlem. She had gone to a series of morning lectures at one of the hotels and one of the lectures had been on furniture—it seemed all of the things in the Harlem apartment were entirely wrong. Carolyn knew this was true, too. Hadn't she been to other homes, where people knew things? They were rich and had—one maid—and she didn't know how to wait on the table—and the family treated her as if she were one of them. And Irving talked back to his father, rather impudently, even when company was there, and the car was a sight—she was ashamed to use it. The least they could have was a new car and a chauffeur.

Irving agreed with all of Carolyn's criticisms, excepting those which concerned himself. He was twenty-three, why shouldn't he have things nicer? Dorothy, going on fourteen, also found the Harlem home distasteful.

"A terrible neighborhood," said Dorothy, who became Dorothea, that year. "It's too far from school and we do need a new car. I'm ashamed to tell anyone where I live. I want a big room and my own bath, so I can ask girls to stay all night, if I want to."

Rose sighed, said the family would break him and times were hard. Mrs. Rose sighed, too. Still, Harlem wasn't such a friendly neighborhood—the other couldn't be worse. And with only one girl there was too much for her to do. If they had a man to drive the car and a cook, maybe—

Carolyn went house-hunting alone. She said she'd take the others with her "when she found something." Two weeks later she took her mother and Dorothea to see the new apartment. It was a foregone conclusion with Carolyn that they would take it—just the formality of mailing the lease for her father's signature.

The apartment was on Riverside Drive, in a huge building of cream-colored brick. At the door was a Negro uniformed in dark green, and another similarly clad attended the mirrored elevator. The halls had Oriental rugs and were lit and draped with an expensiveness that suited even Carolyn. Of course it was pretty far out on the Drive—but it looked rich—and living on the Drive was rather grand, at that. Mrs. Rose was speechless at first, but later the apartment seemed quite satisfying. She liked the ornateness, the grandeur—it was even finer than Yvette's, than any of her friends. Why shouldn't it be, with Abe a partner in a big factory and all—?

The woodwork of the apartment was white enamel. There were little panels in the living room, waiting to be papered, and the dining room had a white enameled plate rail. The lighting fixtures were of the new "inverted" style, on heavy brass chains ending with carved brass holders of white frosted globes, There were French doors of mahogany leading into the living room and dining room, a huge butler's pantry with numerous shelves, a kitchen with a big hooded range and immense white sink, large bed rooms, four baths.

"If—if your Papa will pay for it," Mrs. Rose admitted weakly.

"Oh, he'll pay," said Carolyn, "why shouldn't he—a rich man like him?"

When the men of the family came to see the apartment Irving pronounced it "immense." Mr. Rose looked at the apartment, saw the library that he could have for his own, the big bedroom and bath—and gave in with unexpectedly little persuasion. After all

—his friends were living well—why shouldn't he? He was making money—the family might as well spend it. Didn't the way you live show how well you were doing? Not that he was making so much, of course, but, with Yvette married—if Carolyn wanted the apartment—

Mannie and Dorothea were rather indifferent. Still, Mannie was in prep school and cared most about books—even writing a poem occasionally. He was eighteen. At fourteen, Dorothea didn't care about details as long as they were moving. Her new room was nice and big. Still, they ought to have a new car —Dorothea was quite pouty over the old one.

Carolyn took charge of the furnishings of the new apartment. Mrs. Rose, with uplifted hands, declared her ignorance of periods "and such nonsenses," but begged her daughter not to spend too much money. "You know your Papa. There's a limit even with him."

Irving gave a long-winded dissertation about what to get and told about a fine apartment he had visited, rather down on the drive—two girls he knew, their father was a criminal lawyer. Carolyn didn't listen very closely. She knew what she wanted.

Accompanied by her most intimate friend, Eloise Morton, daughter of S. G. Morton, the box people (both of Eloise's parents had been born in America), Carolyn visited a number of shops. She called the big stores where Yvette traded "middle class," but she was afraid of the decorating shops and called the things in the windows "junk."

"You might like that old stuff," she said to Eloise, "but I can't see anything to it. Old chairs, stiff and funny—a hundred dollars apiece and then a fake, probably. A whole room full of that doesn't look like anything. I like things that show their full value, that you can tell cost a lot of money."

Eloise agreed that her friend had the right idea.

Carolyn didn't allow any mere furniture clerk to suggest or dictate to her. Hadn't she seen a lot of fine homes? Didn't she go to every new show in town and look especially at the stage settings? Hadn't she heard a furniture lecture? Who could advise her?

She didn't want her mother with her, she'd "simply spoil things if she started to talk." Carolyn and Eloise, alone, could give an impression of taste, elegance and riches. Carolyn decided on Adam furniture for the living room. If the ghosts of the brothers Adam groaned a bit Carolyn was too busy to hear. She liked "sets" for living rooms—didn't everyone have them?—so she chose a great davenport of mahogany with cane sides and back, motifs slightly after some of the Adam designs scattered over the woodwork. The upholstery was rose velour. There were two huge chairs of similar design, one a rocking chair. Other chairs were of cane and mahogany, one a Venetian, one a fireside. There was a great oblong table, too, that Carolyn knew showed good judgment, for it was of "dull antique mahogany." It, too, bore motifs of the house of Adam. There was a floor lamp with a rose shade and two table lamps to match and several pieces of "stylish" painted furniture, factory made. Carolyn looked with scorn on the little rugs that had seemed so fine a few years ago. She chose now an immense Oriental in rose and tan for the living room and a Chinese rug in dark blue to combine with the intricately carved Queen Anne furniture of the dining room.

There were elaborately patterned filet lace curtains throughout the house. Before this Mrs. Rose had always hemmed and hung the curtains. Now Carolyn gave the orders for them. The overdrapes and portieres were of rose velour, heavily lined, and, above the windows were elaborate valances, edged with fringe and wide gold braid. There were blue velour curtains in the dining-room.

In the bed rooms Carolyn's imagination had full play. Her parents' room was in mahogany with twin poster beds. Her own room was in ivory, cane inset. Dorothea's was white enameled, painted with blue scenes.

For the walls of the living room, between the panelling, Carolyn chose a scenic paper in grey. On this were to be hung elaborate oil paintings in scalloped gold frames: "A Scene at Twilight," "The Fisherman's Return." In the dining-room the paper was in a tapestry effect, red and blue fruit and flowers.

The family moved into the new apartment in October, 1911. The moving was simple for the old furniture was to be sold and professional movers attended to the packing of ornaments and dishes.

Mrs. Rose and Irving were impressed with the effects wrought by Carolyn's taste and her father's money, but it did not take the family long to settle down to the pleasures of life that Riverside Drive opened to them.

Moving to the Drive, the Roses made the final change in their name. Mannie, usually quiet, was the one to propose it.

"Rose is so—so peculiar," said Mannie. "Anyone could tell it had been something else, Rosen or worse. I'm eighteen and go to college this fall. I'm not going to have a name so—so ordinary. Let's change it to Ross. That's not distinctive, but it isn't queer or foreign. I'm changing my first name just a little, too. I've never been called Emanuel, anyhow. Mannie isn't a name at all. I'm going to register at college as Manning Ross."

There was no letter-box to announce the change, but the elevator man knew that the new occupants of Apartment 31—he wrote the names down with a blurring stub of a pencil to be sure to remember them—were Mr. and Mrs. A. Lincoln Ross, two young Misses Ross and two young men, Irving and Manning.

The family had liked Rose—but there might be something in what Manning had said. But no more changes! Mr. Ross put his foot down, this time. He was meeting important men in business, Gentiles, and he didn't want any more monkey-business about names, Ross was all right and Ross it would have to stay. And it did.

Mrs. Ross took great delight in getting her new servants. It made her feel superior and important, driving up to an employment agent and interviewing prospective retainers. She took Carolyn along for advice and counsel—Carolyn went out a lot and knew about such things.

Carolyn would have liked a retinue, but Ross rebelled—expenses were awful and each servant was another mouth to feed. The old "girl" had got married so they finally chose a cook who was not above helping with other things, a waitress who could combine housework with waiting, and a chauffeur. Besides, the washerwoman would still come in for two days each week.

Soon after the family was settled Mr. Ross bought a big limousine, American made, but one Carolyn thought looked really expensive. The chauffeur was in uniform, of course. He happened to be a young Irish boy and it seemed to Carolyn, sometimes, that he smiled a bit sarcastically and annoyingly as he held the door open for them, especially after her mother had spoken with an accent or her old sing-song.

Mr. Ross didn't object to the new luxuries. It was much more comfortable driving to the office in the limousine than waiting for Irving or one of the girls to take him or depending on less comfortable modes of transportation. He had more room to himself, too. He liked the way the new cook prepared things—he was getting indigestion and had to be careful about what he ate—though he still remembered with real emotion the pot roasts and fish and stuffed goose that Grandma had delighted to prepare. These new dishes—salads and things like that—everything served separately—you could get used to it—it didn't make much difference—here he was, used to a maid in cap and apron, waiting on table—and Minnie used to it, too, excepting when she forgot and talked to her or reached across the table for things. Still, Minnie meant well, a good woman, rather fat these last years, but

a good woman who loved her family—none of this new foolishness some women had, he'd noticed—

Mr. Ross didn't pay much attention to women. He never had. He saw what fine girls his daughters were, that was about all. He couldn't have recognized half a dozen of their best friends, whom he saw constantly at his home, if he had passed them on the street.

His business—that was something. Still, even that didn't keep him busy, the way it used to. This new arrangement, the offices and the factory separated—of course it was for the best. He could always go over to the factory when he wanted to, though there wasn't much need—machinery he didn't understand, everything in such order—with a head for every little department, not to mention the big ones. And, with four partners you couldn't say things as if it were your own business. Mr. Ross was fifty-three, but it hadn't been an easy fifty-three years and things had gone along rather rapidly for a while. Not that he was an old man—far from it. Still, things that had passed seemed pleasanter than they had seemed in the passing—and things to some lacked luster.

This wasn't age—certainly not—he felt as well as he had twenty years ago, practically. Give him some real work to do, you'd find out. But there was so little to do, now. You'd go down to the office about ten and dictate a few letters and potter around with things. You'd examine "swatches" and find that an expert had already given them a chemical analysis. You'd go to luncheon and be careful about what you ate. After luncheon, a little sleepily, you'd dictate more letters, if there were any more and see a few men on business, young upstarts, most likely, or Gentiles who wanted something for nothing—or consult with your partners. Then, you'd drive home after a while and read the paper or listen to Carolyn play on the new player piano or talk with Dorothea, though there wasn't much to talk about. Dinner then, and a game with Adams, though he had rheumatism these last years and wasn't the man he had been. Or Moss would drive over. There was a club, even, if you cared to go to it—a lot of strange men who didn't care anything about you—a club—at least they were of your race—Dorothea was always asking questions about why the family didn't mix with other people—such notions a child gets—

The Rex Suit Company was still progressing. The great factories were outside New York, but the business offices occupied a whole floor of an office building, each partner with his own mahogany furnished office, with its row of bells and its private stenographers. There was an expert to decide each thing. MacDougal was in the sales department and Maurice, the younger Adams boy, was advertising manager—a big advertising agent had charge of all of the advertising, of course. And what advertising the firm did, too! Double pages in the popular weeklies at thousands of dollars a page. Everyone was familiar with the "Kingly Men." Girls cut them out and mounted them for their rooms. "America's Kings in King's Suits" had been familiar enough to get applause at a musical comedy when it was used to introduce two juveniles. "Every Inch a King for the Kings of Creation" and other well-known slogans ran in letters four feet high above the artist's conception of the "Kingly Man" on the billboards.

Each year there was an ornate catalogue of the styles, "for the Prep Youth," "for the College Man," "for the Younger Set," "for the Older Fellows." Hundreds of merchants all over the country displayed King Brand signs and carried King Brand suits. The Rex Company had invented half sizes, adjustable models and the giving with each suit of an extra bit of the goods and two extra buttons for mending. There wasn't much you could plan about for the Rex Company. Likely as not, someone else would have thought of it first, anyway.

Mr. Ross was accustomed to meeting men, now. He liked to meet them, in business. He would listen, weigh what they said, learn from them. He never talked much. He always retained his look of severity. He was known as "a crackerjack of a business man," "a man you couldn't put anything over on," but the other partners were good business men, too. There was nothing for Mr. Ross to work for.

Outside of business he had little. His family still seemed apart, yet he would have done anything to have saved them trouble or pain. He liked Yvette because she was frank and lively, but, these last years he liked Dorothea, too, though there was nothing against Carolyn, a fine girl, if she did like to spend money. Minnie was all right—the boys would be, too, when they got a little older and settled down.

Mr. Ross didn't mind listening to the mechanical piano or the Victrola at home, but he did not care for other kinds of music. Concerts made him miserable and fidgety. He saw nothing in them and after several for charity and one visit to the opera he refused to partake of music outside of the home. He had never learned to like reading. He was still content with the daily papers and glanced, occasionally, at a weekly devoted to current events. He knew nothing about art and said so. He didn't want to be bothered with "such notions." Drama of all kinds bored him and even musical comedies entertained him only for a little while. Usually he got to thinking of business in the midst of things and lost all consciousness of what was going on.

Mr. Ross had no social ambitions, so, with no business worries and no outside interests, his days began to drag unpleasantly. He thought often of other days, of "the other side"; when he had been planning to come to America—he was glad that was over, of MacDougal Street, the hard work he had done there, the long hours, the overtime, the little economies so both ends would meet, then the newer tenement, with things a little easier, the beginnings of the factory—those had been real days, staying awake planning to meet bills, figuring to the dollar how to get enough money to pay the "help" and have enough left for living expenses, then Harlem and now Riverside. It was good to have planned and worked. Still, now he was used to his comforts. He liked space and quiet and the car—but, with nothing to do—

Mrs. Ross had long since relaxed her anxiety over her husband. He had never talked business and he seemed just like always, willing to listen to her stories of how she had spent the day. Mrs. Ross was quite content with the Drive. The aloofness of the neighbors, that had been disagreeable to her in Harlem, became one of her own characteristics now. She became more and more aware of her own importance. She had disliked the way "outsiders" and Gentiles had treated her, years before. Now, her last vestige of humbleness gone, she felt herself more than "as good as anyone." Wasn't she Mrs. A. Lincoln Ross, wife of Ross of the Rex Suit Company, a real figure in New York? Didn't she get her picture in the paper when she gave money to charity? Didn't people treat her with respect as soon as they found out who she was? She was frankly fat, but she didn't mind. She had expensive dressmakers and tailors and she thought the results of her toilet satisfactory. After all, she was nearly fifty.

Her voice had toned down, during the years, as had Yvette's. When talking with those she considered important, she even tried to put an elegant swing into her sentences. Usually, though, her voice was accented, ordinary, uninteresting. She still made errors and sometimes quite a lot of sing-song crept in.

In the morning Mrs. Ross attended to her household affairs, giving directions to the servants, ordering her own provisions over the telephone, even planning meals. She looked into the ice-box to see what provisions remained, rubbed fingers across furniture for dust, examined linens. She was a good

housekeeper. In the afternoon, with Yvette, whom she found most congenial, or an acquaintance, she went for a drive or shopped. She dropped most of her old friends who had not progressed and she had no sentimental regrets concerning them. A few earlier friends she kept up with, asking them for luncheon or for a drive, with a hint of patronage. Through her daughters she met other women of her own age and circumstances. To these she tried to be pleasant, using her best language and manners. She had no intimacies with these women.

During the second year of the family's residence on the Drive, Mrs. Ross was asked to belong to several committees of important charitable organizations. She joined these gladly and gave generous sums. She liked the society of her own race. She did not feel at home with "outsiders" nor know what to say to them—she felt that they were constantly criticizing her. She had decided social ambitions, however, and wanted Mr. Ross to join a well-known club composed of members of his people. She was proud to know women who, a few years ago, or even now, were she less wealthy, would have ignored her. To the arts she was as indifferent as her husband.

Irving was a lawyer now. He had a nice office in one of the newer buildings devoted to professional men, but not much practice. His father found it just as convenient to give him some of the smaller business of the firm as to increase his allowance. When anything important came up Mr. Ross agreed with his partners that it was best to let a better-established lawyer handle the case.

Irving—who became Irwin about this time —could have joined a large firm as a junior member, but he preferred independence. He didn't like to work hard or long and he had heard of the tasks performed by the younger members of big firms. He liked to waste time, browsing around bookstores, walking through the lobbies of hotels, calling on friends. He had a large acquaintance with women and had as many dinner invitations as he could accept. Wasn't he a great catch, a young lawyer with a rich father? And good company.

At twenty-five, Irwin still loved an argument. Although never a great reader, he liked to pose as one, quoting well-known authorities, reading and talking about authors unknown to his hearers. His hair was always immaculately sleeked, though it had just a perceptible wave. He had his favorite manicurist at one of the larger hotels. He smoked an expensive brand of cigarette, carrying them in an elaborate silver and gold case and fitting each one carefully into an extremely long amber cigarette holder before smoking it. He used affected gestures, pounding on a table to emphasize a point he was making. He still wore nose-glasses, now large lensed and tortoise rimmed, and, from habit he held his head too high.

Irwin was proud of his acquaintance with half a dozen actresses of minor importance. These he took to teas, dinners and suppers, talking later as if the engagements had had special significance. He was careful about his acquaintance with other women, choosing those that were, to him, of social importance. He had the same distrust his parents had for those outside of his own race. He never attended services at a synagogue, but to him religion and race were intermingled and he did not attempt to differentiate between them. Since boyhood he had suffered from prejudice far more than his sisters. He was proud to associate with "outsiders," liked to think he looked and spoke and acted like one of them. But he would never have married a Gentile.

Carolyn was now the liveliest member of the Riverside Drive household. She didn't think much of race and creed. She envied other women in some things, but she thought herself all that was desirable and attractive. She liked best the people of her own race, but she preferred them with American or English accents, appearance and accomplishments. She liked to associate only with people of great wealth. Always gowned a bit ahead of the fashion, perfectly groomed, silky, smooth, crisp, she went to the theater, evenings and matinées, to luncheons and to parties, giggling and laughing, quite moderately, of course, and had a gay time. She loved musical comedy and after-theater suppers. She didn't care for the opera, but even the most serious drama could give her something to giggle about afterwards. Her hair and eyes were dark with something of the Orient about them, but her skin was fairer and clearer than her mother's or Yvette's, her round little nose was always white with powder and her eyebrows narrow and smooth, her lips and cheeks pinkly attractive.

You could see Carolyn almost any fair afternoon on the Avenue with Eloise or Helen or Mary Louise, stopping in at one little shop for a bit of lingerie, at another for flowers. They spent money with no thought of its value. Most of them could not remember poverty. Those who could found spending the best method of forgetting. Occasionally they met several of "the boys" for tea. When they didn't they bought tea for themselves at Maillards, usually, or the Plaza. There was always a car waiting and they wore low pumps or slippers and the thinnest of stockings even when the snow was on the ground.

Carolyn "went with" Jack Morton, Eloise's brother. She had met Eloise at the Riverside Drive school. Jack was at Harvard, then, but he was graduated a year later and was "catching on" nicely in his father's box factory. The Mortons thought the Rosses a step below them socially, for the Mortons were a little farther removed from "the old country." Outside of that, they liked Carolyn. So no one was surprised, when, in 1914, when Carolyn was twenty-three, she announced her engagement to Jack. The Rosses thought Carolyn had "done well," as indeed she had, for Jack Morton was a likable fellow, full of practical jokes and fond of poker playing, but on the whole quite a desirable husband.

Ross gave his daughter a diamond laval-liere for an engagement present, and as Carolyn picked it out herself it was quite glittering. He promised her the furniture for her new apartment as a wedding present. The Mortons gave Carolyn a small car, green, with cushions to match, which she pronounced "a young wonder." They had an engagement "at home" and were married a few months later at one of the newer hotels. Carolyn hoped that it was quite evident to the friends of both families that they were both very wealthy.

The young couple took a three weeks' trip to Florida—Jack couldn't stay away from the business longer than that. Then they went to the Astor, but Carolyn wanted to entertain her friends and a hotel does keep you cooped up so. She and Jack finally decided on a small apartment in a high-priced new building in Park Avenue. They had only one maid to start with for they both preferred eating at restaurants. With the little car you could eat at a different place and go to a show or some place every night.

Without Carolyn the Riverside Drive apartment seemed quiet. Manning went to Harvard for a year, dissatisfied with the un-exclusiveness of Columbia.

Dorothea liked school, too, and was now taking a few harmless courses, which gave her something to do, though they didn't satisfy her. Nothing quite pleased Dorothea. She hadn't been satisfied with Carolyn's school—girls of only one creed went there, so narrow. Dorothea said that school was a joke. She had chosen a more expensive school, patronized by daughters of rich men generally. Her new study courses were at Columbia and with private teachers. Mr. Ross didn't like them.

"It isn't as if she had to be a teacher," he said. "A girl can have too much book-learning."

But Dorothy went. She had always been different. Her clothes, for one thing. Couldn't she have had anything she wanted? Look at Carolyn—always dressed like a picture—the family had to admit it, themselves. Even Yvette, though she liked bright colors, was a good dresser. It wasn't as if Dorothea was economical. She spent as much as Carolyn did. Carolyn wore things that "looked expensive," rich broadcloth, elaborate furs—Dorothea preferred rough tweeds. She paid extraordinary sums for little suits that Mrs. Ross thought looked as if she's got them for twenty dollars in Third Avenue. They were of mixed weaves, in grey or tan and she wore big tailored collars over her coats, not mannish looking or freakish, just plain. She paid fifty dollars for her little round velour hats. She wore heavy gloves and shoes, even when she went out with Carolyn, sleek in white gloves, patent leather pumps and furs. Dorothea paid huge prices for plain little evening frocks which she bought at exclusive little places. Even then she was not satisfied.

Dorothea wore a perpetual little pout—something had always just gone wrong. She spent her time wondering what to do, dipping in "courses" on a variety of subjects, at settlement work, "going with people she didn't have to associate with," her mother thought. Clad in a trim-fitting habit she rode whole mornings in Central Park. She exhibited funny little Belgian Griffins at shows. She went to benefits and tournaments. Yet she was always a trifle "put out," a bit bored. Things weren't ever good enough, or quite what she had expected.

For her twenties birthday Dorothea asked for and received a new car, a good-looking foreign-made roadster. About time the family had more than one car! She didn't want a chauffeur. Hadn't she been driving as long as she could remember, learning on the old red one? She liked driving the car best of all.

The family, the family's friends, what anyone said or did—all displeased Dorothea. She made sport of Irwin's pet affectations to his face, to her mother's horror. She called Yvette's things "impossible" and made fun of Carolyn's diamonds. She treated her mother as a person of no consequence, never asking her opinion about things. Although she had nothing in common with her father, she made a great fuss over him and he grew to like her better than any other member of his family. She took him out in her car, though he didn't quite enjoy the rides, expecting to be tipped over at every corner. Dorothea drove perfectly, with the recklessness of a racer.

Dorothea went with "outsiders." She seemed as much at home with members of other races as with her own. She'd bring in unexpected guests, making the family feel ill at ease. While guests were there she'd bring up bits of family history the rest were trying their hardest to keep out of sight.

"Dad," she'd say, "here's someone wants to meet you. He's heard a lot about you. . . . Can you believe that less than twenty-five years ago Dad came to America with no money at all?" Then, with a little gesture and smile, "and now look at him." She'd throw an arm around her father, who, ill at ease, would greet the stranger.

If Mr. Ross had been unsuccessful, he would have looked like any of a thousand of his race whom you can see leaving the shops any evening at the closing hour. But his wealth haloed him. It was impossible to separate him from his money. Thin, stoop-shouldered, solemn, quiet and accented of speech, he stood for success. To Dorothea her father was immensely important. She was the first who had ever made much of him. It embarrassed him—he was a simple old fellow in many ways—but he liked it.

Mrs. Ross thought Dorothea didn't appreciate her.

"It's always her Dad, her Dad," she'd say, "never a word about how I worked when she was small or all I do for her—just Dad this, Dad that—and Irwin don't like—that you're

always bringing up old times, about Papa being a cutter. The other night when that fine Miss Tannenheim was here, you said it, when you was talking to that big blond fellow you brought in. . . ."

"You're a dear, Mother," Dorothea would give her mother the tiniest touch of a kiss on her broad cheek, "but Irv's a mess and he knows it. The Tannenheim person is a cheap old thing with a mean eye and she'll marry him some day, if he isn't watching."

"Dad," said Dorothea, one day. "Let's move. You can't guess how sick I am of Riverside Drive."

"What's the matter? Haven't you got things nice here?"

"Nice—on the Drive?"

"We're alway moving, it seems. Only four years ago. . . ."

"I know, Dad. That's just it. A man of your position ought to have a home. Apartments are nothing. This one is simply awful. Riverside Drive is fearfully ordinary, vulgar—don't you think so? Such a cheap collection of newly-rich. Dad, you ought to have your own home in town, anyhow, and something permanent in the country."

The idea of a home appealed to Mr. Ross He felt, now, that he had always wanted a real home. Dorothea called for him in the car and they explored the streets east of Fifth Avenue. Finally, without consulting the rest of the family, Ross bought a three-story house in East Sixty-fifth Street, just off Fifth Avenue.

"Mother will think this is terrible," Dorothea said as she kissed him, "but you and I like it, don't we? I know it cost an awful lot, Dad, but you can see it's really an investment. After it's made over a bit inside it will do for a family home for years. Imagine you—after all you've done—not having a family home!"

Ross really liked the house. It seemed almost—homelike. The rest of the family were not pleased. The married daughters—of course it was not their affair—but, they wondered if it was just the right thing. Of course, nice people lived in houses, but none of their friends. . . .

"That's why we bought it," said Dorothea.

Irwin "guessed it was all right." Manning was indifferent.

Mrs. Ross held up bejeweled hands and wailed,

"Oh, Dorothea, just as I'm beginning to get into things and can ask people here to a fine apartment on the Drive—an address I can be proud of—and here you buy an old house—I thought, a young girl like you would want things swell—here we've got servants and all—"

"Don't you worry," said Dorothea, "it will be 'swell' enough—awful word. And as for servants—"

The family moved to East Sixty-fifth Street in 1916. Dorothea didn't run around after furniture as those of her family who had chosen furniture before her had done. She turned the whole house over to Miss Lessing, in Madison Avenue. Miss Lessing's corps of exquisitely minded young men came in, looked around, made sketches, brought drapery material and wood finishes, all of which Dorothea examined critically.

"At last we'll have some place we can ask our friends," she said.

The home in East Sixty-fifth Street was rather nice. It was done in English things, mostly, painted walls and rather soft taffetas. There were some big easy chairs that could be pulled around, comfortably, in front of the fireplace. Perhaps because of its seeming simplicity and the plainness of the walls and carpets Mr. Ross liked it more than any home he had ever had. He felt it belonged to him. Mrs. Ross never liked it.

"It's too plain," she said, "nothing to it. No one would believe how much it cost you, Papa. Mrs. Sinsheimer has got an apartment on Park Avenue, just a block from Carolyn. Fourteen rooms. She had a decorator, too, but he got different things than this—gold furniture. It looks like something. We had a fine place on Riverside Drive and Dorothea drags us here, where there ain't even lights enough to see by, at night."

Still, Mrs. Ross found out, from what people said, that there must be something desirable about the new home. She even acquired a bit of the patter Dorothea used, pointing, with something like pride, to "a real Chippendale escritoire, one of the nicest examples in America," and "some Wedgewood placques, three, from an original set of four, you know," and "of course, we are getting old and it's nice we can have a home where we can gather the sort of things we like, as a background."

Irwin "didn't think much of the place, myself," but it was a good idea, the old folks having a home . . . he was glad he didn't have to be ashamed of it, though, for his part . . . now, that country place Dorothea was talking about. . . .

Yes, Dorothea had been talking about a country place. After they were settled in the new home, she continued to talk. They had five servants now—they wouldn't even need two sets—Dad could see now it took just that many to run any kind of a house—and they could just shut up the town house in Spring and open it in Fall. All the family could be there, too, Yvette and the new baby, and Carolyn and their husbands . . . "a real family together. Dad, a permanent family like ours ought to have a decent country place."

The country place was on Long Island, finally. Dorothea picked it out and put the decorations in the hands of the same firm of decorators, who did rather startling things with color wicker, chintz and tiled floors.

It was near a famous country club, and Dorothea knew, as did the rest of them, that none of the men of her family could ever be admitted. It didn't seem fair to her, of course, and yet . . . Dad was a great one—there oughtn't be any place Dad couldn't get into. But Dad didn't care. Though, from things he said, Dorothea knew he had felt things . . . expected them. He hadn't even hoped this much of life. Irwin didn't like being left out of things . . . and yet, Dorothea, looking at Irwin, hearing him argue in his rather nasal tone, gesturing with his long amber cigarette holder, couldn't blame members of the club, exactly. . . . It wasn't because of Irwin's race . . . maybe the members, themselves, weren't so wonderful . . . and yet there were her two brothers-in-law, one rather fat, both slow-minded, card-playing, a bit loud and blatant, always bringing money into the conversation. . . . Yvette, loud, laughing, so heavy, mentally, Carolyn, with her cheap talk of money and spending . . . her mother . . . it wasn't fair to criticize her, her mother'd had a hard time of it when she was young, and yet. . . .

Dorothea knew that, somehow, the man she liked didn't belong to her race. Hamilton Fournier, now . . . of course, if she'd marry him, there be an awful talk, lots of crying and going on about religion . . . that sort of thing. She could hear her mother . . . she remembered when Freda Moss married —"He'll throw it up to you." Yet, if you are proud of your race . . . doesn't that . . . can you have a thing "thrown up to you" that you are proud of? It was a big problem, too big for Dorothea. She felt that she'd always had everything she wanted . . . she could keep on having. . . .

The family settled down comfortably in the new home, Manning with them. He was going to school in town, now.

Mrs. Ross was getting to like the new home better . . . it wasn't Riverside, of course, but people didn't look down on her here. She was even getting in with Mrs. Rosenblatt—now that she lived near her. That crowd—she didn't have their education, but what of it, she was richer than most of them.

Who were they, to be so exclusive? Maybe, by next year, if she donated to their Orphan's Nursery Fund. . . .

Mr. Ross' indigestion seemed a little worse. The doctor came to see him several times each week and he had to be more careful with his diet. There seemed to be less to do at the office. He could retire, of course, but that would take away the only interesting thing he had—the few hours at the office. He even tried outdoor exercise, but after one attempt, he gave up golf as impossible. He gave to organized charities rather liberally and was even appointed on a committee which he attended—he knew it was his money they wanted. He would sit, as he had always sat in the evening, falling asleep over his paper, or bundled up beyond the necessity of the weather, he would climb into the car and spend a few hours with an old friend, or someone would come to see him, playing cards, as always. But a few of the old friends had died, another had moved away . . . there had never been many of them. He was just an old man, and lonesome, with nothing interesting to do or think about. . . .

Manning stopped school the year after the family moved into their new home. He had had a year at Harvard and a year or so at art school. Now, nearly twenty-two, he felt that he was a sculptor. His father was disappointed—Manning had started out a nice boy —it did seem that one of the boys. . . .

But Manning shrugged sensitive shoulders at anything as crude as the clothing business, even wholesale. His soul was not in such things. And Mr. Ross had to admit that the position of model was about the only one in the establishment that Manning could have filled. Manning went in, rather heavily, for the arts that the rest of the family had neglected. Of course Dorothea read, but Manning thought she skimmed too lightly over real literature. And Irwin—an impossible, material fellow.

Manning wore his hair a trifle long. He talked knowingly of Byzantine enamels and the School of Troyes. He knew Della Robbia and the Della-Cruscans. There was nothing he didn't know about French ivories. He knew how champlevé enamelling differed from other methods . . . there were few mysteries for Manning. His personal contributions to Wanty consisted of fantastic heads, influenced slightly by the French of the Fourteenth Century, in bas-relief—very flat relief, of course.

Manning's friends felt they formed a real part of New York's "serious Bohemia." They ate in "unexploited" Greenwich Village restaurants, never complaining about the poorly cooked food, sitting for hours at the bare-painted tables, talking eagerly in the dim candle or lamp light. They expressed disgust when "uptowners" discovered their retreats and sometimes moved elsewhere. You could find them every Saturday and Sunday night in parties of from four to ten, at the Brevoort, sometimes with pretty girls who didn't listen to what they were saying, sometimes with homely little "artistic" ones, hung with soiled embroidered smocks who listened too eagerly, talking of life and art, revolution and undiscovered genius.

There was no question that Manning's father should continue his allowance—there is no money in sincere art these days. Manning knew that even his father must recognize that. Manning spent his summer with the family on Long Island—it was hot in town. But, when one's family is of the bourgeoisie, it does draw one's energy so. In the autumn Manning decided he must have a real studio, some place he could work in and expand, going to "the town house" for week-ends. Having one's family uptown was quite all right, of course—but you couldn't expect an artist to live with them.

Mr. Ross agreed to the studio. He was

getting accustomed to Dorothea's friends, unbelievers though they were. He found he could not accept the artistic friends that Manning thought so delightful.

Manning found his studio, finally. The rent was terrific, of course, but the building had been rebuilt at great expense and was absolutely desirable in location, construction, everything. He furnished it himself in Italian and Spanish renaissance reproduction things. Rather nice! When it was finished—though they probably couldn't "get it," he'd let the family see it.

One Sunday, after a family reunion dinner, Manning announced that his studio was done. If the family liked they might all run down that way—a sort of informal reception—of course, they probably couldn't understand it all.

It was in the Village, of course. Did they think the Village was slumming? Uptown people did. But that's where you'd find real thought, people who accomplished things.

"Why, my new studio has real atmosphere"—Manning ran his fingers through his hair as he spoke. "It's in a wonderful old building, magnificent lines and the architect left them all—it's just the inside he's remodeled. I've the third floor front, two magnificent rooms, a huge fireplace, some lovely Italian things . . . and the view from the window is so quaint and artistic . . . of course you may not understand it . . . this family . . . it's just a block from Washington Square."

"Why, that's where . . ." began Mrs. Ross. Irwin silenced her.

"Don't begin old times, Mamma. Most of us haven't as long memories as you," he said.

"Come on, now that we're all here, let's go down," Manning went on. "I want you to see something really artistic. A friend of mine, DuBroil—I think you've met him—did me a stunning name plate in copper, just my name, Manning Cuyler Ross. I'm so glad I took Cuyler for a middle name last year. And there is just the single word, 'masks.' I thought it was—rather good. And I've a stunning bit of tapestry on the south wall. Come on—you've got your cars here, we'd better get started—"

It was a pleasant drive. The three cars drew up, almost at once, in front of Manning's studio, as he, in the first car, pointed it out to them.

They made quite a party as they turned out in front of the building—a prosperous American family—Mr. and Mrs. Lincoln Ross, well-dressed, commanding, in their fifties, which isn't old these days; Mac-Dougal Adams, plump, pompous; Yvette Ross Adams, in handsome furs and silks; Jack Morton, sleek, black-haired; his always exquisitely gowned wife, Carolyn Ross Morton; Irwin Ross, in a well-fitting cutaway, eyebrows raised inquiringly, chatting alertly; Dorothea Ross, attractive and girlish in rough tan homespun, and Manning Cuyler Ross, their host, pleasantly artistic.

"Here's the place," said Manning. "No elevator, real Bohemia, three flights up, uncarpeted stairs. Come on, Mother."

Mrs. Ross was strangely pale, and on the faces of Yvette and Irwin there were curious shadows. The rest, save for Mr. Ross, were too young to remember. As for him he broke, for the first time in years, into a broad smile. Manning went rattling on.

"This," he proclaimed, "is the way to live! None of your middle-class fripperies. Plain living, high thinking—this is the life!"

They came to the studio at last, and all stood about in silence while Manning explained its charms—the clear light, the plain old woodwork, the lovely view of the square, the remote, old-world atmosphere. In the midst of his oratory Mr. Ross sidled up to Mamma Ross and reached stealthy for her hand.

"Do you remember, Minnie," he whispered, "this room—this old place—those old days—"

"Hush," said Mamma Ross, "the children will hear you."

AMERICANIZATION: A MOVIE
H. L. Mencken was an admirer of the work of WILLIAM GROPPER,
whose appearances in *The Smart Set*
helped launch his career
as a leading magazine illustrator.

Reel I: 0%

Reel II: 10%

Reel III: 50%

Reel IV: 100%

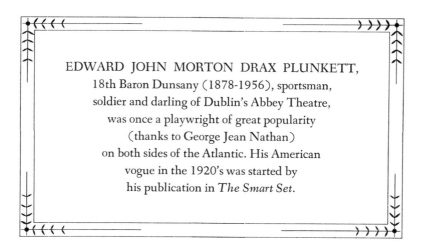

EDWARD JOHN MORTON DRAX PLUNKETT,
18th Baron Dunsany (1878-1956), sportsman,
soldier and darling of Dublin's Abbey Theatre,
was once a playwright of great popularity
(thanks to George Jean Nathan)
on both sides of the Atlantic. His American
vogue in the 1920's was started by
his publication in *The Smart Set*.

The Three Infernal Jokes

LORD DUNSANY

This is the story that the desolate man told to me on the lonely Highland road one autumn evening with winter coming on and the stags roaring.

The saddening twilight, the mountain already black, the dreadful melancholy of the stags' voices, his friendless, mournful face, all seemed to be of some most sorrowful play staged in that valley by an outcast god, a lonely play of which the hills were part and he the only actor.

For long we watch each other drawing out of the solitudes of those forsaken spaces. Then when we met he spoke.

"I will tell you a thing that will make you die of laughter. I will keep it to myself no longer. But first I must tell you how I came by it."

I do not give the story in his words with all his woful interjections and the misery of his frantic self-reproaches, for I would not convey unnecessarily to my readers that atmosphere of sadness that was about all he said, and that seemed to go with him wherever he moved.

It seems that he had been a member of a club, a West-end club he called it, a respectable but quite inferior affair, probably in the city; agents belonged to it, fire insurance mostly, but life insurance and motor agents, too; it was, in fact, a touts' club.

It seems that a few of them one evening, forgetting for a moment their encyclopedias and non-stop tires, were talking loudly over a card-table when the game had ended about their personal virtues, and a very little man with waxed mustaches who disliked the taste of wine was boasting heartily of his temperance. It was then that he who told this mournful story, drawn on by the boasts of others, leaned forward a little over the green baize into the light of the two guttering candles and revealed, no doubt a little shyly, his own extraordinary virtue. One woman was to him as ugly as another.

And the silenced boasters rose and went home to bed leaving him all alone, as he supposed, with his unequalled virtue. And yet he was not alone; for, when the rest had gone, there arose a member out of a deep arm-chair at the dark end of the room and walked across to him, a man whose occupation he did not know and only now suspects.

"You have," said the stranger, "a surpassing virtue."

"I have no possible use for it," my poor friend replied.

"Then doubtless you would sell it cheap," said the stranger.

Something in the man's manner or appearance made the desolate teller of this mournful tale feel his own inferiority, which probably made him feel acutely shy, so that his mind abased itself as an Oriental does his body in the presence of a superior; or perhaps he was sleepy or merely a little drunk. Whatever it was, he only mumbled "Oh, yes," instead of contradicting so mad a remark. And the stranger led the way to the room where the telephone was.

"I think you will find my firm will give you a good price for it," he said; and without more ado he began with a pair of pincers to cut the wire of the telephone and the receiver. The old waiter who looked after the

club they had left shuffling round the other room putting things away for the night.

"Whatever are you doing of?" said my friend.

"This way," said the stranger. Along a passage they went and away to the back of the club, and there the stranger leaned out of a window and fastened the severed wires to the lightning conductor. My friend has no doubt of that, a broad ribbon of copper, half an inch wide, perhaps wider, running down from the roof to the earth.

"Hell," said the stranger, with his mouth to the telephone, then silence for awhile with his ear to the receiver, leaning out of the window. And then my friend heard his poor virtue being several times repeated, and then words like "Yes" and "No."

"They offer you three jokes," said the stranger, "which shall make all who hear them simply die of laughter."

I think my friend was reluctant then to have anything more to do with it; he wanted to go home; he said he didn't want jokes.

"They think very highly of your virtue," said the stranger.

And at that, odd as it seems, my friend wavered, for logically if they thought highly of the goods they should have paid a higher price.

"Oh, all right," he said.

The extraordinary document that the agent drew from his pocket ran something like this: "I, ——— ———, in consideration of three new jokes received from Mr. Montagu-Montague, hereinafter to be called the agent, and warranted to be as by him stated and described, do assign to him, yield, abrogate and give up all recognitions, emoluments, perquisites or rewards due to me here or elsewhere on account of the following virtue, to wit: and that is to say . . . that all women are to me equally ugly." The last eight words being filled in in ink by Mr. Montagu-Montague.

My poor friend duly signed it.

"These are the jokes," said the agent.

They were boldly written on three slips of paper.

"They don't seem very funny," said the other, when he had read them.

"You are immune," said Mr. Montagu-Montague, "but anyone else who hears them will simply die of laughter; that we guarantee."

An American firm had bought at the price of waste paper a hundred thousand copies of the Dictionary of Electricity—written when electricity was new—and it had turned out that even at the time its author had not rightly grasped his subject—the firm had paid £10,000 to a respectable English paper (no other in fact than the *Briton*) for the use of its name; and to obtain orders for the *Briton* Dictionary of Electricity was the occupation of my unfortunate friend. He seems to have had a way with him. Apparently he knew by a glance at a man, or a look round at his garden, whether to recommend the book as "an absolutely up-to-date achievement, the finest thing of its kind in the world of modern science" or as "at once quaint and imperfect, a thing to buy and to keep as a tribute to those dear old times that are gone." So he went on with this quaint though usual business, putting aside the memory of that night as an occasion on which he had "somewhat exceeded" as they say in circles where a spade is called neither a spade nor an agricultural implement, but is never mentioned at all, being altogether too vulgar.

And then one night he put on his suit of dress clothes and found the three jokes in the pocket. That was perhaps a shock. He seems to have thought it over carefully then, and the end of it was he gave a dinner at the club to twenty of the members. The dinner would do no harm, he thought—might even help the business—and if the joke came off he would be a witty fellow, and two jokes still up his sleeve.

Whom he invited or how the dinner went I do not know, for he began to speak rapidly and come straight to the point, as a stick that nears a cataract suddenly goes faster and faster. The dinner was duly served, the port went round, the twenty men were smoking, two waiters loitered, when after carefully reading the worst of the jokes he told it down the table.

They laughed. One man accidentally inhaled his cigar smoke and spluttered; the two waiters overheard and tittered behind their hands; one man, a bit of a raconteur himself, quite clearly wished not to laugh, but his veins swelled dangerously in trying to keep it back and in the end he laughed, too. The joke had succeeded; my friend smiled at the thought; he wished to say little deprecating things to the man on his right, but the laughter did not stop and the waiters would not be silent. He waited, and waited wondering, the laughter went roaring on, distinctly louder now and the waiters as loud as any. It had gone on for three or four minutes when this frightful thought leaped up all at once in his mind: *it was forced laughter!*

How ever could anything have induced him to tell so foolish a joke? He saw its absurdity as in revelation, and the more he thought of it as these people laughed at him, even the waiters, too, the more he felt that he could never lift up his head with his brother touts again. And still the laughter went roaring and choking on. He was very angry. There was not much use in having a friend, he thought, if one silly joke could not be overlooked; he had fed them, too. And then he felt that he had no friends at all, and his anger faded away and a great unhappiness came down on him and he got quietly up and slunk from the room and slipped away from the club.

Poor man, he scarcely had the heart next morning to glance at the papers; but you did not need to glance at them; big type was bandied about that day as though it were common print, the words of the headlines stared at you, and the headlines said Twenty-Two Dead Men at a Club.

Yes, he saw it then: the laughter had not stopped, some had probably burst blood-vessels, some must have choked, some succumbed to nausea, heart-failure must have mercifully taken some, and they were his friends after all, and none had escaped, not even the waiters. It was that infernal joke.

He thought swiftly, and remembers, clear as a nightmare, the drive to Victoria station, the boat train to Dover, and going disguised to the boat; and on the boat, pleasantly smiling, almost obsequious, two constables that wished to speak for a moment with Mr. Watkyn Jones. That was his name.

In a third-class carriage with handcuffs on his wrist, with forced conversation when any, he returned between his captors to Victoria to be tried for murder at the High Court of Bow.

At the trial he was defended by a young lawyer of considerable ability who had gone into the Cabinet in order to enhance his forensic reputation, and he was ably defended. It is no exaggeration to say that the speech for the defense showed it to be usual, even natural and right, to give a dinner to twenty men and to slip away without ever saying a word, leaving all, with the waiters, dead. That was the impression left in the minds of the jury. And Mr. Watkyn Jones felt himself practically free, with all the advantages of his awful experience, and his two jokes intact. But lawyers are still experimenting with the new act which allows a prisoner to give evidence. They do not like to make no use of it for fear they may be thought not to know of the act, and a lawyer who is not in touch with the very latest laws is soon regarded as not being up to date, and he may drop as much as £50,000 a year in fees. And, therefore, though it always hangs their clients they hardly like to neglect it.

Mr. Watkyn Jones was put in the witness box. There he told the simple truth, and a very poor affair it seemed after the impassioned and beautiful things that were uttered by the counsel for the defense. Men and women had wept when they heard that. They did not weep when they heard Watkyn Jones. Some tittered. It no longer seemed a right and natural thing to leave one's guests all dead and to fly the country. Where was Justice, they asked, if anyone could do that? And when his story was told the judge rather happily asked if he could make him die of laughter, too. And what was the joke? For in so grave a place as a Court of Justice no fatal effects need be feared.

And hesitatingly the prisoner pulled from his pocket the three slips of paper; and perceived for the first time that the one on which the first joke had been written had become quite blank. Yet he could remember it, and only too clearly. And he told it from memory to the Court:

"An Irishman once on being asked by his master to buy him a morning paper said in his usual witty way, 'Arrah and begorrah and I will be after wishing you the top of the morning.'"

No joke is quite so good the second time it is told, it seems to lose something of its essence, but Watkyn Jones was not prepared for the awful stillness with which this one was received; nobody smiled; and it had killed twenty-two men. The joke was bad, devilish bad, counsel for the defense was frowning, and an usher was looking in a little bag for something the judge wanted. And at this moment, as though from far away, without his wishing it, there entered the prisoner's head and shone there and would not go, this old bad proverb "As well be hung for a sheep as for a lamb."

The jury seemed to be just about to retire. "I have another joke," said Watkyn Jones, and there and then he read from the second slip of paper. He watched the paper curiously to see if it would go blank, occupying his mind with so slight a thing as men in dire stress very often do, and the words were almost instantly expunged, swept swiftly as if by a hand, and he saw the paper before him as blank as the first. And they were laughing this time, judge, jury, counsel for the prosecution, audience, and all, and the grim men that watched him upon either side. There was no mistake about this joke.

He did not stay to see the end, and walked out with his eyes fixed on the ground, unable to bear a glance to the right or left.

And since then he has wandered, avoiding ports and roaming lonely places. Two years have known him on the Highland roads, often hungry, always friendless, always changing his district, wandering lonely on with his deadly joke.

Sometimes for a moment he will enter inns, driven by cold and hunger, and hear men in the evening telling jokes, and even challenging him, but he sits desolate and silent, lest his only weapon should escape from him and his last joke spread mourning in a hundred cots. His beard has grown and turned gray and is mixed with moss and weeds, so that no one, I think, not even the police, would recognize him now for that dappper tout that sold The Briton Dictionary of Electricity in such a different land.

He paused, his story told; and then his lips quivered as though he would say more, and I believe he intended there and then to yield up his deadly joke on that Highland road and go forth then with his three blank slips of paper, perhaps to a felon's cell with one more murder added to his crimes, but harmless at last to man. I therefore hurried on, and only heard him mumbling sadly behind me, standing, bowed and broken, all alone in the twilight, perhaps telling over and over even then the last infernal joke.

Harvard-educated WITTER BYNNER
was for many years an editor of
McClure's and has won many laurels
as a poet during the past half-
century. Today he lives in New
Mexico. His earliest poems were
published in *The Smart Set*.

Union Square

WITTER BYNNER

Two hags were huddled side by side
    At dawn, in Union Square,
Corrupt and silent. One had died;
    The other waited there.

One lay upon the bench, at rest
    From her nocturnal beat,
Newspapers round her face and breast,
    Her bonnet at her feet.

The other—sunken was her head,
    Her smile was drunk and dreary—
Not even knowing what she said,
    Called to me: "Hullo, dearie!"

FROM VOL. 40, MAY 1913

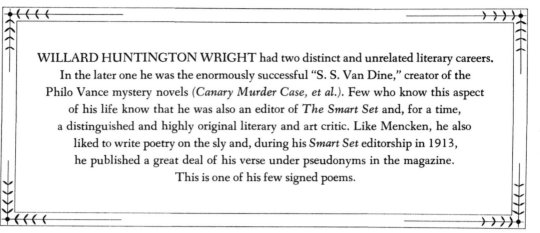

WILLARD HUNTINGTON WRIGHT had two distinct and unrelated literary careers.
In the later one he was the enormously successful "S. S. Van Dine," creator of the
Philo Vance mystery novels (*Canary Murder Case, et al.*). Few who know this aspect
of his life know that he was also an editor of *The Smart Set* and, for a time,
a distinguished and highly original literary and art critic. Like Mencken, he also
liked to write poetry on the sly and, during his *Smart Set* editorship in 1913,
he published a great deal of his verse under pseudonyms in the magazine.
This is one of his few signed poems.

Later

WILLARD HUNTINGTON WRIGHT

I WENT to the place where my youth took birth
In the slow, round kiss of an amorous girl,
When sonnets and lace were the measure of earth
When death was forgotten and life was a whirl.

I addled my brain with the memories flown
Of Heatherby Kaiser and Muriel Moore;
I thought of the women and men I had known,—
The glittering eyes and the bolt on the door—

The warm, gray walls and the odor of musk,
The wine, the piano, the glistening feet,
The eyes grown hazy like shadows at dusk,
The minstreling music that rose from the street.

I thought of Elise with her soft, gold hair;
And the buttonhook hung from the chandelier.
The spirit of passionate youth had been there—
But somehow the dream of it wasn't quite clear,

For the place had been altered; the walls were red,
And the woodwork was stained with a desolate brown;
And they told me a woman had lain in the bed
For a year and a half with the curtains down.

FROM VOL. 40, MAY 1913

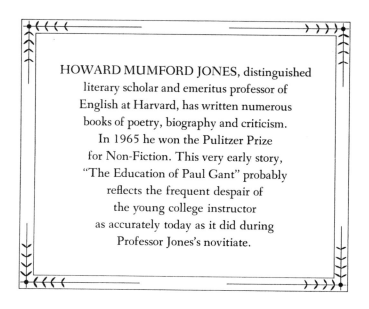

HOWARD MUMFORD JONES, distinguished
literary scholar and emeritus professor of
English at Harvard, has written numerous
books of poetry, biography and criticism.
In 1965 he won the Pulitzer Prize
for Non-Fiction. This very early story,
"The Education of Paul Gant" probably
reflects the frequent despair of
the young college instructor
as accurately today as it did during
Professor Jones's novitiate.

The Education of Paul Gant

HOWARD MUMFORD JONES

Paul Gant, Ph.D., instructor in English, closed his rickety desk in the dingy office in Main Hall, took from its top a faded green bag stuffed with Freshman themes for correction, put on his shabby overcoat, and went out of the building into the chilly November rain. The office he shared with four other harassed instructors in English; and if the light was so bad they had to burn electricity most of the day, they were lucky to have office room at all, since Main Hall, old, stately and inconvenient, was overcrowded with the departments it was supposed to house. The five

of them, one after the other, had visited the oculist, but the university wants classes taught, it is not interested in oculists.

It can not be said that Gant was extremely cheerful as he pushed home through the rain with his coat collar turned up.

In the first place, his overcoat had already outlasted more November rains than its makers ever intended; and in the second place, the bag, with its stuffing of badly scrawled, carelessly phrased compositions which he was vainly trying to keep dry, was a burden alike to his arm, his brain and his heart. And in the

FROM VOL. 58, FEBRUARY 1919

third place, there was the undeniable fact that he and Susan could not live on his salary of $1,200.

Something must be done, or—or—he was not quite sure of the alternative. Finally, he was tired—epically, immorally tired.

Education is a great thing. Especially higher education. The republic is founded on education. Moreover. we believe in lots of education, the higher the better. Every boy and girl is encouraged to go to college and so make the world safe for democracy. This being true, let us consider the case of Paul Gant, Ph.D.

Paul Gant, not yet even B.A., graduated from high school in your town at the head of his class. He was thin, lank, anemic, passionately fond of books. You will recall that you never had much to do with him, but he was always on the debating team, and you told him jocosely "he had swallowed the dictionary." Everybody said it would be a shame if he did not go to college. So he went to college—any college—your college. He spent four years there and was graduated with a B.A. degree. If you will get out your dusty diploma you will see that is the kind of degree you hold. You may remember his name on the Commencement program: "Paul Gant—major subject, English—Honors." You don't remember? Very well. It sounds like bridge but it is not. English is the subject the girls always take because they expect to teach and get married. Paul elected it because he liked to read books.

Now, among the English faculty the professor whom Paul especially admired, became interested in him. That was unfortunate. They talked about books. They would have done better had they talked about plumbing or aviation. The professor, who was a kindly soul, but impractical, told Paul he ought to "continue his studies." And Paul did.

He went to a university noted for the profundity of its scholarship and the size of its library, and enrolled as a candidate for the degree of Master of Arts in English. He bor-

rowed four hundred dollars at four per cent interest to do it. And for a year, in an atmosphere of terrific intellectual pressure, he ground away. He grubbed up the date of Mrs. Browning's birth and discovered it was wrong in most of the text-books, and the relation of Chaucer's final *e*'s to their Anglo-Saxon originals, and the indebtedness of *Selimus* (which is a play and not a patent medicine) to the tragedy of *Locrine*. Also he learned an Old English grammar by heart. Here is a sample: "Before *h* plus a consonant, *r* plus a consonant, *l* plus a consonant, and *h* final, *ae* breaks into *ea*, *ei* breaks into *ie*, and long *i*—."

I have forgotten what happens to long *i*. Also I have probably got it wrong. Let us return to Paul Gant.

When he had any time to spare, he did two things. Most of the time he worked on his master's thesis which bore the fascinating title: "The indebtedness of the Anglo-Saxon Poem of the *Phoenix* to the Latin Poem of Lactantius on the Same Subject." Maybe that wasn't it, but never mind.

And in the rest of his spare time Paul wondered vaguely what all this had to do with reading H. G. Wells and Robert Herrick.

By and by his thesis was "accepted" and he was "examined" by a committee of the graduate faculty. Let us pass over this. Then he stood in line with a herd of other candidates and a gray-haired man in a black gown pronounced a Latin incantation over them, and presto! Paul Gant, B.A. became Paul Gant, M.A. Susan, who had scrimped and saved out of her salary as a high school teacher of French in order to be there, nearly wept when the dean gave Paul his diploma, because she thought that now they could be married. They had been engaged two years. You will have to forgive Susan's unmaidenly boldness. Have you ever taught French in high school?

Paul and Susan were not married that summer. In the first place, there was that four hundred dollars with interest, and in the second place, Paul hadn't his doctor's degree. You have to have a doctor's degree before you can teach about Shelley properly. Paul got him a job in a small college that graciously overlooked his undoctored state in consideration of Paul's receiving $1,000 a year for teaching seventy-five Freshman how to write their mother tongue. Susan returned to her French classes in high school.

II

AT THE end of two years Paul had accomplished a miracle. Do not ask me how he did it. Probably it was education. He not only paid off the four hundred dollars with interest, but he had accumulated four hundred and fifty dollars besides. Also he had given his sister (whom he was partially supporting) two Christmas presents; he had given Susan the silk for a waist and the money for a hat; and, on her birthday, he had presented her with a pair of kid gloves.

Then he went to Susan's town. This was extravagance, but then, he had not seen her for a year and a half.

They concluded not to indulge in the riotous luxury of wedded bliss, but to go after the doctor's degree instead. Then Paul's salary would increase and they could be married. So Paul hied him to an older and even more erudite university and Susan sighed and looked into the mirror twice each morning before going to school. The reason was that Paul was now twenty-six and Susan twenty-five. No, that wasn't the reason. Have you ever taught French in a small town high school in the middle west?

Of course I realize that Paul should have waited on table or sold aluminum ware to the farmers' wives. All the successful men do that to go through college. But the doctor wouldn't let him wait on table and the time was too precious to peddle aluminum ware. Likewise, I realize that Paul should have hunted up another profession. But unfortunately, he thought he could teach. Also, he was right.

When you are in Paul's position, it takes two years—sometimes three, four or five years —to obtain a doctor's degree. They give it to you when they judge you are ready for it, not before. Among other things you have to prepare a suitable thesis—"an original contribution to knowledge" in your "field." You must hunt up somebody sufficiently dead and prove something about him, and the older and deader and more difficult your subject is, the higher your thesis ranks as a contribution to knowledge. Paul liked to write little, graceful essays (he did them rather well), but an original contribution to literature won't do. He gave up reading Arnold Bennett and Galsworthy and other unprofitable authors— what he wanted was a job—and made a study of the prepositions in Anglo-Saxon.

At the end of a year he had done very well. He had a drawer and a half full of Anglo-Saxon prepositions and their Middle English equivalents, all arranged on cards, and he had accumulated a fund of information about authors and books, and dates and editions, and sources that would have dazzled his audience, if he had had one. Also he had a cough.

At the end of three months spent in the summer session, he found one day in the university library a newly received pamphlet by a German student in a university Paul had never heard of, setting forth the doctrine of the Anglo-Saxon preposition completely and exhaustively. Four days later Susan received a letter from the Belleview Hospital, in consequence of which she drew her savings from the bank and traveled night and day to reach Paul before he died. But he didn't die.

III

PERHAPS, however, you are losing interest in this sort of thing. Let us skip a year.

Paul was now twenty-eight and Susan was twenty-seven. In the interval Paul had more or less recovered his health—less rather than more—and he had conceived a brand-new subject for his thesis: A New Theory

Concerning the Latin Works of Walter Mapes. You are still losing interest? So was Paul.

At the end of another eighteen months, Paul sat in a somber recitation hall, looking like a tired and timid victim of the Inquisition facing his judges. Around him and above him, in the tiers of seats, sat the members of the faculty of arts, or such numbers of them as cared to attend the torture. And they asked him questions. They asked him about Milton's theory of church government and about Gottfried von Strassburg and the plays of Hrothswita and Swinburne's religion and the inner meaning of Blake and Orm's *Ormulum* and the probable dates of Marie de France and Byron's relations to three different women and Shakespeare's grammar. And when Paul could, he answered them in a tired, spiritless voice (he had been preparing himself three weeks for the ordeal, using the *Cambridge History of English Literature* in fourteen volumes and quarts of black coffee by way of stimulants); and when he could not answer, he looked at them vaguely and murmured apologetically. Also he wondered whether they were ever going to stop and whether the room was really circular or was it Browning's dates that made it go round.

At length the chief inquisitor relented and the rest said they were satisfied, and Paul promptly fainted. Three weeks later, Paul Gant, M.A., became Paul Gant, Ph.D. And then he and Susan were married.

It is not our business to inquire into the next three weeks. At the end of that time Paul permitted himself an inventory of the situation. He had a debt of $635 with interest at five per cent to pay off; he was required to publish his thesis—it would cost him $150 or $200; and he had discovered that Susan was a dear and wonderful wife, but that two could not live as inexpensively as one.

To offset this side of the ledger, however, he had a position as instructor in English at a university. Let us call it your university. No? Then we will call it a State University. This position paid him $1,200 a year; and as you will see, this was $200 a year more than he had received from his teaching some years before. The difference was, no doubt, attributable to his doctor's degree. The faculty in English numbered sixteen; and in the course of twenty years, if enough older members died or quit or went elsewhere, Paul might hope to become a full professor at the opulent salary of $3,000 a year. This is about the wages of a master plumber.

The Allies were hanging on at Ypres and other unpronounceable names that year. Paul remembered vaguely something about an Austrian archduke, but as he had been reading mediæval Latin all year, you will have to forgive his lack of interest. He did not put the Allies in his inventory at all. That was a mistake.

Susan mothered him a good deal that summer. Paul's nerves were raspy, but he rather liked being fed egg-nogs and hearing Susan read from the works of Mr. Robert W. Chambers. If he had looked at himself with Susan's eyes, he would have seen a pallid, emaciated, "gangly" man with weak eyes and constantly twitching muscles. Or, no—he would not have seen that with Susan's eyes. But if he had looked at Susan with your eyes, dear reader, he would have seen that, though she was only twenty-nine, she looked thirty-five. Fortunately, he did not have your eyes.

IV

Paul was not thinking about his past as he plodded home; he was wondering, instead, about his future. He went over and over what the president of the university, a kindly, brusque, successful man of fifty, had told him in yesterday's interview, when, with the permission of the head of his department, Paul had requested an increase in salary. Gant had been awkward and embarrassed, and the president felt sorry for him.

"It's no use, Dr. Gant," he had said. "This is a war year. You can't get money out of the legislature for anything that does not directly and obviously pertain to the war."

"I've been here two years," timidly expostulated Paul.

"We're very well satisfied," hurriedly returned the president. "And your salary ought to be raised. But, Gant, the appropriations for the college of liberal arts have been cut down $24,000. I'm sorry for you. I'm sorry for anybody who has to struggle along on an income that was already meager in 1914. But I'm helpless—absolutely helpless."

The door of the office had opened at this point and the president's secretary put in his head.

"Major Dennis is here," he said, "about the training corps." It was evident even to Paul that the president was much more interested in the training corps than he was in Gant's salary. Don't blame the president. The training corps would bring an additional 400 students to the university. Paul picked up his hat, he remembered, and the president had made a vague noise in his throat intended to indicate sympathy. Then Gant had left—awkwardly, of course. He had not told Susan about his interview yet; perhaps that was why he kept reviewing the scene as he went home, trying to find some loophole, some unturned stone. But he could not. He would tell Susan tonight. Together, maybe, they could figure out something.

Paul was now near home. It was the same apartment house in which Dr. and Mrs. Paul Gant had been at home after September first, some months before. Before he reaches the doorway, let us indulge in a little figuring.

For the sum of $30 a month the Gants were permitted to occupy a large room with a bed that slid under the china-closet; a bath room containing a tub in which no one but an infant could bathe; a kitchenette intended for persons with Lilliputian appetites; a

dressing room six feet by eight; and two closets. Paul paid the electric light and the gas bills, but the heat, hot and cold water, and a gas range were miraculously furnished.

Paul likewise rented one-thirtieth of a janitor—when he could be found. You will readily see that this arrangement left them $65 a month to squander, but as Paul insisted on putting aside $10 a month to accumulate against his debts, the Gants were left $55 a month with which to buy furniture, dishes, clothes, food, light, books, entertainment, and vacations. Paul had reduced his debt to about $360, but his thesis—alas!—had not yet been printed. He would have made a brilliant financier.

Paul looked up through the rain at the window on the top floor where Susan usually sat waiting. Tonight Susan was not there. Perhaps she had not returned from the Red Cross rooms. Paul felt illogically resentful—he wanted Susan. When he had fitted his key to the lock, he paused and looked absently around him. It was not a nice neighborhood, but Paul had got used to that—except when some club woman asked Susan why they lived way off *there*. Then Paul was willing to murder almost anybody.

He stumbled toward the electric-light button when he entered his apartment. Something was wrong with the room. Was it—oh, the bed had been pulled out into the center of the floor. What was the matter? When Paul had turned the switch, he dropped his bag of themes on the floor where they fell with a dull, mushy sound. Susan was lying, fully dressed, on the bed.

She sat up. She looked at Paul. Paul had never seen her like that before. It was not that she had been crying, it was the hunted look in her eyes. He sat down on the bed beside her. She snuggled up to his wet overcoat.

"It's so co-old and dreary," she moaned.

"I'll telephone for some heat," said Paul

courageously, starting to get up.

"You can't," said Susan without interest. "The janitor got drunk and Mr. Whelpley discharged him, and he's still looking for somebody."

In summoning up his courage, Paul forgot about his interview with the president.

"You're tired, sweetheart," he said. "I'll start supper."

Susan let him get up. When she heard him clattering away in the kitchen, she tidied the bed and pushed it back into the gaping recess in the wall. That made it possible to reach the china-closet. Then she brought forward the dining-room table and spread a cloth on it—one of three. She then proceeded to set the table. When she had denuded a shelf in the china-closet, she paused and, leaning against the table, drew her hand, palm outward, across her forehead. She was a slender, palely attractive woman, still bearing the marks of her former occupation in the form of two deep lines between her eyebrows, a habit of nervously tapping the floor with her foot, and permanently impaired eyesight.

"Paul," she said in a low voice. She was not tapping her foot now. At the sound Gant hastily dropped a pan on the kitchen stove and entered the room. What was the matter? Susan stood with both hands flat on the table, her body slightly inclined toward him so that the electric light clung to her brown hair. Her face looked tired, and in her eyes was still that dumb look of suffering.

"What is it, Sue?" he cried sharply.

"I didn't go to the Red Cross this afternoon," began his wife, hiding her face. "I went to the doctor's."

Paul took a step toward her. Into his eyes came a look of stupefaction! That was replaced by troubled understanding.

"Not—?" he queried elliptically.

"Yes, Paul."

The Gants, husband and wife, stared at each other across the cheap table. The light made little pools of yellow on the dishes and shone dully from the buttons on Paul's vest.

V

A LONG moment went over them. Something was burning on the gas range, but neither was conscious of it. Susan still kept her head down, but now she was playing aimlessly with a knife and a fork. Paul stared at her as if he was never going to see her again. He could hear his watch ticking in his pocket.

"Now, what are we going to do?" he asked dully.

"I don't know, Paul," said Susan, raising her eyes. Then she added irrelevantly. "Bread has gone up to fifteen cents a loaf."

The Allies, being determined to figure in Paul's ledger, had chosen this underhanded method.

"I—I saw the president today," ventured Paul, still staring at his wife with fascinated eyes. "The appropriation for liberal arts has been cut down. And the faculty is going to be reduced. I'm safe, I guess."

"Oh Paul, dear!" cried Susan.

She looked at him. Then she shuddered a little.

"I'm cold," she whimpered, groping her way around the table. Paul put his arms around her and kissed her.

"There, there, sweetheart," he said, and tried to comfort her. It was not a very convincing job. Then he put a shabby coat around her, hauled out the bed half way, made her lie down, and went to do salvage work in the kitchen. On the way he stumbled over his bag of themes. It can not be said that these products of education received the consideration recommended by the books of pedagogy. The fact is, Paul kicked them vigorously against the side of the room. Susan giggled hysterically.

The fried potatoes were a hopeless mess, and the stewed corn no longer recognizable. This did not add to Dr. Gant's optimism. As he cleaned up the stove and began ruefully to prepare another supper, he reflected on his situation, bitterly and without illusion.

His mind went back, for one thing, to the classes he had taught that day; two sections of hopelessly mediocre Freshmen into whose uninterested perceptions he was supposed to pound the fear of comma blunders and respect for the English language. It was incredible that the human intellect could so withstand instruction. A month and a half had gone by, and yet his students, despite the incessant repetitions of the class room, despite patient and continued individual "conferences," despite the simple instructions of the manual of compositions each one possessed, doggedly continued writing sentences without verbs, coupling plural subjects and singular predicates, mistaking adjectives for adverbs, and generally failing to indicate that any progress had been made in them since they left the eighth grade.

Do not be unfair to Paul. His classes were quite as good as the average, and the high schools say they are not to blame. Only, he was grinding out the best years of his life in a wearying battle against stupidity, and even the gods. But the proverb was made in Germany. Paul reflected on the situation. In fact, his mind went into a committee of the whole on the state of this particular union.

And the more he thought, the madder he got. His training and his inclinations were more or less literary: he could write a little; and yet he was set to work, day in and day out, to explain that a verb is conjugated and should never be declined.

He thought about Susan and the long wait to be married; he thought about his studies in the graduate schools; he thought about the way Susan had scrimped and saved; he thought how they had wanted children and had denied themselves for the sake of publishing Paul's thesis; he thought how they could not support the one that was now coming. In fact, he thought so much that he was in danger of burning the potatoes a second time, when Susan's voice recalled him to his surroundings.

"I'm so cold," she whimpered, "I'm freezing."

Paul turned off the gas under the frying pan.

"Where are you going?" asked Susan in alarm.

"I am going," said Paul distinctly from the hall door, "to the furnace room. And I am going to build a fire and get some heat into this damned apartment."

As swearing it was not much, but then, instructors do not have much practice in profanity.

Paul did not build the fire. When he reached the basement, he found Mr. Whelpley, fat, red and perspiring, his head thrust into the maw of the furnace, his voice booming in a series of smothered explosions that should have successfully heated his tenants. But they did not, for on the wall behind him hung the shattered house telephone. He emerged from the furnace and glared at Paul.

"Where's the kindling?" he roared.

"Right over here," said Paul promptly. "And the fine coal is over there."

"Do you know anything about this furnace?" demanded Dr. Gant's landlord, smearing his wet face with black as he brushed back his abundant hair.

"I do," said Paul.

Ordinarily he was timid, but he was still thinking about Freshman composition. "You'll pull out this damper first."

Together they built the fire. Once the telephone jarred faintly, but Mr. Whelpley might have [been] the scriptural idol for all that his ears could hear.

When the furnace had commenced a comfortable purring, Paul turned. It was one of the great moments of his life.

"The janitor is discharged?" he asked crisply. The president of the university would not have known him.

"He is," responded Mr. Whelpley, "good and discharged."

"How much did you pay him?" asked Paul.

"I paid him," said Mr. Whelpley with

growing heat, "one hundred and fifty dollars a month. And I gave him an apartment to live in. I paid him that much because I wanted to keep him. All he had to do was to keep this place clean and warm, and now—"

"Are you thinking of hiring another janitor?" interrupted Paul.

"I am," answered Mr. Whelpley, "if I can find one. Otherwise—"

"Would you hire me?" said Paul.

Let us not dwell on the astonishment of Mr. Whelpley. Also the ensuing conversation between Dr. Gant and his landlord is lost to history.

A half an hour later Dr. Paul Gant stood rummaging through his desk, one foot unconsciously planted on the bag of Freshman themes.

"What have you got?" asked Susan drowsily comfortable with a good supper and plenty of heat.

"I have here," said Paul in his best class-room manner, coming towards her with a handful of papers, "a diploma certifying that I am a Bachelor of Arts. Here is another certifying that I am a Master of Arts. Don't try to read it—it's Latin. And I have here a third document stating that I am a Doctor of Philosophy and may enjoy all the rights and perquisites of that degree. This," he continued, holding forth a smaller paper, "is my appointment as an instructor in English at $100 a month. This," he said triumphantly, drawing a fifth document from his pocket, "is my contract as the janitor of this apartment house at $165 a month. I am now going down to the cellar and start the fire under the water-heater which has not been in operation all day."

"But—" ejaculated the wide-eyed Susan.

"These?" said Paul, following and interpreting her gaze. "These are to start the fire with, under the water-heater."

And he went out with his diplomas in his hand and shut the door.

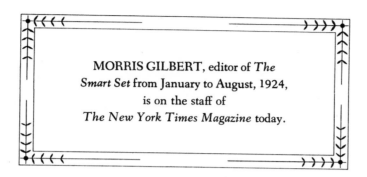

MORRIS GILBERT, editor of *The Smart Set* from January to August, 1924, is on the staff of *The New York Times Magazine* today.

Cats

—•—

MORRIS GILBERT

CATS have no sense of humor, but like gray
Back-yard Iagos, brood and fiercely shrink,
Stroking grim prickly whiskers as they think
About affairs, revenges, brawls, and prey.

Cats to red gusty passions oft give way;
They haunt old tarnished thresholds and they slink
Along, intensely frustrate, on the brink
Of antic doom, like banshees lithe and fey.

The only cat that ever smiled was he
That grinned in sunny Cheshire formerly.
If cats should suddenly sprout up about
Six times as big as they are now, no doubt
The bold behemoth and the jaguar
Would be less awful then than cats, by far.

FROM VOL. 50, OCTOBER 1916

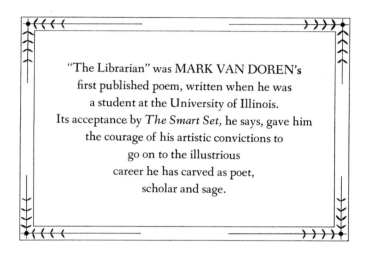

"The Librarian" was MARK VAN DOREN's
first published poem, written when he was
a student at the University of Illinois.
Its acceptance by *The Smart Set,* he says, gave him
the courage of his artistic convictions to
go on to the illustrious
career he has carved as poet,
scholar and sage.

The Librarian

MARK VAN DOREN

WHEN first in that still treasure-house of books
I saw the dread librarian come and go,
And never deign to loosen with soft looks
Her spell o'er us who would her secret know;
When next, behind her frosted iron shield,
I saw her move along the friendly halls,
Rebuking with a single glance congealed—
Ignoring such as stood against the walls;
I, wondering then if king or god did hold
Possession of her queenly heart and mind,
Resolved to be incontinently bold,
And ask her if she be of mortal kind.
I did,—and lo! this answer did she fling:
"I'm just a girl, and fit for anything!"

FROM VOL. 47, OCTOBER 1915

DAMON RUNYON (1884-1946), the
author of *Guys and Dolls* and many
another successful story of the worlds
inhabited by gangsters, promoters,
professional ballplayers and others
outside "the pale" of respectable society
in his time, was a novice newspaperman in
Denver and still an aspiring poet when
this work appeared. A New York newspaper
editor cut his first name two years
after this poem was published and Runyon
kept it that way thereafter.

Roses of a Dream

THE BALLAD OF A BEACH-COMBER

ALFRED DAMON RUNYON

A WOMAN'S a scent of perfume; a snatch of a passing song,
And loving a haze of hasheesh for making the brain go wrong;
Dear Christ! But I loved the odor, the music spoke heaven to me—
(Hark! that's the pound of the breakers and the roar of the open sea!)

Somehow I'm thinking of roses—but blessing the coral bar
That sends me the song of the breakers—my thinking might wander too far;
Somehow I'm thinking of roses—and dreaming—and dreaming— Ah, me!
(Hark! there's the throb of the breakers and the sound of the open sea!)

Somehow I'm thinking of roses and scenting a rose perfume;
Oh, this is the Springtime yonder and roses are coming to bloom!
And soon it will be white Summer—but what can it mean to me?—
(Hark! there's the song of the breakers and the voice of the open sea!)

Somehow I'm thinking of roses and lights and a lilting song—
(But loving's a haze of hasheesh for making the brain go wrong.)
Of roses of white and crimson—of dusk and a friendly tree—
(Hark! there's the sound of the breakers and the roar of the open sea!)

Aye, a woman's a scent of perfume, the breath of a fading rose—
And music don't last forever, however sweetly it goes;
But somehow I'm thinking of roses that carry an ancient plea—
(Thank God! there's the throb of the breakers and the roar of the open sea!)

A woman's a scent of perfume, a snatch of a passing song—
And loving a haze of hasheesh for making the brain go wrong—
Did I say that I loved the odor?—Ah, well, let the roses be—
(Hark! there's the wail of the breakers and the sigh of the open sea!)

FROM VOL. 25, JUNE 1908

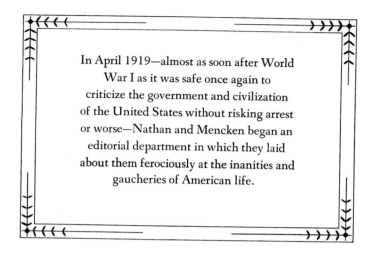

In April 1919—almost as soon after World War I as it was safe once again to criticize the government and civilization of the United States without risking arrest or worse—Nathan and Mencken began an editorial department in which they laid about them ferociously at the inanities and gaucheries of American life.

Répétition Générale *

SELECTIONS

GEORGE JEAN NATHAN and H. L. MENCKEN

Announcement.—Urged by friends, customers and large numbers of the miscellaneous gentry in all parts of the United States, including the late Confederate States, the editors of this favorite family magazine announce their candidacy for the offices of President and Vice-President of the United States. Neither has any active preference for either office; after the election, or before, if it is legally necessary, the matter may be determined satisfactorily by shooting dice. The platform upon which they propose to stand contains, so far, the following planks:

1

They promise, if elected, to procure the immediate restoration of the saloon, exactly as it existed before Prohibition—by the repeal, if it is possible, of the Eighteenth Amendment, but, if it is not possible, in spite of it.

FROM VOL. 71, JUNE 1923

* SIC

2

They agree to veto all bills enacted by Congress embracing appropriations of public money, and to refuse to execute them in case they are passed over their veto, saving only bills for the upkeep of the Army and Navy.

3

They agree, within 24 hours after their induction into office, to discharge and dismiss, without pensions, at least half of the judges now sitting in the Federal courts of the Republic, and to make every feasible effort to railroad the discharged jurists to jail.

4

They agree to discharge and dismiss the whole diplomatic corps of the United States, and to prevent, if possible, the return of any member of the existing corps to the United States.

5

They agree to close at once all the public offices in Washington, save only the War Department, the Navy Department and the Postoffice, and to have all persons now holding appointments in such offices run out of Washington within 24 hours.

6

They agree to stop the payment of interest on all public obligations of the United States, save such as were bought at the time of issue by persons who now hold no more than $10,000 worth apiece.

7

They agree to liberate at once all persons now held in Federal prisons for so-called political offenses, save those of whom it may be proved that they are not guilty. ·

8

They agree to abrogate and nullify any existing Tariff Act or any Tariff Act to be passed by Congress during their term, by discharging and dismissing all collectors of customs, tidewaiters, appraisers, inspectors and other such blackmailers.

9

They agree to put into execution at once a scheme of universal military service, whereby every resident of the United States, male or female, citizen or foreigner, shall join the colors on reaching the age of 21 years, and serve continuously for at least two years.

10

They agree to hang at least 10,000 labor leaders a year.

11

They agree to suppress the Y.M.C.A., Columbia University, the Sons of the Revolution, and the Anti-Saloon League.

12

They agree to prevent, by the use of the full military and naval forces of the United States, any interference with the free exercise of any of the fine arts, or of any orderly sport.

13

They promise to restore free speech absolutely, without any reservation whatsoever. They agree to send the Army to seize, and, if necessary, execute, any person or persons who shall offer to interfere with the exercise of free speech and free assemblage by any other person or persons.

14

They agree to insure the utmost conceivable religious freedom. They engage to protect every resident of the United States in his right to worship any god, devil or other supernatural bugaboo in any manner agreeable to him, so long as it does not involve the dissemination of noises or odors offensive to nearby persons.

15

They agree to abrogate and nullify all laws prohibiting the free activity of quack doctors, sellers of patent medicines, bogus mine stocks, Polish government bonds, etc.

16

They agree to deport all Armenians from the United States.

17

They agree to bend their best efforts to the restoration of chattel slavery in the South, and to extend it to the North, and to make it include white slaves as well as colored ones.

18

They agree to seize all persons who acted as Y.M.C.A. secretaries or Red Cross agents during the late war, and to cause them to serve in the Army for at least five years, unless sooner killed on the field of honor.

19

They agree to collect all war debts owed to the United States by foreign powers, by force and in full.

20

They agree to abolish the Interstate Commerce Commission, and to appoint a captain in the Army, with a file of 10 soldiers armed with loaded muskets, to regulate railroad rates by private conferences with the presidents of the railroads.

21

They agree to reduce the membership of the United States Senate by 50% and of the House of Representatives by 75%, and to provide military funerals, with General Pershing in attendance in full uniform, for the members eliminated.

22

They agree to burn Harvard University.

23

They agree to shove Cal Coolidge, Henry Cabot Lodge and Charles E. Hughes into the Army.

24

They agree to serve without pay, to provide their own subsistence, and to remain in office, regardless of the Constitutional limitation, until assassinated.

[In succeeding issues, these planks were continued until eventually there were some one hundred and fifty.]

Section 4

Optimistic Note: Five Years After.—From a circular entitled "The Patriotism of Saving," issued by the Bureau of Publicity of the Treasury Department in 1918:

The epoch of conservation upon which we are now entering will not have the spacious picturesqueness of the epoch of exploitation which we are leaving behind. But it will not be without its compensations. Greed, which has been such a dominating motive in our industrial growth, *will necessarily come to play a smaller part,* because greed is waste. Fewer men will work merely for money, *and more will work for love of work, for love of country, and for the gratitude of their fellows.*

Section 6

Two Definitions.—Atheist: one who is not half so atheistic as he says he is. Christian: one who is not half so Christian as he tries to look.

Section 9

The Higher Learning in America—When the Rev. Dr. Billy Sunday, the whooping evangelist, recently arrived in Columbia, S. C., to alarm the white and black morons, the general chairman of the committee appointed to welcome him was Dr. W. D. Melton, president of the University of South Carolina. Dr. Melton was accompanied to the station by Dr. W. S. Currell, former president of the University and now dean of the Graduate School.

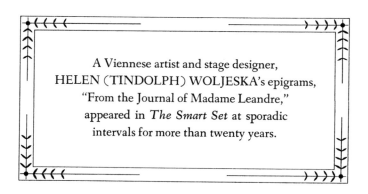

A Viennese artist and stage designer,
HELEN (TINDOLPH) WOLJESKA's epigrams,
"From the Journal of Madame Leandre,"
appeared in *The Smart Set* at sporadic
intervals for more than twenty years.

From the Journal of Madame Leandre *

HELEN WOLJESKA

When we mourn the death of a friend, we mourn the death of part of ourselves. That aspect of us which he had conceived is no more.

Do not expect any love to last. And let go away everybody and everything that wishes to leave you. As soon as you struggle to retain, you become small, and foolish, and commonplace.

Everything that is most beautiful in life and art owes its existence to impulse—not to intention.

The more I like people the less I wish to meet their kith and kin.

Debts are bad every way. If you take them lightly, they coarsen you. If you take them seriously, they worry you.

I do not love you. I love in you a certain quality or combination of qualities that has power to attract me. Every woman is at the mercy of a certain type of man.

To care for people on account of their attractive appearance only is like frequenting a house where you like the facade better than the hostess.

FROM VOL. 19, AUGUST 1906

* SIC

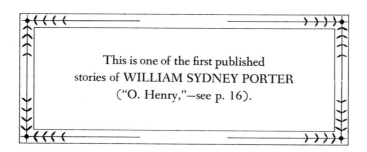

This is one of the first published
stories of WILLIAM SYDNEY PORTER
("O. Henry,"—see p. 16).

A Ghost of a Chance

O. HENRY

"Actually, a *hod!*" repeated Mrs. Kinsolving, pathetically.

Mrs. Bellamy Bellmore arched a sympathetic eyebrow. Thus she expressed condolence and a generous amount of apparent surprise.

"Fancy her telling, everywhere," recapitulated Mrs. Kinsolving, "that she saw a ghost in the apartment she occupied here—our choicest guest-room—a ghost, carrying a hod on its shoulder—the ghost of an old man in overalls, smoking a pipe and carrying a hod! The very absurdity of the thing shows her malicious intent. There never was a Kinsolv-

ing that carried a hod. Every one knows that Mr. Kinsolving's father accumulated his money by large building contracts, but he never worked a day with his own hands. He had this house built from his own plans; but—oh, a hod! Why need she have been so cruel and malicious?"

"It is really too bad," murmured Mrs. Bellmore, with an approving glance of her fine eyes about the vast chamber done in lilac and old gold. "And it was in this room she saw it! Oh, no, I'm not afraid of ghosts. Don't have the least fear on my account. I'm glad you put me in here. I think family ghosts so

FROM VOL. 9, JANUARY 1903

interesting! But, really, the story does sound a little inconsistent. I should have expected something better from Mrs. Fischer-Suympkins. Don't they carry bricks in hods? Why should a ghost bring bricks into a villa built of marble and stone? I'm so sorry, but it makes me think that age is beginning to tell upon Mrs. Fischer-Suympkins."

"This house," continued Mrs. Kinsolving, "was built upon the site of an old one used by the family during the Revolution. There wouldn't be anything strange in its having a ghost. And there was a Captain Kinsolving who fought in General Greene's army, though we've never been able to secure any papers to vouch for it. If there is to be a family ghost, why couldn't it have been his, instead of a bricklayer's?"

"The ghost of a Revolutionary ancestor wouldn't be a bad idea," agreed Mrs. Bellmore; "but you know how arbitrary and inconsiderate ghosts can be. Maybe, like love, they are 'engendered in the eye.' One advantage of those who see ghosts is that their stories can't be disproved. By a spiteful eye, a Revolutionary knapsack might easily be construed to be a hod. Dear Mrs. Kinsolving, think no more of it. I am sure it was a knapsack."

"But she told everybody!" mourned Mrs. Kinsolving, inconsolable. "She insisted upon the details. There is the pipe. And how are you going to get out of the overalls?"

"Sha'n't get into them," said Mrs. Bellmore, with a prettily suppressed yawn; "too stiff and wrinkly. Is that you, Felice? Prepare my bath, please. Do you dine at seven at Clifftop, Mrs. Kinsolving? So kind of you to run in for a chat before dinner! I love those little touches of informality with a guest. They give such a home flavor to a visit. So sorry; I must be dressing. I am so indolent I always postpone it until the last moment."

Mrs. Fischer-Suympkins had been the first large plum that the Kinsolvings had drawn from the social pie. For a long time, the pie itself had been out of reach on a top shelf.

But the purse and the pursuit had at last lowered it. Mrs. Fischer-Suympkins was the heliograph of the smart society parading corps. The glitter of her wit and actions passed along the line, transmitting whatever was latest and most daring in the game of peep-show. Formerly, her fame and leadership had been secure enough not to need the support of such artifices as handing around live frogs for favors at a cotillion. But, now, these things were necessary to the holding of her throne. Besides, middle-age had come to preside, incongruous, at her capers. The sensational papers had cut her space from a page to two columns. Her wit developed a sting; her manners became more rough and inconsiderate, as if she felt the royal necessity of establishing her autocracy by scorning the conventionalities that bound lesser potentates.

To some pressure at the command of the Kinsolvings, she had yielded so far as to honor their house by her presence, for an evening and night. She had her revenge upon her hostess by relating, with grim enjoyment and sarcastic humor, her story of the vision carrying the hod. To that lady, in raptures at having penetrated thus far toward the coveted inner circle, the result came as a crushing disappointment. Everybody either sympathized or laughed, and there was little to choose between the two modes of expression.

But, later on, Mrs. Kinsolving's hopes and spirits were revived by the capture of a second and greater prize.

Mrs. Bellamy Bellmore had accepted an invitation to visit at Clifftop, and would remain for three days. Mrs. Bellmore was one of the younger matrons, whose beauty, descent and wealth gave her a reserved seat in the holy of holies that required no strenuous bolstering. She was generous enough thus to give Mrs. Kinsolving the accolade that was so poignantly desired; and, at the same time, she thought how much it would please Terence. Perhaps it would end by solving him.

Terence was Mrs. Kinsolving's son, aged twenty-nine, quite good-looking enough, and with two or three attractive and mysterious traits. For one, he was very devoted to his mother, and that was sufficiently odd to deserve notice. For others, he talked so little that it was irritating, and he seemed either very shy or very deep. Terence interested Mrs. Bellmore, because she was not sure which it was. She intended to study him a little longer, unless she forgot the matter. If he was only shy, she would abandon him, for shyness is a bore. If he was deep, she would also abandon him, for depth is precarious.

On the afternoon of the third day of her visit, Terence hunted up Mrs. Bellmore, and found her in a nook actually looking at an album.

"It's so good of you," said he, "to come down here and retrieve the day for us. I suppose you have heard that Mrs. Fischer-Suympkins scuttled the ship before she left. She knocked a whole plank out of the bottom with a hod. My mother is grieving herself ill about it. Can't you manage to see a ghost for us while you are here, Mrs. Bellmore—a bang-up, swell ghost, with a coronet on his head and a cheque-book under his arm?"

"That was a naughty old lady, Terence," said Mrs. Bellmore, "to tell such stories. Perhaps you gave her too much supper. Your mother doesn't really take it seriously, does she?"

"I think she does," answered Terence. "One would think every brick in the hod had dropped on her. It's a good mammy, and I don't like to see her worried. It's to be hoped that the ghost belongs to the hod-carriers' union, and will go out on a strike. If he doesn't, there will be no peace in this family."

"I'm sleeping in the ghost-chamber," said Mrs. Bellmore, pensively. "But it's so nice I wouldn't change it, even if I were afraid, which I'm not. It wouldn't do for me to submit a counter story of a desirable, aristocratic shade, would it? I would do so, with pleasure, but it seems to me it would be too obviously an antidote for the other narrative to be effective."

"True," said Terence, running two fingers thoughtfully into his crisp, brown hair; "that would never do. How would it work to see the same ghost again, minus the overalls, and have gold bricks in the hod? That would elevate the spectre from degrading toil to a financial plane. Don't you think that would be respectable enough?"

"There was an ancestor who fought against the Britishers, wasn't there? Your mother said something to that effect."

"I believe so; one of those old chaps in raglan vests and golf trousers. I don't care a continental for a continental, myself. But the mother has set her heart on pomp and heraldry and pyrotechnics, and I want her to be happy."

"You are a good boy, Terence," said Mrs. Bellmore, sweeping her silks close to one side of her, "not to beat your mother. Sit here by me, and let's look at the album, just as people used to do twenty years ago. Now, tell me about every one of them. Who is this tall, dignified gentleman leaning against the horizon with one arm on the Corinthian column?"

"That old chap with the big feet?" inquired Terence, craning his neck. "That's great-uncle O'Brannigan. He used to keep a rathskeller on the Bowery."

"I asked you to sit down, Terence. If you are not going to amuse, or obey, me, I shall report in the morning that I saw a ghost wearing an apron and carrying schooners of beer. Now, that is better. To be shy, at your age, Terence, is a thing that you should blush to acknowledge."

At breakfast on the last morning of her visit, Mrs. Bellmore startled and entranced every one present by announcing positively that she had seen the ghost.

"Did it have a—a—a—?" Mrs. Kinsolving, in her suspense and agitation, could not bring out the word.

"No, indeed—far from it."

There was a chorus of questions from others at the table. "Weren't you frightened?" "What did it do?" "How did it look?" "How was it dressed?" "Did it say anything?" "Didn't you scream?"

"I'll try to answer everything at once," said Mrs. Bellmore, heroically, "although I'm frightfully hungry. Something awakened me —I'm not sure whether it was a noise or a touch—and there stood the phantom. I never burn a light at night, so the room was quite dark, but I saw it plainly. I wasn't dreaming. It was a tall man, all misty white from head to foot. It wore the full dress of the old, colonial days—powdered hair, baggy coat skirts, lace ruffles and a sword. It looked intangible and luminous in the dark, and moved without a sound. Yes, I was a little frightened at first—or startled, I should say. It was the first ghost I had ever seen. No, it didn't say anything. I didn't scream. I raised up on my elbow, and then it glided silently away, and disappeared when it reached the door."

Mrs. Kinsolving was in the seventh heaven. "The description is that of Captain Kinsolving, of General Greene's army, one of our ancestors," she said, in a voice that trembled with pride and relief. "I really think I must apologize for our ghostly relative, Mrs. Bellmore. I am afraid he must have badly disturbed your rest."

Terence sent a smile of pleased congratulation toward his mother. Attainment was Mrs. Kinsolving's, at last, and he loved to see her happy.

"I suppose I ought to be ashamed to confess," said Mrs. Bellmore, who was now enjoying her breakfast, "that I wasn't very much disturbed. I presume it would have been the customary thing to scream and faint, and have all of you running about in picturesque costumes. But, after the first alarm was over, I really couldn't work myself up to a panic. The ghost retired from the stage quietly and peacefully, after doing its little turn, and I went to sleep again."

Nearly all who listened, politely accepted Mrs. Bellmore's story as a made-up affair, charitably offered as an offset to the unkind vision seen by Mrs. Fischer-Suympkins. But one or two present perceived that her assertions bore the genuine stamp of her own convictions. Truth and candor seemed to attend upon every word. Even a scoffer at ghosts—if he were very observant—would have been forced to admit that she had, at least in a very vivid dream, been honestly aware of the weird visitor.

Soon, Mrs. Bellmore's maid was packing. In two hours, the auto would come to convey her to the station. As Terence was strolling upon the east piazza, Mrs. Bellmore came up to him, with a confidential sparkle in her eye.

"I didn't wish to tell the others all of it," she said, "but I will tell you. In a way, I think you should be held responsible. Can you guess in what manner that ghost awakened me last night?"

"Rattled chains," suggested Terence, after some thought, "or groaned? They usually do one or the other."

"Do you happen to know," continued Mrs. Bellmore, with sudden irrelevancy, "if I resemble any one of the female relatives of your restless ancestor, Captain Kinsolving?"

"Don't think so," said Terence, with an extremely puzzled air. "Never heard of any of them being noted beauties."

"Then, why," said Mrs. Bellmore, looking the young man gravely in the eye, "should that ghost have kissed me, as I'm sure it did?"

"Heavens!" exclaimed Terence, in wide-eyed amazement; "you don't mean that, Mrs. Bellmore! Did he actually kiss you?"

"I said it," corrected Mrs. Bellmore. "I hope the impersonal pronoun is correctly used."

"But why did you say I was responsible?"

"Because you are the only living male relative of the ghost."

"I see. 'Unto the third and fourth generation.' But, seriously, did he—did it—how do you — ?"

"Know? How does any one know? I was asleep, and that is what awakened me, I'm almost certain."

"Almost?"

"Well, I awoke just as—oh, can't you understand what I mean? When anything arouses you suddenly, you are not positive whether you dreamed, or—and yet you know that—Dear Me, Terence, must I dissect the most elementary sensations in order to accommodate your extremely practical intelligence?"

"But, about kissing ghosts, you know," said Terence, humbly, "I require the most primary instruction. I never kissed a ghost. Is it—is it — ?"

"The sensation," said Mrs. Bellmore, with deliberate, but slightly smiling, emphasis, "since you are seeking instruction, is a mingling of the material and the spiritual."

"Of course," said Terence, suddenly growing serious, "it was a dream or some kind of a hallucination. Nobody believes in spirits, these days. If you told the tale out of kindness of heart, Mrs. Bellmore, I can't express how grateful I am to you. It has made my mother supremely happy. That Revolutionary ancestor was a stunning idea."

Mrs. Bellmore sighed. "The usual fate of ghost-seers is mine," she said, resignedly. "My privileged encounter with a spirit is attributed to lobster salad or mendacity. Well, I have, at least, one memory left from the wreck—a kiss from the unseen world. Was Captain Kinsolving a very brave man, do you know, Terence?"

"He was licked at Yorktown, I believe," said Terence, reflecting. "They say he skedaddled with his company, after the first battle there."

"I thought he must have been timid," said Mrs. Bellmore, absently. "He might have had another."

"Another battle?" asked Terence, dully.

"What else could I mean? I must go and get ready now; the auto will be here in an hour. I've enjoyed Clifftop immensely. Such a lovely morning, isn't it, Terence?"

On her way to the station, Mrs. Bellmore took from her bag a silk handkerchief, and looked at it with a little, peculiar smile. Then she tied it in several very hard knots, and threw it, at a convenient moment, over the edge of the cliff along which the road ran.

In his room, Terence was giving some directions to his man, Brooks. "Have this stuff done up in a parcel," he said, "and ship it to the address on that card."

The card was that of a New York costumer. The "stuff" was a gentleman's costume of the days of '76, made of white satin, with silver buckles, white silk stockings and white kid shoes. A powdered wig and a sword completed the dress.

"And look about, Brooks," added Terence, a little anxiously, "for a silk handkerchief with my initials in one corner. I must have dropped it somewhere."

It was a month later when Mrs. Bellmore and one or two others of the smart crowd were making up a list of names for a coaching trip through the Catskills. Mrs. Bellmore looked over the list for a final censoring. The name of Terence Kinsolving was there. Mrs. Bellmore ran her prohibitive pencil lightly through the name.

"Too shy!" she murmured, sweetly, in explanation.

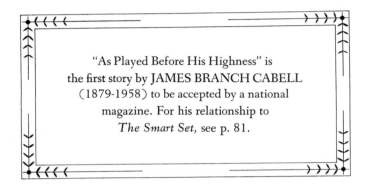

"As Played Before His Highness" is
the first story by JAMES BRANCH CABELL
(1879-1958) to be accepted by a national
magazine. For his relationship to
The Smart Set, see p. 81.

As Played Before His Highness

JAMES BRANCH CABELL

The idea," said the baroness, "is preposterous!"

"Admirably put!" cried the grand duke. "We will execute it tonight."

The baroness stared at him coldly, and added:

"Besides, one could only take a portmanteau."

"They hold very little," his highness agreed; "I assure you, after I had packed my coronet there was hardly room for a change of linen. And I had to choose between my family tree and a tooth-brush."

FROM VOL. 6, MARCH 1902

"Louis, Louis," sighed the baroness, "can you never be serious? You are about to throw away a duchy, and you laugh like a schoolboy."

"Ma foi!" retorted the grand duke, looking out on the moonlit gardens, "as a loyal Noumarian, I rejoice at the good fortune that is to befall my country. Morality demands my abdication," he added, virtuously, "and for once I agree with morality."

The Baroness von Altenburg was not disposed to argue the point; for she with the rest of the world knew that the Grand Duke

of Noumaria had in his time left little un-
done that tended to jeopardize both his dignity and his grand duchy. His latest scheme,
however, threatened to dispense with both.

It was Homeric in its simplicity. To eluci-
date it he had led the baroness to the
Summer-house that good Duke Ludwig
erected in the Gardens of Breschau, close
to the fountain of the Naiads, and had in a
few words explained his plan. There were
post-horses in Noumaria; there was an entirely unobstructed road that led to Vienna,
and thence to the world outside; and he
proposed, in short, to quiet the grumbling of
the discontented Noumarians by the sudden
and complete disappearance of their grand
duke. As a patriot, the baroness could not
fail to perceive the inestimable benefit that
would thus be conferred on her country.

He stipulated, however, that his exit from
public life should be made in company with
this the latest lady on whom he had bestowed
his somewhat fickle affections. Remembering
these things, the baroness, without exactly
encouraging or discouraging his scheme, was
at least not prone to insist on his morality.

She contented herself with a truism. "Indeed, your highness, the example you set
your subjects is bad."

"Yet they protest," said the grand duke.
"I have done the things I ought not to have
done, and left unread the papers I have
signed. What more can one ask of a grand
duke?"

"You are indolent," remonstrated the lady.

"You are adorable," said his highness.

"And that injures your popularity."

"Which vanished with my waist."

"You create scandals."

"'The woman tempted me,'" quoted the
grand duke, and added, reflectively, "It is
singular—"

"I am afraid," said the baroness, "it is
plural."

The grand duke waved a dignified dissent,
and continued:

"—that I could never resist green eyes of
a peculiar shade."

The baroness, becoming vastly interested
in the structure of her fan, went on, with
some severity:

"Your reputation—"

"*De mortuis—*" pleaded the grand duke.

"—is bad; and you go from bad to worse."

"By no means," said his highness; "when I
was nineteen—"

"I won't believe it of you!" cried the lady.

"I assure you," protested his highness,
gravely, "I was a devil of a fellow! She was
only twenty, and she had brown eyes."

"By this time," said the lady, spitefully,
"she may have grandchildren."

"I am thirty-five!" said the grand duke,
with dignity.

"Then the Almanach de Gotha—"

"'Tis a misprint!" cried the grand duke.
"I will explain it in Vienna."

"I am not going to Vienna."

"'And Sapphira,'" murmured his highness, "'fell down straightway at his feet, and
yielded up the ghost.' Beware, Amalia!"

"I am not afraid, your highness."

"Nor I. Let Europe frown and journalists
moralize, while I go straight on the road that
leads to Vienna and heaven."

"Or—" suggested the baroness helpfully.

"There is no 'or.' Once out of Noumaria,
we leave all things save happiness behind."

"Among these things, your highness, is a
duchy."

"*Hein?*" said the grand duke; "what is it?
A black-spot on the map, a pawn in the game
of politics. I give up the pawn and take—the
queen."

"That is unwise," said the baroness, with
composure; "and besides, you are hurting my
hand. Apropos of the queen—the grand
duchess—"

"Will thank God heartily for her deliver-
ance. She will renounce me before the world,
and—almost—love me in secret."

"A true woman," said the baroness, oracularly, "will follow a husband——"

"Till his wife makes her stop," said the grand duke, his tone implying that he knew whereof he spoke.

"If the grand duchess loved you——"

"I don't think she would ever mention it," said the grand duke, turning this new idea over in his mind. "She has a great regard for appearances."

"Nevertheless——"

"She will be regent," chuckled the grand duke. "I can see her now—Marie Antoinette, with a dash of Boadicea. Noumaria will be a temple of all the virtues. Charles will be brought up on moral aphorisms and health-foods, with me as a forcible example of what to avoid. Deuce take it, Amalia," he added, "a father must furnish an example to his children!"

"Pray," asked the baroness, "do you owe it to the prince to take this trip to Vienna?"

"*Ma foi!*" retorted the grand duke, "I owe that to myself."

"It will break the grand duchess's heart."

"Indeed!" observed his highness. "You seem strangely in the confidence of my wife."

The baroness descended to aphorism.

"All women are alike, your highness."

"I have heard," said the grand duke, "that seven devils were cast out of Magdalene."

"Which means—?"

"I have never heard of this being done to any other woman."

"Beware, your highness, of the crudeness of cynicism!"

"I am old," complained the grand duke, "and one reaches years of indiscretion early in life."

"You admit, then, that discretion is desirable?"

"I admit that," said his highness, with firmness, "of you alone."

"Am I, then," queried the baroness, "desirable?"

"More than that," said the grand duke, "you are dangerous. You are a menace to the peace of my court. The young men make sonnets to your eyes and the ladies are ready to tear them out. You corrupt us. There is Châteauroux, now——"

"I assure you," protested the baroness, "he is not the sort of a person to——"

"At twenty-five," interrupted the grand duke, "one is always that sort of a person. Besides, he makes verses."

"Not like yours, your highness. In that line you need fear no rival."

"You confess, then," interrogated the grand duke, "that I have no rival?"

"I said in that line, your highness."

His highness frowned.

"At least," he reflected, "my lines are cast in pleasant places; but I had rather make love to you than verses."

"It is difficult," agreed the baroness, "to do both convincingly; and you were born a poet."

"I was not consulted," cried the grand duke; "and in time one may live down an epic. Besides, my verses are destined to oblivion. Had I been driven by hunger rather than *ennui*—who knows? As it is, my verses are unread, just as my proclamations are unreadable."

"Phrases, your highness."

"Phrases or not, it is decided. You shall make no more bad poets."

"You will," said the baroness, "put me to a vast expense for curlpapers."

"You shall create no more heartburnings."

"My milliner will be inconsolable."

"In short, you must leave Noumaria."

"You will break my heart."

"As misery loves company, I will go with you. We should never forget," added his highness, with considerable kindliness, "always to temper justice with mercy."

"You will do no such thing!"

"I have ordered a carriage to be ready at dawn."

"I trust your highness will enjoy your drive."

"In good company," said the grand duke, "anything is endurable."

152

The baroness reflected; the grand duke smiled.

"I will not go," she said.

"Remember Sapphira," said the grand duke, "and by no means forget the portmanteau."

"I have no intention of going," reiterated the baroness, firmly.

"I would never suspect you of such a thing. Still a portmanteau, in case of emergency—"

"But—"

"Exactly."

"I am told the sunrise is very beautiful from the Gardens of Breschau."

"It is well worth seeing," agreed the grand duke, "on certain days—Thursday, for instance. The gardeners make a specialty of them on Thursdays."

"By a curious chance," murmured the baroness, "this is Wednesday."

"Indeed!" said the grand duke; "I believe it is."

"And I shall be here on your highness' recommendation; but only," she added, "to see the sunrise."

"Of course," said the grand duke, "to see the sunrise—with a portmanteau!"

The baroness was silent.

"With a portmanteau," entreated the grand duke. "I am a connoisseur of portmanteaux. Say that I may see yours."

The baroness smiled.

"Say yes, Amalia," whispered the grand duke. "I adore portmanteaux."

The baroness bent toward him and said:

"I am sorry to inform your highness that there is someone at the door of the Summer-house."

II

INASMUCH as all Noumaria knew that the grand duke, once closeted with the lady whom he delighted to honor, did not love intrusions; inasmuch as a discreet court had learned to regard the Summer-house as sacred to his highness and the Baroness von Altenburg—for these reasons the grand duke

was inclined to resent this disturbance of his privacy as he peered out into the gardens.

His countenance was less severe as he turned again to the baroness; it smacked more of bewilderment.

"It is only the grand duchess," he said.

"And the Comte de Châteauroux," said the baroness.

"Precisely," said the grand duke.

There was no impropriety in the situation, but there is no denying that their voices were somewhat lowered. The rather severely classic beauty of the grand duchess was plainly visible from where they sat. With the Comte de Châteauroux, whose uniform of the Cuirassiers glittered in the moonlight, she made an undeniably handsome picture. It was possibly the grand duke's esthetic taste that held him immovable for a moment.

"After all—" he began, and rose.

"I am afraid that the grand duchess—" murmured the baroness.

"It is the duty of a good husband," said the grand duke, "to conceal from his wife any knowledge that may cause her pain."

Thereupon he sat down.

"I do not," said the baroness, "approve of eavesdropping."

"If you put it that way—" agreed the grand duke, and rose once more, when the voice of Châteauroux stopped him.

"My God!" he cried, "I can't and won't give you up, Victoria!"

"I have heard," said his highness, "that the moonlight is bad for the eyes." Saying this, he seated himself composedly in the darkest corner of the Summer-house.

"This is madness!" cried the grand duchess; "sheer madness!"

"Madness, if you will," persisted Châteauroux, "but a madness too strong for us to resist. Listen, Victoria," and he waved his hand toward the palace, whence music, softened by the distance, stole through the lighted windows; "don't you remember? They used to play that at Godesberg."

The grand duchess was silent.

"Ah, dear heart," he continued, "those were happy times, were they not, when we were boy and girl together? I have danced that so many times with you! It brings back so many things—the scent of your hair, the soft cheek that sometimes brushed mine, the white shoulders that I longed to kiss so many times before I dared."

"*Hein?*" muttered the grand duke.

"We aren't boy and girl now," said the grand duchess, and her voice was regretful. "All that lies behind us, dear. It was a dream —a foolish dream that we must forget."

"Can you forget?" whispered Château-roux; "can you forget it all, Victoria?—that night at Ingolstadt, when you told me that you loved me; that day at Godesberg when we were lost in the palace gardens?"

"*Mon Dieu,* what a memory!" murmured the grand duke. "He makes love by the almanac."

"Ah, dearest woman in the world," continued Châteauroux, "you loved me once, and you have not quite forgotten, I know. We were happy then—ah, so happy—and now—"

"Life," said the grand duchess, "cannot always be happy."

"Ah, no, dear heart! But what a life has been this of mine—a life of dreary days, filled with sick, vivid dreams of our youth that is hardly past as yet! And so many dreams, woman of my heart! The least remembered trifle brings back in a flash some corner of the old castle and you as I saw you there—laughing, or insolent, or it may be tender, though the latter comes but seldom. Just for a moment I see you and my blood leaps up in homage to my dear lady. Then—ah, the vision disappears quickly as it came, and I hunger more than ever for the sight of your loved face."

"This," said the grand duke, "is insanity."

"But," went on Châteauroux, more softly, "I love better the dreams of the night. They are not made all of memories, sweetheart; rather they are romances that my love weaves out of many memories of you—wild, fantastic stories of just you and me that always end happily if I am let to dream them out in comfort. For there is a woman in these dreams who loves me, whose heart and body and soul are mine, all mine. It is a wonderful vision while it lasts, though it is only in dreams that I am master of my heart's desire, and the waking is very bitter. Ah, Victoria, have pity! Don't let it be only a dream!"

"Not but what he does it rather well, you know," whispered the grand duke to the baroness, "though his style is a trifle florid. That last speech was quite in my earlier manner."

The grand duchess did not stir as Châteauroux bent over her jeweled hand.

"Come, dear love!" he said. "Don't let us lose our only chance of happiness. You will go?"

"I cannot," whispered the grand duchess, "I cannot, dear. We have our work to do in the world."

"You will go?" said Châteauroux again.

"My husband —"

"A man who leaves you for each new caprice, who flaunts his mistresses in the face of Europe."

"My children —"

"Dear God! are they or aught else to stand in my way, think you? You love me!"

"It would be criminal."

"You love me!"

"You act a dishonorable part, Château-roux."

"You love me!"

"I will never see you again," said the grand duchess, firmly. "Go! I loathe you, I loathe you, monsieur, even more than I loathe myself for stooping to listen to you."

"You love me!" said Châteauroux and took her in his arms.

Then it was granted to the Baroness von Altenburg and the Grand Duke of Noumaria to behold a wonderful sight, for the grand duchess rested her head on his shoulder, and said:

"Yes, dear, better than all else beside."

"Really," said the grand duke, "I would never have thought it of Victoria."

"You will come, then?" said Châteauroux.

And the grand duchess answered, quietly:

"It shall be as you say."

Then, while the grand duke and the baroness craned their necks, Châteauroux bent over her upturned lips; but the grand duchess struggled away from him, saying, hurriedly:

"Hush, Philippe! I heard someone—something stirring."

"It was the wind, dear heart."

"Come—I am afraid—it is madness to wait here."

"At dawn, then—in the gardens?"

"Yes, dear. But come, Philippe. I dare not wait." And they disappeared in the direction of the palace.

III

THE grand duke looked dispassionately on their retreating figures; inquiringly on the baroness; reprovingly on the moon, as if he rather suspected it of having treated him with injustice.

Ma foi," said his highness at length, "I have never known such a passion for sunrises. We shall have them advertised shortly as 'Patronized by the Nobility.'"

"Indeed," said the baroness, "I think we shall"; and added, "her own cousin, too."

"Victoria," observed the grand duke, "has always had the highest regard for her family; but she is going too far."

"Yes," said the baroness; "as far as Vienna."

"She has taken leave of her senses."

"I am much afraid," sighed the baroness, "that she has taken leave of her husband."

"I never dreamed of Victoria—" began the grand duke.

"Precisely," interrupted the baroness; "you never dreamed of Victoria; and it seems that Châteauroux did."

"I shall tell her that there are limits. Yes,"

repeated the grand duke, emphatically, "that there are limits."

"If I am not mistaken, she will reply that there are—baronesses."

"I shall appeal to her better nature."

"You will find it," said the baroness, "strangely hard of hearing."

"I shall have Châteauroux arrested."

"On what grounds, your highness?"

"In fact," admitted the grand duke, "we do not want a scandal."

"It is not," said the baroness, "altogether a question of what we want."

"There will be a horrible one."

"The papers will thrive on it."

"International complications."

"The army has very little to do."

"A divorce."

"The lawyers will call you blessed. At least," added the baroness, conscientiously, "your lawyers will. I am afraid that hers—"

"Will not be so courteous?" queried the grand duke.

"It is possible," admitted the baroness, "that they may discover some other adjective."

"In short," his highness summed it up, "there will be the deuce to pay."

"Precisely," said the baroness.

The grand duke lost his temper. "If she goes," he thundered, "I'll be—"

"You will be," said the baroness, hastily, "whether she goes or not; and she will go."

"You forget," said his highness, recovering his rumpled dignity, "that I am the grand duke."

"You forget," retorted the baroness, "that Châteauroux is twenty-five."

"I must stop them," said the grand duke.

"It will be difficult," said the lady.

"Without scandal."

"It will be impossible."

The grand duke frowned, and lapsed into a most unducal sullenness.

"Your highness," murmured the baroness, "I cannot express my sympathy for you."

"Madame," said the grand duke, "I cannot express my sympathy for myself. At least, not in the presence of a lady."

"But I have a plan."

"I," said the grand duke, "have any number of plans; but Châteauroux has a carriage; and Victoria," he added, reflectively, "has the deuce of a temper."

"My plan," said the baroness, "is a good one."

"It needs to be," said the grand duke.

Thereupon, the Baroness von Altenburg unfolded to his highness her scheme for preserving peace in the reigning family of Noumaria; and the grand duke heard and marveled.

"Amalia," he said, when she had ended, "you should be prime minister—"

"Ah, your highness," said the lady, "you flatter me."

"—though, indeed," reflected the grand duke, "what would a mere prime minister do with lips like yours?"

"You agree, then, to my plan?" the baroness questioned.

"*Ma foi,* yes!" said the grand duke. "In the gardens, at dawn."

"At dawn," said the baroness, "in the gardens."

IV

THE grand duke glanced discontentedly over the scene; in the gray light that heralded the day he found the world a strangely cheerless place. The Gardens of Breschau were deserted, save for a traveling carriage that stood not a hundred yards from the Summerhouse.

"It seems," he said, "that I am the first on the ground, and that Châteauroux is a dilatory lover. Young men degenerate."

Saying this, he seated himself on a convenient bench, where Châteauroux found him a few minutes later, smoking a contemplative cigarette, and promptly dropped a portmanteau at the ducal feet.

"Monsieur le comte," said the grand duke, "this is an unforeseen pleasure."

"Your highness!" cried Châteauroux, in astonishment.

"Precisely," said the grand duke.

Châteauroux caressed his chin reflectively. The grand duke inhaled his cigarette in an equally meditative fashion.

"I did not know," said the grand duke, "that you were such an early riser. Or perhaps," he continued, "you are late in retiring. Fie, fie, monsieur, you must be careful! You will create a scandal in our court." He shook his finger knowingly at Châteauroux.

"Your highness—" said the latter, and stammered into silence.

"You said that before, you know," remarked the grand duke.

"An affair of business—"

"Ah," said the grand duke, casting his eye first on the portmanteau and then on the carriage, "can it be that you are leaving Noumaria? We shall miss you, comte."

"I was summoned very hastily, or I should have paid my respects to your highness."

"Indeed," said the grand duke, "it is somewhat sudden."

"It is imperative, your highness."

"And yet," pursued the grand duke, "travel is beneficial to young men."

"I shall not go far, your highness."

"I would not for the world intrude on your secrets, comte—"

"My estates, your highness—"

"—for young men will be young men, I know."

"My steward, your highness, is imperative."

"Stewards are," agreed the grand duke, "somewhat unreasonable at times. I trust she is handsome."

"Ah, your highness!" cried Châteauroux.

"And you have my blessing. Go in peace."

The grand duke was smiling benevolently on the discomfited Châteauroux when the Baroness von Altenburg suddenly appeared between them, in traveling costume and carrying a portmanteau.

"Heyday!" said the grand duke; "it seems

that the steward of our good baroness is also importunate."

"Your highness!" cried the baroness, and dropped her portmanteau.

"Everyone," said the grand duke, "appears to doubt my identity this morning."

Châteauroux turned from the one to the other in bewilderment.

"This," said the grand duke, after a pause, "is painful. It is unworthy of you, Châteauroux."

"Your highness!" cried the latter.

"Again?" said the grand duke, pettishly.

The baroness applied her handkerchief to her eyes, and said plaintively:

"You do not understand, your highness."

"I am afraid," said the grand duke, "that I understand only too clearly."

"We will not deceive you—" cried the baroness.

"It would be unwise," agreed the grand duke, "to attempt it."

"—and I confess that I was here to meet Monsieur de Châteauroux."

"Good God!" cried the latter.

"Precisely," observed the grand duke; "to compare portmanteaux; and you have selected the interior of this carriage, no doubt, as a suitable spot."

"And I admit to your highness—"

"His highness already knowing," interpolated the grand duke.

"That we were about to elope."

"I assure you—" began Châteauroux.

"I will take the lady's word for it," said the grand duke, "though it grieves me."

"We knew you would never give your consent," murmured the baroness.

"Undoubtedly," said the grand duke, "I would never have given my consent."

"And we love each other."

"Fiddle-de-dee!" said his highness.

Châteauroux passed his hand over his brow. "This," he said, "is some horrible mistake."

"It is," assented the grand duke; "a mistake—but one of your making."

"I did not expect the baroness—"

"So early?" continued his highness, sympathetically. "It was unfortunate."

"Indeed, your highness—" began Châteauroux.

"Do you deny, Monsieur le comte," asked the grand duke, coldly, "that you were awaiting a lady?"

Châteauroux was silent.

"Or perhaps," suggested the grand duke, "it was someone else you were expecting."

Still silence.

"Ah, Philippe!" entreated the baroness, "confess to his highness."

"If I do—" said Châteauroux.

"Stop, sir!" said the grand duke, "you have already brought scandal to our court. Do not add profanity to your other crimes. I protest," he continued, "even the grand duchess has heard of it."

Indeed, the grand duchess, hurrying from the palace, was already within a few feet of the trio, and had only then perceived her husband's presence.

"I should not be surprised," said the grand duke, raising his eyes to heaven, "if it were all over the palace by this time."

Then, as the grand duchess paused in astonishment, he asked, gravely:

"You, too, have heard of this sad affair, Victoria?"

"Your highness!" cried the grand duchess.

"Of what these two young fools have planned? Ah, I see you have, and come in haste to prevent it. You have a good heart, Victoria."

"I did not know—" began the grand duchess.

"Until the last moment," finished the grand duke. "I understand. But perhaps," he continued hopefully, "it is not yet too late to bring them to their senses."

Turning to the baroness and Châteauroux, he said:

"I will not stop you, but—"

"Believe me," said the baroness, "we are heartily grateful for your highness's magnanimity. We may, then, depart with your permission?"

"But I beg you to reflect—"

"We have reflected," said the baroness; and handed her portmanteau to the unwilling Châteauroux.

"To you," said his highness, frowning on Châteauroux, "I have nothing to say. Under the cover of hospitality you have endeavored to steal away the fairest ornament of our court; I leave you to the pangs of conscience, if indeed you have a conscience. But the baroness is young; she has been misled by your sophistry and specious pretense of affection. She has evidently been misled," he said kindly, to the grand duchess, "as any woman might be."

"As any woman might be!" echoed the grand duchess.

"I shall therefore," continued the grand duke, "do all in my power to dissuade her from this ruinous step. I shall appeal to her better nature, and not, I trust, in vain."

He hurried to the carriage, where the baroness had seated herself.

"Amalia," he whispered, "you are an admirable actress."

The baroness smiled.

"It is now time," said his highness, "for me to appeal to your better nature. I shall do so in a loud voice, for I have prepared a most virtuous homily that I am unwilling the grand duchess should miss. You will be overcome with remorse, burst into tears, throw yourself at my feet—remember that the left is the gouty one—and be forgiven. You will then be restored to favor, while Châteauroux drives off alone and in disgrace. Your plan works wonderfully."

"It is true," said the baroness, doubtfully, "that was the plan."

"And a magnificent one," said the grand duke.

"But I have altered it, your highness."

"And this alteration, Amalia?"

"Involves a trip to Vienna."

"Not yet, Amalia. We must wait."

"I am going," said the baroness, "with Monsieur de Châteauroux."

The grand duke supported himself by grasping the carriage door.

"Preposterous!" he cried.

"You have given your consent," protested the baroness, "and in the presence of the grand duchess."

"But that," said the astonished grand duke, "was part of the plan."

"Indeed, your highness," said the baroness, "it was a most important part. You must know," she continued, with some diffidence, "that I have had the misfortune to fall in love with Monsieur de Châteauroux."

"Who is in love with the grand duchess."

"I have reason to believe," said the baroness, modestly, "that he is in love with me."

"Especially after hearing him last night," suggested the grand duke.

"That scene, your highness, he had carefully rehearsed with me."

The grand duke gazed meditatively at the baroness, who had the grace to blush.

"Then it was," he asked, slowly, "a comedy for my benefit?"

"You would never have consented, you know," she began. But the grand duke's countenance, which was slowly altering to a dusky green, caused her to pause.

"You will get over it in a week, Louis," she murmured; "and you will find other—baronesses."

"Probably," said his highness, grinning in a ghastly fashion. "Nevertheless," he added, "it was a mean trick to play on the grand duchess."

"I do not think the grand duchess will complain," said the baroness.

Then a light broke slowly on the grand duke. "You planned all this beforehand?" he inquired, with a carefully modulated voice.

"Precisely, your highness."

"And Châteauroux helped you?"

"Precisely, your highness."

"And the grand duchess knew?"

"The grand duchess suggested it, your highness."

The grand duke turned his back to her. "Monsieur de Châteauroux," he called, "I find the lady is adamant. I wish you a pleasant journey." He held open the door of the carriage for Châteauroux to enter.

"You will forgive us, your highness?" asked the latter.

"You will forget?" murmured the baroness.

"I will do both," said the grand duke. *"Bon voyage, mes enfants!"*

With a cracking of whips the carriage drove off.

"Victoria," said the grand duke, with admiration, "you are a remarkable woman. I think that I will walk for a while in the gardens, and meditate on the perfections of my wife."

He strolled off in the direction of the woods. As he reached the summit of a slight incline, he turned and looked over the road that leads from Breschau to Vienna. A cloud of dust showed where the carriage had disappeared.

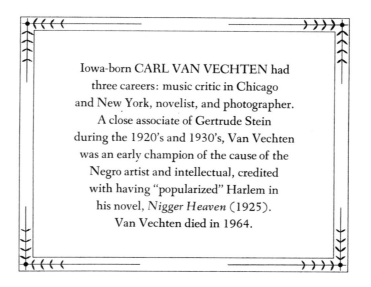

Iowa-born CARL VAN VECHTEN had
three careers: music critic in Chicago
and New York, novelist, and photographer.
A close associate of Gertrude Stein
during the 1920's and 1930's, Van Vechten
was an early champion of the cause of the
Negro artist and intellectual, credited
with having "popularized" Harlem in
his novel, *Nigger Heaven* (1925).
Van Vechten died in 1964.

How the Twelve Best Sellers Ended

CARL VAN VECHTEN

Slowly she closed the window upon which the driving rain was beating, pulling down the shade, hid the sight of his retreating figure from her eyes."

"The woman still wore her hyacinths, but the man had lost his soul."

"As the plum-blossoms fell in clouds of pink, he took her in his arms and pressed hot kisses on her red mouth."

"Then the two fled down the dark road,

one sobbing and the other cursing, while all night long a tear-stained baby lay by the dead fire."

"Drawing on one glove, Hilda carelessly threw the other over her shoulder back at Meacham, who was watching her with eager eyes. It was her answer to his unuttered question."

"God is good to some men, but to women He is merciless, and He gave none of his pity to Marian."

FROM VOL. 24, MARCH 1908

" 'Muriel, my dear,' said the duchess, 'you are perfectly right. The gentleman should return by the earlier train.' "

"The blood-red sun had sunk into the sea, and the sudden darkness of the tropics blotted out all trace of the island. As they stood together looking over the rail, Pierce drew his hands before his eyes and tried to forget both the woman by his side and the woman whom he had left behind."

"Humbled and broken, Judith fell to the ground, bowing her aching temples to the hot sand. The camel-driver threw four pieces of silver into her burnoose and rode away into the desert."

"Twice again they met: once on Broadway when Harold raised his hat, and once in Sherry's, when she was with her husband, and this time Harold gave no sign that he knew her."

"The time came when he found himself glad to have lived it all—to have known so glorious a woman, and to have forgotten her."

"He flung the hideous thing away from him and then fell dead at Andrea's feet."

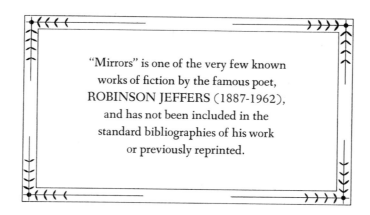

"Mirrors" is one of the very few known
works of fiction by the famous poet,
ROBINSON JEFFERS (1887-1962),
and has not been included in the
standard bibliographies of his work
or previously reprinted.

Mirrors

ROBINSON JEFFERS

About Adair? It's a curious story—perhaps I can tell you more of it than anyone else. For it was to me that Adair came to unburden his soul, the night before he smashed all his mirrors and sailed for Africa.

Insane? Not at all. But he was excitable, you remember, and highly sensitive. Things irritated him—little things that you or I would barely notice. He had the vision of an artist, and the nerves of a decadent; but he had no art, no work—the artist's safety valve.

Adair used to visit me often in the evenings, and talk. He had strange theories, and a wonderful power of making them appear reasonable. There was a vividness in him . . . I can see him now—his very expression—the whiteness of his long features. He used to sit in the big wicker chair, there by the hearth, and prove to me, step by step, that evolution is a progressive degeneracy, that man is less happy, less beautiful, less perfect, than an ichthyosaurus. Then he would light another cigarette—he smoked them interminably. He used to come in without knocking, silently, like a ghost, any time between nine and midnight. Often he would talk until dawn, and go home under the rising sun. Or he would sit silent until dawn.

FROM VOL. 40, AUGUST 1913

But his last visit was different from the others. About eleven in the evening I heard a step before the door, and a knock, and Adair's voice calling me.

"Come in," I said.

But he wouldn't come in; I had to go to the door. Adair was standing in the passage, violently excited.

"You have a mirror," he whispered, "on the wall, to the right of the bookcase."

"Yes?" I asked, wondering.

"Take it down," he said. "Take it down—out of the room. Then I'll come in." And, as a matter of fact, the mirror had to be removed before he would enter.

Then, "Shut the door," Adair said; and began to pace the floor with great strides. Three steps from that window to the opposite wall; three steps from the wall to the window; back and forth, back and forth, without speaking. And in each three steps his heel would strike twice on the rug, softly, and once, with a sharp tap, on the hardwood floor. Thud, thud, tap; tap, thud, thud—a queer rhythm which got on my nerves.

Then Adair spoke, and so abruptly that I was startled.

"Have you ever hated mirrors?"

"No," I gasped. "No. What—"

"Neither have I," he said, "till tonight. It never occurred to me. But why not? Why not? They're contemptible. Everything's contemptible."

Then suddenly, with a plunge and jerk, Adair was in the middle of his story. He talked so rapidly that my mind was outdistanced at once, and tagged along out of breath, always half a dozen words behind his meaning.

"You remember Millie Gaspard," he said. And before I could quite recall the blonde little actress, Adair was already speaking of Miss Converse, whom people regarded as his fiancée. Then Adair's talk veered back to the actress.

"You know that two years ago I was intimate with Millie Gaspard."

I nodded. That intimacy had been the root of a scandal which even Adair's inherited money was barely able to hush up.

"Millie had queer pet names to employ when she was feeling affectionate. She used to call me 'Baby of Love,' and 'Joy Child' " —Adair was speaking tragically, without a smile—"and she used to pat my hand, three little quick pats, holding it tightly in her own.

"My God!" he burst out incoherently. "I thought I was rid of her! I gave her ten thousand dollars, and thought I was rid of her.

"But the memory sticks. We're like everybody we meet. Once I heard a coachman roar at his horse—filthy words. Ten months later I heard myself shouting the same words at my terrier.

"And tonight, Alice—Miss Converse—caught my hand and patted it three little quick pats. And said, 'Baby of Love.' That was tonight, when I was leaving her."

Adair paused for breath, and I interrupted him. "But," I said, "Miss Converse—how did she—"

"She learned it from me," Adair answered. "Just as I had learned it from Millie Gaspard, who had learned it from God knows what brute when she was young.

"Alice learned it from me. I remember now that once I patted her hand—and was hot with shame, remembering from whom I had the trick. And once—perhaps twice—I called her—by the pet name."

"But why," I said—"what do you—"

"Idiot!" Adair whispered. "Do you think I can marry a woman who has learned the tricks of Millie Gaspard?

"Yet," he said, "that isn't the worst of it. The worst of it is that I know we are all mirrors—senseless mirrors—blank spaces which reflect. If I do a thing, or say a thing, it is only because someone else has done it, said it. Nothing but mirrors.

"And the sky and the earth and the water," Adair went on, "are mirrors. If I am happy, the sky is happy. If I am sorrowful, the world droops. Everywhere I look—my own face.

"And you, too," he said, raging at me with his dark eyes, "you are a mirror. You are bewildered because I am bewildered. You are exasperated because I am exasperated. If I should smile, you would smile. Bah!

"And," he whispered hopelessly, "God is a mirror. . . . My own face. My own face always. Or Millie's pet names."

With that, Adair tossed up one hand in a curiously final gesture and dropped into a chair—that wicker chair by the hearth.

But when I began to answer him—some foolish thoughts of remonstrance and consolation—Adair burst once more into speech, and raved like a mad prophet, tearing heaven and earth into shreds of similarity. "Everything is like everything else—everything reflects everything else—" So that it came to me to understand why Nero sought to destroy the world—because it looked like himself.

"There is nothing so terrible," I was thinking, "or so contemptible as one's own likeness. That is why monkeys seem unclean to us."

Then, through the cloud of my thought, I heard Adair bidding me good-bye.

"I shall sail tomorrow," he said, "for Europe, and get to Africa as quickly as possible. Perhaps in the desert, in the jungle, things won't look like myself. Good-bye."

So Adair went away the next afternoon, and has spent his life shooting big animals. Now and then he ships hunting trophies to his friends on this side. I hear that he has sent Miss Converse a rhinoceros head.

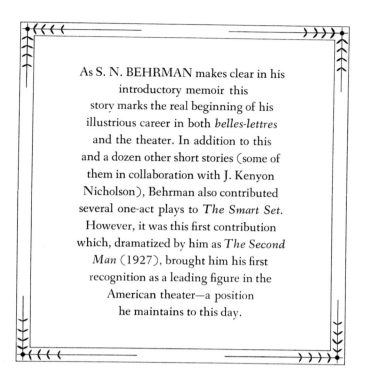

As S. N. BEHRMAN makes clear in his
introductory memoir this
story marks the real beginning of his
illustrious career in both *belles-lettres*
and the theater. In addition to this
and a dozen other short stories (some of
them in collaboration with J. Kenyon
Nicholson), Behrman also contributed
several one-act plays to *The Smart Set.*
However, it was this first contribution
which, dramatized by him as *The Second
Man* (1927), brought him his first
recognition as a leading figure in the
American theater—a position
he maintains to this day.

That Second Man

S. N. BEHRMAN

"*. . . for, together with, and, as it were behind, so much pleasurable emotion, there is
always that other strange second man in me,
calm, critical, observant, unmoved, blaséodi-
ous.*"—LORD LEIGHTON: Letter to his sister.

As Clark Storrey rang the bell of Courtney's narrow marble house he thought with
pleasure of the mournful expression with
which, he knew, Courtney would greet him.
When Courtney was gay Storrey did not find
him amusing but in his fits of depression—
lately very frequent with him—there was
something, to Storrey, almost jocund. The

sag in his plump, pasty cheeks, the little
whine that crept into his voice, the limp
droop of his big body—the spectacle of Courtney as a forlorn lover, a plump Malvolio,
appealed to Storrey's sense of humor, but,
more piquantly, to a less amiable sense.

The pleasure he derived from the contem-
plation of Courtney in his present condition,
his own role of splendid fellow and good
friend, forced him to dissimulate but it lost
little of its zest on this account. To think
that Courtney—who was a first-rate scientist,
master of a hidden vivid world which, he,
Storrey, could not enter—was at the mercy of
an emotion which made him abjectly ridic-

ulous as any clerk mooning over a post-card picture of an actress! It vindicated a notion he had long harbored that Courtney, despite his renown, was essentially quite commonplace. The notion of cold superiority that people entertained about him was a myth that Monica had completely melted.

That was pleasing to Courtney [Storrey?], who had always a bit envied and rather despised him. And it was also pleasing to him that before him alone of all people, Courtney made no effort to hide his absurd frailty.

Courtney's telegram had read:

"Must see you at once. Courtney."

So, although he was having a good time at the Seldens' house-party, he had decided to come in, especially as pretty Mrs. Morton had volunteered to motor him to town. Courtney must be in a bad way to send him a wire like that; evidently Monica had been unusually definite with him this time. . . . He hoped not too definite; Courtney mustn't be frightened off. But he felt confident he could patch things up; he smiled again at the thought of how easy it would be for him to restore Courtney's confidence. . . .

As he opened the door of the gloomy study, his smile disappeared; he advanced into the room wearing an expression of grave concern.

"Just got your wire. . . ."

Courtney gave him a limp hand and said nothing.

"I was afraid you might be ill—"

"It's Monica. She's refused me."

"Nonsense!"

"She has, I tell you. Point blank."

"You asked her to marry you?"

"I offered her everything—put my life at her feet, my work—" Courtney mopped his brow with a handkerchief he had in his hand.

"I guess I'd better try to forget her," he said miserably.

"Nonsense!" repeated Storrey cheerfully. "But tell me why? Why did she refuse you!"

His voice sounded as though he were quite surprised and not a little indignant.

Courtney made a helpless gesture.

"Doesn't love me."

"Does she love someone else?"

"That's the worst of it. She does."

"Who?"

"Wouldn't tell me. Do you know who it is?"

"Yes. It's no one. It's a lie. She doesn't love anyone."

"What makes you think so?" Eagerness leaped back into his voice and eyes.

Storrey improvised reasons. . . . He enjoyed the scene: Courtney slumped in a high-back chair looking very pale and sickly as though he were suffering from indigestion, the long table covered with neatly ordered piles of scientific journals from nearly every country in Europe, abstruse journals filled with curiously patterned figure-formulas covering whole pages.

But Courtney refused to believe, refused to be comforted. Finally Storrey, unable to resist the temptation to be ever so little malicious, said soothingly:

"After all, you have your science, old man."

Courtney responded magnificently to the prod: he turned haggard eyes at Storrey.

"Science! You think science means anything to me now? When I've lost her! I tell you I can't work since I've known her—I can't work. The books that formerly fascinated me, my researches—nothing matters to me now. When I start to do anything and get thinking of her I can't go on. I—I—get a headache," he finished miserably.

Storrey liked to hear Courtney denounce his profession in this way. What an illusion this was of the cold mastery of scientific men! They were as helpless as babies. . . .

"Of course," said Storrey after a moment, "this is all nonsense. If you want her, really want her, you can get her."

"That's what you always say. You keep telling me that. But it's not true—"

Storrey lit a cigarette.

"No doubt about it. Not in the least—"

Storrey's tone carried conviction. In spite of all Monica had said to him, Courtney felt slightly better already. He began to lift his head.

"But she told me," he began, "last night—"

"A mere child," said Storrey with finality. "Doesn't in the least know what she wants. Won't till after she's married. That's up to you."

"But she's not attracted to me—"

"She doesn't understand you. She has no appreciation of your intellectual gifts."

"It's true. Prohelium means nothing to her."

Prohelium was the name of the new element Courtney had discovered. "You must make it mean something to her. You must teach her to see how wonderful it is to widen the boundaries of knowledge, the deep mystery and elusiveness of the things you work with, the marvelous delicacy of your experiments. . . ."

Courtney sighed heavily. "If I could only talk like you, Storrey!"

"Talk! That's it—talk! By their sensitiveness to mere words women demonstrate their intellectual inferiority—and their right to the vote."

"If she only understood me—as you do!"

"My dear chap—she shall be made to."

"How?"

Storrey lit another cigarette.

"How?" repeated Courtney tensely.

Storrey slid forward comfortably in the dark leather chair till he seemed to be resting on the tip of his spine—a pose, he had read, often assumed by Arthur Balfour.

"Maternal pressure," he replied. "I'll wager you anything a poor poet can pay that Mrs. Gray doesn't know Monica's refused you."

"What if she did?"

"She'd raise Cain. You see Gray—mère—no pun intended, old chap—is desperately afraid—of guess what?"

"What?"

"That Monica will marry *me!*"

Courtney said nothing. But his face went a shade grayer. His plump cheeks hung like dew-laps.

"Of course you see how absurd it is. Monica and I—"

"I wonder you don't marry her," said Courtney a bit breathlessly. "She likes you. She likes you better than me, that's plain." Courtney's voice was not without a touch of bitterness.

"Nonsense. She doesn't—really. Fancy my being married to Monica! She'd leave me in six months. By which time I should certainly have left her. Monica couldn't stand the poverty of my ménage and," he laughed bitterly, "neither could I."

"It's strange you're not in love with Monica."

"There speaks the eternal lover. I think it strange you *are* in love with her. She's pretty—I grant you that. But—Great Heavens, man—so young!"

"She's young," said Courtney softly. His voice sounded suddenly like a far, gentle echo.

"And so full of spirits!"

"Isn't she!"

"Her laughter gets on my nerves. Like the constant ringing of chimes."

"Yes," said Courtney. "It is like chimes."

There was a silence.

Courtney seemed lost in tender revery. Storrey broke into it.

"That's the thing to do," he said. "There's no doubt of it."

"What is?"

"Monica's stepmother must be persuaded that *I* want to marry Monica. She'll never rest then until Monica is married to you."

"What makes you think so?" asked Courtney doubtfully.

"No doubt about it. The old lady is cracked about the idea of having you for a stepson-in-law. Oh, it's not your scientific eminence.

It's not even your family, though of course that has something to do with it. It's your money, my friend, your lucre, your multitudinous boodle—"

Courtney lifted a deprecating hand.

"That's what it is, old man. The Grays are mighty hard up—Monica's been dressing shamefully of late."

"She looks better—" said Courtney truculently.

"I know, old man. Niftier in gingham than a fine lady in velvet. How extraordinary, Courtney, that a chit of a girl like Monica can make a man of your eminence talk like a hack writer!"

"I don't like you to talk about Monica that way."

"Why not? She is an impudent minx, isn't she, shallow as a platter? Her lack of appreciation of you proves that."

"She's young. I sometimes think I'm too old for her," he said pathetically.

"You're only thirty-six."

"She's twenty-two. But it's not that alone. She's so gay, full of fun. I can't—prattle, Storrey. I don't follow her small talk. . . ."

"I don't wonder. Her talk is not small. It is infinitesimal. Your microscopic training should help you—"

"I don't do the things she likes, dance, play tennis—you know—"

"You're not a jazz figure, Courtney," admitted Storrey judiciously. "But you'd better marry her. If you don't she'll run away with a tenor or somebody."

"I wish to Heaven I could marry her," groaned Courtney.

"You shall. I'll begin showering attentions on Monica immediately. Poor Mrs. Gray. She'll be frightened to death."

"You're sure about this, Storrey?"

"No doubt of it."

"But if Monica doesn't love me! She told me last night she didn't—never could."

"Just marry her. She'll change her mind."

Courtney rose.

"You know, Storrey," he said, "I used to think—when I thought about it—not often, you understand, until I met Monica—that I'd never marry unless the woman wanted me as much I wanted her. But that was before I wanted any woman—as I want Monica. I'd marry her on any terms, Storrey. You understand?"

"Of course I understand, old fellow. And you shall. Mighty good thing for Monica, too."

"You really think so?"

"You have only to persist. You'll win her, as the military men say, by attrition. I've got to run now, old man—keep the pot boiling—"

"Forgive me for taking you away from the Seldens. But I just had to see you."

"That's all right, old boy. I was glad of an excuse to get away. Awful bore."

"You always make it so easy for your friends to impose on you," said Courtney earnestly. "No wonder everybody's crazy about you. . . ."

II

STORREY left Courtney's house in singularly good humor. He did not turn downtown, but cut across the avenue into Central Park. He wanted to be out in the cool sunshine, dallying pleasantly with his thoughts.

He walked along buoyantly, swinging his cane, a smile playing about his lips. He was thinking of Courtney's complete and almost pathetic reliance upon him: this man who possessed a knowledge and a skill, a sensitiveness to the hidden forces of nature, that Courtney could not help admiring. . . . Courtney's discovery had brought him the highest fame in scientific circles, he was elected an honorary F. R. S. in England and had even been mentioned for the Nobel prize. . . . . And with all this Courtney had inherited an immense fortune from his father. Courtney had met Monica at a house-party to which his mother had dragged him and the man of science had fallen hopelessly in love at first sight with the beautiful, golden-haired girl, not, Storrey reflected, as a man of the world falls in love, with a certain genial deprecation of his irrationality, but as an awkward schoolboy falls in love.

In Monica's presence Courtney would become tongue-tied; he could do nothing but silently register adoration. . . . He would sit dumbly staring at her; once when the three of them were having tea together Monica asked Courtney whether he was trying to hypnotize her. . . . She took a certain delight in torturing him; she was always unnecessarily risqué in his presence, would talk of having "affairs" with the blithe ingenuousness of a child prattling of storks.

"When are you and I going to have an affair, Storrey?" she would ask. "You're awfully slow about it. . . ."

Her virginal beauty made her audacities irresistibly piquant, but they hurt Courtney so that he often begged her to stop. . . . An avowed materialist Courtney professed the belief that creation was the result of a fortuitous and not altogether happy combination of circumstances.

"A slight change in the temperature," he was fond of quoting, "and we should have been at the mercy of the ants."

Lately Storrey had twitted him with his conservatism in the field of morals; was it really so important that Monica should make a fetish of monogamy in view of the Creator's carelessness about more fundamental things.

But Courtney had not pursued the subject, reiterating stubbornly: "I don't like her to talk that way. Of course I know she wouldn't do anything—well—you know—wrong. She couldn't. She's too pure, too good. But I don't like her to talk that way."

Nevertheless Monica kept on talking that way and Storrey enjoyed Courtney's discomfiture as much as she did.

. . . Storrey detested this Puritanism in Courtney; he knew it was the instinct for exclusive possession that made him want to forbid Monica the sharing of even verbal intimacies with others. . . . The girl he wanted for himself must be "as chaste as ice, as pure as snow." . . . It made Storrey indignant to think of it; what right had Courtney to desire for himself alone this beautiful creature full of high spirits and laughter—this desiccated thinking-machine, as intelligent as a mole inside his scientific burrow, but quite helpless and uninteresting once out of it? . . .

Storrey's vindictiveness was partly the result of his envy at Courtney's distinctions, the place he had won for himself in the world; actually he knew that Courtney's activities were not mole-like, but the result of thought-processes as beautifully crystalline as a poem of George Meredith. Storrey's mind was not as superficial as his life and work, which was his tragedy.

The truth was that in an obscure way he was jealous of Courtney; jealous of the place he had won for himself in the intellectual world, jealous of his money, jealous of the fact that he would marry Monica. For of course he would marry Monica. There was no way out of it for her—unless he himself married her. . . .

For a moment he toyed with that temptation of taking her away from Courtney. Monica was lovely—and really a dear. Storrey liked her better, after all, than any girl he knew. She never really got on his nerves; when she began to bore him she would always know it and say: "All right, Storrey, I'm leaving."

Moreover there was something quite brave and fine about Monica; Storrey knew that, too. She had been going the pace rather swiftly of late, but chiefly because there was nothing else for her to do.

"We're too poor to refuse invitations, mother and I," she had said to him one day.

And another time, when she described the antics of a gay party she had attended:

"I'd have done anything that night. An antidote to the Genesis-man. He'd spent the afternoon with me."

The sobriquet had been applied to Courtney by Monica after his first attempt to initiate her into modern scientific theories of evolution. He had asked her how she thought it all began and she had replied innocently with the orthodox recital culminating in the Garden of Eve. Courtney, who had taken her quite seriously, brushed away the myth with indulgent superiority and devoted a half hour to the nebular theory.

"So you see, Monica," he had said in conclusion, "it's not true what you've read in the Bible."

"But I like the Bible ever so much better," she had answered quickly; "there's a girl like me in it. . . ."

Storrey's smile, which had disappeared as he thought of Courtney's unapproachable eminence, returned as he recalled this recital. She was a demure little witch! It might be the best thing he could do, after all, to marry Monica. He would settle down, quit this awful business of pretending to be something he wasn't, "a snapper up of unconsidered trifles," quit wrapping banal ideas in adroitly turned verse, and get down to brass tacks artistically and actually. . . .

He was sick of being tame cat to half the people in New York, sick of playing the good fellow to people he despised. . . .

But a moment's consideration and he banished the thought. It was too late to change. He should lead exactly the same sort of life if he married Monica as he led now. He would probably be unfaithful and Monica would probably be jealous. . . . No, it was better to continue in his present role in life, a spectator who occasionally manipulated a few strings. . . .

It would be interesting after all to see Monica and Courtney married. An odd couple. Monica would be bored to death. What would be her revenge?

He repeated the question to himself. . . . His smile deepened.

"How funny!" he exclaimed inwardly. "Poor old Courtney. . . . !"

III

WHEN he got to his rooms he found a telephone message from Monica. He was not surprised. The message said: "Very important." That, too, was a cry for help; the second he had received that day. How simple people were, how helpless; they could be turned as easily as a rhyme. . . . Of course Monica had called him up to tell him that she had refused Courtney, that she had foolishly told her mother about it, that there had been a volcanic scene. . . . She wanted to get support from him to help her through the crisis. Poor Monica. She would have to succumb. . . . He thought for a moment of calling her, but decided to wait till she called him again.

He sat down in a great easy chair, pushed a specially prepared arm around so that it made a broad wooden bridge over his knees, reached for a pad and fountain pen and began to write.

He sat slumped down in the chair—he could adjust the angle of the impromptu desk by turning a screw on the side. He always wrote this way; in the same position he assumed when he smoked his after dinner cigar.

"I wonder if I'd do better work if I really had to earn a living by this stuff," he asked himself. "Probably I'd do better work. Or perhaps I'd just turn out a lot more of the same stuff. . . ."

Very comfortably Storrey began to write . . . a faint smile hovering about his lips as he toyed with the words. . . . A few nights before, at a dance at the Seldens, he had taken a walk in the moonlight with a girl; they had been dancing and he asked her to go outside with him. They stepped out through the open French windows, crossed the lawn, and walked down a narrow path between high poplars, with the stars quite close, and the moon showing between them. . . .

It was a most curious moon, red-bronze in color, wafer-thin, exquisitely curved, like a tiny scimitar, a shaving of a moon. God, Courtney had said, must be a curious person to fashion such a moon, a butcher with artistic leanings. Or was He an artist suffering from a sadistic atavism? Which did she think? The girl thought it was slightly chilly and hadn't they better go back to the ball-room?

They went back to the ball-room. . . . Storrey put the walk and the talk into a poem. While writing he struck off several figures that rather pleased him; one was that the tree-tops looked like hedges in the sky between which the stars grew like buttercups. There was a hint of nostalgia, the wavering suggestion of sensuousness as the man and the girl stood for a moment on the brink of understanding, then the sophisticated monologue on the moon breaking the spell! At the end the usual ironic fillip: the mask of convention drawn on with the white gloves, a polite request for a waltz from an ancient dowager. . . .

Storrey played with his ideas lazily, pared them off, tucked them in. He had written that poem a good many times before. And, when he had nearly finished modeling it, the telephone rang.

Storrey was glad. The interruption was welcome. He had had enough of creation. He reached out and took the 'phone from the tabouret. Monica's voice sounded strained, a bit breathless.

"Hello, kiddie!" he said heartily.

She reproached him for not responding to her message.

"Is it really so important?" he asked.

"Very. I've simply *got* to see you, Storrey."

They made a luncheon engagement. He got together the written sheets and put them into a drawer. He was pleased that he had done some work and that he was going to see Monica.

There had been a gravity in her voice today that was quite unusual for her and quite appealing. She must really be upset at the idea of marrying Courtney. One

couldn't exactly blame her; Courtney would forever fill her ears with halting expositions of scientific theory, not because he was interested in her mental development, but that she might have the background to appreciate the splendor of his achievement.

It was absurd, thought Storrey, to think that scientists were less egoists than artists. Their deeper consciousness of the tragic insignificance of man, of the feebleness of his cry amid the vast solitudes of time and space, did not mitigate the intensity of their appetites and vanities. Nor were their minds different from other peoples'; they were reputed more rational because, since the problems they attack take longer to solve, they have less leisure for the gratification of instinct. . . .

He met Monica in the lounge just off the lobby of the Ritz. Storrey's income was small enough to require husbanding, but he never economized on food. Dining at smart houses had sharpened an instinctive epicureanism. Besides, he liked to be seen at the right places. But today Monica would not lunch in the hotel with him:

"Please," she said. "Let's go to some place quiet. I want to *talk* to you."

"That means," he said lightly, "that you want me to talk to you, to give you advice. I can give you advice here as well as anywhere."

"I want you alone today. We'll meet people we know here. I always meet you in crowds." Already they were walking out of the hotel.

"I know a nice little place in Fifty-first Street," she said. "The dearest old ladies come there to drink iced tea."

"So that's it? You want a setting that will show off your youth."

She looked swiftly at him, smiling with arch gravity.

He had never seen her so subdued. He had never seen her quite so perfect. Sometimes he thought her coloring a bit too vivid, but today she was pale. Her golden hair peeped out from beneath a small toque, two dark-blue bird's wings, shaped like a helmet.

He told her she was looking charming, but she did not seem as pleased as usual at a compliment from him.

"I've read your St. Augustine," she said suddenly. "Most of it."

"I wanted you to read all of it," he said severely.

He had reproached her the last time for a wicked remark she had made about Courtney and he had told her it was sacrilegious for a girl named after the mother of St. Augustine to talk that way. She had not known that Monica was the name of St. Augustine's mother and she had become greatly interested in the career of the Saint. She wanted to know whether Monica, the Saint's mother, had written anything and Storrey told her that she was not a writer so far as he knew, having more important work to do. But her son had written a rather well-known work called the Confessions and the title had so intrigued Monica that she had made him promise to send her a copy.

"Yes," she said eagerly, "I read it nearly all. I thought it would be dull, but it wasn't, because you know he started off very badly, this saint. He only gets good—when he gets tired. . . . Is that it?"

She looked at him questioningly, her eyes quite serious.

"Tell me," she repeated, "I want to know."

"It is difficult, little ingénue, to determine in such cases, whether renunciation or satiety is the cause. But what are such delicate problems to you? If I thought you'd have stopped with the conversion—"

"I know. You wanted me to be just edified. Am I so very wicked?"

"Not wicked. Merely not discriminating."

She pouted.

"Why am I?"

"Because," he said, "the cream of humanity worships you, and you spend your time lunching with a—a footnote."

"What do you mean, a footnote?" She frowned adorably when she was perplexed.

"A scribbler," he said, borrowing easily from a much-read novel, "is a mere footnote to reality."

"Oh, but I like footnotes," she said eagerly. "You know why. Because once we—a girl I knew at school and myself—got hold of some dry-looking translation of a novel by—oh, I forget—one of those wicked old Romans. Every few seconds or so there were stars in the text and down the bottom of the page there were little paragraphs that really belonged where the stars were. Only they were in Latin! We got a Latin dictionary—Lois and I. . . ."

She chattered on telling of their difficulties with the dictionary. . . . They turned into the restaurant, Monica nodding gaily to the waitresses; she seemed to know them all. They passed through the long dining-room and into an open space in the rear where there were small tables under colored umbrellas.

"So you see, Storrey, I'm just a light, giddy creature and I love footnotes. Now what are you going to do about it?"

He did not answer for a moment.

"You're incorrigible, Monica," he said finally.

"I know what you're thinking: that I ought to go in for solider things, heavy textbooks. Oh, Storrey, imagine living all your life with a textbook—how bored you'd get!"

"Wouldn't be bad. If you had an occasional footnote to relieve the monotony."

"I know what you want, Storrey. You want all the fun and none of the responsibility."

He leaned close to her and touched her hand.

"Don't talk like that, kiddie," he said. "I'm terribly fond of you—today."

"Just today?"

"Always."

"Then you might prove it."

"I am proving it."

"If you are, then you'll do me the favor I've come to ask of you."

"What is it?"

"It's such a little thing." She looked at him with troubled eyes. "It's—that you should marry me."

He was astonished. He was astonished because she wasn't laughing, because there was no laughter in her eyes. He was uncomfortable. He was sorry he had come. It was a mistake.

"I'll be ever so good, Storrey, really. I'm fond of you, you know. I won't bother you—ever. I'll just sit in a corner and not make a sound all the time while you write your wonderful poems—"

That was one thing about Monica he didn't entirely like. She really thought his poems wonderful and devoured them as they appeared, like caramels. . . .

Fortunately the waitress came. . . .

They ordered consomme and creamed chicken and a salad, leaving the dessert to be decided on later. The waitress disappeared to fetch the consomme.

"What do you say, Storrey?" she resumed. "You see how persistent I am—"

She was smiling now. Storrey solemnly assured her that he would love her for ever and a day but that he would certainly not marry her.

"All right for you!" said Monica and began nibbling a biscuit, quite angry with him.

"The trouble is you don't understand anything about anything," said Storrey.

"The trouble is that you're damn selfish," said Monica. "Yes, you are. You like to go around and be petted by people. You're afraid I'll interfere." Her tone changed suddenly. "But I wouldn't interfere. Really I wouldn't. You could do anything you liked. You see, I know you're really fonder of me than of anyone. Just as I know that I'm fonder of you than I ever shall be of anyone."

"The very young," he said, "especially when female, are subject to obsessions."

"You might think you're so old yourself. You're only thirty. . . . Mother always calls you 'that young fellow Storrey'! . . ."

Suddenly Monica held an imaginary lorgnette to her eyes and began speaking in a high, strained falsetto: "'That rather conceited young fellow—er—what's his name—oh, yes, Storrey. Storrey . . . ! Curious name, very curious. Writes. What? Poetry? You mean verses, my dear, verses. Has anyone ever read them? I'm sure I haven't. No time for such trash, you know—'" Monica lowered the lorgnette. Her mimicry was delightful.

"Your stepmother is an intelligent woman. Monica. She doesn't even squander her time recklessly."

"Stingy old thing! She wants me to marry that old encyclopedia just because he's rich!"

"You refer to Courtney?"

"You know I do," said Monica savagely. "This shows—how much you like me! You're always playing with me. You're always making fun of me. I ask you to marry me and—instead of being glad—and saying yes—you—you—keep me in suspense." A tear glistened on her eyelash.

"I don't think it's fair of you to ask me to luncheon and take advantage of my absurdly sympathetic nature by threatening to cry. Please remove that teardrop, Monica—unobtrusively. . . ."

"Gosh, I am sloppy! I'm sorry, old boy. But I've been yawning with the old lady till I'm half hysterical. Honest, I don't know whether I'm coming or going." She dabbed her eyes furtively with a bit of handkerchief, "Like a manicurist at a movie, aren't I, Storrey?" She grimaced.

"You're a dear child, Monica, and I'm terribly in love with you, and to show you that I am I'm going to take you for a drive in the park in a hansom cab and make you feel ashamed of yourself—"

She clapped her hands joyfully.

"Oh, Storrey!" she gasped ecstatically. "That's just what I've always wanted you to do to me. Is it a promise?"

"You're incorrigible," said Storrey, with decorum.

IV

PEOPLE liked Clark Storrey for various reasons, some because he didn't take himself seriously; others because, though a writer, he was a "regular fellow"; others still because they thought him singularly detached in his judgments of things; and everybody liked him because they thought him a loyal and disinterested friend. Few people understood the true source of these things they deemed his virtues.

It was true, for example, that Storrey did not take himself seriously but that sprang not so much from the absence of conceit in him as from the absolution it offered him from the struggle to attain a perfect and unhackneyed form of expression, from struggle of any sort whatever. If he was a "regular fellow" it was because, among business men and society women, he commanded thereby an adulation other artists would not have yielded him. If he was detached in his judgments it was because it helped him to justify his frailities to see them mirrored in others. The virtue attributed to him by everybody, that he was a loyal friend, was sheer nonsense and he despised the people who believed it. No man manipulated his friends as he did: he got from them everything he wanted, from a yachting cruise in the Mediterranean to the loan of a motor-car, things his luxury-loving soul demanded but that he was too poor to get for himself.

In the hansom with Monica, Storrey thought about these things and, what was unusual with him, he thought about them with a certain compunction. He knew the truth about himself, and now, for the first time, with Monica sitting beside him, her hand resting on his, the knowledge gave him a certain twinge of discomfort.

After all, wasn't he running a serious risk in going on this way? Mightn't he become terribly bored, with a growing sense of emptiness, isolation, stealing up around him? . . . No, there was small danger of that: he loved material comforts too much, and, while he had them he could not remain long unhappy. . . .

He looked at Monica's pure profile. . . . Why should he give her up to Courtney? It was ridiculous to give her up to Courtney. If he didn't marry Monica he would never marry anyone; that he knew. To think of her married to Courtney was a little like thinking of her wearing an eternal dead-white mask and hideous clothes. Courtney would not become her. . . .

And yet he had just been telling her that it was eminently fitting for her to marry Courtney, that he would provide her with the exquisite background her loveliness needed.

"I can't marry him, Storrey, I can't," she was saying.

"He'll be a wonderful husband for you. Just the best. Won't bother you. Spends ages in the laboratory, you know."

"But he'll come back from the laboratory. I'm sure he doesn't sleep in the laboratory."

She looked at him with eyes of unblemished innocence. He patted her cheek. He liked her best when she looked like that. . . . Why didn't he take her in his arms? Why didn't he kiss her? Why didn't he carry her off and live with her and fashion poems for her? No. That sort of idyl wasn't possible for him. If she were rich—very rich—perhaps. Or if he were. . . . But limited means drove people too much together. "I mustn't do it," he kept telling himself.

"I've told mother, you know," said Monica finally, as though she had just remembered something.

"Told her what?"

"That I love you."

"You didn't!"

"Yes," she said tranquilly.

"And what did you say—about me?"

"I told her you loved me, too. And that you had asked me to marry you."

"You impertinent—! How dared you tell such a lie!"

"I'll tell you. I thought that if I told

mother that you had asked me that you would be—well—sort of compromised—and you'd *have* to ask me. I'm trying to get it—sort of spread around. Now wait—" She put her hand over his mouth to silence his protest. "You see, I'm doing it for your good. I know that you do love me. I know that you do want to marry me. I know the reason you haven't asked me yourself is because you think you haven't enough money and that I want all sorts of frivolous things. It's just like you—you're so splendid and always thinking of other people. But you misjudge me, Storrey. I could be most awfully happy on just what you have. And so could you. So I'm just telling everybody that we're engaged. . . ."

"You wretched child! You make me furious with you! But you're not really doing it!"

"Oh, but I am! Isn't it jolly? I'm thinking of sending an announcement to the papers. Of course! That's *just* what I'll do."

"You'll do nothing of the sort."

She laughed joyously.

"I've got you, Storrey. I've got you at last!"

She was maddening. . . .

"You'll do no such thing," he repeated stupidly, not knowing what to say to her.

"Yes, I will. I've told everyone, so it might as well be in the papers!"

"You little goose! Don't you see that now you'll have to marry Courtney? Your stepmother despises me. She'll disown you if you don't marry Courtney now. You'll have to marry him because you'll have to marry someone. I certainly shan't. Your stepmother will insist on it—to keep you from marrying me." He was genuinely frightened now.

"But how is she going to keep me from marrying you?"

"She won't have to. I'll disappear. I'll go away. I'll abandon you."

"You wouldn't, Storrey!"

"I won't let you ruin your life. . . ." He didn't want to make that hypocritical speech. But habit was too strong. . . .

"You wouldn't have people say you jilted me? And have them laugh at me. . . . ?"

"That's just what I'm going to do," he said fiercely.

Twilight had fallen. . . . In the half-darkness that had descended on them swiftly while they jogged along in the hansom, he saw her lips tremble slightly.

He touched her face with his hands and then drew her to him, kissing her eyes and cheeks and her. . . .

She sighed and rested in his arms contentedly, like a tired child. . . . "Oh, Storrey," she whispered, "you make me so happy, Storrey. . . ."

V

THEY were married in the country on the lawn of Fairview, overlooking the Hudson. Courtney believed in quiet weddings, so there were only a few people, immediate relatives and intimate friends. Storrey was best man.

It was a fine June day. The guests gathered on the terrace in front of the house, chatting and laughing together in little groups of twos and threes. A string orchestra played from a bay window screened with foliage. The long, low-set, rambling house had an air of having settled itself comfortably on the crest of the hill, like an old hen sitting on an egg.

Inside, the Bishop who was to perform the ceremony stood with his back to the great rubble fireplace in the living-room, dressed in full regalia (Courtney's mother was High Church), his surplice blowing in the breeze that swept through the open windows. The Bishop, in a deep, rich voice, was saying things about weddings. . . .

Storrey felt uncomfortable, nervous, irritated. He walked into the library to smoke a cigarette. Courtney jumped at him from the chair in which he had been sitting:

"I'm frightfully nervous, Storrey!"

Storrey regarded him coldly. An intense dislike of Courtney had taken possession of him.

"I was going to send for you, Storrey," continued Courtney. "I wanted you near me."

"You'd better go in. I think you're wanted inside—"

Storrey found it unbearable to be talking to him.

"Wanted? Already?" He seized Storrey's hand. "All right. But I want you to know that I'll never forget what you've done for me. I owe it all to you. The happiest man in the world—"

He fumbled away, muttering gratitudes. . . . Storrey, singularly unhappy, walked on through the library and came out on the veranda, encircling the rear of the house. . . . Well, he'd done it! He'd thrown her away! Why? Why had he done it? Why had he given her up? He did not know. . . .

A quick picture of Monica rose up before him, as she had been that last time—looking beseechingly at him and saying:

"You wouldn't abandon me, Storrey?"

"Damn him!" His fists clenched as he cursed Courtney under his breath. "Damn him! Damn him!" And after a moment: "What's the matter with you? You're being beastly. You're being sentimental. You're being jealous."

And he repeated to himself over and over the thousand reasons why marriage with Monica was impossible for him. If the whole thing were to do over he would do again exactly what he had done. There was no doubt of it. And yet. . . .

And yet he could not shake off his mood, the deepening sense he felt that in throwing Monica into Courtney's arms he had repressed the finest impulse he had ever had. . . . But of course it wasn't that at all. It was jealousy. Plain jealousy. It was that he didn't want Courtney to have her. What had Courtney done to deserve her. . . .?

"Damn that fellow," he said to himself, thinking suddenly of Courtney's scientific distinction. "He'll probably discover the Riddle of the Universe some weekend. . . ."

What was the matter with him? Was he losing his sense of humor? What should he do with Monica on his hands?

It was just like Courtney to be rotten with money. If only he had Courtney's money. What a time he could give Monica with it!

A clear soprano sounded suddenly. . . . "Oh, Promise Me. . . ." Storrey stood by the rail of the veranda, his hands in his pockets, staring off into space. . . . He would go on forever, he supposed, writing nice little verses to titillate the fancies of middle-aged virgins . . . eating other peoples' dinners and being pleasant to everybody. He would probably get fat. . . . Yes, he would certainly get fat. . . . Already his collar was getting too tight for him. . . .

What a life! He wished he were blamed well out of it!

Courtney rushed in on him, seized him. . . .

"For Heaven's sake, Storrey," he almost gasped. "We're all ready—waiting for you. Ten minutes late. . . ."

Storrey addressed a remark to Courtney, which, happily, Courtney did not hear. Then he followed him inside.

VI

THE Bishop was still talking about marriage. He was delivering generalizations to his clients. . . . "It is an honorable estate . . ." he was assuring them. Did the Bishop really believe that? Hadn't he read Shaw?

Then, for the first time, Storrey looked at Monica. She was standing with raised head looking the Bishop square in the eyes. There was something defiant in her bearing, something, too, unconquered and unconquerable.

"She's wonderful," Storrey said to himself. He looked at Courtney. He was standing limply, his big body looking flabbier than ever, his eyes fixed on the ground.

The Bishop's voice rose and fell. He was talking now about sharing things. . . . Storrey wondered what Monica was thinking. Was she aware of him? Of course she must be. Did she hate him? Would she continue to hate him? Did she understand him now or did she still believe that in renouncing her he was actuated by altruism? Would they ever resume the old camaraderie? Not for a year, alas, certainly. . . . But, maybe, sometime. Ennui might probably set in. When Courtney's talk about the nebular hypothesis might probably make her feel like jumping out of a window.

Storrey's depression began to lift. . . . Yes, Courtney might probably try to make an intellectual of Monica, not because he liked intellectual women, but in order to stimulate appreciation of his own achievements. And one day his hesitating expositions might probably drive her into hysterics and she might throw a book at him and run out of the room to be away from him. . . . And then she might probably telephone to him, Storrey. And he might probably meet her somewhere, perhaps in the old ladies' rendezvous in Fifty-first Street and he might see the desperation in Monica's eyes and he would understand. He would be gentle. He would be silent. He would be comforting. . . .

". . . Let him speak now or forever after hold his peace . . ." boomed the Bishop.

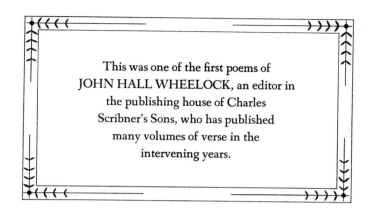

This was one of the first poems of
JOHN HALL WHEELOCK, an editor in
the publishing house of Charles
Scribner's Sons, who has published
many volumes of verse in the
intervening years.

A Persian Love Song

JOHN HALL WHEELOCK

WOULD that I might become you,
Losing myself, my sweet.
So longs the dust that lies
About the rose's feet.

So longs the last dim star
Hung on the verge of night;
She moves, she melts, she slips,
She trembles into the light.

FROM VOL. 37, JUNE 1912

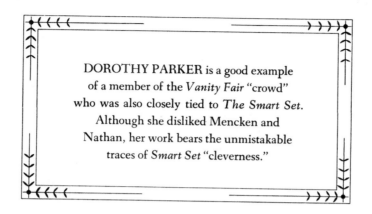

DOROTHY PARKER is a good example
of a member of the *Vanity Fair* "crowd"
who was also closely tied to *The Smart Set.*
Although she disliked Mencken and
Nathan, her work bears the unmistakable
traces of *Smart Set* "cleverness."

Too Bad

DOROTHY PARKER

"My dear," Mrs. Marshall said to Mrs. Ames, "I never was so surprised in my life. Never in my life. Why, Grace and I were like that—just like *that.*"

She held up her right hand, the upstanding first and second fingers rigidly close together, in illustration.

Mrs. Ames shook her head sadly, and offered the cinnamon toast.

"Imagine!" said Mrs. Marshall, refusing it, though with a longing eye. "We were going to have dinner with them last Tuesday night, and then I got this letter from Grace from this little place up in Connecticut, saying she was going to be up there she didn't know how long, and she thought, when she came back, she'd probably take just one big room with a kitchenette. Ernest was living at the Athletic Club, she said."

"But what did they do about their apartment?" Mrs. Ames' voice was high with anxiety.

"Why, it seems his sister took it, furnished and all—by the way, remind me, I must go and see her," said Mrs. Marshall. "They wanted to move into town, anyway, and they were looking for a place."

"Doesn't she feel terribly about it—his sister?" asked Mrs. Ames.

"Oh—terribly," Mrs. Marshall dismissed

the word as inadequate. "My dear, think how everybody that knew them feels. Think how I feel. I don't know when I've had a thing depress me more. If it had been anybody but the Weldons!"

Mrs. Ames nodded.

"That's what I said," she retorted.

"That's what everybody says." Mrs. Marshall quickly took away any undeserved credit. "To think of the Weldons separating! Why, I always used to say to Jim, 'Well, there's one happily married couple, anyway,' I used to say, 'so congenial, and with that nice apartment, and all.' And then, right out of a clear sky, they go and separate. I simply can't understand what on earth made them do it. It just seems too awful!"

Again Mrs. Ames nodded, slowly and sadly.

"Yes, it always seems too bad, a thing like that does," she said. "It's too bad."

II

Mrs. Ernest Weldon wandered about the orderly living-room, giving it some of those little feminine touches. She was not especially good as a touch-giver. The idea was pretty, and appealing to her. Before she was married, she had dreamed of herself as moving softly about her new dwelling, deftly moving a vase here or straightening a flower there, and thus transforming it from a house to a home. Even now, after seven years of marriage, she liked to picture herself in the gracious act.

But, though she conscientiously made a try at it every night as soon as the silk-shaded lamps were lit, she was always a bit bewildered as to how one went about performing those tiny miracles that make all the difference in the world to a room. The living-room, it seemed to her, looked good enough as it was—as good as it would ever look, with that mantelpiece and the same old furniture. Delia, one of the most thoroughly feminine of creatures, had subjected it to a long series

of emphatic touches earlier in the day, and none of her handiwork had since been disturbed. But the feat of making all the difference in the world, so Mrs. Weldon had always heard, was not a thing to be left to servants. Touch-giving was a wife's job. And Mrs. Weldon was not one to shirk the business she had entered.

With an almost pitiful air of uncertainty, she strayed over to the mantel, lifted a small Japanese vase, and stood with it in her hand, gazing helplessly around the room. The white-enameled bookcase caught her eye, and gratefully she crossed to it and set the vase upon it, carefully rearranging various ornaments to make room. To relieve the congestion, she took up a framed photograph of Mr. Weldon's sister in evening gown and eye-glasses, again looked all about, and then set it timidly on the piano. She smoothed the piano-cover ingratiatingly, straightened the copies of "A Day in Venice," "To a Wild Rose," and "Three O'Clock in the Morning," which stood ever upon the rack, walked over to the tea-table and effected a change of places between the cream-jug and the sugarbowl.

Then she stepped back, and surveyed her innovations. It was amazing how little difference they made to the room.

Sighing, Mrs. Weldon turned her attention to a bowl of daffodils, slightly past their first freshness. There was nothing to be done there; the omniscient Delia had refreshed them with clear water, had clipped their stems, and removed their more passé sisters. Still Mrs. Weldon bent over them pulling them gently about.

She liked to think of herself as one for whom flowers would thrive, who must always have blossoms about her, if she would be truly happy. When her living-room flowers died, she almost never forgot to stop in at the florist's, the next day, and get a fresh bunch. She told people, in little bursts of confidence, that she loved flowers. There was something almost apologetic in her way of uttering her tender avowal, as if she would beg her listeners not to consider her too bizarre in her taste. It seemed rather as though she expected the hearer to fall back, startled, at her words, crying, "Not really! Well, what *are* we coming to?"

She had other little confessions of affection, too, that she made from time to time; always with a little hesitation, as if understandably delicate about baring her heart, she told her love for color, the country, a good time, a really interesting play, nice materials, well-made clothes, and sunshine. But it was her fondness for flowers that she acknowledged oftenest. She seemed to feel that this, even more than her other predilections, set her apart from the general.

Mrs. Weldon gave the elderly daffodils a final pat, now, and once more surveyed the room, to see if any other repairs suggested themselves. Her lips tightened as the little Japanese vase met her gaze; distinctly, it had been better off in the first place. She set it back, irritation that the sight of the mantel always gave her, welling within her.

She had hated the mantelpiece from the moment they had first come to look at the apartment. There were other things that she had always hated about the place, too—the long, narrow hall, the dark dining-room, the inadequate closets. But Ernest had seemed to like the apartment well enough, so she had said nothing, then or since. After all, what was the use of fussing? Probably there would always be drawbacks, wherever they lived. There were enough in the last place they had had.

So they had taken the apartment on a five-year lease—that was four years and three months still to go. Mrs. Weldon felt suddenly weary. She lay down on the davenport, and pressed her thin hand against her dull brown hair.

Mr. Weldon came down the street, bent almost double in his battle with the wind from the river. His mind went over its nightly dark thoughts on living near Riverside Drive, five blocks from a subway station—two of those blocks loud with savage gales. He did not much like their apartment, even when he reached it. As soon as he had seen that dining-room, he had realized that they must always breakfast by artificial light—a thing he hated. But Grace had never appeared to notice it, so he had held his peace. It didn't matter much, anyway, he explained to himself. There was pretty sure to be something wrong, everywhere. The dining-room wasn't much worse than that bedroom on the court, in the last place. Grace had never seemed to mind that, either.

Mrs. Weldon opened the door at his ring.

"Well!" she said, cheerily.

They smiled brightly at each other.

"Hel-lo," he said. "Well! You home?"

They kissed, slightly. She watched with polite interest while he hung up his hat and coat, removed the evening papers from his pocket, and handed one to her.

"Bring the papers?" she said, taking it.

She preceded him along the narrow hall to the living-room, where he let himself slowly down into his big chair, with a sound between a sigh and a groan. She sat opposite him, on the davenport. Again they smiled brightly at each other.

"Well, what have you been doing with yourself today?" he inquired.

She had been expecting the question. She had planned, before he came in, how she would tell him all the little events of her day—how the woman in the grocer's shop had had an argument with the cashier, and how Delia had tried out a new salad for lunch, with but moderate success, and how Alice Marshall had come to tea and it was quite true that Norma Matthews was going to have another baby. She had woven them into a lively little narrative, carefully choosing amusing phrases of description; had felt that she was going to tell it well and with spirit, and that he might laugh at the account of the occurrence in the grocer's. But now, as she considered it, it seemed to her a long, dull story. She had not the energy to begin it. And he was already smoothing out his paper.

"Oh, nothing," she said, with a gay little laugh. "Did you have a nice day?"

"Why—" he began. He had had some idea of telling her how he had finally put through that Detroit thing, and how tickled J. G. had seemed to be about it. But his interest waned, even as he started to speak. Besides, she was engrossed in breaking off a loose thread from the silk flowers on one of the pillows beside her.

"Oh, pretty fair," he said.

"Tired?" she asked, anxiously.

"Not so much," he answered. "Why—want to do anything tonight?"

"Why, not unless you do," she said, brightly. "Whatever you say."

"Whatever *you* say," he corrected her, chivalrously.

The subject closed. There was a third exchange of smiles, and then he hid most of himself behind his paper.

Mrs. Weldon, too, turned to the newspaper. But it was an off night for news—some sort of tariff business, a failure in Wall Street, an impending strike, a four-day-old murder mystery. No one she knew had died or become engaged or married, or had attended any social functions. The fashions depicted on the woman's page were for Miss Fourteen-to-Sixteen. The advertisements ran mostly to bread, and sauces, and foot remedies, and sales of kitchen utensils. She put the paper down.

She wondered how Ernest could get so much enjoyment out of a newspaper. He could occupy himself with one for almost an hour, and then pick up another and go all through the same news with unabated interest. She wished that she could. She wished, even more than that, that she could think of something to say. She glanced

around the room for inspiration.

"See my pretty daffy-down-dillies?" she said, finding it. To anyone else, she would have referred to them as daffodils.

Mr. Weldon looked in the direction of the flowers.

"M-m-mm," he said appreciatively, and returned to the news.

She looked at him, and shook her head despondently. He did not see, behind the paper; nor did she see that he was not reading. He was waiting, his hands gripping the printed sheet till their knuckles were blue-white, for her next remark.

It came.

"I love flowers," she said, in one of her little rushes of confidence.

Her husband did not answer. He sighed, his grip relaxed, and he went on reading.

Mrs. Weldon searched the room for another suggestion.

"Ernie," she cooed, "I'm so comfortable. Wouldn't you like to get up and get my handkerchief off the piano for me?"

He rose instantly.

"Why, certainly," he said.

The way to ask people to fetch handkerchiefs, he thought as he went back to his chair, was to ask them to do it, and not try to make them think that you were giving them a treat. Either come right out and ask them, would they or wouldn't they, or else get up and get your handkerchief yourself.

"Thank you ever so much," his wife said enthusiastically.

Delia appeared in the doorway. "Dinner," she murmured bashfully, as if it were not quite a nice word for a young woman to use, and vanished.

"Dinner, Ern," cried Mrs. Weldon gaily, getting up.

"Just minute," issued indistinctly from behind the newspaper.

Mrs. Weldon waited. Then her lips compressed, and she went over and playfully took the paper from her husband's hands. She smiled carefully at him, and he smiled back at her.

"You go ahead in," he said, rising. "I'll be right with you. I've just got to wash up."

She looked after him, and something like a volcanic eruption took place within her. You'd think that just one night—just one little night—he might go and wash before dinner was announced. Just one night—it didn't seem much to ask. But she said nothing. God knew it was aggravating, but after all, it wasn't worth the trouble of fussing about.

She was waiting, cheerful and bright, courteously refraining from beginning her soup, when he took his place at the table.

"Oh, tomato soup, eh?" he said, animatedly.

"Yes," she answered. "You like it, don't you?"

"Who—me?" he said. "Oh, yes. Yes, indeed."

She smiled at him.

"Yes, I thought you liked it," she said.

"You like it, too, don't you?" he inquired.

"Oh, yes," she assured him. "Yes, I like it ever so much. I'm awfully fond of tomato soup."

"Yes," he said, "there's nothing much better than tomato soup on a cold night."

She nodded.

"I think it's nice too," she confided.

They had had tomato soup for dinner probably three times a month during their married life.

The soup was finished, and Delia brought in the meat.

"Well, that looks pretty good," said Mr. Weldon, carving it. "We haven't had steak for a long time."

"Why, yes, we have, too, Ern," his wife said eagerly. "We had it—let me see, what night were the Baileys here? — we had it Wednesday night — no, Thursday night. Don't you remember?"

"Did we?" he said. "Yes, I guess you're right. It seemed longer, somehow."

Mrs. Weldon smiled politely. She could not think of any way to prolong the discussion.

What did married people talk about, anyway, when they were alone together? She had seen married couples—not dubious ones but people she really knew were husbands and wives—at the theatre or in trains, talking together as animatedly as if they were just acquaintances. She always watched them marvelingly, wondering what on earth they found to say.

She could talk well enough to other people. There never seemed to be enough time for her to finish saying all she wanted to to her friends; she recalled how she had run on to Alice Marshall, only that afternoon. Both men and women found her attractive to listen to, not brilliant, nor particularly funny, but still 'amusing and agreeable. She was never at a loss for something to say, never conscious of groping around for a topic. She had a good memory for bits of fresh gossip, or little stories of some celebrity that she had read or heard somewhere, and a knack of telling them entertainingly. Things people said to her stimulated her to quick replies, and more amusing narratives. They weren't especially scintillating people, either; it was just that they talked to her.

That was the trick of it. If nobody said anything to you, how were you to carry on a conversation from there? Inside, she was always bitter and angry at Ernest for not helping her out.

Ernest, too, seemed to be talkative enough when he was with others. People were always coming up and telling her how much they had enjoyed meeting her husband, and what fun he was. They weren't just being polite. There was no reason why they should go out of their way to say it.

Even when she and Ernest had another couple in to dinner or bridge, they both talked and laughed easily, all evening long. But as soon as the guests said good night and what an awfully nice evening it had been, and the door had closed behind them, there the Weldons were again, without a word to say to each other. It would have been intimate and amusing to have talked over their guests' clothes and skill at bridge and probable domestic and financial affairs, and she would do it the next day, with great interest, too, to Alice Marshall, or some other one of her friends. But she couldn't do it with Ernest. Just as she started to, she found she simply couldn't make the effort.

So they would put away the cardtable and empty the ash-receivers, with many "Oh, I beg your pardon's" and "No, no—I was in your way's," and then Ernest would say, "Well, I guess I'll go along to bed," and she would answer, "All right—I'll be in in a minute," and they would smile cheerfully at each other, and another evening would be over.

She tried to remember what they used to talk about before they were married, when they were engaged. It seemed to her that they never had had much to say to each other. But she hadn't worried about it then; indeed, she had felt the satisfaction of the correct, in their courtship, for she had always heard that true love was inarticulate. Then, besides, there had been always kissing and things, to take up your mind. But it had turned out that true marriage was apparently equally dumb. And you can't depend on kisses and all the rest of it to while away the evenings, after seven years.

You'd think that you would get used to it, in seven years, would realize that that was the way it was, and let it go at that. You don't though. A thing like that gets on your nerves. It isn't one of those cozy, companionable silences that people occasionally fall into together. It makes you feel as if you must do something about it, as if you weren't performing your duty. You have the feeling a hostess has when her party is going badly, when her guests sit in corners and refuse to mingle. It makes you nervous and self-conscious, and you talk desperately about tomato

soup, and say things like "daffy-down-dilly."

Mrs. Weldon cast about in her mind for a subject to offer her husband. There was Alice Marshall's new system of reducing—no, that was pretty dull. There was the case she had read in the morning's paper about the man of eighty-seven who had taken, as his fourth wife, a girl of twenty—he had probably seen that, and as long as he hadn't thought it worth repeating, he wouldn't think it worth hearing. There was the thing the Baileys' little boy had said about Jesus—no, she had told him that the night before.

She looked over at him, desultorily eating his rhubarb pie. She wished he wouldn't put that smeary stuff on his head. Perhaps it was necessary, if his hair really was falling out, but it did seem that he might find some more attractive remedy, if he only had the consideration to look around for one. Anyway, why must his hair fall out? There was something a little disgusting about people with falling hair.

"Like your pie, Ernie?" she asked vivaciously.

"Why, I don't know," he said, thinking it over. "I'm not so crazy about rhubarb, I don't think. Are you?"

"No, I'm not so awfully crazy about it," she answered. "But then, I'm not really crazy about any kind of pie."

"Aren't you really?" he said, politely surprised. "I like pie pretty well—some kinds of pie."

"Do you?" The polite surprise was hers now.

"Why, yes," he said. "I like a nice huckleberry pie, or a nice lemon meringue pie, or a—" He lost interest in the thing himself, and his voice died away.

He avoided looking at her left hand, which lay on the edge of the table, palm upward. The long, gray-white ends of her nails protruded beyond the tips of her fingers, and the sight made him uncomfortable. Why in God's name must she wear her fingernails that heathenish length, and file them to those horrible points? If there was anything that he hated, it was a woman with pointed fingernails.

They returned to the living-room, and Mr. Weldon again eased himself down into his chair, reaching for the second paper.

"Quite sure there isn't anything you'd like to do tonight?" he asked solicitously. "Like to go to the movies, or anything?"

"Oh, no," she said. "Unless there's something you want to do."

"No, no," he answered. "I just thought maybe you wanted to."

"Not unless you do," she said.

He began on his paper, and she wandered aimlessly about the room. She had forgotten to get a new book from the library, and it had never in her life occurred to her to re-read a book that she had once completed. She thought vaguely of playing Canfield, but she did not care enough about it to go to the trouble of getting out the cards, and setting up the table. There was some sewing that she could do, and she thought that she might presently go into the bedroom and fetch the camisole that she was making for herself. Yes, she would probably do that, in a little while.

Ernest would read industriously, and, along toward the middle of the paper, he would start yawning aloud. Something snapped inside Mrs. Weldon when he did this. She would murmur that she had to speak to Delia, and hurry to the kitchen. She would stay there rather a long time, looking vaguely into jars and inquiring half-heartedly about laundry lists, and when she returned, he would have gone in to get ready for bed.

In a year, three hundred of their evenings were like this. Seven times three hundred is more than two thousand.

Mrs. Weldon went into the bedroom, and brought back her sewing. She sat down, pinned the pink satin to her knee, and began whipping narrow lace along the top of the halfmade garment. It was fussy work. The fine thread knotted and drew, and she could not get the light adjusted so that the shadow of her head did not fall on her work. She grew a little sick, from the strain on her eyes.

Mr. Weldon turned a page, and yawned aloud. "Wah-huh-huh-huh-huh," he went on, on a descending scale.

Something snapped inside Mrs. Weldon.

III

"My dear," Mrs. Ames said to Mrs. Marshall, "don't you really think that there must have been some other woman?"

"Oh, I simply couldn't think it was anything like that," said Mrs. Marshall. "Not Ernest Weldon. So devoted—home every night at half-past six, and such good company, and so jolly, and all. I don't see how there *could* have been."

"Sometimes," observed Mrs. Ames, "those awfully jolly men at home are just the kind."

"Yes, I know," Mrs. Marshall said. "But not Ernest Weldon. Why, I used to say to Jim, 'I never saw such a devoted husband in my life,' I said. Oh, not *Ernest Weldon.*"

"I don't suppose," began Mrs. Ames, and hesitated. "I don't suppose," she went on, intently pressing the bit of sodden lemon in her cup with her teaspoon, "that Grace—that there was ever anyone—or anything like that?"

"Oh, Heavens, no," cried Mrs. Marshall. "Grace Weldon just gave her whole life to that man. It was Ernest this and Ernest that every minute. I simply can't understand it. If there was one earthly reason—if they ever fought, or if Ernest drank, or anything like that. But they got along so beautifully together—why, it just seems as if they must have been crazy to go and do a thing like this. Well, I can't begin to tell you how blue its made me. It seems so awful!"

"Yes," said Mrs. Ames, "it certainly is too bad."

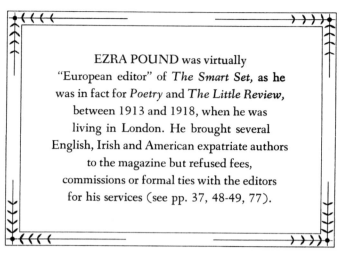

EZRA POUND was virtually
"European editor" of *The Smart Set,* as he
was in fact for *Poetry* and *The Little Review,*
between 1913 and 1918, when he was
living in London. He brought several
English, Irish and American expatriate authors
to the magazine but refused fees,
commissions or formal ties with the editors
for his services (see pp. 37, 48-49, 77).

Pan Is Dead

EZRA POUND

PAN is dead. Great Pan is dead.
Ah, bow your heads, ye maidens all,
And weave ye him his coronal.

There is no summer in the leaves,
And withered are the sedges;
How shall we weave a coronal,
Or gather floral pledges?

That I may not say, ladies.
Death was ever a churl.
That I may not say, ladies.
How should he show a reason,
That he has taken our Lord away
Upon such hollow season?

FROM VOL. 41, SEPTEMBER 1913

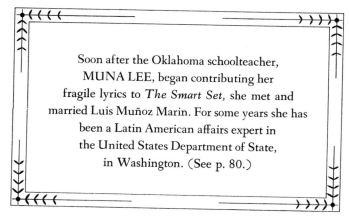

Soon after the Oklahoma schoolteacher,
MUNA LEE, began contributing her
fragile lyrics to *The Smart Set,* she met and
married Luis Muñoz Marin. For some years she has
been a Latin American affairs expert in
the United States Department of State,
in Washington. (See p. 80.)

Nina

MUNA LEE

SHE lives in St. Francis,
She is like a nun.
Her cheeks are pale as a white, white rose,
Her lips are sweet as one.

If I lived in St. Francis,
I'd take a painting brush
And paint upon her rose white cheek
A little pink rose flush.

If I lived in St. Francis,
For all she's like a nun,
I'd kiss her lips to the red of a rose
That have the sweet of one.

FROM VOL. 50, SEPTEMBER 1916

"Violets," was among several poems and
stories in *The Smart Set* with which the
controversial author of *Lady Chatterley's
Lover*, etc. founded his American reputation.
Lawrence's work was particularly prized
in those years by Ezra Pound, who brought
him to the magazine and by Editor
Willard H. Wright, who admired its
strength and frankness.

Violets

D. H. LAWRENCE

SISTER, tha knows while we was on the planks
Aside o' th' grave, while th' coffin wor lyin' yet
On the yaller clay, an' th' white flowers top of it
   Tryin' to keep off'n him a bit o' th' wet,

An' parson makin' haste, an' a' the black
Huddlin' close together a cause o' th' rain,
Did t' 'appen ter notice a bit of a lass away back
By a headstun, sobbin' an' sobbin' again?

—How should I be lookin' round
An' me standin' on the plank
Beside the open ground,
Where our Ted 'ud soon be sank?

D. H. Lawrence

Yi, an' 'im that young,
Snapped sudden out of all
His wickedness, among
Pals worse n'r ony name as you could call.

Let be that; there's some o' th' bad as we
Like better nor all your good, an' 'e was one.
An' cos I liked him best, yi, bett'r nor thee,
I canna bide to think where he is gone.

Ah know tha liked 'im bett'r nor me. But let
Me tell thee about this lass. When you had gone
Ah stopped behind on t' pad i' th' drippin' wet
An' watched what 'er 'ad on.

Tha should ha' seed her slive up when we'd gone,
Tha should ha' seed her kneel an' look in
At th' sloppy wet grave—an' 'er little neck shone
That white, an' 'er shook that much, I'd like to begin

Scraightin' mysen as well. 'En undid her black
Jacket at th' bosom, an' took from out of it
Over a double 'andful of violets, all in a pack
Ravelled blue and white—warm, for a bit

O' th' smell come waftin' to me. 'Er put 'er face
Right intil 'em and scraighted out again,
Then after a bit 'er dropped 'em down that place,
An' I come away, because o' the teemin' rain.

FROM VOL. 41, SEPTEMBER 1913

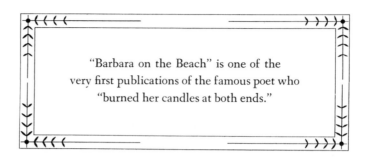

"Barbara on the Beach" is one of the
very first publications of the famous poet who
"burned her candles at both ends."

Barbara on the Beach

EDNA ST. VINCENT MILLAY

I found Barbara sitting on the beach, delectable in white icing, her quite unbelievable hair shining in the sun, and her rather sizable but very graceful feet crossed in front of her.

"Good morning, Barbara," said I, not throwing away my cigar. "Do you love me today, Barbara?"

"No, Peter," said the girl of my heart, "no, indeed, Peter. But I think you are very nice looking."

"H'm!" said I. "Well, now, you're not so bad yourself, you know. Would you be pleased if I should seat myself at your rather

sizable but very graceful feet and sing to you?"

"You can sit down if you want to," said Barbara, which was not answering my question at all; "but you'll have to keep still because I'm thinking."

So I dropped down in Barbara's lee, and smoked, and watched her think.

This is the way she did it:

First she leaned back on both hands and frowned at the horizon. Then she raised her brows and pouted. After which she caught one corner of her under-lip crookedly between her teeth and squinted the opposite

FROM VOL. 44, NOVEMBER 1914

eye. Then she drew up her feet sidewise, leaned on the opposite hand, and looked at me with a cold, glassy stare. After which she shrugged, dropped her eyes to my collar, and smiled whimsically. Having done which she shrugged again, very crossly, scowled at the water, scowled at the sky, and looked back at me with an expression of acute distress.

It was very evidently a painful operation.

"Do you want me to hold your hand?" said I.

Barbara straightened out her face and smiled at me.

"No, you perfect dear," she said, "but I *should* like to have you lie up behind my back and be a dune. Would it be too much trouble?"

I know that's what she said, because I afterwards remembered having heard her say it. But at the time I didn't notice. I was too busy watching her smile.

You have never seen Barbara smile, which is a pity. But doubtless you know some nice girl whose smile you like to watch, so that you will understand what I am about to tell you. O yes, there are other nice girls, lots of 'em; though Barbara is the nicest. Barbara is so nice that she doesn't have to pretend to be a bit nicer than she is; wherefore she is a pleasant person to sit on the beach with.

But, as I was saying, Barbara smiled, and I watched her. Barbara can say more in a smile than most women can in an hour, and these are some of the things she said:

"Why, hello, Peter! I'd forgotten all about you. What an old dear you are, to be sure! We've been pals for a long time, haven't we, Peter? Ever since we were kiddies. You were an awful kid, Peter. Isn't it great that we always see the joke? And isn't it a great day, anyway?"

Those are just some of the things she smiled at me. And there was a dimple, too, not a big fat cupid dimple, but a—a *different* dimple, as you might say—a very small, very round, quite unexpected dimple at the left-hand corner of her mouth. It never shows

unless she is really amused at something, when it always comes out (what it actually does, I suppose, is *go in*) for a minute to see what the fun is all about. It is just about big enough to hold a poppy seed.

You will remember that Barbara had asked me a question. Doesn't it seem to you a long time since she asked it? Now, doubtless, that is just the way it seemed to her. But I didn't notice. I was thinking of something else. And when she spoke to me again I blushed. Sometimes I think Barbara knows I like that dimple.

"Well?" said Barbara.

"Er—I beg your pardon," said I.

"Aren't you going to?"

"Going to what?"

"Lie up behind my back and be a dune."

"Barbara," I said, for the goodness-knows-how-manyth time, "will you marry me?"

"Certainly not," said Barbara. "Why should I?"

So there now! Take that! "Certainly not. Why should I?"

Well, there was really no reason why she should. In fact, when you get right down to it, there were several perfectly good reasons why she should not. But they didn't make the thought of it any more pleasant. "Certainly not." O, well, she didn't have to, you know; etc., etc. "Why should I?" H'm! Some people had thought, etc., etc. And I guessed I could get along without her anyhow, etc., etc., etc. "Certainly not. Why should I?" To the devil with the girl!

"Well," said Barbara, "aren't you going to?"

"No," I said, "I'll be darned if I do. You can lean on your elbow. I won't—I won't—er—lie doon—"—Barbara groaned—"I won't lie doon," I went on with dignity, "and be leaned on by any girl except the girl I'm going to marry. It isn't seemly."

"Hmfhthfh!" said Barbara, not without scorn.

And there was a heavy silence.

"O, Barbara," I said brightly, after several

minutes had passed over our heads with leaden feet, "I have an idea!"

Barbara looked incredulous.

"Let's go for a swim?"

"Dowanno," said Barbara.

Now wasn't that hateful of her? Such a good chance to be decent, too!

But there was a reason, and the reason—do you know Rolfe Alling, dammim!—well, he was the reason. It isn't only swims he's queered for me.

"Rolfe Alling is coming down tomorrow," said Barbara, "and I want my hair nice. Perhaps, after he's gone — but then, you'll be gone before he is."

I said nothing.

Barbara waited.

"What did you say?" asked Barbara.

I repeated.

"Speak!" said Barbara.

"Bow!" said I. Then I hugged my knees up under my chin and looked out at the homely green water, and the day was all clouded up and everything was spoiled.

After a minute Barbara began again, rather meekly, but choosing the wrong words.

"Rolfe Alling—"

"Damn him!" said I, and turned on her suddenly. "You can bet your life I'll be gone before he is. I'll go before he comes."

Whereupon I got to my feet and started off.

I was going, and Barbara knew it. And she didn't want me to go, and I knew it. So I kept on going.

"Peter!"

I didn't stop.

"Peter, aren't you going to say good-bye?"

"Yes," said I, "good-bye," and kept on going.

Barbara had to run to catch up with me, and when she had caught up with me she had to go some to keep up with me.

"Peter, I don't want you to go!"

I quickened my step.

"O, Peter, what makes you so *mee*-an?"

"Barbara," I said, and stopped so suddenly that she had to turn around to answer me. "Will you marry me?"

This time she didn't say "Certainly not." She didn't even say "No." What she did say was, "O, Peter!"

I eyed her gloomily.

"Barbara," I said at last, "if you don't care anything about me, why do you care if I go?" Which was certainly a sensible question.

But Barbara was evasive.

"Why, Peter, I do care something about you. I think you are lovely."

"Hmfhthfh!" said I.

Barbara looked startled.

"Looker here," I went on, "if you think I'm going to stick around here and play obbligato to that—that—to Mr. Alling, you've missed count. This beach isn't wide enough for us both. When he comes on I go off, or somebody's likely to get his feet wet. You can stay with him or come with me, but you can't bunch us."

Barbara was silent.

Things were getting stale again, and I played my last card.

"I shall be at Alison's if you should want me for anything. She's got a whole lot of folks over there."

"Who?" said Barbara. Aha!

"Oh, the Cutlers, and Dicky, and the Noyes girls, and Sue and John West, and Jane Crittenden, and—"

"Oh," said Barbara, "that crowd."

After a pause, "Which of the two Noyes girls do you think nicer?" asked Barbara.

"Neither," said I promptly, just as she had known I would do. She knew I disliked them both.

"I'm afraid you won't have an awfully good time," said Barbara; "that is, unless you like Jane Crittenden. Do you like Jane Crittenden?" Aha!

"Very much," said I fervently.

"Oh! perhaps you think her handsome?"

"Well, no, not handsome — but there's something about her, you know, something you can't explain—"

"Oh," said Barbara, "no, I didn't know. But it's all very interesting, I'm sure."

"Yes, isn't it?" I was enthusiastic.

Barbara looked at me.

And there was another pause.

Then, "Are you sure Jane Crittenden is going to be there?" she asked.

"O, yes," I said, "or I should not—"

"Should not what?" Aha!

"Should not have told you so."

"Oh," said Barbara.

All at once she turned and started off up the beach. I was too astonished at first to move. She walked very fast and very straight, and I noticed that her head kept going higher and higher.

"Barbara!" I called, and started after her.

And just as I spoke her name, I saw her fall, quietly, softly, forward into the sand.

And I was on my knees beside her.

"Barbara!" I said sharply.

But she did not move. She was lying perfectly still.

What I went through in that instant it would be impossible to describe. It seemed a year ago that we had sat together back there on the beach. All the light words we had spoken became a mist in my mind, far away and unreal. And this moment, and Barbara and myself, and the water and sky, seemed somehow terribly detached from anything that had ever happened before or would ever happen again.

"Barbara," I said, "for God's sake, speak!"

"B-bow!" said Barbara quaveringly.

I started back as if I had been shot. And then I stared at her. Had she said that, or—but yes, that was certainly what she had said.

Just then I loved her so that it seemed to me I must die. But instead I laughed.

"Barbara," I said, "you only girl, what are you crying about?"

I tell you now that to this day I haven't the slightest idea what she *was* crying about, or why she turned and went just when she did.

But at that she began to cry in very earnest. And I knelt beside her; and her sobs hurt my throat and her tears stung my eyes, but I did not touch her because I had not the right.

After a while she sat up shakily with her back to me and began fumbling at her belt. I put my handkerchief into her hand.

And in a little while she turned, with one arm over her face, and reached out gropingly with the other hand. It touched my sleeve, and I felt my face go white. But I did not move. I must remember that Barbara was not herself—I must remember—her hand went to my shoulder and I set my teeth, but I did not move. There must be no mistake about this—I had waited too long—there must be no mistake. I felt her arm go about my neck and tighten, and the sweat started out on my forehead, but I clenched my hands and gave her her last chance.

"Barbara," I said, "do you know what you are doing?"

And "Yes," said Barbara, "I know per-per-fectly well."

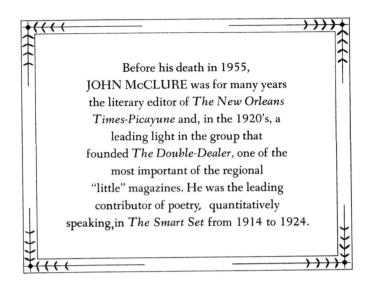

Before his death in 1955,
JOHN McCLURE was for many years
the literary editor of *The New Orleans
Times-Picayune* and, in the 1920's, a
leading light in the group that
founded *The Double-Dealer,* one of the
most important of the regional
"little" magazines. He was the leading
contributor of poetry, quantitatively
speaking,in *The Smart Set* from 1914 to 1924.

The Needy Poet Invoketh the Gods

JOHN McCLURE

M AY all the hidden deities
Of fair luck befriend
My toe that peepeth coyly
From my shoe's end!

My toe that peepeth coyly
Like a wee maid
Void of worldly wickedness
And somewhat afraid,

My toe that peepeth coyly
Fearing sore to get,
Scratched upon a cobblestone
Or damnably wet.

May all the hidden deities
Of fair luck befriend
My toe that peepeth coyly
From my shoe's end!

FROM VOL. 46, MAY 1915

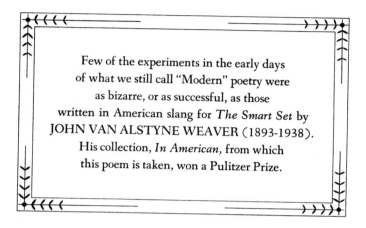

Few of the experiments in the early days
of what we still call "Modern" poetry were
as bizarre, or as successful, as those
written in American slang for *The Smart Set* by
JOHN VAN ALSTYNE WEAVER (1893-1938).
His collection, *In American,* from which
this poem is taken, won a Pulitzer Prize.

Riot

JOHN V. A. WEAVER

T HERE was me, walkin' peaceful down the alley,
Smokin' a pipe. The sun was blazin' down,
It was all quiet, like any reg'lar noonday.
I squats down in a bar'l, lights a match,
An' "Bang-bang-bang!" I hears, an' drops the pipe.

A guy runs at me, hollers, "You! Where is he?
You seen him!" I just sets there. "Keep your shirt on,"
I says, "Where's who?"

"The nigger! Where's he at?"
They gangs around me. I just sets there dumb.
More on 'em runs up, yelpin' "Get the coon!"
They jams aroun' the cellar; they's a yell,
They dashes down the steps. . . . A dozen shots . . .
The white guy next me pitches up his mitts
And flops down. . . . Then . . .

195

Listen, I wanta ast you,
You been down to the zoo, feedin' time?
You seen the keeper thrun a hunk o' steak,
You hearn the awful snarl the tiger gi'n?
. . . That mob . . . !

They drags this pore ol' nigger out,
They kicks his face in right before my eyes,
They plugs him full o' bullets,
What's left ain't even quiverin' no more.
I seen it, me! The wagon comes a-clangin',
Nobody left but me to tell about it,
Me an' the half-kilt bum. . . .

And now you come,
Tryin' to make me swear before a judge
This pore ol' alley-cat was goin' gunnin',
An' murderin' white guys . . . !

FROM VOL. 61, MARCH 1920

"A Little Cloud" and "The Boarding House,"
two of the *Dubliners* stories, were
JAMES JOYCE's first publications in the
United States (see pp. 48-49).

A Little Cloud

JAMES JOYCE

Eight years before he had seen his friend off at the North Wall and wished him godspeed. Gallaher had got on. You could tell that at once by his traveled air, his well-cut tweed suit, and fearless accent. Few fellows had talents like his and fewer still could remain unspoiled by such success. Gallaher's heart was in the right place and he had deserved to win. It was something to have a friend like that.

Little Chandler's thoughts ever since lunch time had been of his meeting with Gallaher, of Gallaher's invitation and of the great city London, where Gallaher lived. He was called Little Chandler because, though he was but slightly under the average stature, he gave one the idea of being a little man. His hands were white and small, his frame was fragile, his voice was quiet and his manners were refined. He took the greatest care of his fair, silken hair and moustache and used perfume discreetly on his handkerchief. The half moons of his nails were perfect and when he smiled you caught a glimpse of a row of childish white teeth.

As he sat at his desk in the King's Inns he thought what changes those eight years had brought. The friend whom he had known

FROM VOL. 46, MAY 1915

under a shabby and necessitous guise had become a brilliant figure on the London Press. He turned often from his tiresome writing to gaze out of the office window. The glow of a late autumn sunset covered the grass plots and walks. It cast a shower of kindly golden dust on the untidy nurses and decrepit old men who drowsed on the benches; it flickered upon all the moving figures—on the children who ran screaming along the gravel paths and on everyone who passed through the gardens. He watched the scene and thought of life; and (as always happened when he thought of life) he became sad. A gentle melancholy took possession of him. He felt how useless it was to struggle against fortune, this being the burden of wisdom which the ages had bequeathed to him.

He remembered the books of poetry upon his shelves at home. He had bought them in his bachelor days and many an evening, as he sat in the little room off the hall, he had been tempted to take one down from the bookshelf and read out something to his wife. But shyness had always held him back; and so the books had remained on their shelves. At times he repeated lines to himself and this consoled him.

When his hour had struck he stood up and took leave of his desk and of his fellow-clerks punctiliously. He emerged from under the feudal arch of the King's Inns, a neat, modest figure, and walked swiftly down Henrietta Street. The golden sunset was waning and the air had grown sharp. A horde of grimy children populated the street. They stood or ran in the roadway or crawled up the steps before the gaping doors or squatted like mice upon the thresholds. Little Chandler gave them no thought. He picked his way deftly through all that minute vermin-like life and under the shadow of the gaunt spectral mansions in which the old nobility of Dublin had roystered. No memory of the past touched him, for his mind was full of a present joy.

He had never been in Corless's but he knew the value of the name. He knew that people went there after the theater to eat oysters and drink liqueurs; and he had heard that the waiters there spoke French and German. Walking swiftly by at night he had seen cabs drawn up before the door and richly dressed ladies, escorted by cavaliers, alight and enter quickly. They wore noisy dresses and many wraps. Their faces were powdered and they caught up their dresses, when they touched earth, like alarmed Atalantas. He had always passed without turning his head to look. It was his habit to walk swiftly in the street even by day, and whenever he found himself in the city late at night he hurried on his way apprehensively and excitedly. Sometimes, however, he courted the causes of his fear. He chose the darkest and narrowest streets and, as he walked boldly forward, the silence that was spread about his footsteps troubled him; and at times a sound of low, fugitive laughter made him tremble like a leaf.

He turned to the right towards Capel Street. Ignatius Gallaher on the London Press! Who would have thought it possible eight years before? Still, now that he reviewed the past, Little Chandler could remember many signs of future greatness in his friend. People used to say that Ignatius Gallaher was wild. Of course, he did mix with a rakish set of fellows at that time, drank freely and borrowed money on all sides. In the end he had got mixed up in some shady affair, some money transaction: at least, that was one version of his flight. But nobody denied him talent. There was always a certain . . . something in Ignatius Gallaher that impressed you in spite of yourself. Even when he was out at elbows and at his wits' end for money he kept up a bold face. Little Chandler remembered (and the remembrance brought a slight flush of pride to his cheek) one of Ignatius Gallaher's sayings when he was in a tight corner:

"Half time, now, boys," he used to say light-heartedly. "Where's my considering cap?"

That was Ignatius Gallaher all out; and damn it, you couldn't but admire him for it.

Little Chandler quickened his pace. For the first time in his life he felt himself superior to the people he passed. For the first time his soul revolted against the dull inelegance of Capel Street. There was no doubt about it: if you wanted to succeed you had to go away. You could do nothing in Dublin. As he crossed Grattan Bridge he looked down the river towards the lower quays and pitied the poor stunted houses. They seemed to him a band of tramps, huddled together along the river banks, their old coats covered with dust and soot, stupefied by the panorama of sunset and waiting for the first chill of night to bid them arise, shake themselves and begone. He wondered whether he could write a poem to express his idea. Perhaps Gallaher might be able to get it into some London paper for him. Could he write something original? He was not sure what idea he wished to express, but the thought that a poetic moment had touched him took life within him like an infant hope. He stepped onward bravely.

Every step brought him nearer to London, farther from his own sober, inartistic life. A light began to tremble on the horizon of his mind. He was not so old—thirty-two. His temperament might be said to be just at the point of maturity. There were so many different moods and impressions that he wished to express in verse. He felt them within him. He tried to weigh his soul to see if it was a poet's soul. Melancholy was the dominant note of his temperament, he thought, but it was a melancholy tempered by recurrences of faith and resignation and simple joy. If he could give expression to it in a book of poems perhaps men would listen. He would never be popular: he saw that. He could not sway the crowd but he might appeal to a little circle of kindred minds. The English critics, per-

haps, would recognize him as one of the Celtic school by reason of the melancholy tone of his poems; besides that, he would put in allusions. He began to invent sentences and phrases from the notice which his book would get. *"Mr. Chandler has the gift of easy and graceful verse."* . . . *"A wistful sadness pervades these poems."* . . .*"The Celtic note."* It was a pity his name was not more Irish-looking. Perhaps it would be better to insert his mother's name before the surname: Thomas Malone Chandler, or better still: T. Malone Chandler. He would speak to Gallaher about it.

He pursued his revery so ardently that he passed his street and had to turn back. As he came near Corless's his former agitation began to overmaster him and he halted before the door in indecision. Finally he opened the door and entered.

The light and noise of the bar held him at the doorways for a few moments. He looked about him, but his sight was confused by the shining of many red and green wine glasses. The bar seemed to him to be full of people and he felt that the people were observing him curiously. He glanced quickly to right and left (frowning slightly to make his errand appear serious) but when his sight cleared a little he saw that nobody had turned to look at him: and there, sure enough, was Ignatius Gallaher leaning with his back against the counter and his feet planted far apart.

"Hallo, Tommy, old hero, here you are! What is it to be? What will you have? I'm taking whisky: better stuff than we get across the water. Soda? Lithia? No mineral? I'm the same. Spoils the flavor. . . . Here, *garçon*, bring us two halves of malt whisky, like a good fellow. . . . Well, and how have you been pulling along since I saw you last? Dear God, how old we're getting! Do you see any signs of aging in me—eh, what? A little gray and thin on the top—what?"

Ignatius Gallaher took off his hat and displayed a large, closely-cropped head. His face was heavy, pale and clean-shaven. His eyes, which were of bluish slate-color, relieved his unhealthy pallor and shone out plainly above the vivid orange tie he wore. Between these rival features the lips appeared very long and shapeless and colorless. He bent his head and felt with two sympathetic fingers the thin hair at the crown. Little Chandler shook his head as a denial. Ignatius Gallaher put on his hat again.

"It pulls you down," he said, "Press life. Always hurry and scurry, looking for copy and sometimes not finding it: and then, always to have something new in your stuff. Damn proofs and printers, I say, for a few days. I'm deuced glad, I can tell you, to get back to the old country. Does a fellow good, a bit of a holiday. I feel a ton better since I landed again in dear dirty Dublin. . . . Here you are, Tommy. Water? Say when."

Little Chandler allowed his whisky to be very much diluted.

"You don't know what's good for you, my boy," said Ignatius Gallaher. "I drink mine neat."

"I drink very little as a rule," said Little Chandler modestly. "An odd half-one or so when I meet any of the old crowd: that's all."

"Ah, well," said Ignatius Gallaher, cheerfully, "here's to us and to old times and old acquaintance."

They clinked glasses and drank the toast.

"I met some of the old gang to-day," said Ignatius Gallaher. "O'Hara seems to be in a bad way. What's he doing?"

"Nothing," said Little Chandler. "He's gone to the dogs."

"But Hogan has a good sit, hasn't he?"

"Yes; he's in the Land Commission."

"I met him one night in London and he seemed to be very flush. . . . Poor O'Hara! Booze, I suppose?"

"Other things, too," said Little Chandler shortly.

Ignatius Gallaher laughed.

"Tommy," he said, "I see you haven't changed an atom. You're the very same serious person that used to lecture me on Sunday mornings when I had a sore head and a fur on my tongue. You'd want to knock about a bit in the world. Have you never been anywhere, even for a trip?"

"I've been to the Isle of Man," said Little Chandler.

Ignatius Gallaher laughed.

"The Isle of Man!" he said. "Go to London or Paris: Paris, for choice. That'd do you good."

"Have you seen Paris?"

"I should think I have! I've knocked about there a little."

"And is it really so beautiful as they say?" asked Little Chandler.

He sipped a little of his drink while Ignatius Gallaher finished his boldly.

"Beautiful?" asked Ignatius Gallaher, pausing on the word and on the flavor of his drink. "It's not so beautiful, you know. Of course, it is beautiful. . . . But it's the life of Paris; that's the thing. Ah, there's no city like Paris for gaiety, movement, excitement. . . ."

Little Chandler finished his whisky and, after some trouble, succeeded in catching the barman's eye. He ordered the same again.

"I've been to the Moulin Rouge," Ignatius Gallaher continued when the barman had removed their glasses, "and I've been to all the Bohemian cafés. Hot stuff! Not for a pious chap like you, Tommy."

Little Chandler said nothing until the barman returned with the two glasses: then he touched his friend's glass lightly and reciprocated the former toast. He was beginning to feel somewhat disillusioned. Gallaher's accent and way of expressing himself did not please him. There was something vulgar in his friend which he had not observed before. But perhaps it was only the result of living in London amid the bustle and competition of the Press. The old personal charm was still there under this new gaudy manner. And, after all, Gallaher had lived, he had seen the world. Little Chandler looked at his friend enviously.

"Everything in Paris is gay," said Ignatius Gallaher. "They believe in enjoying life—and don't you think they're right? If you want to enjoy yourself properly you must go to Paris. And, mind you, they've a great feeling for the Irish there. When they heard I was from Ireland they were ready to eat me, man."

Little Chandler took four or five sips from his glass.

"Tell me," he said, "is it true that Paris is so . . . immoral as they say?"

Ignatius Gallaher made a catholic gesture with his right arm.

"Every place is immoral," he said. "Of course you do find spicy bits in Paris. Go to one of the students' balls, for instance. That's lively, if you like, when the cocottes begin to let themselves loose. You know what they are, I suppose?"

"I've heard of them," said Little Chandler.

Ignatius Gallaher drank off his whisky and shook his head.

"Ah," he said, "you may say what you like. There's no woman like the Parisienne —for style, for go."

"Then it is an immoral city," said Little Chandler, with timid insistence—"I mean, compared with London or Dublin?"

"London!" said Ignatius Gallaher. "It's six of one and half a dozen of the other. You ask Hogan, my boy. I showed him a bit about London when he was over there. He'd open your eye. . . . I say, Tommy, don't make punch of that whisky: liquor up."

"No, really. . . ."

"Oh, come on, another one won't do you any harm. What is it? The same again, I suppose?"

"Well . . . all right."

"Francois, the same again. . . . Will you smoke, Tommy?"

Ignatius Gallaher produced his cigar-case. The two friends lit their cigars and puffed at them in silence until their drinks were served.

"I'll tell you my opinion," said Ignatius Gallaher, emerging after some time from the clouds of smoke in which he had taken refuge, "It's a rum world. Talk of immorality! I've heard of cases—what am I saying?—I've known them: cases of . . . immorality. . . ."

Ignatius Gallaher puffed thoughtfully at his cigar and then, in a calm historian's tone, he proceeded to sketch for his friend some pictures of the corruption which was rife abroad. He summarized the vices of many capitals and seemed inclined to award the palm to Berlin. Some things he could not vouch for (his friends had told him), but of others he had had personal experience. He spared neither rank nor caste. He revealed many of the secrets of religious houses on the Continent and described some of the practises which were fashionable in high society and ended by telling, with details, a story about an English duchess—a story which he knew to be true. Little Chandler was astonished.

"Ah, well," said Ignatius Gallaher, "here we are in old jog-along Dublin where nothing is known of such things."

"How dull you must find it," said Little Chandler, "after all the other places you've seen!"

"Well," said Ignatius Gallaher, "it's a relaxation to come over here, you know. And, after all, it's the old country, as they say, isn't it? You can't help having a certain feeling for it. That's human nature. . . . But tell me something about yourself. Hogan told me you had . . . tasted the joys of connubial bliss. Two years ago, wasn't it?"

Little Chandler blushed and smiled.

"Yes," he said. "I was married last May twelve months."

"I hope it's not too late in the day to offer my best wishes," said Ignatius Gallaher. "I didn't know your address or I'd have done so at the time."

He extended his hand, which Little Chandler took.

"Well, Tommy," he said, "I wish you and

yours every joy in life, old chap, and tons of money, and may you never die till I shoot you. And that's the wish of a sincere friend, an old friend. You know that?"

"I know that," said Little Chandler.

"Any youngsters?" said Ignatius Gallaher. Little Chandler blushed again.

"We have one child," he said.

"Son or daughter?"

"A little boy."

Ignatius Gallaher slapped his friend sonorously on the back.

"Bravo," he said, "I wouldn't doubt you, Tommy."

Little Chandler smiled, looked confusedly at his glass and bit his lower lip with three childishly white front teeth.

"I hope you'll spend an evening with us," he said, "before you go back. My wife will be delighted to meet you. We can have a little music and—"

"Thanks awfully, old chap," said Ignatius Gallaher, "I'm sorry we didn't meet earlier. But I must leave tomorrow night."

"Tonight, perhaps . . . ?"

"I'm awfully sorry, old man. You see I'm over here with another fellow, clever young chap he is, too, and we arranged to go to a little card party. Only for that. . . ."

"Oh, in that case. . . ."

"But who knows?" said Ignatius Gallaher considerately. "Next year I may take a little skip over here now that I've broken the ice. It's only a pleasure deferred."

"Very well," said Little Chandler, "the next time you come we must have an evening together. That's agreed now, isn't it?"

"Yes, that's agreed," said Ignatius Gallaher. "Next year if I come, *parole d'honneur.*"

"And to clinch the bargain," said Little Chandler, "we'll just have one more now."

Ignatius Gallaher took out a large gold watch and looked at it.

"Is it to be the last?" he said. "Because you know, I have an a.p."

"Oh, yes, positively," said Little Chandler.

"Very well, then," said Ignatius Gallaher, "let us have another one as a *deoc an doruis*—that's good vernacular for a small whisky, I believe."

Little Chandler ordered the drinks. The blush which had risen to his face a few moments before was establishing itself. A trifle made him blush at any time: and now he felt warm and excited. Three small whiskies had gone to his head and Gallaher's strong cigar had confused his mind, for he was a delicate and abstinent person. The adventure of meeting Gallaher after eight years, of finding himself with Gallaher in Corless's surrounded by lights and noise, of listening to Gallaher's stories and of sharing for a brief space Gallaher's vagrant and triumphant life, upset the equipoise of his sensitive nature. He felt acutely the contrast between his own life and his friend's, and it seemed to him unjust. Gallaher was his inferior in birth and education. He was sure that he could do something better than his friend had ever done, or could ever do, something higher than mere tawdry journalism if he only got the chance. What was it that stood in his way? His unfortunate timidity! He wished to vindicate himself in some way, to assert his manhood. He saw behind Gallaher's refusal of his invitation. Gallaher was only patronizing him by his friendliness just as he was patronizing Ireland by his visit.

The barman brought their drinks. Little Chandler pushed one glass towards his friend and took up the other boldly.

"Who knows?" he said, as they lifted their glasses. "When you come next year I may have the pleasure of wishing long life and happiness to Mr. and Mrs. Ignatius Gallaher."

Ignatius Gallaher, in the act of drinking, closed one eye expressively over the rim of his glass. When he had drunk he smacked his lips decisively, set down his glass and said:

"No blooming fear of that, my boy. I'm going to have my fling first and see a bit of life and the world before I put my head in the sack—if I ever do."

"Some day you will," said Little Chandler calmly.

Ignatius Gallaher turned his orange tie and slate-blue eyes full upon his friend.

"You think so?" he said.

"You'll put your head in the sack," repeated Little Chandler stoutly, "like everyone else if you can find the girl."

He had slightly emphasized his tone and he was aware that he had betrayed himself; but, though the color had heightened in his cheek, he did not flinch from his friend's gaze. Ignatius Gallaher watched him for a few moments and then said:

"If ever it occurs, you may bet your bottom dollar there'll be no mooning and spooning about it. I mean to marry money. She'll have a good fat account at the bank or she won't do for me."

Little Chandler shook his head.

"Why, man alive," said Ignatius Gallaher, vehemently, "do you know what it is? I've only to say the word and tomorrow I can have the woman and the cash. You don't believe it? Well, I know it. There are hundreds—what am I saying?—thousands of rich Germans and Jews, rotten with money, that'd only be too glad. . . . You wait a while, my boy. See if I don't play my cards properly. When I go about a thing I mean business, I tell you. You just wait."

He tossed his glass to his mouth, finished his drink and laughed loudly. Then he looked thoughtfully before him and said in a calmer tone:

"But I'm in no hurry. They can wait. I don't fancy tying myself up to one woman, you know."

He imitated with his mouth the act of tasting and made a wry face.

"Must get a bit stale, I should think," he said.

Little Chandler sat in the room off the hall, holding a child in his arms. To save money they kept no servant but Annie's young sister Monica came for an hour or so

in the morning and an hour or so in the evening to help. But Monica had gone home long ago. It was a quarter to nine. Little Chandler had come home late for tea and, moreover, he had forgotten to bring Annie home the parcel of coffee from Bewley's. Of course she was in a bad humor and gave him short answers. She said she would do without any tea, but when it came near the time at which the shop at the corner closed she decided to go out herself for a quarter of a pound of tea and two pounds of sugar. She put the sleeping child deftly in his arms and said:

"Here. Don't waken him."

A little lamp with a white china shade stood upon the table and its light fell over a photograph which was enclosed in a frame of crumpled horn. It was Annie's photograph. Little Chandler looked at it, pausing at the thin, tight lips. She wore the pale blue summer blouse which he had brought her home as a present one Saturday. It had cost him ten and elevenpence; but what an agony of nervousness it had cost him! How he had suffered that day, waiting at the shop door until the shop was empty, standing at the counter and trying to appear at his ease while the girl piled ladies' blouses before him, paying at the desk and forgetting to take up the odd penny of his change, being called back by the cashier, and, finally, striving to hide his blushes as he left the shop by examining the parcel to see if it was securely tied. When he brought the blouse home Annie kissed him and said it was very pretty and stylish; but when she heard the price she threw the blouse on the table and said it was a regular swindle to charge ten and elevenpence for it. At first she wanted to take it back, but when she tried it on she was delighted with it, especially with the make of the sleeves, and kissed him and said he was very good to think of her.

Hm! . . .

He looked coldly into the eyes of the photograph and they answered coldly. Certainly they were pretty and the face itself was pretty. But he found something mean in it. Why was it so unconscious and lady-like? The composure of the eyes irritated him. They repelled him and defied him: there was no passion in them, no rapture. He thought of what Gallaher had said about rich Jewesses. Those dark Oriental eyes, he thought, how full they are of passion, of voluptuous longing! . . . Why had he married the eyes in the photograph?

He caught himself up at the question and glanced nervously round the room. He found something mean in the pretty furniture which he had bought for his house on the hire system. Annie had chosen it herself and it reminded him of her. It, too, was prim and pretty. A dull resentment against his life awoke within him. Could he not escape from his little house? Was it too late for him to try to live bravely like Gallaher? Could he go to London? There was the furniture still to be paid for. If he could only write a book and get it published that might open the way for him.

A volume of Byron's poems lay before him on the table. He opened it cautiously with his left hand lest he should waken the child and began to read the first poem in the book:

> *"Hushed are the winds and still the eve-*
> *ning gloom,*
> *Not e'en a Zephyr wanders through*
> *the grove,*
> *Whilst I return to view my Margaret's*
> *tomb*
> *And scatter flowers on the dust I love."*

He paused. He felt the rhythm of the verse about him in the room. How melancholy it was! Could he, too, write like that, express the melancholy of his soul in verse? There were so many things he wanted to describe: his sensation of a few hours before on Grattan Bridge, for example. If he could get back again into that mood. . . .

The child awoke and began to cry. He turned from the page and tried to hush it: but it would not be hushed. He began to rock it to and fro in his arms but its wailing cry grew keener. He rocked it faster while his eyes began to read the second stanza:

> *"Within this narrow cell reclines her*
> *clay,*
> *That clay where once . . ."*

It was useless. He couldn't read. He couldn't do anything. The wailing of the child pierced the drum of his ear. It was useless, useless! He was a prisoner for life. His arms trembled with anger and suddenly bending to the child's face he shouted:
"Stop!"

The child stopped for an instant, had a spasm of fright and began to scream. He jumped up from his chair and walked hastily up and down the room with the child in his arms. It began to sob piteously, losing its breath for four or five seconds, and then bursting out anew. The thin walls of the room echoed the sound. He tried to soothe it but it sobbed more convulsively. He looked at the contracted and quivering face of the child and began to be alarmed. He counted seven sobs without a break between them and caught the child to his breast in fright. If it died! . . .

The door was burst open and a young woman ran in, panting.

"What is it? What is it?" she cried.

The child, hearing its mother's voice, broke out into a paroxysm of sobbing.

"It's nothing, Annie . . . it's nothing. . . . He began to cry. . . ."

She flung her parcels on the floor and snatched the child from him.

"What have you done to him?" she cried, glaring into his face.

Little Chandler sustained for one moment the gaze of her eyes and his heart closed together as he met the hatred in them. He began to stammer:

"It's nothing. . . . He . . . he began to

cry. . . . I couldn't . . . I didn't do anything. . . . What?"

Giving no heed to him she began to walk up and down the room, clasping the child tightly in her arms and murmuring:

"My little man! my little mannie! Was 'ou frightened, love? . . . There now, love! There now! . . . Mamma's little lamb of the world! . . . There now!"

Little Chandler felt his cheeks suffused with shame and he stood back out of the lamplight. He listened while the paroxysm of the child's sobbing grew less and less; and tears of remorse started to his eyes.

Topical cartoons became a feature of *The Smart Set*
during the last years of the Nathan-Mencken regime.
The most frequent contributor was
the satirical expressionist HANS STENGEL (1894-1928).

I. "I don't know nothing about music, but I know what I like."

II. "If you don't like this country, why don't you go where you came from?"

III. "Something must be done to save Christianity from the Turks."

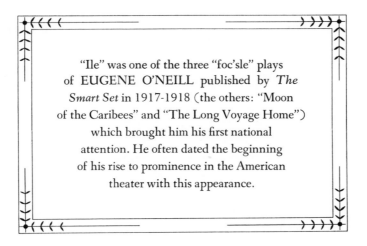

"Ile" was one of the three "foc'sle" plays of EUGENE O'NEILL published by *The Smart Set* in 1917-1918 (the others: "Moon of the Caribees" and "The Long Voyage Home") which brought him his first national attention. He often dated the beginning of his rise to prominence in the American theater with this appearance.

Ile

—◆—

EUGENE O'NEILL

First produced by the Provincetown Players at the
Provincetown Playhouse, New York City,
on November 30, 1917.

CHARACTERS
BEN, the cabin boy
THE STEWARD
CAPTAIN KEENEY
SLOCUM, second mate
MRS. KEENEY
JOE, a harpooner

Members of the crew of the steam whaler
Atlantic Queen.

FROM VOL. 50, MAY 1918

Scene—CAPTAIN KEENEY'S *cabin on board the steam whaling ship* Atlantic Queen—*a small, square compartment about eight feet high with a skylight in the center looking out on the poop deck. On the left (the stern of the ship) a long bench with rough cushions is built in against the wall. In front of the bench, a table. Over the bench, several curtained portholes.*

In the rear, left, a door leading to the captain's sleeping quarters. To the right of the door a small organ, looking as if it were brand new, is placed against the wall.

On the right, to the rear, a marble-topped sideboard. On the sideboard, a woman's sewing basket. Farther forward, a doorway leading to the companionway, and past the officer's quarters to the main deck.

In the center of the room, a stove. From the middle of the ceiling a hanging lamp is suspended. The walls of the cabin are painted white.

There is no rolling of the ship, and the light which comes through the skylight is sickly and faint, indicating one of those gray days of calm when ocean and sky are alike dead. The silence is unbroken except for measured tread of some one walking up and down on the poop deck overhead.

It is nearing two bells—one o'clock—in the afternoon of a day in the year 1895.

At the rise of the curtain there is a moment of intense silence. Then the STEWARD *enters and commences to clear the table of the few dishes which still remain on it after the* CAPTAIN's *dinner. He is an old, grizzled man dressed in dungaree pants, a sweater, and a woolen cap with ear flaps. His manner is sullen and angry. He stops stacking up the plates and casts a quick glance upward at the skylight; then tiptoes over to the closed door in rear and listens with his ear pressed to the crack. What he hears makes his face darken and he mutters a furious curse. There is a noise from the doorway on the right and he darts back to the table.*

BEN *enters. He is an over-grown, gawky boy with a long, pinched face. He is dressed in sweater, fur cap, etc. His teeth are chattering with the cold and he hurries to the stove, where he stands for a moment shivering, blowing on his hands, slapping them against his sides, on the verge of crying.*

THE STEWARD (*in relieved tones—seeing who it is*). Oh, 'tis you, is it? What're ye shiverin' 'bout? Stay by the stove where ye belong and ye'll find no need of chatterin'.

BEN. It's c-c-cold (*Trying to control his chattering teeth—derisively.*) Who d'ye think it were—the Old Man?

THE STEWARD (*makes a threatening move—* BEN *shrinks away*). None o' your lip, young un, or I'll learn ye. (*More kindly.*) Where was it ye've been all of the time—the fo'c's'tle?

BEN. Yes.

THE STEWARD. Let the Old Man see ye up for'ard monkeyshinin' with the hands and ye'll get a hidin' ye'll not forget in a hurry.

BEN. Aw, he don't see nothin'. (*A trace of awe in his tones—he glances upward.*) He just walks up and down like he didn't notice nobody—and stares at the ice to the no'th'ard.

THE STEWARD (*the same tone of awe creeping into his voice*). He's always starin' at the ice. (*In a sudden rage, shaking his fist at the skylight.*) Ice, ice, ice! Damn him and damn the ice! Holdin' us in for nigh on a year—nothin' to see but ice—stuck in it like a fly in molasses!

BEN (*apprehensively*). Ssshh! He'll hear ye.

THE STEWARD (*raging*). Aye, damn him, and damn the Arctic seas, and damn this stinkin' whalin' ship of his, and damn me for a fool to ever ship on it! (*Subsiding as if realizing the uselessness of this outburst—shaking his head—slowly, with deep conviction.*) He's a hard man—as hard a man as ever sailed the seas.

BEN (*solemnly*). Aye.

THE STEWARD. The two years we all signed up for are done this day. Blessed Christ! Two years o' this dog's life, and no luck in the fishin', and the hands half starved with the food runnin' low, rotten as it is; and not a sign of him turnin' back for home! (*Bitterly.*) Home! I begin to doubt if ever I'll set foot on land again. (*Excitedly.*) What is it he thinks he's goin' to do? Keep us all up here after our time is worked out till the last man of us is starved to death or frozen? We've grub enough hardly to last out the voyage back if we started now. What are the men goin' to do 'bout it? Did ye hear any talk in the fo'c's'tle?

BEN (*going over to him—in a half whisper*). They said if he don't put back` south for home today they're goin' to mutiny.

THE STEWARD (*with grim satisfaction*). Mutiny? Aye, 'tis the only thing they can do; and serve him right after the manner he's treated them—'s if they wern't no better nor dogs.

BEN. The ice is all broke up to s'uth'ard. They's clear water 's far 's you can see. He ain't got no excuse for not turnin' back for home, the men says.

THE STEWARD (*bitterly*). He won't look nowheres but no'th'ard where they's only the ice to see. He don't want to see no clear water. All he thinks on is gettin' the ile—'s if it was our fault he ain't had good luck with the whales. (*Shaking his head.*) I think the man's mighty nigh losin' his senses.

BEN (*awed*). D'you really think he's crazy?

THE STEWARD. Aye, it's the punishment o' God on him. Did ye ever hear of a man who wasn't crazy do the things he does? (*Pointing to the door in rear.*) Who but a man that's mad would take his woman—and as sweet a woman as ever was—on a stinkin' whalin' ship to the Arctic seas to be locked in by the rotten ice for nigh on a year, and maybe lose her senses forever—for it's sure she'll never be the same again.

BEN (*sadly*). She useter be awful nice to me before—(*His eyes grow wide and frightened.*) She got—like she is.

THE STEWARD. Aye, she was good to all of us. 'Twould have been hell on board without her; for he's a hard man—a hard, hard man—a driver if there ever was one. (*With a grim laugh.*) I hope he's satisfied now—drivin' her on till she's near lost her mind. And who could blame her? 'Tis a

God's wonder we're not a ship full of crazed people—with the damned ice all the time, and the quiet so thick you're afraid to hear your own voice.

BEN (*with a frightened glance toward the door on right*). She don't never speak to me no more—jest looks at me 's if she didn't know me.

THE STEWARD. She don't know no one —but him. She talks to him—when she does talk—right enough.

BEN. She does nothin' all day long now but sit and sew—and then she cries to herself without makin' no noise. I've seen her.

THE STEWARD. Aye, I could hear her through the door a while back.

BEN (*tiptoes over to the door and listens*). She's cryin' now.

THE STEWARD (*furiously—shaking his fist*). God send his soul to hell for the devil he is! (*There is the noise of some one coming slowly down the companionway stairs. The* STEWARD *hurries to his stacked up dishes. He is so nervous from fright that he knocks off the top one, which falls and breaks on the floor. He stands aghast, trembling with dread.* BEN *is violently rubbing off the organ with a piece of cloth which he has snatched from his pocket.* CAPTAIN KEENEY *appears in the doorway on right and comes into the cabin, removing his fur cap as he does so. He is a man of about forty, around five-ten in height but looking much shorter on account of the enormous proportions of his shoulders and chest. His face is massive and deeply lined, with gray-blue eyes of a bleak hardness, and a tightly clenched, thin-lipped mouth. His thick hair is long and gray. He is dressed in a heavy blue jacket and blue pants stuffed into his seaboots. He is followed into the cabin by the* SECOND MATE, *a rangy six-footer with a lean weather-beaten face. The* MATE *is dressed about the same as the captain. He is a man of thirty or so.*)

KEENEY (*comes toward the* STEWARD— *with a stern look on his face. The* STEWARD *is visibly frightened and the stack of dishes rattles in his trembling hands.* KEENEY *draws back his fist and the* STEWARD *shrinks away. The fist is gradually lowered and* KEENEY *speaks slowly).* 'Twould be like hitting a worm. It is nigh on two bells, Mr. Steward, and this truck not cleared yet.

THE STEWARD (*stammering*). Y-y-yes, sir.

KEENEY. Instead of doin' your rightful work ye've been below here gossipin' old woman's talk with that boy. (*To* BEN, *fiercely.*) Get out o' this, you! Clean up the chart room. (BEN *darts past the* MATE *to the open doorway.*) Pick up that dish, Mr. Steward!

THE STEWARD (*doing so with difficulty*). Yes, sir.

KEENEY. The next dish you break, Mr. Steward, you take a bath in the Bering Sea at the end of a rope.

THE STEWARD (*trembling*). Yes, sir. (*He hurries out. The* SECOND MATE *walks slowly over to the* CAPTAIN.)

MATE. I warn't 'specially anxious the man at the wheel should catch what I wanted to say to you, sir. That's why I asked you to come below.

KEENEY (*impatiently*). Speak your say, Mr. Slocum.

MATE (*unconsciously lowering his voice*). I'm afeared there'll be trouble with the hands by the look o' things. They'll likely turn ugly, every blessed one o' them, if you don't put back. The two years they signed up for is up to-day.

KEENEY. And do you think you're tellin' me somethin' new, Mr. Slocum? I've felt it in the air this long time past. D'you think I've not seen their ugly looks and the grudgin' way they worked?

(*The door in rear is opened and* MRS. KEENEY *stands in the doorway. She is a slight, sweet-faced little woman primly dressed in black. Her eyes are red from weeping and her face drawn and pale. She takes in the cabin with a frightened glance and stands as if fixed to the spot by some nameless dread, clasping and unclasping her hands nervously. The two men turn and look at her.*)

KEENEY (*with rough tenderness*). Well, Annie?

MRS. KEENEY (*as if awakening from a dream*). David, I—— (*She is silent. The* MATE *starts for the doorway.*)

KEENEY (*turning to him—sharply*). Wait!

MATE. Yes, sir.

KEENEY. D'you want anything, Annie?

MRS. KEENEY (*after a pause, during which she seems to be endeavoring to collect her thoughts*). I thought maybe—I'd go up on deck, David, to get a breath of fresh air. (*She stands humbly awaiting his permission. He and the* MATE *exchange a significant glance.*)

KEENEY. It's too cold, Annie. You'd best stay below to-day. There's nothing to look at on deck—but ice.

MRS. KEENEY (*monotonously*). I know —ice, ice, ice! But there's nothing to see down here but these walls. (*She makes a gesture of loathing.*)

KEENEY. You can play the organ, Annie.

MRS. KEENEY (*dully*). I hate the organ. It puts me in mind of home.

KEENEY (*a touch of resentment in his voice*). I got it jest for you.

MRS. KEENEY (*dully*). I know. (*she turns away from them and walks slowly to the bench on left. She lifts up one of the curtains and looks through a porthole; then utters an exclamation of joy.*) Ah, water! Clear water! As far as I can see! How good it looks after all these months of ice! (*She turns round to them, her face transfigured with joy.*) Ah, now I must go up on deck and look at it, David.

KEENEY (*frowning*). Best not to-day, Annie. Best wait for a day when the sun shines.

MRS. KEENEY (*desperately*). But the sun never shines in this terrible place.

KEENEY (*a tone of command in his voice*). Best not to-day, Annie.

MRS. KEENEY (*crumbling before this command—abjectly*). Very well, David. (*She stands there staring straight before her as if in a daze. The two men look at her uneasily.*)

KEENEY (*sharply*). Annie!

MRS. KEENEY (*dully*). Yes, David.

KEENEY. Me and Mr. Slocum has business to talk about—ship's business.

MRS. KEENEY. Very well, David. (*She goes slowly out, rear, and leaves the door three-quarters shut behind her.*)

KEENEY. Best not have her on deck if they's goin' to be any trouble.

MATE. Yes, sir.

KEENEY. And trouble they's goin' to be I feel it in my bones. (*Takes a revolver from the pocket of his coat and examines it.*) Got your'n?

MATE. Yes, sir.

KEENEY. Not that we'll have to use 'em —not if I know their breed of dog—jest to frighten 'em up a bit. (*Grimly.*) I ain't never been forced to use one yit; and trouble I've had by land and by sea's long as I kin remember, and will have till my dyin' day, I reckon.

MATE (*hesitantly*). Then you ain't goin' —to turn back?

KEENEY. Turn back! Mr. Slocum, did you ever hear o' me pointin' s'uth for home with only a measly four hundred barrel of ile in the hold?

MATE (*hastily*). No, sir—but the grub's gittin' low.

KEENEY. They's enough to last a long time yit, if they're careful with it; and they's plenty o' water.

MATE. They say it's not fit to eat—what's left; and the two years they signed on fur is up to-day. They might make trouble for you in the courts when we git home.

KEENEY. To hell with 'em! Let them make what law trouble they kin. I don't give a damn 'bout the money. I've got to git the ile! (*Glancing sharply at the* MATE.) You ain't turnin' no damned sea lawyer, be you, Mr. Slocum?

MATE (*flushing*). Not by a hell of a sight, sir.

KEENEY. What do the fools want to go home fur now? Their share o' the four hundred barrel wouldn't keep 'em in chewin' terbacco.

MATE (*slowly*). They wants to git back to their folks an' things, I s'pose.

KEENEY (*looking at him searchingly*). 'N you want to turn back, too. (*The* MATE *looks down confusedly before his sharp gaze.*) Don't lie, Mr. Slocum. It's writ down plain in your eyes. (*With grim sarcasm.*) I hope, Mr. Slocum, you ain't agoin' to jine the men agin me.

MATE (*indignantly*). That ain't fair, sir, to say sich things.

KEENEY (*with satisfaction*). I warn't much afeard o' that, Tom. You been with me nigh on ten year and I've learned ye whalin'. No man kin say I ain't a good master, if I be a hard one.

MATE. I warn't thinkin' of myself, sir— 'bout turnin' home, I mean. (*Desperately.*) But Mrs. Kenney, sir—seems like she ain't jest satisfied up here, ailin' like—what with the cold an' bad luck an' the ice an' all.

KEENEY (*his face clouding—rebukingly but not severely*). That's my business, Mr. Slocum. I'll thank you to steer a clear course o' that. (*A pause.*) The ice'll break up soon to no'th'ard. I could see it startin' to-day. And when it goes and we git some sun Annie'll perk up. (*Another pause—then he bursts forth:*) It ain't the damned money what's keepin' me up in the Northern seas, Tom. But I can't go back to Homeport with a measly four hundred barrel of ile. I'd die fust. I ain't never come back home in all my days without a full ship. Ain't that truth?

MATE. Yes, sir; but this voyage you been icebound, an'—

KEENEY (*scornfully*). And d'you s'pose any of 'em would believe that—any o' them skippers I've beaten voyage after voyage? Can't you hear 'em laughin' and sneerin'— Tibbots 'n' Harris 'n' Simms and the rest—

and all o' Homeport makin' fun o' me? "Dave Keeney what boasts he's the best whalin' skipper out o' Homeport comin' back with a measly four hundred barrel of ile?" (*The thought of this drives him into a frenzy, and he smashes his fist down on the marble top of the sideboard.*) Hell! I got to git the ile, I tell you. How could I figger on this ice? It's never been so bad before in the thirty year I been acomin' here. And now it's breakin' up. In a couple o' days it'll be all gone. And they's whale here, plenty of 'em. I know they is and I ain't never gone wrong yit. I got to git the ile! I got to git it in spite of all hell, and by God, I ain't agoin' home till I do git it! (*There is the sound of subdued sobbing from the door in rear. The two men stand silent for a moment, listening. Then* KEENEY *goes over to the door and looks in. He hesitates for a moment as if he were going to enter—then closes the door softly.* JOE, *the harpooner, an enormous six-footer with a battered, ugly face, enters from right and stands waiting for the captain to notice him.*)

KEENEY (*turning and seeing him*). Don't be standin' there like a gawk, Harpooner. Speak up!

JOE (*confusedly*). We want—the men, sir—they wants to send a depitation aft to have a word with you.

KEENEY (*furiously*). Tell 'em to go to — (*Checks himself and continues grimly.*) Tell 'em to come. I'll see 'em.

JOE. Aye, aye, sir. (*He goes out.*)

KEENEY (*with a grim smile*). Here it comes, the trouble you spoke of, Mr. Slocum, and we'll make short shift of it. It's better to crush such things at the start than let them make headway.

MATE (*worriedly*). Shall I wake up the First and Fourth, sir? We might need their help.

KEENEY. No, let them sleep. I'm well able to handle this alone, Mr. Slocum. (*There is the shuffling of footsteps from outside and five of the crew crowd into the cabin, led by* JOE. *All are dressed alike—*

sweaters, seaboots, etc. *They glance uneasily at the* CAPTAIN, *twirling their fur caps in their hands.*)

KEENEY (*after a pause*). Well? Who's to speak fur ye?

JOE (*stepping forward with an air of bravado*). I be.

KEENEY (*eyeing him up and down coldly*). So you be. Then speak your say and be quick about it.

JOE (*trying not to wilt before the* CAPTAIN's *glance and avoiding his eyes*). The time we signed up for is done to-day.

KEENEY (*icily*). You're tellin' me nothin' I don't know.

JOE. You ain't pintin' fur home yit, far 's we kin see.

KEENEY. No, and I ain't agoin' to till this ship is full of ile.

JOE. You can't go no further no'th with the ice afore ye.

KEENEY. The ice is breaking up.

JOE (*after a slight pause during which the others mumble angrily to one another*). The grub we're gittin' now is rotten.

KEENEY. It's good enough fur ye. Better men than ye are have eaten worse. (*There is a chorus of angry exclamations from the crowd.*)

JOE (*encouraged by this support*). We ain't agoin' to work no more less you puts back for home.

KEENEY (*fiercely*). You ain't, ain't you?

JOE. No; and the law courts'll say we was right.

KEENEY. To hell with your law courts! We're at sea now and I'm the law on this ship. (*Edging up toward the harpooner.*) And every mother's son of you what don't obey orders goes in irons. (*There are more angry exclamations from the crew.* MRS. KEENEY *appears in the doorway in rear and looks on with startled eyes. None of the men notice her.*)

JOE (*with bravado*). Then we're agoin' to mutiny and take the old hooker home ourselves. Ain't we, boys? (*As he turns his head to look at the others,* KEENEY's *fist shoots out to the side of his jaw.* JOE *goes down in a heap and lies there.* MRS. KEENEY *gives a shriek and hides her face in her hands. The men pull out their sheath knives and start a rush, but stop when they find themselves confronted by the revolvers of* KEENEY *and the* MATE.)

KEENEY (*his eyes and voice snapping*). Hold still! (*The men stand huddled together in a sullen silence.* KEENEY's *voice is full of mockery.*) You've found out it ain't safe to mutiny on this ship, ain't you? And now git for'ard where ye belong, and——(*He gives* JOE's *body a contemptuous kick.*) Drag him with you. And remember the first man of ye I see shirkin' I'll shoot dead as sure as there's a sea under us, and you can tell the rest the same. Git for'ard now! Quick! (*The men leave in cowed silence, carrying* JOE *with them.* KEENEY *turns to the* MATE *with a short laugh and puts his revolver back in his pocket.*) Best get up on deck, Mr. Slocum, and see to it they don't try none of their skulkin' tricks. We'll have to keep an eye peeled from now on. I know 'em.

MATE. Yes, sir. (*He goes out, right.* KEENEY *hears his wife's hysterical weeping and turns around in surprise—then walks slowly to her side.*)

KEENEY (*putting an arm around her shoulder—with gruff tenderness*). There, there, Annie. Don't be afeard. It's all past and gone.

MRS. KEENEY (*shrinking away from him*). Oh, I can't bear it! I can't bear it any longer!

KEENEY (*gently*). Can't bear what, Annie?

MRS. KEENEY (*hysterically*). All this horrible brutality, and these brutes of men, and this terrible ship, and this prison cell of a room, and the ice all around, and the silence. (*After this outburst she calms down and wipes her eyes with her handkerchief.*)

KEENEY (*after a pause during which he looks down at her with a puzzled frown*). Remember, I warn't hankerin' to have you come on this voyage, Annie.

MRS. KEENEY. I wanted to be with you, David, don't you see? I didn't want to wait back there in the house all alone as I've been doing these last six years since we were married—waiting, and watching, and fearing—with nothing to keep my mind occupied—not able to go back teaching school on account of being Dave Keeney's wife. I used to dream of sailing on the great, wide, glorious ocean. I wanted to be by your side in the danger and vigorous life of it all. I wanted to see you the hero they make you out to be in Homeport. And instead — (*Her voice grows tremulous.*) All I find is ice and cold—and brutality! (*Her voice breaks.*)

KEENEY. I warned you what it'd be, Annie. "Whalin' ain't no ladies' tea party," I says to you, and "you better stay to home where you've got all your woman's comforts." (*Shaking his head.*) But you was so set on it.

MRS. KEENEY (*wearily*). Oh, I know it isn't your fault, David. You see, I didn't believe you. I guess I was dreaming about the old Vikings in the story books and I thought you were one of them.

KEENEY (*protestingly*). I done my best to make it as cozy and comfortable as could be. (MRS. KEENEY *looks around her in wild scorn.*) I even sent to the city for that organ for ye, thinkin' it might be soothin' to ye to be playin' it times when they was calms and things was dull like.

MRS. KEENEY (*wearily*). Yes, you were very kind, David. I know that. (*She goes to left and lifts the curtains from the porthole and looks out—then suddenly bursts forth:*) I won't stand it—I can't stand it—pent up by these walls like a prisoner. (*She runs over to him and throws her arms around him, weeping. He puts his arm protectingly over her shoulders.*) Take me away from here, David! If I don't get away from here, out of this terrible ship, I'll go mad! Take me home, David! I can't think any more. I feel as if the cold and the silence were crushing down on my brain. I'm afraid. Take me home!

KEENEY (*holds her at arm's length and looks at her face anxiously*). Best go to bed, Annie. You ain't yourself. You got fever. Your eyes look so strange like. I ain't never seen you look this way before.

MRS. KEENEY (*laughing hysterically*). It's the ice and the cold and the silence—they'd make any one look strange.

KEENEY (*soothingly*). In a month or two, with good luck, three at the most, I'll have her filled with ile and then we'll give her everything she'll stand and pint for home.

MRS. KEENEY. But we can't wait for that—I can't wait. I want to go home. And the men won't wait. They want to get home. It's cruel, it's brutal for you to keep them. You must sail back. You've got no excuse. There's clear water to the south now. If you've a heart at all you've got to turn back.

KEENEY (*harshly*). I can't, Annie.

MRS. KEENEY. Why can't you?

KEENEY. A woman couldn't rightly understand my reason.

MRS. KEENEY (*wildly*). Because it's a stupid, stubborn reason. Oh, I heard you talking with the second mate. You're afraid the other captains will sneer at you because you didn't come back with a full ship. You want to live up to your silly reputation even if you do have to beat and starve men and drive me mad to do it.

KEENEY (*his jaw set stubbornly*). It ain't that, Annie. Them skippers would never dare sneer to my face. It ain't so much what any one'd say—but——(*He hesitates, struggling to express his meaning.*) You see—I've always done it—since my first voyage as skipper. I always come back—with a full ship—and—it don't seem right not to—somehow. I been always first whalin' skipper out o' Homeport, and——Don't you see my meanin', Annie? (*He glances at her. She is not looking at him but staring dully in front of her, not hearing a word he is saying.*) Annie! (*She comes to herself with a start.*) Best turn

in, Annie, there's a good woman. You ain't well.

MRS. KEENEY (*resisting his attempts to guide her to the door in rear*). David! Won't you please turn back?

KEENEY (*gently*). I can't, Annie—not yet awhile. You don't see my meanin'. I got to get the ile.

MRS. KEENEY. It'd be different if you needed the money, but you don't. You've got more than plenty.

KEENEY (*impatiently*). It ain't money I'm thinkin' of. D'you think I'm as mean as that?

MRS. KEENEY (*dully*). No—I don't know—I can't understand——(*Intensely.*) Oh, I want to be home in the old house once more and see my own kitchen again, and hear a woman's voice talking to me and be able to talk to her. Two years! It seems so long ago—as if I'd been dead and could never go back.

KEENEY (*worried by her strange tone and the far-away look in her eyes*). Best go to bed, Annie. You ain't well.

MRS. KEENEY (*not appearing to hear him*). I used to be lonely when you were away. I used to think Homeport was a stupid, monotonous place. Then I used to go down on the beach, especially when it was windy and the breakers were rolling in, and I'd dream of the fine free life you must be leading. (*She gives a laugh which is half a sob.*) I used to love the sea then. (*She pauses; then continues with slow intensity:*) But now—I don't ever want to see the sea again.

KEENEY (*thinking to humor her*). 'Tis no fit place for a woman, that's sure. I was a fool to bring ye.

MRS. KEENEY (*after a pause—passing her hand over her eyes with a gesture of pathetic weariness*). How long would it take us to reach home—if we started now?

KEENEY (*frowning*). 'Bout two months, I reckon, Annie, with fair luck.

MRS. KEENEY (*counts on her fingers—then murmurs with a rapt smile*). That would be August, the latter part of August, wouldn't it? It was on the twenty-fifth of

August we were married, David, wasn't it?

KEENEY (*trying to conceal the fact that her memories have moved him—gruffly*). Don't *you* remember?

MRS. KEENEY (*vaguely—again passes her hand over her eyes*). My memory is leaving me—up here in the ice. It was so long ago. (*A pause—then she smiles dreamily.*) It's June now. The lilacs will be all in bloom in the front yard—and the climbing roses on the trellis to the side of the house—they're budding. (*She suddenly covers her face with her hands and commences to sob.*)

KEENEY (*disturbed*). Go in and rest, Annie. You're all wore out cryin' over what can't be helped.

MRS. KEENEY (*suddenly throwing her arms around his neck and clinging to him*). You love me, don't you, David?

KEENEY (*in amazed embarrassment at this outburst*). Love you? Why d'you ask me such a question, Annie?

MRS. KEENEY (*shaking him—fiercely*). But you do, don't you, David? Tell me!

KEENEY. I'm your husband, Annie, and you're my wife. Could there be aught but love between us after all these years?

MRS. KEENEY (*shaking him again—still more fiercely*). Then you do love me. Say it!

KEENEY (*simply*). I do, Annie.

MRS. KEENEY (*gives a sigh of relief—her hands drop to her sides.* KEENEY *regards her anxiously. She passes her hand across her eyes and murmurs half to herself*): I sometimes think if we could only have had a child. (KEENEY *turns away from her, deeply moved. She grabs his arm and turns him around to face her—intensely.*) And I've always been a good wife to you, haven't I, David?

KEENEY (*his voice betraying his emotion*). No man has ever had a better, Annie.

MRS. KEENEY. And I've never asked for much from you, have I, David? Have I?

KEENEY. You know you could have all I got the power to give ye, Annie.

MRS KEENEY (*wildly*). Then do this

once for my sake, for God's sake—take me home! It's killing me, this life—the brutality and cold and horror of it. I'm going mad. I can feel the threat in the air. I can hear the silence threatening me—day after gray day and every day the same. I can't bear it. (*Sobbing.*) I'll go mad, I know I will. Take me home, David, if you love me as you say. I'm afraid. For the love of God, take me home! (*She throws her arms around him, weeping against his shoulder. His face betrays the tremendous struggle going on within him. He holds her out at arm's length, his expression softening. For a moment his shoulders sag, he becomes old, his iron spirit weakens as he looks at her tear-stained face.*)

KEENEY (*dragging out the words with an effort*). I'll do it, Annie—for your sake—if you say it's needful for ye.

MRS. KEENEY (*with wild joy—kissing him*). God bless you for that, David! (*He turns away from her silently and walks toward the companionway. Just at that moment there is a clatter of footsteps on the stairs and the* SECOND MATE *enters the cabin.*)

MATE (*excitedly*). The ice is breakin' up to no'the'ard, sir. There's a clear passage through the floe, and clear water beyond, the lookout says.

(KEENEY *straightens himself like a man coming out of a trance.* MRS. KEENEY *looks at the* MATE *with terrified eyes.*)

KEENEY (*dazedly—trying to collect his thoughts*). A clear passage? To no'the'ard?

MATE. Yes, sir.

KEENEY (*his voice suddenly grim with determination*). Then get her ready and we'll drive her through.

MATE. Aye, aye, sir.

MRS. KEENEY (*appealingly*). David!

KEENEY (*not heeding her*). Will the men turn to willin' or must we drag 'em out?

MATE. They'll turn to willin' enough. You put the fear o' God into 'em, all. They're meek as lambs.

KEENEY. Then drive 'em—both watches (*With grim determination.*) They's whale t'other side o' this floe and we're going to git 'em.

MATE. Aye, aye, sir. (*He goes out hurriedly. A moment later there is the sound of scuffling feet from the deck outside and the* MATE'S *voice shouting orders.*)

KEENEY (*speaking aloud to himself—derisively*). And I was goin' home like a yaller dog!

MRS. KEENEY (*imploringly*). David!

KEENEY (*sternly*). Woman, you ain't adoin' right when you meddle in men's business and weaken 'em. You can't know my feelin's. I got to prove a man to be a good husband for ye to take pride in. I got to git the ile, I tell ye.

MRS. KEENEY (*supplicatingly*). David! Aren't you going home?

KEENEY (*ignoring this question—commandingly*). You ain't well. Go and lay down a mite. (*He starts for the door.*) I got to git on deck. (*He goes out. She cries after him in anguish:*) David! (*A pause. She passes her hand across her eyes—then commences to laugh hysterically and goes to the organ. She sits down and starts to play wildly an old hymn.* KEENEY *re-enters from the doorway to the deck and stands looking at her angrily. He comes over and grabs her roughly by the shoulders.*)

KEENEY. Woman, what foolish mockin' is this? (*She laughs wildly and he starts back from her in alarm.*) Annie! What is it? (*She doesn't answer him.* KEENEY'S *voice trembles.*) Don't you know me, Annie? (*He puts both hands on her shoulders and turns her around so that he can look into her eyes. She stares up at him with a stupid expression, a vague smile on her lips. He stumbles away from her, and she commences softly to play the organ again.*)

KEENEY (*swallowing hard—in a hoarse whisper, as if he had difficulty in speaking*). You said—you was a-goin' mad—God! (*A long wail is heard from the deck above.*) Ah

bl-o-o-o-ow! (*A moment later the* MATE'S *face appears through the skylight. He cannot see* MRS. KEENEY.)

MATE (*in great excitement*). Whales, sir —a whole school of 'em—off the star'b'd quarter 'bout five miles away—big ones!

KEENEY (*galvanized into action*). Are you lowerin' the boats?

MATE. Yes, sir.

KEENEY (*with grim decision*). I'm a-comin' with ye.

MATE. Aye, aye, sir. (*Jubilantly.*) You'll git the ile now right enough, sir. (*His head is withdrawn and he can be heard shouting orders.*)

KEENEY (*turning to his wife*). Annie! Did you hear him? I'll git the ile. (*She doesn't answer or seem to know he is there. He gives a hard laugh, which is almost a groan.*) I know you're foolin' me, Annie. You ain't out of your mind — (*Anxiously.*) Be you? I'll git the ile now right enough —jest a little while longer, Annie—then we'll turn hom'ard. I can't turn back now, you see that don't ye? I've got to git the ile. (*In sudden terror.*) Answer me! You ain't mad, be you? (*She keeps on playing the organ, but makes no reply. The* MATE'S *face appears again through the skylight.*)

MATE. All ready, sir. (KEENEY *turns his back on his wife and strides to the doorway, where he stands for a moment and looks back at her in anguish, fighting to control his feelings.*)

MATE. Comin' sir?

KEENEY (*his face suddenly grown hard with determination*). Aye. (*He turns abruptly and goes out.* MRS. KEENEY *does not appear to notice his departure. Her whole attention seems centered in the organ. She sits with half-closed eyes, her body swaying a little from side to side to the rhythm of the hymn. Her fingers move faster and faster and she is playing wildly and discordantly as*

THE CURTAIN FALLS

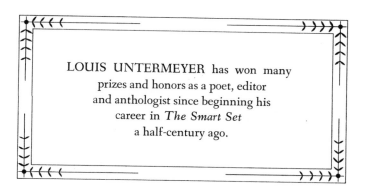

LOUIS UNTERMEYER has won many
prizes and honors as a poet, editor
and anthologist since beginning his
career in *The Smart Set*
a half-century ago.

In the Subway

LOUIS UNTERMEYER

CHAOS is conquered even as we ride;
The rock is rent, the darkness torn aside
And all the horrors of the deep defied.

The centuries disclose their secret graves;
Riding in splendor through a world of waves,
The ancient elements become our slaves.

Uncanny fancies whisper to and fro,
Terror and night surround us here below,
And through the house of death we come and go.

And here, oh, startling note of irony,
I see the men and women facing me
Reading their papers calmly, leisurely.

FROM VOL. 35, SEPTEMBER 1911

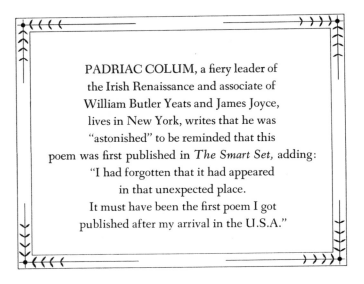

PADRIAC COLUM, a fiery leader of
the Irish Renaissance and associate of
William Butler Yeats and James Joyce,
lives in New York, writes that he was
"astonished" to be reminded that this
poem was first published in *The Smart Set,* adding:
"I had forgotten that it had appeared
in that unexpected place.
It must have been the first poem I got
published after my arrival in the U.S.A."

The Beggar-woman Sings

PADRAIC COLUM

MAVOURNEEN, we'll go far away
From the net of the crooked town
Where they grudge us the light of the day.

Around my neck you will lay
Two tight little arms of brown.
Mavourneen, we'll go far away
From the net of the crooked town.

And what will we hear on the way?
The stir of wings up and down, says she,
In nests where the little birds stay!

Mavourneen, we'll go far away
From the net of the crooked town,
Where they grudge us the light of the day!

FROM VOL. 46, MAY 1915

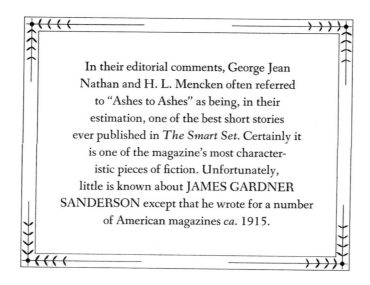

In their editorial comments, George Jean
Nathan and H. L. Mencken often referred
to "Ashes to Ashes" as being, in their
estimation, one of the best short stories
ever published in *The Smart Set*. Certainly it
is one of the magazine's most characteristic pieces of fiction. Unfortunately,
little is known about JAMES GARDNER
SANDERSON except that he wrote for a number
of American magazines *ca.* 1915.

"Ashes to Ashes"

JAMES GARDNER SANDERSON

Jules withdrew the silver cover of the *entrée* deferentially, but with a respectful flourish—a flourish subtly expressive, a flourish of subdued confidence and faith. The Baron drew his chair as close as his physical being permitted and inspected the offering in silence.

"Is it well, *chéri?*" asked his companion anxiously.

"One never knows," responded the Baron heavily. "We shall see."

With unostentation, he reserved the delicacies of the dish for his own plate and served his waiting consort. Jules filled the glasses and retired; for a few moments conversation ceased.

"*Tiens!*" exclaimed the girl at last. "A little lightness, a little gaiety! Is a dinner with me a funeral?"

The Baron regarded her gloomily. "It is the fifteenth, Coralie," he said. "Thou knowest that on the fifteenth I am never gay."

"Là la!" cried Coralie tartly. "Is it, then, the thought of her you have lost? Thou hast been but a bear tonight, at dinner a bear; at

FROM VOL. 45, JANUARY 1915

the comedy a bear; at supper"—the palms turned slightly upward. "I care not to sup with bears who dream of lost bearmates."

"A thousand thunders!" exploded the Baron. "Do I care that she has gone? No! Life was hell with her. She was *bourgeoise*. Figure to yourself—she expected me, the Baron d'Artois, to follow her peasantry and to be gallant to none other."

"An ignorant woman-pig," commented Coralie, sympathetically.

"Say thou an American; it is enough," the Baron retorted, tucking his napkin further into the rolls of his titled neck. "And this is of the month the fifteenth." He glanced uneasily toward the door of the room as he spoke.

"Is it not worth what thou must pay?" asked Coralie.

"It is not the payment, though the good God knows I have sought to avoid it. I do not cavil at twenty-five hundred francs. It was for my honor that I scorned the *procès-verbal*. We soil ourselves with these *canaille*. Yet, though I refused to submit, the recreant judge dared to place it upon the books that each month I—Gustav d'Artois—must pay twenty-five hundred francs. For what? For whom? For *her*. No longer of my house, no longer under my protection, no longer Madame la Baronne, and yet must I pay her such money. It is of the most damnable." The Baron gulped bitterly of his wine.

"I have defied them. 'Pouf!' I have said, when first the paper came. Then came a gendarme in uniform, with a hat like a bowl. I threw him across the apartment he dared defile and soon there came three, five, ten others. Am I Samson? They knelt upon me, bound me with steel as a criminal and drove me in a grated wagon away to vile incarceration. I lay with one named Bowery Mike, who fought for prizes, and with another such, called Paddy the Sneak. They called me Frenchy."

The Baron paused and shuddered heavily at the memory. Coralie shrugged a pair of gleaming shoulders in commiseration.

"Also there were vermin," the Baron continued wearily. "In the morning I paid—accursed alimony of an accursed country."

"Yet a d'Artois need not miss the paltry money," suggested Coralie smoothly.

"It was not the money," said the Baron, a trifle peevishly. "That thou knowest, Tender Chicken; for hast thou not had ten times as much, given from my heart? Of a certainty, I did not wish to pay it, but still it was not the money."

"She is an animal," commented Coralie, with sudden conviction. "Otherwise this money thou mightest have given me as well."

"Truly," assented the Baron.

Jules removed the *entrée* and presented a capon for inspection. The Baron nodded gloomily and wiped his forehead. The waiter noiselessly served the course and melted, pad-footed, into the colors of the velvet hangings.

"*Mon ami*, why stay in this provincial city? Let us depart," said Coralie.

"To what good?" asked her companion. "The fifteenth is the fifteenth. I know it. The second time it came I buried myself, I went to Philadelphia, I humiliated myself to hide. She watched through the eyes of a secret agent and the Prefect of Police, and they broke down the door of my apartment. I paid."

"In Paris," suggested Coralie wistfully, "one may live apart from Cattle."

"So some day, Present Angel of my Soul, shall we live. But now I may not go. On the third fifteenth I placed myself in *La Gascogne* and there came a man and brought me from my cabin back to the judge, saying that I was about to flee. They made me sign a paper whereby if I fail to pay they may strip me bare as a featherless chicken. No. It is inexorable; it is fate. Accursed woman and accursed land! I paid."

"Drink thou to forgetfulness," said Coralie, thirstily raising her wine.

The Baron drank noisily, mopping his

mustachios with all his napkin, and the watchful Jules slid with stealth from the gloom and refilled the glasses. The violins exulted in the *crescendo* climax of Broadway's latest Viennese waltz, and, after the applause, the interval fell upon the *café* with its usual silently noisy contrasts. The clatter of knives, forks and dishes rose into insistent existence; the swift steps of the servitors, passing and repassing, became softly audible. Above them mimic clouds drifted gently over the mimic sky; at their sides the fountain tossed sparkling drops prismatically into its pool, and over all hung the hum of many voices, rising louder as the laughter-loving theater contingent drifted more swiftly in.

The Baron turned apprehensively with the entrance of each newcomer. The hour was drawing near. Both pudgy hands lay on the spotless cloth of his table, and the light, glowing up from below, threw dancing shadows where the finger-tips drummed in nervous anticipation.

"The fifteenth," wailed the Baron. "She will come."

"*Peste!*" scowled Coralie. "Let a thousand like her come."

"She will come," the Baron asserted, unheeding. "She will come alone and she will take but tea. They will serve her and she will sit—and sit. Then will they bring to her a silver tray—" His voice broke suddenly. Directly across the narrow room an unoccupied table had been placed facing him. The Baron's roving eye looked upon it with quick horror. So might a murderer gaze from his cell upon the waiting scaffold.

The table's single chair lay tilted forward in reservation. Its napery, glass and silver shone in severest simplicity, and even the central decoration—a single American Beauty rose in a tall, slender vase—marked the differentiation from its neighbors. At the wall behind it stood a tall waiter immovably biding the arrival of its occupant. In all the *café* lay no other vacant chair. And in the lobby without crowds waited.

"It has come," said the Baron tragically. "Again it has come. It will always come, see thou!"

Coralie attacked her salad. The tragedy was not in her life, and she was hungry.

"When next thou suppest, sup alone," she said tartly. "Am I less than nothing?"

But the Baron's eyes widened and he began to breathe heavily through his flattened nose. The strain was telling, and, in anticipation of greater danger, even the possible loss of Coralie paled to insignificance.

"Little Crab of the Brooks," he said with an effort, "thou art all. But I have paid her *such* money today—twenty-five h u n d r e d francs—and she will come. She always comes; it is the fifteenth. Let us depart."

"I shall wait; there is a Biscuit Tortoni," said Coralie calmly.

"*Soit!*" said the Baron. "It is fate. I can never go, and she always comes. And I have paid her such money."

The maître d'hôtel passed them, honoring a guest, and the Baron's figure stiffened in swift fear.

"It is she!" he whispered.

In the functionary's wake an unattended girl walked with quiet unconcern. The eyes of the curious diners swept her impudently up and down, but she made her way to her waiting seat in cool disregard of the sensation which her entrance created, and, as she sank gracefully in her place, thanked the solicitous maître with a smile. The lounging waiter sprang into galvanized action, and the girl, without consulting the *carte,* gave him a short command. Then her glance roamed idly over the *café* until it rested briefly and impersonally upon the Baron.

The Baron's eyes burned. Gaily he raised his glass. "Coralie, to thy blue eyes," he cried. "To thy lips, *Petite Amie!* Drink!" He clinked her glass.

"Art a muttonhead?" asked Coralie amazed.

"La la la la la," laughed the Baron rapidly. "Let us be gay. *Vive la France!*"

"Thou are *dronk,*" announced Coralie.

"With love of thee," cried the Baron, with a fluttering upward gesture of his hand. "Sweet poultry, canst not see my beating heart?" He bowed and placed his hands over the organ mentioned. Coralie noted the beads of perspiration standing out upon them, and passed from astonishment to angry comprehension.

"*Cochon!*" she hissed in jealousy. "Seek not to defend yourself with me."

The cool eyes of the girl across the room rested briefly upon him again, and he clenched his teeth in a last effort to demonstrate indifference.

"Fool!" he snapped, smiling. "Laugh! Be gay. *A votre santé.*"

But Coralie refused to raise her glass. There are limits to feminine endurance.

"I shall leave you," she said angrily, "so soon as I have had my Biscuit Tortoni."

The waiter across the way set down a dainty dish of toast and a pot of tea with its cup and saucer, and the girl sipped it in apparent abstraction. The Baron sat crumpled in his seat, spent with his effort at masking.

"It is well," he said, hollowly, to Coralie's statement. "But look—*vois-tu.*"

"*Tutoyer* me never again," said Coralie. "Besides, I have already seen her." She glanced across the room at the girl in high-necked black. "And the robe is most abominable," she added.

"Thou hast seen her, yes," the Baron said, oblivious to her injunction against further intimacy. "But never hast thou seen what soon will be. It is the inexorable fifteenth. Six times have I seen it and six times six times and more shall I see it. It is as the eternal ocean. Always shall I pay and always watch."

The girl across the room sipped her tea; one would have said that she was slightly bored, and distinctly not of the *café's* habitués. The rich severity of her black gown, cut high in the neck and bearing but a single pearl for ornament, contrasted sharply with the powdered ivory, the dancing jewels and the colors at the other tables. The curve of her lips suggested a shadow of mockery, of disdain and perhaps of self-contempt, as she held immovably and with lowered glance to the apparent justification of her unattended presence, and the battery of eyes, opened in force at the sight of tea and toast in a New York *café* at midnight, made seemingly no whit of indentation upon the Harveyized steel of her poise.

The Baron watched her slightest movement in agony of soul. There had been a divorce—banal and usual result of an international marriage, forced by progenitors equally so—and the Baron was free and enriched by the settlement. But the stern hand of the American law had decreed alimony, and the alimony monthly decreased the patrimony of matrimony. If that had been all! Seven months had passed since the jury had gallantly given its verdict, and on the fifteenth of each month succeeding she who had been by the grace of god of ambition Madame la Baronne d'Artois had dined where the Baron dined.

The girl leaned back slightly and the waiter bent to catch her commands. He paused in respectful bewilderment, and the girl repeated her low-toned order sharply. Across the room the Baron sucked in his breath.

"It has come!" he cried in a mighty voice of anguish.

Coralie finished her sweet. "I am done," she said. "See how all regard you with eyes amused. Come! I will make you a nauseating drink of ammonia, and you shall sleep." She crumpled her napkin, pushing away her chair.

The Baron half rose, but dropped back heavily. "Sour Apple Tart of my soul," he replied dully, "it is too late. I am bound. I cannot move. I *must* watch."

The tall waiter had removed the tea and toast; in its place lay a silver tray bearing the lighted lamp of a chafing dish with nothing more. The girl opened a purse of chained gold and drew therefrom five crisp one-hundred-dollar bills.

"My money," moaned the Baron. "My own money!"

For a fleeting moment the girl looked across and laughed.

"Seven times," whispered the Baron, "and seventy times seven will come. God of my Israel!"

Then, one by one, calmly and without hesitation, the girl fed the crackling bills to the flame. The ashes dropped gently to the tray. The Baron, heedless of the throng, rose and extended pleading, supplicating hands. The fifth bill burned slowly, but at length it, too, followed the others, and the girl listlessly stirred the ashes with her fingertip.

For a moment the Baron groped blindly; then he fell, dragging the cloth, glasses and dishes with him. They came, and Coralie touched him scornfully with a dainty slippered toe.

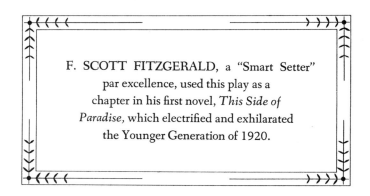

F. SCOTT FITZGERALD, a "Smart Setter"
par excellence, used this play as a
chapter in his first novel, *This Side of
Paradise,* which electrified and exhilarated
the Younger Generation of 1920.

The Débutanté *

F. SCOTT FITZGERALD

A ONE-ACT PLAY

*Scene I:—A large and dainty bedroom in
the Connage house—a girl's room; pink walls
and curtains and a pink bedspread on a
cream-colored bed. Pink and cream are the
motifs of the room, but the only article of
furniture in full view is a luxurious dressing
table with a glass top and a three-sided mirror. On the walls we have an expensive print
of "Cherry Ripe," a few polite dogs by Land-
seer, and the "King of the Black Isles" by
Maxfield Parrish.*

Great disorder consisting of the following
*items: (1) seven or eight empty cardboard
boxes, with tissue paper tongues hanging
panting from their mouths; (2) an assortment of street dresses mingled with their
sisters of the evening, all upon the table, all
evidently new; (3) a roll of tulle, which
has lost its dignity and wound itself tor-
tuously around everything in sight; and (4)
upon the two small chairs, a collection of
lingerie that beggars description. One would
enjoy seeing the bill called forth by the fin-
ery displayed and one is possessed by a desire to see the princess for whose benefit—
Look! There's someone!—Disappointment!*

FROM VOL. 60, NOVEMBER 1919

* SIC

This is only a maid looking for something— she lifts a heap from a chair—Not there; another heap, the dressing table, the chiffonier drawers. She brings to light several beautiful chemises and an amazing pajama, but this does not satisfy her—she goes out.

An undistinguishable mumble from the next room.

Now, we are getting warm. This is Mrs. Connage, ample, dignified, rouged to the dowager point and quite worn out. Her lips move significantly as she looks for it. Her search is less thorough than the maid's, but there is a touch of fury in it that quite makes up for its sketchiness. She stumbles on the tulle and her "damn" is quite audible. She retires, empty-handed.

More chatter outside and a girl's voice, a very spoiled voice, says: "Of all the stupid people"—

After a pause a third seeker enters, not she of the spoiled voice but a younger edition. This is Cecelia Connage, sixteen, pretty, shrewd and constitutionally good-humored. She is dressed for the evening in a gown the obvious simplicity of which probably bores her. She goes to the nearest pile, selects a small pink garment and holds it up appraisingly.

CECELIA:

Pink?

ROSALIND:

Yes!
Very snappy?
Yes!

CECELIA:

I've got it!
(She sees herself in the mirror of the dressing table and commences to tickle-toe on the carpet.)

ROSALIND:

(Outside.) What are you doing— trying it on?

(Cecelia ceases and goes out, carrying the garment at the right shoulder. From the other door, enters Alec Connage, about twen-

ty-three, healthy and quite sure of the cut of his dress clothes. He comes to the center of the room and in a huge voice shouts:)

Mamma!

(There is a chorus of protest from next door and encouraged he starts toward it, but is repelled by another chorus.)

ALEC:

So *that's* where you all are! Amory Blaine is here.

CECELIA:

(Quickly.) Take him down stairs.

ALEC:

Oh he *is* down stairs.

MRS. CONNAGE:

Well, you can show him where his room is. Tell him I'm sorry that I can't meet him now.

ALEC:

He's heard a lot about you all. I wish you'd hurry. Father's telling him all about the war and he's restless. He's sort of temperamental.
(This last suffices to draw Cecelia into the room)

CECELIA:

(Seating herself high upon lingerie.) How do you mean temperamental)?

ALEC:

Oh, he writes stuff.

CECELIA:

Does he play the piano?

ALEC:

I don't know. He's sort of ghostly, too— makes you scared to death sometimes—you know, all that artistic business.

CECELIA:

(Speculatively.) Drink?

ALEC:

Yes—nothing queer about him.

CECELIA:

Money?

ALEC:

Good Lord—ask him. No, I don't think so. Still he was at Princeton when I was at New Haven. He must have some.

MRS. CONNAGE:

(Enter Mrs. Connage.) Alec, of course, we're glad to have any friend of yours, but you must admit this is an inconvenient time, and he'll be a little neglected. This is Rosalind's week you see. When a girl comes out she needs all the attention.

ROSALIND:

(Outside.) Well, then prove it by coming here and hooking me.
(Exit Mrs. Connage.)

ALEC:

Rosalind hasn't changed a bit.

CECELIA:

(In a lower tone.) She's awfully spoiled.

ALEC:

Well, she'll meet her match tonight.

CECELIA:

Who—Mr. Amory Blaine?
(Alec nods.)
Well Rosalind has still to meet the man she can't out-distance. Honestly, Alec, she treats men terribly. She abuses them and cuts them and breaks dates with them and yawns in their faces—and they come back for more.

ALEC:

They love it.

CECELIA:

They hate it. She's a—she's a sort of vampire, I think—and she can make girls do what she wants usually—only she hates girls.

ALEC:

Personality runs in our family.

CECELIA:

(Resignedly.) I guess it ran out before it got to me.

ALEC:

Does Rosalind behave herself?

CECELIA:

Not particularly well. Oh, she's average—smokes sometimes, drinks punch, frequently kissed—Oh, yes—common knowledge—one of the effects of the war you know.
(Emerges—Mrs. Connage.)

MRS. CONNAGE:

Rosalind's almost finished and I can go down and meet your friend.
(Exeunt Alec and his mother.)

ROSALIND:

(Outside.) Oh, mother—

CECELIA:

Mother's gone down.
(Rosalind enters, dressed—except for her flowing hair. Rosalind is unquestionably beautiful. A radiant skin with two spots of vanishing color, and a face with one of those eternal mouths, which only one out of every fifty beauties possesses. It is sensual, slightly, but small and beautifully shaped. If Rosalind had less intelligence her "spoiled" expression might be called a pout, but she seems to have sprung into growth without that immaturity that "pout" suggests. She is wonderfully built, one notices immediately, slender and athletic, yet lacking under-development. Her voice, scarcely musical, has the ghost of an alto quality and is full of vivid instant personality.)

ROSALIND:

Honestly there are only two costumes in the world I really enjoy being in—(combing her hair at the dressing table) a hoop skirt dress with pantaloons or a bathing suit. I'm quite charming in both of them.

CECELIA:

Are you glad you're coming out?

ROSALIND:

Delighted.

226

CECELIA:

(*Cynically.*) So you can get married and live on Long Island with the *fast younger married set?* You want life to be a chain of flirtation, with a man for every link.

ROSALIND:

Want it to be one!—you mean I've *found* it one.

CECELIA:

Ha!

ROSALIND:

Cecelia, darling, you don't know what a trial it is to be—like me—I've got to keep my face like steel in the street to keep men from winking at me. If I laugh hard from a front row at the theater, the comedian plays to me for the rest of the evening. If I drop my voice, my eyes, my handkerchief at a dance my partner calls me up on the phone every day for a week.

CECELIA:

It must be an awful strain.

ROSALIND:

The unfortunate part is that the only men who interest me at all are the totally ineligible ones. Ah—if I were poor, I'd go on the stage. That's where my type belongs.

CECELIA:

Yes, you might as well get paid for the amount of acting you do.

ROSALIND:

Sometimes when I've felt particularly radiant I've thought—why should this be wasted on one man—?

CECELIA:

Often when you're particularly sulky, I've wondered why it should all be wasted on just one family.
(*Getting up.*) I think I'll go down and meet Mr. Amory Blaine. I like temperamental men.

ROSALIND:

My dear girl, there aren't any. Men don't know how to be really angry or really happy —and the ones that do go to pieces.

CECELIA:

Well I'm glad I don't have all your worries, I'm engaged.

ROSALIND:

(*With a scornful smile.*) Engaged? Why you little lunatic. If mother heard you talking like that she'd send you off to boarding school where you belong.

CECELIA:

You won't tell her though, because I know things I could tell—and you're too selfish.

ROSALIND:

(*A little annoyed.*) Run along little girl!— Who are you engaged to, the iceman?—the man that keeps the candy store?

CECELIA:

Cheap wit—good-bye, darling, I'll see you later.

ROSALIND:

Oh be *sure* and do that—you're *such* a help.
(*Exit Cecelia. Rosalind finished her hair and rises, humming. She goes up to the mirror and starts to dance in front of it, on the soft carpet. She watches not her feet, but her eyes—never casually but always intently, even when she smiles.*)
(*The door suddenly opens and then slams behind a good-looking young man, with a straight, romantic profile, who sees her and melts to instant confusion.*)

HE:

Oh I'm sorry, I thought—

SHE:

(*Smiling radiantly.*) Oh, you're Armory Blaine, aren't you?

HE:

(*Regarding her closely.*) And you're Rosalind?

SHE:

I'm going to call you Amory—oh, come in —it's all right—mother'll be right in—(*under her breath*) unfortunately.

HE:

(*Gazing around.*) This is sort of a new wrinkle for me.

SHE:

This is No Man's Land.

HE:

This is where you—you—(*embarrassment.*)

SHE:

Yes—all those things.
(*She crosses to the bureau.*) See, here's my rouge—eye pencils.

HE:

I didn't know you were that way.

SHE:

What did you expect?

HE:

I thought you'd be sort of—sort of—sexless; you know, swim and play golf.

SHE:

Oh I do—but not in business hours.

HE:

Business?

SHE:

Six to two—strictly.

HE:

I'd like to have some stock in the corporation.

SHE:

Oh it's not a corporation—it's just "Rosalind, Unlimited." Fifty-one shares, name, good will and everything goes at $25,000 a year.

HE:

(*Disapprovingly.*) Sort of a chilly proposition.

SHE:

Well, Amory, you don't mind—do you? When I meet a man that doesn't bore me to death after two weeks, perhaps it'll be different.

HE:

Odd, you have the same point of view on men that I have on women.

SHE:

I'm not really feminine, you know—in my mind.

HE:

(*Interested.*) Go on.

SHE:

No, you—you go on—you've made me talk about myself. That's against the rules.

HE:

Rules?

SHE:

My own rules—but you—oh, Amory, I hear you're brilliant. The family expects so much of you.

HE:

How encouraging.

SHE:

Alec said you'd taught him to think. Did you? I don't believe anyone could.

HE:

No. I'm really quite dull.
(*He evidently doesn't intend this to be taken quite seriously.*)

SHE:

Liar.

HE:

I'm—I'm religious—I'm literary. I've—I've even written poems.

SHE:

Vers libre—splendid. (*She declaims.*)
Trees are green,
The birds are singing in the trees,
The girl sips her poison
The bird flies away; the girl dies.

HE:

(*Laughing.*) No, not that kind.

SHE:

(*Suddenly.*) I like you.

HE:

Don't.

SHE:

Modest too—

HE:

I'm afraid of you. I'm always afraid of a girl —until I've kissed her.

SHE:

(*Emphatically.*) My dear boy, the war is over.

HE:

So I'll always be afraid of you.

SHE:

(*Rather sadly.*) I suppose you will.
(*A slight pause on both their parts.*)

HE:

(*After due consideration.*) Listen. This is a frightful thing to ask.

SHE:

(*Knowing what's coming.*) After five minutes.

HE:

But will you—kiss me?—Or are you afraid?

SHE:

I'm never afraid—but your reasons are so poor.

HE:

Rosalind, I really *want* to kiss you.

SHE:

So do I.
(*They kiss—definitely and thoroughly.*)

HE:

(*After a breathless second.*) Well, your curiosity is satisfied.

SHE:

Is yours?

HE:

No, it's only aroused.
(*He looks it.*)

SHE:

(*Dreamily.*) I've kissed dozens of men, I suppose I'll kiss dozens more.

HE:

(*Abstractedly.*) Yes, I suppose you could— like that.

SHE:

Most people like the way I kiss.

HE:

(*Remembering himself.*) Good Lord, yes. Kiss me once more, Rosalind.

SHE:

No—my curiosity is generally satisfied at one.

HE:

(*Discouraged.*) Is that a rule?

SHE:

I make rules to fit the cases.

HE:

You and I are somewhat alike—except that I'm years older in experience.

SHE:

How old are you?

HE:

Twenty-three. You?

SHE:

Nineteen—just.

HE:

I suppose you're the product of a fashionable school.

SHE:

No—I'm fairly raw material. I was expelled from Spence—I've forgotten why.

HE:

What's your general trend?

SHE:

Oh, I'm bright, quite selfish, emotional when aroused, fond of action—

HE:

(*Suddenly.*) I don't want to fall in love with you—

SHE:

(Raising her eyebrows.) No one's asked you to.

HE:

(Continuing calmly)—But I probably will. I love your mouth.

SHE:

Hush—please, don't fall in love with my mouth—hair, eyes, shoulders, tempers—but not my mouth. Everybody falls in love with my mouth.

HE:

It's quite beautiful.

SHE:

It's too small.

HE:

No it isn't—let's see.
(He kisses her again with the same thoroughness.)

SHE:

(Rather moved.) Say something sweet!

HE:

(Frightened.) Lord help me.

SHE:

(Drawing away.) Well, don't—if it's so hard.

HE:

Shall we pretend? So soon?

SHE:

We haven't the same standards of time as other people.

HE:

Already it's—other people.

SHE:

Let's pretend.

HE:

No—I can't—it's sentimental.

SHE:

You're not sentimental?

HE:

No, I'm romantic—a sentimental person thinks things will last—a romantic person hopes against hope that they won't. Sentiment is emotional.

SHE:

And you're not? (with her eyes half closed.) You probably flatter yourself that that's a superior attitude.

HE:

Well—Oh Rosalind, Rosalind, don't argue —kiss me again.

SHE:

(Quite chilly now.) No—I have no desire to kiss you.

HE:

(Openly taken aback.) You wanted to kiss me a minute ago.

SHE:

This is now.

HE:

I'd better go.

SHE:

I suppose so.
(He goes toward the door.)

SHE:

Oh!
(He turns.)

SHE:

(Laughing.) Score Home Team, 100— Opponents, Zero.
(He starts back.)
(Quickly.) Rain—no game!
(He goes out.)
(She goes quickly to the chiffonier, takes out a cigarette case and hides it in the side drawer of a desk. Her mother enters—note book in hand.)

MRS. CONNAGE:

Good—I've been wanting to speak to you alone before we go down stairs.

ROSALIND:

Heavens, you frighten me.

MRS. CONNAGE:

Rosalind, you've been a very expensive proposition.

ROSALIND:

(*Resignedly.*) Yes.

MRS. CONNAGE:

And you know your father hasn't what he once had.

ROSALIND:

(*Making a wry face.*) Oh please don't talk about money.

MRS. CONNAGE:

You can't do anything without it. This is our last year in this house—and unless things change, Cecelia won't have the advantages you've had.

ROSALIND:

(*Impatiently.*) Well—what is it?

MRS. CONNAGE:

So I ask you to please mind me in several things I've put down in my note book. The first one is: Don't disappear with young men. There may be a time when it's valuable, but at present I want you on the dance floor where I can find you. There are certain men I want to have you meet and I don't like finding you in some corner of the conservatory exchanging silliness with anyone—or listening to it.

ROSALIND:

(*Sarcastically.*) Yes, listening to it *is* better.

MRS. CONNAGE:

And don't waste a lot of time with the college set—little boys nineteen and twenty years old. I don't mind a prom or a football game, but staying away from advantageous parties to eat in the little cafés down town with Tom, Dick and Harry—

ROSALIND:

(*Offering her code, which is by the way quite as high as her mother's.*) Mother, it's done—one can't run everything now the way one did in the early nineties.

MRS. CONNAGE:

(*Paying no attention.*) There are several bachelor friends of your father's that I want you to meet tonight—youngish men.

ROSALIND:

(*Nodding wisely.*) About forty-five?

MRS. CONNAGE:

(*Sharply.*) Why not?

ROSALIND:

Oh, *quite* all right—they know life and are so adorably tired looking—(*shakes her head*) but they *will* dance.

MRS. CONNAGE:

I haven't met Mr. Blaine—but I don't think you'll care for him. He doesn't sound like a money maker.

ROSALIND:

Mother, I never *think* about money.

MRS. CONNAGE:

You never keep it long enough to think about it.

ROSALIND:

(*Sighs.*) Yes, I suppose some day I'll marry a ton of it—out of sheer boredom.

MRS. CONNAGE:

(*Referring to note book.*) I had a wire from Hartford. Dawson Ryder is coming up. Now there's a young man I like, and he's floating in money. It seems to me that since you seem tired of Howard Gillespie, you might give Mr. Ryder some encouragement. This is the third time he's been up in a month.

ROSALIND:

How did you know I was tired of Howard Gillespie?

MRS. CONNAGE:

The poor boy looks so miserable every time he comes.

ROSALIND:

That was one of those romantic pre-battle affairs. They're all wrong.

MRS. CONNAGE:

(*Her say said.*) At any rate make us proud of you tonight.

ROSALIND:

Don't you think I'm beautiful?

MRS. CONNAGE:

You know you are.

(*From downstairs is heard a shriek of a violin being tuned, the rattle of a drum. Mrs. Connage turns quickly to her daughter.*)

MRS. CONNAGE:

Come.

ROSALIND:

One minute.

(*Her mother leaves. Rosalind goes to the glass, where she gazes at herself with great satisfaction. She kisses her hand and touches her mirrored mouth with it. Then she turns out the lights and leaves the room.*

Silence for a moment. A few chords from the piano, the discreet message of faint drums, the rustle of new silk, all blend on the staircase outside and drift in through the partly opened door. Bundled figures pass in the lighted hall. The laughter heard below becomes doubled and multiplied. Then some one comes in from the side, switches on the lights and closes the door. It is Cecelia. She goes to the chiffonier, looks in the drawers, hesitates—then to the desk whence she takes the cigarette case and selects one. She lights it and puffing and blowing walks toward the mirror.)

CECELIA:

(*In tremendously sophisticated accents.*) Oh, yes, coming out is *such* a farce nowadays you know. One really plays around *so* much

before one is seventeen, that it's positively anti-climax.

(*Shaking hands with a visionary, middle-aged nobleman.*)

Yes, your grace—I b'lieve I've heard my sister speak of you. Have a puff—they're very good. They're—they're Coronas. You don't smoke? What a pity! The King doesn't allow it I suppose. Yes, I'll dance.

(*So she dances around the room to a tune from downstairs. Her arms outstretched to an imaginary partner. The cigarette waving in her hand. Darkness comes quickly down and the lights stay low until—*)

SCENE II

Draperies cut off the stage to a corner of a den downstairs, filled by a very comfortable leather lounge. A small light is on each side above and in the middle; over the couch hangs a painting of a very old, very dignified gentleman, period 1860. Outside the music is heard in a fox trot.

Rosalind is seated on the lounge and on her left is Howard Gillespie, a shallow youth of about twenty-four. He is obviously very unhappy and she quite bored.

GILLESPIE:

(*Feebly.*) What do you mean I've changed? I feel the same toward you.

ROSALIND:

But you don't look the same to me.

GILLESPIE:

Three weeks ago you used to say that you liked me because I was so blasé, so indifferent—I still am.

ROSALIND:

But not about me. I used to like you because you had brown eyes and thin legs.

GILLESPIE:

(*Helplessly.*) They're still thin and brown.

ROSALIND:

I used to think you were never jealous. Now you follow me with your eyes wherever I go.

GILLESPIE:

I love you.

ROSALIND:

(*Coldly.*) I know it.

GILLESPIE:

And you haven't kissed me for two weeks. I had an idea that after a girl was kissed she was—was—won.

ROSALIND:

Those days are over. I have to be won all over again every time you see me.

GILLESPIE:

Are you serious?

ROSALIND:

About as usual. There used to be two kinds of kisses: First when girls were kissed and deserted, second when they were engaged. Now there's a third kind where the man is kissed and deserted. If Mr. Jones of the nineties bragged he'd kissed a girl everyone knew he was through with her. If Mr. Jones of 1919 brags the same, everyone knows it's because he can't kiss her any more. Given a decent start any girl can beat a man nowadays.

GILLESPIE:

Then why do you play with men?

ROSALIND:

(*Leaning forward confidentially.*) For that first moment, when he's interested. There *is* a moment—Oh, just before the first kiss, a whispered word—something that makes it worth while.

GILLESPIE:

And then?

ROSALIND:

Then after that you make him talk about himself. Pretty soon he thinks of nothing but being alone with you.—He sulks, he won't fight, he doesn't want to play—Victory.

(*Enter Dawson Ryder, twenty-six, hand-some, rather cold, wealthy, faithful to his own, a bore perhaps, but steady and sure of success.*)

RYDER:

I believe this is my dance. Rosalind.

ROSALIND:

Very well, Dawson. Mr. Ryder this is Mr. Gillespie. (*They shake hands and Gillespie leaves tremendously downcast.*)

RYDER:

Your party is certainly a success.

ROSALIND:

Is it—I haven't seen it lately. I'm weary— Do you mind sitting out?

RYDER:

Mind—I'm delighted. You know I loath this "rushing" idea. See a girl yesterday, today, tomorrow.

ROSALIND:

Dawson!

RYDER:

What?

ROSALIND:

I wonder if you know you love me.

RYDER:

(*Startled.*) What—Oh—I say, you're re-markable.

ROSALIND:

Because you know I'm an awful proposi-tion. Anyone who marries me would have his hands full. I'm mean—mighty mean.

RYDER:

Oh, I wouldn't say that.

ROSALIND:

Oh, yes I am—especially to the people near-est to me.
(*She rises.*)
Come, let's go. I have changed my mind and I want to dance. Mother is probably hav-ing a fit.

233

(They start out.)
Does one shimmy in Hartford?
(Exeunt.)
(Enter Alec and Cecelia.)

CECELIA:

Just my luck to get my own brother for an intermission.

ALEC:

(Gloomily.) I'll go if you want me to.

CECELIA:

Good heavens no—who would I begin the next dance with?
(Sighs.)
There's no color in a dance since the French officers went back.

ALEC:

I hope Amory doesn't fall in love with Rosalind.

CECELIA:

Why, I had an idea you wanted him to.

ALEC:

I did, but since seeing these girls—I don't know. I'm awfully attached to Amory. He's sensitive and I don't want him to break his heart over somebody who doesn't care about him.

CECELIA:

He's very good looking.

ALEC:

She won't marry him, but a girl doesn't have to marry a man to break his heart.

CECELIA:

What does it? I wish I knew the secret.

ALEC:

Why, you cold-blooded little kitty. It's lucky for some that the Lord gave you a pug nose.
(Enter Mrs. Connage.)

MRS. CONNAGE:

Where on earth is Rosalind?

ALEC:

(Brilliantly.) Of course you've come to the best people to find out. She'd naturally be with us.

MRS. CONNAGE:

Her father has marshalled eight bachelor millionaires to meet her.

ALEC:

You might form a squad and march through the halls.

MRS. CONNAGE:

I'm perfectly serious—for all I know she may be at the Cocoanut [sic] Grove with some football player on the night of her debut. You look left and I'll—

ALEC:

(Flippantly.) Hadn't you better send the butler through the cellar?

MRS. CONNAGE:

(Perfectly serious.) Oh, you don't think she'd be there!

CECELIA:

He's only joking, mother.

ALEC:

Mother had a picture of her tapping a keg of beer with some high hurdler.

MRS. CONNAGE:

Let's look right away.
(They go out. Enter Rosalind with Gillespie.)

GILLESPIE:

Rosalind—Once more I ask you. Don't you care a blessed thing about me?
(Enter Amory.)

AMORY:

My dance.

ROSALIND:

Mr. Gillespie, this is Mr. Blaine.

GILLESPIE:

I've met Mr. Blaine. From Dayton, aren't you?

AMORY:

Yes.

GILLESPIE:

(*Desperately.*) I've been there. It's rather awful.

AMORY:

(*Spicily.*) I don't know. I always felt that I'd rather be provincial hot-tamale than soup without seasoning.

GILLESPIE:

What?

AMORY:

Oh, no offense.
(*Gillespie bows and leaves.*)

ROSALIND:

He's too much *people.*

AMORY:

I was in love with a *people* once.

ROSALIND:

So?

AMORY:

Oh yes, some fool—nothing at all to her, except what I read into her.

ROSALIND:

What happened?

AMORY:

Finally I convinced her that she was smarter than I was—then she threw me over. Said I was impractical, you know.

ROSALIND:

What do you mean, impractical?

AMORY:

Oh—drive a car, but can't change a tire.

ROSALIND:

What are you going to do?

AMORY:

Write—I'm going to start here in New York.

ROSALIND:

Greenwich Village.

AMORY:

Good heavens no—I said write—not drink.

ROSALIND:

I like business men. Clever men are usually so homely.

AMORY:

I feel as if I'd known you ages.

ROSALIND:

Oh, are you going to commence the "pyramid" story?

AMORY:

No—I was going to make it French. I was Louis 14th and you were one of my—my—(*Changing his tone.*) Suppose—we fell in love.

ROSALIND:

I've suggested pretending.

AMORY:

If we did it would be very big.

ROSALIND:

Why?

AMORY:

Because selfish people are in a way terribly capable of great loves.

ROSALIND:

Pretend. (*Turning her lips up.*) (*Very deliberately they kiss.*)

AMORY:

I can't say sweet things. But you are beautiful.

ROSALIND:

Not that.

AMORY:

What then?

ROSALIND:

(*Sadly.*) Oh, nothing—only I want sentiment, real sentiment—and I never find it.

AMORY:

I never find anything else in the world—and I loathe it.

ROSALIND:

It's so hard to find a male to gratify one's artistic taste. (*Someone has opened a door and the music of a waltz surges into the room. Rosalind rises.*)

ROSALIND:

Listen, they're playing "Kiss Me Again." (*He looks at her.*)

AMORY:

Well?

ROSALIND:

Well?

AMORY:

(*Softly—the battle lost.*) I love you.

ROSALIND:

I love you. (*They kiss.*)

AMORY:

Oh, God, what have I done?

ROSALIND:

Nothing. Oh, don't talk. Kiss me again.

AMORY:

I don't know why or how, but I love you—from the moment I saw you.

ROSALIND:

Me too—I—I—want to belong to you. (*Her brother strolls in, starts and then in a loud voice says, "Oh, excuse me," and goes.*)

ROSALIND:

(*Her lips scarcely stirring.*) Don't let me go—I don't care who knows.

AMORY:

Say it.

ROSALIND:

I love you. (*They part.*)

ROSALIND:

Oh—I am very youthful, thank God—and rather beautiful, thank God—and happy, thank God, thank God—(*She pauses and then in an odd burst of frankness adds.*) Poor Amory! (*He kisses her again.*)

CURTAIN.

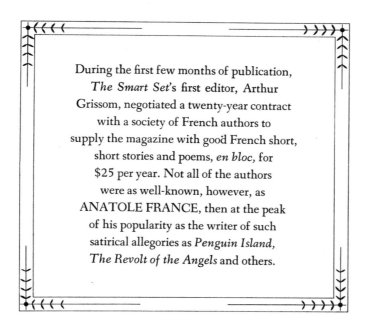

During the first few months of publication, *The Smart Set*'s first editor, Arthur Grissom, negotiated a twenty-year contract with a society of French authors to supply the magazine with good French short, short stories and poems, *en bloc,* for $25 per year. Not all of the authors were as well-known, however, as ANATOLE FRANCE, then at the peak of his popularity as the writer of such satirical allegories as *Penguin Island, The Revolt of the Angels* and others.

La Dame a L'Eventail *

—◆—

ANATOLE FRANCE

TCHOUANG-TSEN, du pays de Soung, était un lettré qui poussait la sagesse jusqu'au détachement de toutes les choses périssables, et comme, en bon Chinois qu'il était, il ne croyait point, d'ailleurs, aux choses éternelles, il ne lui restait pour contenter son âme que la conscience d'échapper aux communes erreurs des hommes qui s'agitent pour acquérir d'inutiles richesses ou de vains honneurs. Mais il faut que cette satisfaction soit profonde, car il fut, après sa mort, proclamé heureux et digne d'envie. Or, pendant les jours que les génies inconnus du monde lui accordèrent de passer sous un ciel vert, parmi des arbustes en fleurs, des saules et des bambous, Tchouang-Tsen avait coutume de se promener en rêvant dans ces contrées où il vivait sans savoir ni comment ni pourquoi. Un matin qu'il errait à l'aventure sur les pentes fleuries de la montagne Nam-Hoa, il se trouva insensiblement au milieu d'un cimetière où les morts reposaient, selon l'usage du pays, sous des monticules de terre battue. A la vue des tombes innombrables qui s'étendaient par delà l'horizon, le lettré médita sur la destinée des hommes.

"Hélas!" se dit-il, "voici le carrefour où aboutissent tous les chemins de la vie. Quand

FROM VOL. 7, AUGUST 1902

* SIC

une fois on a pris place dans le séjour des morts, on ne revient plus au jour."

Cette idée n'est point singulière, mais elle résume assez bien la philosophie de Tchouang-Tsen et celle des Chinois. Les Chinois ne connaissent qu'une seule vie, celle où l'on voit au soleil fleurir les pivoines. L'égalité des humains dans la tombe les console ou les désespère selon qu'ils sont enclins à la sérénité ou à la mélancolie. D'ailleurs, ils ont, pour les distraire, une multitude de dieux verts ou rouges qui, parfois, ressuscitent les morts et exercent la magie amusante. Mais Tchouang-Tsen, qui appartenait à la secte orgueilleuse des philosophes, ne demandait pas de consolation à des dragons de porcelaine. Comme il promenait ainsi sa pensée à travers les tombes, il rencontra soudain une jeune dame qui portait des vêtements de deuil, c'est-à-dire une longue robe blanche d'une étoffe grossière et sans coutures. Assise près d'une tombe, elle agitait un éventail blanc sur la terre encore fraîche du tertre funéraire.

Curieux de connaître les motifs d'une action si étrange, Tchouang-Tsen salua la jeune dame avec politesse et lui dit:

"Oserai-je, madame, vous demander quelle personne est couchée dans ce tombeau, et pourquoi vous vous donnez tant de peine pour éventer la terre qui la recouvre? Je suis philosophe; je recherche les causes, et voilà une cause qui m'échappe."

Le jeune dame continuait à remuer son éventail. Elle rougit, baissa la tête et murmura quelques paroles que le sage n'entendit point. Il renouvela plusieurs fois sa question, mais en vain. La jeune femme ne prenait plus garde à lui et il semblait que son âme eût passé tout entière dans la main qui agitait l'éventail.

Tchouang-Tsen s'éloigna à regret. Bien qu'il connût que tout n'est pas vanité, il était, de son naturel, enclin à rechercher les mobiles des actions humaines, et particulièrement de celles des femmes; cette petite espèce de créature lui inspirait une curiosité malveil-lante, mais très vive. Il poursuivait lentement sa promenade en détournant la tête pour voir encore l'éventail qui battait l'air comme l'aile d'un grand papillon, quand, tout à coup, une vieille femme qu'il n'avait point aperçue d'abord lui fit signe de la suivre. Elle l'entraîna dans l'ombre d'un tertre plus élevé que les autres et lui dit:

"Je vous ai entendu faire à ma maîtresse une question à laquelle elle n'a pas répondu. Mais moi je satisferai votre curiosité par un sentiment naturel d'obligeance, et dans l'espoir que vous voudrez bien me donner en retour de quoi acheter aux prêtres un papier magique qui prolongera ma vie."

Tchouang-Tsen tira de sa bourse une pièce de monnaie, et la vieille parla en ces termes:

"Cette dame que vous avez vue sur un tombeau est Madame Lu, veuve d'un lettré nommé Tao, qui mourut, voilà quinze jours, après une longue maladie, et ce tombeau est celui de son mari. Ils s'aimaient tous deux d'un amour tendre. Même en expirant, Monsieur Tao ne pouvait se résoudre à la quitter, et l'idée de la laisser au monde dans la fleur de son âge et de sa beauté lui était tout à fait insupportable. Il s'y résignait, pourtant, car il était d'un caractère très doux et son âme se soumettait volontiers à la nécessité. Pleurant au chevet du lit de Monsieur Tao, q'elle n'avait point quitté durant sa maladie, Madame Lu attestait les dieux qu'elle ne lui survivrait point, et qu'elle partagerait son cercueil comme elle avait partagé sa couche.

"Mais Monsieur Tao lui dit:

"'Madame, ne jurez point cela.'

"'Du moins,' reprit-elle, 'si je dois vous survivre, si je suis condamnée par les génies à voir encore la lumière du jour quand vous ne la verrez plus, sachez que je ne consentirai jamais à devenir la femme d'un autre, et que je n'aurai qu'un époux comme je n'ai qu'une âme.'

"Mais Monsieur Tao lui dit:

"'Madame, ne jurez point cela.'

"'Oh! Monsieur Tao, Monsieur Tao! laissez-moi jurer du moins que de cinq ans entiers je ne me marierai.'

"Mais Monsieur Tao lui dit:

"'Madame, ne jurez point cela. Jurez seulement de garder fidèlement ma mémoire tant que la terre n'aura pas séché sur mon tombeau.'

"Madame Lu en fit un grand serment. Et le bon Monsieur Tao ferma les yeux pour ne plus les rouvrir. Le désespoir de Madame Lu passa tout ce qu'on peut imaginer. Ses yeux étaient dévorés de larmes ardentes. Elle égratignait, avec les petits couteaux de ses ongles, ses joues de porcelaine. Mais tout passe, et le torrent de cette douleur s'écoula. Trois jours après la mort de Monsieur Tao la tristesse de Madame Lu était devenue humaine. Elle apprit qu'un jeune disciple de Monsieur Tao désirait lui témoigner la part qu'il prenait à son deuil. Elle jugea avec raison qu'elle ne pouvait se dispenser de le recevoir. Elle le reçut en soupirant. Ce jeune homme était très élégant et d'une belle figure; il lui parla un peu de Monsieur Tao et beaucoup d'elle-même; il lui dit qu'il sentait bien qu'il l'aimait; elle le lui laissa dire. Il promit de revenir. En l'attendant, Madame Lu, assise auprès du tertre de son mari, où vous l'avez vue, passe tout le jour à sécher la terre de la tombe au souffle de son éventail."

Quand la vieille eut terminé son récit, le sage Tchouang-Tsen songea:

"La jeunesse est courte; l'aiguillon du désir donne des ailes aux jeunes femmes et aux jeunes hommes. Après tout, Madame Lu est une honnête personne qui ne veut pas trahir son serment."

C'est un exemple à proposer aux femmes blanches de l'Europe.

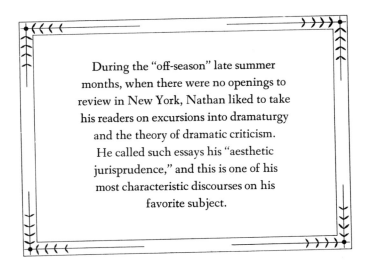

During the "off-season" late summer
months, when there were no openings to
review in New York, Nathan liked to take
his readers on excursions into dramaturgy
and the theory of dramatic criticism.
He called such essays his "aesthetic
jurisprudence," and this is one of his
most characteristic discourses on his
favorite subject.

The Seventh Veil

ABRIDGED

GEORGE JEAN NATHAN

As a critic, it has never been my aim or purpose to convince anybody, including myself. My sole effort has been to express personal opinions grounded upon such training and experience and the philosophy deduced therefrom as I may possess. Since I personally am not fool enough to believe finally in everything that I happen at the moment to believe, however stoutly, I am not fool enough to wish to convince anyone finally in matters that, at their very best, are in all probability of a dubious truth. I please myself to believe that the critic who has another aim is a vainglorious and often absurd figure. One is a good critic in the degree that one is able to answer vacillating and quibbling doubt with determined and per-

suasively positive doubt. Criticism is the prevailing of intelligent skepticism over vague and befuddled prejudice and uncertainty. It answers no riddle: it merely poses an oppugnant and contradictory riddle. When the critic ceases to have self-doubts, he ceases to be a critic and becomes a college professor.

II

THE critic who is expert in the manipulation of logic appreciates the infinitely superior value of the tricky and specious argument as opposed to the simple and sound argument. Sound arguments, in the assault of logic upon the herd head, are doomed to more or less dismal failure. If the

FROM VOL. 72, SEPTEMBER 1923

straight-line reasoning but evidential sky-rockets, pin-wheels and flower-pots. The critic of the arts, if he is of the species that wishes to convert his readers to his way of thinking—if he is, in other words, idiotically imbued with the messiah-pox—must conduct himself much the same as a propagandist in wartime. He must lie convincingly; he must deftly distort the facts; he must perform elaborately as a country fair hypnotist performs; but he must not permit himself to be found out. His criticism must be a shrewd, deceptive, plausible and irresistibly spurious amalgam of esthetic gold bricks, spook photography, death-bed visions, covered carpet tacks and Hindoo mango-tree growing set into a frame of substantial but mild and very easily assimilable dialectics. The so-called influential critic is not the critic who tells the truth as he sees it in terms of the truth, but more often the one who tells the truth as he sees it in terms of the truth as others see it. He may write what he believes, but he is careful first to filter it through the minds of those whom he is addressing. This is the "as we all well know," "as you will surely agree," "those of us who," "as for the rest of us" type of critic. One finds him everywhere. He is the critical go-getter, good-mixer, backslapper. And, like a competent shoe drummer, he gets what he goes after.

In the matter of the value of the showy argument as against the sound, I am always reminded of a murder trial that I covered eighteen or nineteen years ago in a little town in New Jersey. A physician was charged with having killed his wife by giving her drugs whose action and effect were indistinguishable from those of ptomaine poisoning. Things looked pretty bad for the defendant and, up to the time the counsel for the defense began its cross-examination of the star witness for the State, the odds were heavy on the man's conviction for murder in the first degree. The testimony of the star witness for the prosecution had dangerously riddled the defensive armor. This witness had previously sworn that he, a stranger in the little town, had arrived in town on the night of the alleged murder. It was the first time he had ever been in the little town. He had left the next morning and had not been back since summoned as a witness by the prosecution. On the night in question, he testified, he had got off the train at the depot and had walked up the main street of the town and gone directly to the accused's house. If the defense could shoot a hole through this testimony, it well appreciated that it would go a long way toward convincing the jury of the innocence of its client.

Among the four attorneys for the accused was a little, bewhiskered, taciturn yokel of some fifty years who, it had been observed, hadn't so much as opened his mouth once since the beginning of the trial. None of the newspapermen present could solve the mystery of his presence: he seemed a sheer wanton waste of good money on the part of the defendant. The cross-examination of the important star witness for the State proceeded—the usual questionings and re-questionings. These all centered upon his presence in the little town on the night in point. The cross-examination had been going on for about five weary hours when suddenly the little bewhiskered yokel lawyer who hadn't thus far spoken a single word hopped to his feet, brushed back the other attorneys for the defense, and approached the man in the witness box.

"You say that you got out at the depot and walked directly up the main thoroughfare of this city to the defendant's residence?" he inquired.

The witness nodded.

"Well, then," asked the little lawyer, "tell the gentlemen of the jury what you saw when you walked up the main thoroughfare."

The witness, somewhat perplexed, replied that he had seen nothing.

"What, nothing!" exclaimed the little lawyer. "You saw *nothing?*"

Nothing, answered the witness.

"Do you mean to say that you can face the jury and deliberately say that you saw nothing"—here the little lawyer paused dramatically—"nothing *unusual?*"

The witness, nonplussed, again made negative answer.

The little lawyer turned to the jury:

"You have heard the witness say, gentlemen of the jury, that he walked up the main street of our city and yet saw absolutely nothing in the least unusual. I ask you, gentlemen, can you therefore for one moment believe that this witness has told the truth that he actually was in our city on the night he says he was? You certainly cannot. For if he had been here and had, as he says, walked up the main thoroughfare he could not possibly—he could not *conceivably*—have missed seeing the fine three-story school-building which we have recently erected!"

The jury, composed of villagers who had paid out their good taxes for the little school-building and were immensely proud of it as one of the real sights of their little town, smiled back their agreement. Their eventual verdict—a unanimous one—was not guilty.

III

It is often argued against the dramatic critic that his judgment becomes warped through a surfeit of the theatre, that since he is compelled to go to play upon play night upon night that judgment, calloused through repetition and satiety, is bound to become unduly influenced and hence devitalized by the man's personal impatience, cumulatively blasé point of view and physical fatigue. This is nonsense. Were it true, the same argument might be applied with equal force against the reliability of the doctor, surgeon and criminal lawyer in constant practice. If my critical judgment and prac-tising skill are corrupted by my being forced to sit successively through fifty idiotic plays, what of the critical judgment and practising skill of the doctor who is called upon successively to attend fifty women whose only trouble is that they do not love their husbands, of the surgeon who is forced successively to perform fifty minor operations in the region of the spankspot, and of the criminal lawyer who is compelled successively to defend fifty plainly innocent clients against the eloquence of some shyster prosecutor in a poke collar?

IV

Very young men and very old men alone are cocksure. The soundest of critics is thus the man of middle years. He has temporarily outgrown the cocksureness of his youth and he is still this side of the cocksureness of age. He is temporarily free from empty prejudice, free from youth's revolt and from age's revolt against revolt, and beset by a healthy skepticism and doubt. He is of open mind; he is without indignations; he doesn't give a damn.

V

The value of a detached point of view in artistic creation seems to me to be absurdly overestimated. Truly great art is the product of passionate interest and hot enthusiasm. That interest and enthusiasm may affect a cool and self-condescending smile, and that smile may in turn be interpreted as the smile of detachment, but it is never—save in the instance of the second-grade artist—anything of the kind. A tonic detached philosophy is not necessarily the fruit of a detached point of view. It is more often the fruit of a positive point of view which, to its own pleasurable inexpectation and disconcertment, has found itself cut into, half-frustrated and divided into two by the sudden incursion of a point of view that appears to be equally positive in its approach to the truth. . .

242

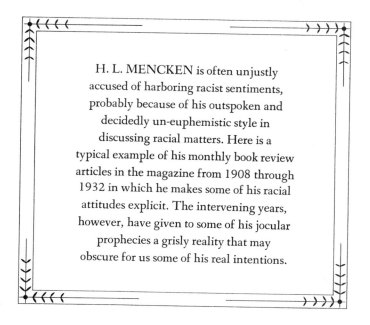

H. L. MENCKEN is often unjustly accused of harboring racist sentiments, probably because of his outspoken and decidedly un-euphemistic style in discussing racial matters. Here is a typical example of his monthly book review articles in the magazine from 1908 through 1932 in which he makes some of his racial attitudes explicit. The intervening years, however, have given to some of his jocular prophecies a grisly reality that may obscure for us some of his real intentions.

Si Mutare Potest Aethiops Pellum Suam

ABRIDGED

H. L. MENCKEN

Two late books intrigue me, not only because they are of intrinsic virtue, but also and chiefly because they expose a problem that will haunt this great Calvinist republic, in the days to come, like a persistent glycosuria or night sweat. I allude, of course, to the race question, now beautifully expanding and mellowing, and in particular to that part of it which has to do with the niggero. What, ladies and gentlemen, in hell or out of it, are we to do with the Ethiop? Who shall answer the thunderous demands of the emerging coon? For emerging he is, both quantitatively and qualitatively, and there will come a

FROM VOL. 53, SEPTEMBER 1917

morn, believe me or not, when those with ears to hear and hides to feel will discover that he is to be boohed and put off no longer—that he has at last got the power to exact a square answer, and that the days of his docile service as minstrel, torch and goat are done. When that morn dawns, I pray upon both knees, I shall be safe in the Alps, and not below the Potomac River, hurriedly disguised with burnt cork and trying to get out on the high gear. Soon or late, I agree with William Archer (see his "Through Afro-America," 1910) it will come to rough work—and perhaps sooner than most of us fancy. The

Southerners, even the honest ones, have botched the business abominably, and unless Providence intervenes with a miracle I suspect that it will jolly well botch the South.

I speak, not as a villainous Yankee and Abolitionist, but as one of Southern birth, and of Southerners born. I was brought up (or, in the local dialect, raised) among darkeys; I played with darkey boys in my nonage; I know hundreds of darkeys today; I am on good terms with them; I have never had a serious quarrel with an individual among them. I thus qualify, I hope, as a Southern gentleman, or, at all events, as a Southerner. More, I am and always have been in favor of slavery, not only for blacks, but also for all save a small and shrinking minority of whites. Yet more, I regard Stonewall Jackson as a great general, and believe that Ben Butler has never reached heaven, and prefer batter-bread to *petit pain,* and voted for Bryan, and am sound on infant damnation and the crime of '73, and have the hookworm and used to write editorials for the Baltimore *Sunpaper.* I bore you with these qualifications in self-defense. It would shock and grieve me to be called a Yankee, and, what is worse, it would libel me. I hate everyone born north of the Mason and Dixon line, whether man or woman. I regard the surrender of General Robert E. Lee as the most calamitous human event since the discovery of America. I would rather be chained by the leg in the common jail of Yazoo City, Miss., fed only upon hoecake and coca-cola, than smothered in violets by all the gals of Boston. . . .

Nevertheless, it seems to me that the South has failed to solve the problem of the *Homo noir,* and that the completeness of its failure is growing more visible day by day. Not only is the coon not come to equilibrium; he is jumping up and rocking the boat more and more. For thirty or forty years after the war it was simply a question of how much should be given to him—freely or haltingly, generously or grudgingly, as you choose. But now it is fast becoming a question of how much he will demand and take—if possible, peaceably; if not, by force. And why the change? Simply because the niggero has been making fast and secure progress, not in mere education, but in competence, in self-confidence, in wealth—because he has begun to find out that he can make his way, Southerners or no Southerners—because, in all that is essential and lasting, he has shown better progress than the Southern whites. A harsh fact, but still a fact. The South likes to think that it has recovered from the Civil War—the whole region, in truth, swarms with wind-machines who keep on trying to demonstrate it—but a glance at the evidence is enough to fill any impartial judge with doubts. Those four years were more terrible than anyone knew. They wiped out the old civilization, and they left the soil so sterile that a new one has never sprung up.

Consider, for example, Virginia—in the old days undoubtedly the premier American state, the mother of Presidents and statesmen, the hatchery of national ideas and ideals, the home of the first American university worthy of the name, the *arbiter elegantiarum* of the western world. Well, observe Virginia today. It is years since a first-rate man has come out of it; it is years since an idea has come out of it. The *ancien régime* went down the red gullet of war; the poor white trash are now in the saddle. Politics in Virginia are cheap, ignorant, parochial, idiotic; there is scarcely a man in office above the rank of a petty job-seeker, the political doctrine that prevails is made up of hand-me-downs from the bumpkinry of the Middle West—Bryanism, prohibition, vice crusading, all that sort of claptrap; the administration of the law is turned over to professors of Puritanism and espionage; a Washington or a Jefferson, dumped there by some act of God, would be denounced as a scoundrel and jailed overnight. Elegance, *esprit,* culture? Virginia has no art, no literature, no philosophy, no mind or aspiration of her own. Her education has

244

sunk to the Baptist seminary level; not a single contribution to human knowledge has come out of her colleges in twenty-five years; she spends less than half upon her common schools, per capita, than any Northern state spends. In brief, an intellectual desert, a paradise of the fourth-rate. There remains, at the top, a ghost of the old urbanity, a bit wistful and infinitely charming. But there is no thought under it, no cultural pressure and vigor, no curiosity and enterprise. The mind of the state, as it is revealed to the nation, is pathetically naif and inconsequential; it no longer reacts with energy and elasticity to great problems; it seems fallen to the bombastic trivialities of the camp-meeting and the Chautauqua. A Lee or a Poe or a Jefferson would be almost as unthinkable in the Virginia of today as a Huxley or a Nietzsche in Nicaragua.

I choose the Old Dominion, not because I disdain it, but precisely because I esteem it. It is, by long odds, the most civilized of the Southern states, now as always. If one turns to such a commonwealth as Georgia the picture becomes far darker. Here the liberated lower orders of whites have borrowed the worst commercial bumptiousness of the Yankee and superimposed it upon a culture that, at bottom, is little removed from barbarism. Georgia is not only ignorant and stupid; it is vicious. A self-respecting and educated European, going there to live, would not only find intellectual stimulation utterly lacking; he would actually feel a certain insecurity. The Leo Frank affair was no isolated phenomenon, no accident; it fitted into its frame very snugly; it was a natural expresssion of Georgian ideas of the true, the good and the beautiful. There is a state with more than half of the area of Italy and more population than either Denmark or Norway, and yet, in thirty years it has not produced a single first-class book or picture or poem or scientific discovery or political or philosophical idea, or other sound contribution to human advancement. If it had been destroyed by an earth-

quake in 1875, the world would be exactly where it is today. If the whole of its present population were to be transplanted to Mars tomorrow, the news would be of no more interest to civilization than the news that a distillery had burned down in Kentucky.

If you want to get some notion of the intellectual and social backwardness of Georgia, turn to the last edition of "Who's Who in America," and particularly to page 15, on which the assembled *aluminados* are sorted out according to their places of birth. Georgia, with a population of 2,609,121, contributes 243; Michigan, with a population of 2,810,173, contributes 551; Vermont, with a population of 355,956, contributes 363. But we forget that Georgia is half black—we must chalk off the Moors. Very well, let us match that half of Georgia which is white against that part of the northern populace which is at least half American. (Georgia herself has very few foreign whites.) The result is almost as striking. The 1,300,000 whites of Georgia contribute 242 Whoswhoistas; the 1,433,375 inhabitants of Massachusetts who have "one or both parents native" offer 2,002. In New Jersey (perhaps the least civilized Northern state) the 1,213,601 American and semi-American whites give "Who's Who" 501 names—more than twice as many as Georgia. Here, remember, I always regard birthplace, and not place of residence. Georgia is no new state; it had half a million population in 1825, and more than a million before the Civil War. Yet it is now left far behind, both relatively and actually, by such new states as Wisconsin, Iowa and Michigan, none of which got on its legs until after the war.

Apply any other test and you will unearth the same sluggishness. The Southern white is falling behind the procession; not only is the Northern white forging ahead of him, but also the Southern *procyon lotor*. I turn to page 68 of the third revised edition of Ely's "Outlines of Economics," just published, and find this:

In the South during the last census decade the number of Negro farmers increased more rapidly than the number of white farmers; the acreage of land operated by white farmers decreased while that operated by Negro farmers increased 10 per cent; the value of farm land and buildings owned by whites increased 117 per cent, but the value of farm land and buildings owned by Negroes increased 156 per cent; while the number of Negro farm owners increased 17 per cent as contrasted with an increase of 12 per cent in the white owners of farms.

More, the niggero is making equal, if not actually greater strides, in commerce and industry. When he learns to read and write he no longer sets up shop as a shyster lawyer, a quack doctor or a grafting ecclesiastic; he applies himself to a trade, or opens a store, or begins swindling his fellow blacks with some banking or insurance scheme. The number of such enterprises increases enormously in all the Southern states; there are whole towns given over to darkey business, and soon there will be whole regions. And then? Well, and then the band will begin to play. The black has learned the capital lesson that property is necessary to self-respect, that he will never get anywhere so long as he is poor. Once he is secure in that department he will take up the business of getting back his plain constitutional rights. Will he produce leaders fit for so great and delicate a venture? The answer is held *in petto* by the gods—but it is not to be forgotten that he produced a leader fit for the work of preparation. The Southern whites have pondered and debated the negro question for fifty years; it has been their first and almost only permanent concern; they offer its difficulties as the explanation of all their lack of progress. But let us not forget here that it was a black man, Booker Washington, who worked out the only intelligible solution so far heard of, and that he forced the whites, for all the concentrated horsepower of their joint meditation, to accept it. Booker liberated the niggeroes by teaching them the value of skill and money. Some later prophet may go a step further.

The day he arises I shall retire to Interlaken.

All these lofty thoughts are inspired by the two books before mentioned—"His Own Country," by Paul Kester (*Bobbs-Merrill*), and "The Autobiography of an Ex-Colored Man" (*Sherman-French*), the first a novel and the second a record of fact. Mr. Kester's narrative runs to nearly 700 pages, but in structure it is quite simple. A young quadroon, the natural son of a Virginia planter, goes to Canada in his youth, acquires an education, accumulates money, and marries a white wife. Then, through an agent, he buys the decayed plantation of his old master, and returns as a gentleman of leisure. The circumambient gentry are horrified—what, a coon at Comorn Hall! But the worst is yet to come. The prodigal demands social recognition, goes into the courts to obtain his rights, defies the local *noblesse,* attracts the attention of the Northern newspapers, takes to the Chautauquas, horns into national politics, lunches at the White House, founds a black party, collects a war fund of millions, and tries to organize into one compact whole the financial, voting and even military strength of his 10,000,000 fellows. Alas, too soon! A cog slips, and down he goes, just as success seems yielding to his prehension. His Black Crusaders blow up, the newspapers turn upon him, his following falls away, he himself is amiably butchered by his white neighbors, and his son and daughter with him. . . . "'My son,' he gasped. 'My daughter—I have given all.' . . . Above Comorn rolled the [*sic*] leaped the sombre smoke and crimson flame. Against even the brightening glory of the morning sky the Black Crusader had unfurled and flung the awful challenge of his sable flag." . . .

A mere shocker? A book to harrow fat women? Nay, you mistake it. It is a serious attempt, by a man of Northern birth, long resident in the South, to project an experimental beam into the sinister and much muddled future. It is careful, thoughtful, persuasive, provocative; it stands as far above

246

the gaudy balderdash of a Thomas Dixon as a novel by Dreiser stands above the boudoir goods of Robert W. Chambers. There is in it no sentimental propaganda, no childish tickling of the blackamoor. One sees in Brent, the Black Crusader, not only the unsuspected potentialities of the emerging negro, but also his deficiencies—his lack of self-restraint, his savage passion, his almost Jewish impudence and obnoxiousness. And in the lesser blacks of the chronicle these deficiencies are made even plainer; examine them carefully, if you are not a Southerner, and you will get some notion of what it means to live among such evil and intolerable Anthropoidea. Nor are the whites overdone in stupidity and hunkerousness. They are not the barbaric white trash of Georgia, but Virginians of gentle birth and rearing—the only genuine gentleman, perhaps, now extant in this moral republic. And they approach their problem, despite its final descent to bloodshed, in decency and soberness of mind, and with as much charity as human beings in trouble ever show. In brief, the story is artfully planned; there is no special pleading in it; it is an honest and discreet attempt to put living drama into a work of the imagination, and it comes, in places, to a very high level of achievement.

"The Autobiography of an Ex-Colored Man" is less sophisticated and reflective; all the author seeks to do is to tell his own story, with certain generalizations by the way. He is, like most Afro-Americans of any intelligence, chiefly white and of good blood, more, he is so nearly pure white that, in the end, he marries a white wife and passes over from the one race into the other. The value of his tale lies in the accuracy of its details—its pictures of the social life of the negro, North and South. He distinguishes three classes, (*a*) the tough niggeroes, (*b*) the order of niggero servants, dependent on the whites, and (*c*) the new order of well-to-do, industrious, self-respecting and aspiring niggeroes. It is the misfortune of the South that the first

class is still numerous, and that the second is shrinking. It is the double misfortune of the South that the white Southerners still exhibit a vain and passionate intolerance of the third class. The brunette Napoleon (or Rockefeller, or Roosevelt, or Carranza, or Garrison), when he comes, will come out of Class III. . . . The anonymous author handles the question of miscegenation somewhat gingerly, though it is, in a sense, the main matter of his book. Interbreeding is going out of fashion in the South; it is no longer customary down there for every gentleman to have his xanthous mistress. But that is not because the Southerners have re-enacted the seventh commandment, but because the more slightly yellow girls have improved in education and aspiration and self-respect, and are thus less willing to enter into concubinage. A compensatory movement, not to be mentioned in a family magazine, shows itself in the North. You will find some notice of it in the present work. . . .

II

"THE MYSTERIOUS STRANGER" having escaped the public hangman, Albert Bigelow Paine now ventures upon the open publication of Mark Twain's "What Is Man?" (*Harper*). Of this book I have often discoursed at length; Mark wrote it back in the '80's, but did not print it until 1906, and then only in an edition limited to 250 copies, and not for sale. It contains, in brief, two ideas, neither of them very startling, the first being that man, in Dr. Crile's phase, is an adaptive mechanism, and the second being that altruism, when analyzed, always turns out to be self-interest in a long-tailed coat. These ideas, as I say, are not startling—most men of any intelligence subscribe to them today—but when they first occurred to Mark they were less prevalent, and so they shook him up a bit, and he set them down with the air of a boy pulling the cat's tail, and was afraid to circulate them. Even now they meet with horrified opposition from such pillars of forgotten nonsense as the New York *Times Review of Books*. In the issue for June 3 there is a long editorial denouncing them as naughty, and stating that "one refuses to believe that the book voices the setttled, mature convictions held by Mr. Clemens—at least one does not wish to believe it." Refuses? On what ground? No more than a glance at Paine's life of Mark is sufficient to prove that he not only held to them to the last, but that he was fond of extending them and reinforcing them. If he was anything at all in this world, he was an absolute skeptic and determinist; nothing offended and enraged him more than the sloppy idealism and optimism which the *Times* now seeks to ram down his aesophagus [*sic*]. That such bosh should be seriously printed as criticism is surely a sorry indication of the depths to which criticism is sunk in These States.

But let us not be impatient. The fact that Mark was an intelligent man is one that will penetrate the caputs of the national grand-mas of letters only slowly. They began by greeting him as a childish buffoon; they proceeded to hail him a purveyor of refined entertainment; they are now in the stage of praising him as a chaser of the blues—in the *Times* phrase, one "who has done so much, through his joyous humor, to lighten the burdens of his generation." Such judgments are worse than errors; they are indecencies. It is as if Italian organ-grinders should essay to estimate Beethoven. The truth about Mark is that he was a colossus, that he stood head and shoulders above his country and his time, that even the combined pull of Puritanism without and Philistinism within could not bring him down to the national level. The result is that he remains mysterious—a baffling puzzle to the critics of the country. Read Howells' "My Mark Twain" if you would see how even the utmost personal intimacy can leave a second-rate man with only a vague and inaccurate picture of a first-rate man. . . .

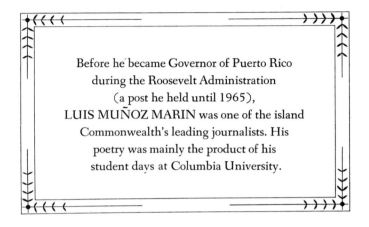

Before he became Governor of Puerto Rico
during the Roosevelt Administration
(a post he held until 1965),
LUIS MUÑOZ MARIN was one of the island
Commonwealth's leading journalists. His
poetry was mainly the product of his
student days at Columbia University.

Leaves

LUIS MUÑOZ MARIN

WE shall forget our words,
We shall forget our hearts,
And in forgetting these, we forget all
For we have words, then hearts, then . . . nothing more.

But these trees, my love, that have heard us,
These trees that are good and trusting and deep
With the eternal spirit of the earth,
Shall they forget?
I dread the reproach of their everlasting leaves.

FROM VOL. 62, MAY 1920

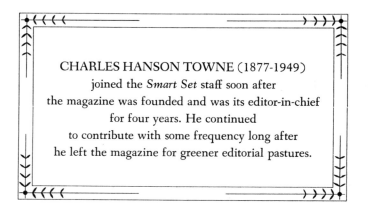

CHARLES HANSON TOWNE (1877-1949)
joined the *Smart Set* staff soon after
the magazine was founded and was its editor-in-chief
for four years. He continued
to contribute with some frequency long after
he left the magazine for greener editorial pastures.

After Reading Keats

CHARLES HANSON TOWNE

Down his great corridors of sumptuous sound
Today I wandered once again; each word
Seemed like the lyric rapture of a bird
Singing in Spring above the burgeoning ground.
Oh, once again that old delight I found,
Once more the marvel of his voice I heard
Until my spirit with new joy was stirred,
Hearing such music through his halls resound.

How beautiful thy place, Poet blest!—
That room wherein is set thy Grecian Urn,
Thy Nightingale that sings at set of sun
Out in thy garden where my tired feet turn;
And in one chamber, back from his long quest,
That passionate lover, young Endymion!

FROM VOL. 22, JULY 1907

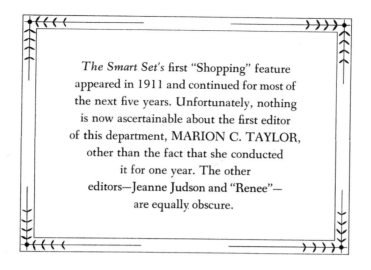

The Smart Set's first "Shopping" feature
appeared in 1911 and continued for most of
the next five years. Unfortunately, nothing
is now ascertainable about the first editor
of this department, MARION C. TAYLOR,
other than the fact that she conducted
it for one year. The other
editors—Jeanne Judson and "Renee"—
are equally obscure.

Shopping for The Smart Set

ABRIDGED

MARION C. TAYLOR

The writer will be glad to offer suggestions or answer questions regarding
shopping and the New York shops. Readers of THE SMART SET inquiring
for names of shops where articles described are purchasable should enclose
a stamped self-addressed envelope for reply, and state page and month.

WELL, the Horse Show is over and the
opening night of the Opera is a month or
so past, so we may assume that the social
season is well under way. Every day the
Avenue is congested with carriages and
motors from early morning till still earlier
the next day, and now that Thanksgiving is
over almost everyone in town is busy with
holiday shopping. It is well nigh impossible
to get a table in any of the fashionable
restaurants, and the theaters are crowded at
night, Everyone is wearing his best bib and
tucker, the vexations of fittings at tailor and
dressmaker being past, and the fashionable
world is quite ready for the usual strenuous season.

At the many smart November weddings
the fashion of gowning the bride in artistic
period costumes seemed predominant—most
of the young women selected the styles best
suited to their individual requirements, and
the results were generally happy; simplicity
in outline, graceful drapery and richness of
material seemed the dominant notes. The
veils were nearly all worn in the new cap-
like effect which in the case of a lace veil—
and they are undoubtedly the modish thing
to wear—makes a charming frame for the
face. The bridesmaids at most of the fashionable London weddings have been wearing
little caps of various nets with short veils in
back, but we seem to prefer hats, or hair

FROM VOL. 33, FEBRUARY 1911

ornaments in the case of any evening wedding, which is an infrequent occurrence. Many of the bridesmaids this fall have worn charming Watteau costumes or Romney effects, the most beautiful part of them being the marvelous color combinations, which grow more beautiful each year. Some of the wedding processions are veritable pageants of gorgeous color effects.

At the Horse Show I was struck by the really wonderful furs and fur wraps worn, and the quiet, soft tones of many of the costumes worn in the evening, in contrast to the gorgeous Oriental effects seen at the Opera. I heard these colors referred to the other day as "joyous colors" and I know of no more suitable term. Deep, rich crimsons, glowing, flamelike tones, warm, deep yellows, and a beautiful orange are all marvelously treated so that the result is rich and harmonious, never glaring or bold as one might imagine. The colder colors, cerise and the like, seem less popular than those of brilliant depth.

A ribbon is frequently wound in the hair or a wide band of bugle trimming or something similar is frequently worn.

PARISIAN HINTS

One of the newest French ideas is that of colored heels to one's shoes and slippers. The very smartest women are wearing red and green heels to black shoes. These shoes frequently show cloth uppers of white or in a cloth to match the costume. I haven't the slightest idea whether the style will catch on over here or not. I can imagine some charming adaptations of it but I also fear some dreadful results if it does. Many ultra fashionable women who affect First Empire, Empress Josephine costumes wear with them the heelless slippers of that period, and if one has a small slender foot the idea is charming.

Picturesque evening gowning is to my mind decidedly an artistic achievement, and one sees more and more of it each season.

Gloves are almost always discarded with these period costumes as the idea is wholly incongruous. One's hair is frequently dressed in a modified style of the period, and one's jewels should be in keeping.

Speaking of hair, French women are wearing the hair rather close to the head to display rather than hide its charming contour. I hear that the bang is coming back—a regular child's bang, too, youthful no doubt but not universally becoming. Everything tends toward a low forehead, and little if any part of the ears is to be seen; however, the soft waves of hair loosely arranged are as becoming as any mode I know of.

FURS AND FUR BAGS

One of the winter's most charming ideas is the bag or purse of fur to match one's cloak or set or the trimming on one's suit or frock. They are seen mostly in the flatter furs, seal, mole, broadtail and the like, and are rather large—long and graceful with rounded corners. The mountings are very handsome gold ones, usually engraved and frequently gem-studded. I have also seen a few in the longer-haired furs, chinchilla, mink and sable; and except that they are a little bulkier, the idea lends itself splendidly to even skunk, American opossum and badger, all of which are very popular. The extensive use of ermine abroad has been felt over here, as has the pretty fashion of having the skins of short-haired furs such as seal and mole made up in opposite directions, which is a conservatively decorative idea suggesting a host of charming conceptions.

Ermine and *"taupe,"* as the French call mole, are still as successful from a fashion standpoint as they promised to be early in season. In the cheaper furs red fox did not make the hit its sponsors hoped, nor has fitch in my opinion been much of a success. Badger, American opossum, cross fox and dyed raccoon, which closely resembles the more expensive skunk, seem to be the most popular of the cheaper furs. Natural raccoon is becoming quite common; Australian opossum is dying out; and I see less white fox this year than ever before; but it is essentially a fur winter nevertheless, and I see more fur used in every possible way than ever before.

A New French Fur Fashion

This is a tiny capelike affair called *"camail"* which clings closely to the shoulders not unlike a coachman's cape. I described in my November number a Francis wrap of black satin and velvet which accompanied a very smart black satin gown. This wrap had one of these little capelike affairs and is still the only thing of the sort I have seen over here, but the photographs and sketches from abroad represent them as charming accessories which will possibly be welcomed next spring.

The Art of Corset Making

Some months ago I casually mentioned a corset made by a woman who had studied every known science that would help her to make a truly successful corset. I had but little space to devote to it that month and could not really do the matter justice. I have since found the corset to be, besides healthful and sensible, a perfect fitting garment, so well made to suit each individual customer's requirements that it is rapidly becoming immensely popular here in town among women who demand the last word in this most important art. Many of the leading dressmakers and tailors are recommending it because it is so cleverly boned that the ugly mark where the corset leaves off is avoided and the absolute smoothness so much sought after is the result.

To Teach Temperance

A truly humorous suggestion is offered by a tall glass which has three rings around it about a half-inch apart. The first one measures a moderate drink. Resting on the top

one is a fat little pig. The card which accompanies it says:

Pig, Whiskey Soda, 1st line (for spirit) Moderation. 2nd line (for spirit) Generous allowance. If the second line be exceeded the suggestion is obvious.

These also come with tiny donkeys instead of pigs; both are bound to cause fun and are attractive additions to the cellarette.

A Real Novelty

Here is something I quite fell in love with the other day—a tiny flat glass tube about two inches long, with a wire around the top, having a hook which fastened it to the buttonhole to hold water and keeps one's boutonniere fresh. When the flower is in it this little hook cannot be seen, and the device enables one to go about all day with a perfectly fresh flower. The idea is originally Russian, has had quite a vogue in England and France, where the fashion of a flower in the buttonhole is even more popular than in America, and is not an unknown one over here; but I know of no other shop in town where these little arrangements can be found, although I have no doubt they will be copied in silver and gold as the idea is a splendid one for cotillion favors and the like. It would be useful to both men and women, for so many of the latter invariably wear a single flower with a simple walking suit.

Keeping Abreast of the Times

I have heard of all sorts of wonderful conveniences offered by department stores, and of all sorts of wonderful things sold by them, but it did surprise me a little the other day when I was told I might buy a Curtiss type aeroplane just as easily and quickly as two spools of silk. Now I don't suppose for a moment that there is going to be any great rush in that department nor any bargain sales in aeroplanes just yet. It is a little early to expect that, but the fact is nevertheless a practical example of the up-to-next-week business methods in vogue today.

253

I saw in this shop a very attractive fern dish of cut glass and silver with an electrolier or candles in the center. You can readily see the possibilties of this innovation. The shop in question has already seen them and has patented the device, which was an idea of the buyer in that particular department—another encouraging illustration of the co-operation between employer and employee in progressive firms today.

The Beauty of Hammered Silver

One of the leading silversmiths is showing a collection of the most marvelous pieces of hammered silver, a collection unequalled in America in its size and the beauty of the work. Each article is carved out of a single piece of silver, which, when one sees the delicate beauty of the finished designs and the perfection of the work, seems almost impossible, and, when one actually sees the work done, seems even more marvelous. Of course the silver is naturally expensive, but it is one of the few genuine products of the age which simply cannot be commercialized. Each piece is the work of an artist who put the very best that was in him in his work, and is an honest piece of the very finest known work in silver. For a wedding or Christmas gift I know of nothing which of necessity more clearly reflects the truly artistic taste of the giver, and nothing surer of proper appreciation, for the artistic beauty of the work compels admiration.

New Ideas for the Motorist

In a shop devoted to motor apparel and accessories I came across three things especially noteworthy. The first was a splendid icebox of galvanized iron, covered with patent leather. It has a top tray with one large and two small compartments for sandwiches and other food stuffs, and the bottom has a large center space for the ice and two small deep ones for bottles or anything else one desires. The second was a bag to fasten on the brass rod at the back of the front seat; it closes with patent clamps and may be opened without removing it from the rod, and discloses a complete set of toilet articles, also needles, thread and a thimble. They are so handy and convenient that the bag is sure to be liked. A second bag to hang on the rod has a center space for a luncheon box, and two outer ones for Thermos bottles. Both of these come in various kinds and colors of leather.

The New Records

Some of the so-called popular records for the phonograph are very good this month. They include the duet "Alma" from "Alma, Where Do You Live?" and some of the best music from "The Girl in the Train" and "Our Miss Gibbs." Pryor's band gives a very good rendering of the "Adagio Lamentosa" from Tschaikowsky's "Sonata." Then I liked the charming duet "Let Us Talk Politics" from "La Fille de Mme. Angot," which was so successfully revived last winter at the Manhattan Opera House. Gadski sings two splendid records, one from "Don Giovanni," the other from "The Magic Flute," and I also admired a Lemmone flute record called "Andalouse."

The Season's Shopping Bags

The popularity of enamel is beautifully illustrated in the fittings of some of the new bags. They are in the most fascinating shades of enamel and are quite the prettiest fittings I have come across. The bags themselves are preferably plain when they have such elaborate fittings but of soft and beautiful leather lined with a color to blend harmoniously with the enamel.

Another handsome bag is an imported novelty of the season—in fact, most of the handsomest bags come from Vienna. This one is of morocco, which I think the prettiest leather for general use (with the possible exception of lizard, which is much more expensive) and has silver corners. As the corners wear out more quickly than any other part of the bag, this is a sensible as well as a smart idea. There is a very large tortoise shell button at the top which opens the bag, and a very thin double strap handle. I consider this the very handsomest bag I have seen this year, for it is simple yet inexpressibly smart, and comes in a variety of desirable shades.

Boudoir Baskets

One of the Avenue shops noted for its exclusive things is showing some scrap baskets aptly called "boudoir baskets." They are of white enamel, a plain conservative shape with a wide gold-plated rim at the top. Midway between the top and bottom is an opening, through which a ribbon may be laced corresponding in color to one's decorations. I know of no handsomer or more appropriate basket for a woman's room than one of this sort, and if one wished to fill it with flowers for a holiday gift I'm sure its beauty would find a welcome for it. They show here a very fine line of those smart wicker baskets with a leather rim around the top and a brass monogram at one side which are ideal for living room or den. I also saw a bridge trump indicator which attracted me. A little metal stand held a miniature goal—posts and bar, across which dropped on either side tiny ivory flaps with the suits stamped on them in color. It is as attractive an indicator as I've seen and something different from the usual ones.

AFTERWORD

It must be obvious to anyone who has read this book that it could not have been written without the help and cooperation of a great many individuals. Indeed, I have been the lucky recipient of so much open-handed assistance and encouragement from so many sources that I despair of being able properly to acknowledge, let alone thank, them all here.

My use of published material is acknowledged below in a separate section in the form of descriptive notes. In addition, there are considerable collections of unpublished manuscripts and letters relating to *The Smart Set*

in the university libraries at Cornell, Princeton and Yale and the New York Public Library. For permission to read and reproduce these I wish to thank the curators and librarians concerned.

Where no specific sources are cited in the notes and the matter is not obviously taken from the magazine itself, my information has been gleaned from personal interviews or correspondence. In the "Foreword" to this volume I have already alluded to the enormous aid given to me by the late Burton Rascoe (in 1955-1957), the late H. L. Mencken (in 1955) and the late George Jean Nathan (dur-

256

ing 1955-1958) without which this work, had it ever been written at all, would have had quite a different character and substance. Each of these "central figures" in the story granted me interviews, answered my questions by telephone and letter, and generously gave me quotation privileges—the raw material from which my account was developed. Similar assistance of the utmost value was given me in interviews and correspondence by S. N. Behrman, Morris Gilbert, Will F. Jenkins, Muna Lee, Charles G. Shaw, Mark Van Doren, the late Carl Van Vechten, Eltinge F. Warner, and the late Mrs. Warner and the late Thyra Samter Winslow. All of these people deserve my highest gratitude which I hope I have in some small measure repaid by accurately reporting the data with which they provided me.

Only slightly less important are the numerous letters I have received over the past decade—some of them containing valuable documents and mementos or very detailed personal reminiscences running to several pages—from former contributors to *The Smart Set,* including: Franklin P. Adams, Faith Baldwin, Lillian Foster Barrett, Richmond Brooks Barrett, Morris Bishop, Marion L. Bloom, Phyllis Bottome, Berton Braley, Harold Brighouse, Kenneth Burke, Witter Bynner, James Branch Cabell, Elizabeth J. Coatsworth (Mrs. Henry Beston), Padraic Colum, Floyd Dell, Babette Deutsch, Glenn Ward Dresbach, Lord Dunsany, Paul Eldridge, Paul Hervey Fox, Waldo Frank, John T. Frederick, Henry S. Haskins, Leslie Nelson Jennings, Howard Mumford Jones, S. Jay Kaufman, Alexander King, Jacques LeClercq, Muna Lee, Oscar Lewis, Ludwig Lewisohn, David Morton, Thomas Moult, Gorham B. Munson, Maj. Frank Pease, Ben Ray Redman, William Seagle, Louise deForest Shelton, Odell Shepard, Sigmund Spaeth, Vincent Starrett, Nancy Byrd Turner, Louis Untermeyer, Blanche Shoemaker Wagstaff, John Hall Wheelock,

Margaret Widdemer, Louis Wilkinson and Edmund Wilson.

I am also grateful for helpful information provided me in conversation or letters by Betty Adler (editor of *Menckeniana,* Enoch Pratt Free Library, Baltimore), Hayden Carruth (grandson and namesake of a favorite *Smart Set* humorist), Charley May (Mrs. John Gould) Fletcher, Professor Guy J. Forgue, Mrs. Arthur Guiterman, Alfred A. Knopf, the late Mrs. John Lohrfinck (secetary to H. L. Mencken for many years), William Manchester, August Mencken, Harlan Miller, Upton Sinclair, Bradford F. Swan, Peter Viereck and Mrs. W. Carl Whitlock.

My special thanks also go to Napir Wilt and Walter Blair, of the University of Chicago, for giving me just the right combination of latitude and pressure to develop a doctoral dissertation from a portion of this research (in 1957); to Jacques Barzun, of Columbia University, Mr. Charles A. Pearce, of New York, and my colleague, Cecil McCulley, of the College of William and Mary, who read portions of various versions of the manuscript at different stages of composition and made useful suggestions; and to Herr Heinrich Icksstadt, of the Free University of Berlin, who did some of the final checking and clerical leg work.

Indispensable help was given me in countless ways by my friend, James A. Servies, Librarian of the College of William and Mary, and especially by his assistant, Gene Lanier, who perfected the ingenious method whereby the anthologized selections were photocopied from microfilms. To them and to the Committee on Faculty Research of the College of William and Mary for a summer grant in 1960 to continue my research on *The Smart Set,* I am very grateful. .

I wish, however, to absolve any and all of the above-mentioned of complicity in crimes committed herein against literature, literary history or common sense. The gaffes and gaucheries are strictly my own.

NOTES TO THE HISTORY

The chief source of information is obviously the magazine itself (Vols. 1 to 89, March 1900 to April 1930), available in the original or on microfilm only in a few of the largest metropolitan, university and research libraries. For full understanding, *The Smart Set* should be supplemented by at least random browsing through *Ainslee's Magazine* (September 1902-December 1909), *The Dial* (1913-1924), *Judge* (1900-1924), *Life* (1900-1924), *The Little Review* (March 1914-Spring 1924), *Poetry: A Magazine of Verse* (1912-1924), *Puck* (1900-1924), *Town Topics* (1900-1920), *Vanity Fair* (1913-1924) and *The American Mercury* (1924-1933).

The indispensable general reference work for magazines of this period (although it does not cover *The Smart Set*) is Frank Luther Mott, *A History of American Magazines,* Vol. 4: 1885-1905 (Harvard, 1957), supplemented by Frederick J. Hoffman, Charles Allen and Carolyn F. Ulrich, *The Little Magazine: A History and a Bibliography* (Princeton, 1946). James Playsted Wood, *Magazines in the United States,* 2nd ed. (Ronald Press, 1956), Chap. 15, unfortunately abounds in factual errors about *The Smart Set*, as do all other reference books which mention the magazine.

Useful general works on literary and historical backgrounds are: Grant C. Knight,

The Strenuous Age in American Literature, 1900-1910 (University of North Carolina Press, 1954); Henry F. May, *The End of American Innocence* (Knopf, 1959); and Frederick J. Hoffman, *The Twenties* (Viking, 1955).

Studies specific to *The Smart Set* are: Burton Rascoe and Groff Conklin, *The Smart Set Anthology* (Reynal & Hitchcock, 1934), pp. i-xxxiv, and Carl R. Dolmetsch, *A History of the Smart Set Magazine, 1914-1923* (Unpublished Ph.D. dissertation, University of Chicago, 1957).

Caviar for Dilettantes

The fullest account of Colonel William D'Alton Mann (1839-1920) and *Town Topics* is: Andy Logan, "That Was New York," *The New Yorker*, XLI, August 14, 1965, 37-91; August 21, 1965, 41-98. Miss Logan has made exhaustive use of all the contemporary newspaper accounts as well as such "secondary" sources as Mott, pp. 459-460 and 751-755; Ludwig Lewisohn, *Expression in America* (Harper, 1932), pp. 314-316; Lloyd Morris, *Postscript to Yesterday* (Random House, 1947), pp. 19-21; and the personal memoirs of Charles Hanson Towne, Mark Sullivan and Norman Hapgood. For the story of Col. Mann's encounter with Booth Tarkington, see James Woodress, *Booth Tarkington: Gentleman from Indiana* (Lippincott), p. 123. *M'lle. New York* and other "little" magazines of that period are described in Mott, p. 86, as well as in Hoffman, Allen, and Ulrich. The best source of information concerning the early *Smart Set*, however, remains Charles Hanson Towne's memoirs, *So Far So Good* (Messner, 1945), pp. 89-115. A sketch of Arthur Grissom (1868-1902), the magazine's first editor, is in: LaTouche Hancock, "The Poets of Printing House Square," *The Bookman*, XV, May 1902, 268-273; for Grissom's escapades in Kansas City and especially his part in the founding of *The Independent* there, see Mott, pp. 97-98.

The Colonel versus Mrs. Grundy

Marvin Dana is one of those discussed by Zona Gale in "Editors of the Younger Generation," *The Critic*, XLIV, April 1904, 318-331. The information on *Ainslee's* here is from Vol. X of that magazine, with background facts from Mott, p. 49. Joe Lee Davis, *James Branch Cabell* (Twayne, TUSAS No. 12, 1962) is the best short account of Cabell. For the *Collier's-Town Topics* feud and the ensuing libel and perjury trials see Andy Logan's two-part *New Yorker* article (cited above) and *Collier's Weekly*, Vols. XXXIV-XXXVI (1904-1906) and *Town Topics*, Vols. LII-LIV (same period). For the early career of Damon Runyon see Edwin P. Hoyt, *A Gentleman of Broadway* (Little, Brown, 1964). Sinclair Lewis' early career in *The Smart Set* is fully detailed in Mark Schorer, *Sinclair Lewis: An American Life* (Simon & Schuster, 1961), pp. 124, 178, 230, *et passim*. According to Schorer (p. 801), Lewis returned to writing verses in his early *Smart Set* manner near the end of his life. The *Smart Set* correspondence of Henry Sydnor Harrison is now in the Duke University Library and is quoted here by the kind permission of Mr. Harrison's sister and executrix, Mrs. George Curry, of Columbia, S.C.

"For Minds That Are Not Primitive"

H. L. Mencken's association with *The Smart Set* can be traced in Betty Adler and Jane Wilhelm, *H. L. M.: The Mencken Bibliography* (Johns Hopkins, 1961), Guy Jean Forgue, ed., *The Letters of H. L. Mencken* (Knopf, 1961), pp. 5-262, *et passim*, and in the only available phonograph recording of Mencken's voice, an interview with Donald H. Kirkley, Sr., at the Library of Congress, Washington, D.C., June 30, 1948 (Caedmon LP-1082). The best secondary sources on Mencken and *The Smart Set* are: William R. Manchester, "A Critical Study of the Work of H. L. Mencken as Literary Critic for *The Smart Set* Magazine, 1908-1914," (Unpublished M. A. thesis, University of Missouri, 1947); and three full-length biographies—Isaac Goldberg, *The Man Mencken* (Simon & Schuster, 1925); Edgar Kemler, *The Irreverent Mr. Mencken* (Little, Brown, 1950); and William Manchester, *Disturber of the Peace* (Harper, 1950).

The *Smart Set* career of George Jean Nathan may be followed only in outline—in Isaac Goldberg, *The Theatre of George Jean Nathan* (Simon & Schuster, 1926), pp. 149-152; Constance Frick, *The Dramatic Criticism of George Jean Nathan* (Cornell, 1943); and Charles Angoff, ed., *The World of George Jean Nathan* (Knopf, 1952). [A full-fledged biographical-critical study of Nathan is under preparation by the author for the Twayne United States Authors Series.]

The only detailed source of information concerning John Adams Thayer is his "business" autobiography: *Astir: A Publisher's Life Story* (Small, Maynard, 1910), the second edition of which, entitled *Out of the Rut: A Business Life Story* (G. W. Dillingham, 1912) contains an account of his purchase of *The Smart Set*, pp. 303-307, as used here.

The only extant file of the English edition of *The Smart Set* known is in The British Museum, London.

OWEN HATTERAS IN ERUPTION

There is very little reliable information about Willard Huntington Wright ("S. S. Van Dine," 1888-1939), other than the standard reference works (*Who's Who . . . ,* Kunitz and Haycroft, *Twentieth Century Authors,* etc.) or the few newspaper accounts referred to: *The New York Times,* October 5, 1917, p. 20, col. 3; April 13, 1929, p. 23, col. 1; April 14, 1939 (editorial), p. 22, col. 3. For information about Wright's relationship with Mencken, see Forgue, ed., *The Letters of H. L. Mencken,* pp. 10-112, *et passim* (there are also unpublished letters used here

in the Princeton University Library). Wright's later life was detailed to the author by the late Burton Rascoe in New York in 1955. Percival Pollard's book is *Masks and Minstrels of New Germany* (John W. Luce, 1911); its influence was attested to in interviews with the late Burton Rascoe, H. L. Mencken, George Jean Nathan and a dozen others.

"GOOD LORD, DELIVER Us!"

For the literary and artistic situation in the United States on the eve of World War I (1912-1914), see especially Margaret Anderson, *My Thirty Years' War* (Covici, Friede, 1930); Van Wyck Brooks, *The Confident Years, 1885-1915* (Dutton, 1952); Alfred Kazin, *On Native Grounds* (Reynal & Hitchcock, 1942) and the works mentioned above by Lewisohn, May and Morris. The story of Nathan's meeting with Warner on the *Imperator* was first recorded in a letter sent by Nathan to Dr. Isaac Goldberg in 1925 (now in the New York Public Library) and used by Goldberg and several others in biographies of Nathan and Mencken. It was confirmed to the author by Mr. and Mrs. Eltinge Warner in an interview at Easthampton, L.I. in July 1955, as were the other details of the Warner regime given here. The Mencken letters to Willard Huntington Wright, Ernest Boyd and Theodore Dreiser quoted in this chapter and elsewhere in this work are in the Princeton library. Some of them have been published in the Forgue edition of Mencken's letters, but permission to quote or reprint them antedates their publication elsewhere. *The New York Times* story quoted ("Smart Set Changes Hands") is from August 16, 1914, Sec. 2, p. 12, col. 8. The list of Mencken pseudonyms is from a letter by him to Harry Leon Wilson, January 26, 1915 (Forgue, p. 60); a further list given in the Alder and Wilhelm *Bibliography* (pp. 348-349) is open to question because some of the names listed were also used by Nathan and other *Smart Set* contributors and were not solely Mencken's property. Some of the manuscripts of Lord Dunsany's early *Smart Set* contributions (including his earliest one) are in a box of *Smart Set* materials in the Manuscript Division of the New York Public Library. For Joyce's associations with the magazine, see Forgue, ed., pp. 64, 70, 73, 104 and D. D. Paige, ed., *The Letters of Ezra Pound: 1907-1941*, (Harcourt, 1950), *passim*, the same source, of course, details Pound's activities as virtual "foreign editor" of the magazine between 1913 and about 1920. The tenure of the Nathan-Mencken editorship of the three "parasite" magazines (as they called them) was as follows: *Parisienne* (July 1915-November 1916), *Saucy Stories* (August-November 1916) and *Black Mask* (April-November 1920). The Owen Hatteras "Litany for Magazine Editors" is typical of the Nathan-Mencken collaborations, most of which are not easily recognizable in their essentials as the work of either; this one, for instance, was printed under Nathan's signature in *The Bookman* (Vol. 43, May 1916, pp. 280-283) and under Mencken's in his *Book of Burlesques* (Lane, 1916).

PISTOLS FOR TWO

Mencken's letters to Ernest Boyd and others quoted here are in the collections at the Firestone Library, Princeton University, and are quoted by permission of the late Mr. Mencken. The quotations of Nathan's "credo" are from his *Smart Set* article of August 1922, pp. 131-137. Nathan's ideas were expounded in *The Critic and The Drama* (Knopf, 1922) and throughout seven other books published between 1915 and 1925. Mencken's most explicit statements of critical theory, quoted here, may be found in his monthly *Smart Set* article for August 1917 (pp. 138 ff.) and his views on poetry in "Exeunt Omnes," December 1919, pp. 138 ff. (reprinted with a few changes in *Prejudices*, 2nd Ser.).

"THE ARISTOCRAT AMONG MAGAZINES"

Most of the material used here on the actual editorial conduct of the magazine was obtained in interviews with George Jean Nathan, in New York, May 1955, and with H. L. Mencken, in Baltimore, August 1955. The office memos were published in *The Intimate Notebooks of George Jean Nathan* (Knopf, 1932), pp. 48-50 and the letter from L. M. Hussey to Nathan (November 22, 1921) is in the Cornell University Library. The *Smart Set* letters to Vincent Starrett and Carl Van Vechten are in the New York Public Library and that to Will F. Jenkins is in Mr. Jenkins' possession. The letter to Louis Untermeyer is also printed in his reminiscences, *From Another World* (Harcourt, Brace, 1939), p. 194. The comment by Leslie Nelson Jennings is contained in a letter by Mrs. Jennings to the author, August 15, 1964. The information on Thyra Samter Winslow was given the author by Mrs. Winslow in a series of interviews in New York in March and April 1955, supplemented by Mrs. Winslow's obituary notice in *The New York Times*, December 3, 1961. Little is known about Lucia Bronder ("Lilith Benda"), so the author has had to rely on statements made by Messrs. Mencken and Nathan in interviews (dates above); the note from Mencken to Nathan is quoted in *The Intimate Notebooks . . .* (v.s.), p. 47. Among the most helpful informants for this period were Miss Lillian Foster Barrett and Richmond Brooks Barrett in letters to the author in 1955 and 1964; the genesis of "The Sins of the Father" is Nathan's story. Burton Rascoe's *A Bookman's Daybook* (Liveright, 1929) is the chief source of reliable information about Achmed Abdullah. The decor in the *Smart Set* office was described to the author by Mr. Richmond Brooks Barrett and Mr. Nathan. Miss Muna Lee granted the author an interview in Washington, April 13, 1955, in which the biographical facts presented here were related. The best account to date of *The Double Dealer* and its relationship to *The Smart Set* is a Ph.D. dissertation by Frances Bowen Durett, "The New Orleans Double Dealer: 1921-May 1926/ A Critical History" (Vanderbilt University, 1954) reprinted, in part, in *Reality and Myth: Essays in American Literature in Memory of Richmond Croom Beatty* (Vanderbilt University Press, 1964), Chap. XI. Cabell's special relationship to *The Smart Set*, including the genesis of *Jurgen,* etc., may be followed in Padraic Colum and Margaret Freeman Cabell, eds., *Between Friends: Letters of James Branch Cabell and Others* (Harcourt, Brace & World, 1962), *passim*. The role of *The Smart Set* in O'Neill's career was first outlined by Barrett H. Clark in *Eugene O'Neill: The Man and His Plays* (Dover, rev. ed., 1947), pp. 51-53 and elaborated by several later biographers, including Agnes Boulton (the first Mrs. Eugene O'Neill and a *Smart Set* contributor herself) and the Gelbs, most recently. Fitzgerald's early appearances in *The Smart Set* were first recounted by him in *The Crack-Up,* ed. by Edmund Wilson (New Directions, 1942), pp. 85-86 and reiterated with some added details by Mizener, Trumbull and the other biographers of Fitzgerald. The story of how "Miss Thompson" came to *The Smart Set* is recounted in part by Burton Rascoe in his *Smart Set Anthology,* in part in his *Before I Forget* (Doubleday, 1937, p. 360) and further elaborated and emended by Mr. Nathan in an interview in New York, May 8, 1955.

THE COSTS OF CLEVERNESS

For varying contemporary estimates of *The Smart Set* in the early 1920's see and compare: Rascoe, *Bookman's Daybook* (pp. 21-22); Mary Kolars, "Some Modern Periodicals," *Catholic World,* CXVI, March 1923, pp. 781-89 (a very useful commentary) and Horace Gregory and Marya Zaturenska, *A History of American Poetry: 1900-1940* (New York, 1946, p. 364) where Kenneth Fearing is quoted as saying that when he was a student at the University of Wisconsin all the students read either *The Smart Set* or *The Dial* and the more literary-minded ones read the latter. The best description of the fads and fancies of the Young Intellectuals of the early Twenties remains: Malcolm Cowley, *Exile's Return* (Viking, 1951). *The Little Review* is the subject of Margaret Anderson's *My Thirty Years' War* (Covici, 1930) and *The Reviewer* (a "branch" of *The Smart Set* in Richmond) of Emily Clark's *Innocence Abroad* (Knopf, 1931). The account of the last days of the Nathan-Mencken regime on *The Smart Set* is taken principally from an interview granted the author by Mr. and Mrs. Eltinge F. Warner, at Easthampton, L.I., July 12, 1955, as emended in interviews with Messrs. Nathan and Mencken and a letter to the author by Mr. Alfred A. Knopf in which Mr. Knopf denies having tried to purchase *The Smart Set* but suggests that it "might have been my father." For the beginnings of *The American Mercury* see M. K. Singleton *H. L. Mencken and The American Mercury Adventure* (Duke University Press, 1962), an adequate although confused study which must be supplemented by the Forgue edition of the Mencken letters (v.s.) for greatest accuracy. Morris Gilbert's editorship of *The Smart Set* was recounted to the author by Mr. Gilbert in New York, May 18, 1955, and confirmed in almost all details by Messrs. Nathan and Mencken. The comment by Burton Rascoe quoted here concerning Gilbert was made to the author privately by Mr. Rascoe. The negotiations on the sale of *The Smart Set* to Hearst may be followed in the letters addressed to Nathan (and one to Mencken) by Warner, James P. Brady, and A. W. Sutton in the Cornell University Library if anyone is interested in the purely financial matters. The material on the very last days of *The Smart Set*—the merger with *McClure's*, etc.—is taken from Wood, *Magazines in the United States* (v.s.).